MOUNTAINEERING WOMEN

MOUNTAINEERING WOMEN

Climbing Through History

Joanna Croston

Foreword by Jasmin Paris
Contributions by Nandini Purandare and Ashima Shiraishi
Illustrated by Tessa Lyons

with 160 illustrations

CONTENTS

FOREWORD Jasmin Paris — 6
INTRODUCTION Nandini Purandare — 8

CLIMBER STORIES — 17

Junko Tabei and the First Women's Ascent of Everest — 18
Gwen Moffat, the UK's First Female Mountain Guide — 28
Catherine Destivelle Versus the Dru — 38
Wasfia Nazreen and the Seven Summits — 46
Wanda Rutkiewicz and Her Obsession with K2 — 54
Pat Deavoll Faces Karim Sar — 64
Brette Harrington and Her Free-Solo of Chiaro di Luna — 72
Lynn Hill and the First Free Ascent of the Nose — 98
Gerlinde Kaltenbrunner and the Race for the 8,000-metre Peaks — 108
Ines Papert and the Ice Climb of Her Dreams — 116
Élisabeth Revol's Fight for Survival on Nanga Parbat — 126
Kei Taniguchi Climbs Kamet — 134
Sarah Hueniken on Ice — 142
Alison Hargreaves Tackles the Alps — 150
Pasang Lhamu Sherpa and the Climb of Her Life — 178
Hazel Findlay, with Strong Body and Mind — 186
Juliana García's Journey to be Latin America's First Certified Mountain Guide — 194
Sharon Wood's Discoveries in the Andes — 202
Lydia Bradey and Her Solo Ascent of Everest — 210
Tamara Lunger's Love and Loss on K2 — 218

THE FUTURE OF CLIMBING Ashima Shiraishi — 240

Glossary — 243
Timeline — 244
Mountain Profiles — 249
More Mountaineering Women — 250
Notes — 252
Index — 252
Picture Credits — 255
About the Contributors — 255
Author Acknowledgments — 255

FOREWORD

Jasmin Paris

There was a moment on the last loop of the Barkley Marathons when my attention briefly shifted from the urgency of the race to the still, forested summit I had just reached. In that moment, I was suddenly acutely aware of the living, breathing mass of trees around me. I could feel the damp on my skin, smell the soil and leaves on the ground beneath my feet. I was part of the landscape, insignificant. Then my focus was back and I was hurtling down the hill, jacket catching on branches, legs stretching to avoid rocks and tree trunks, arms flailing like a windmill to maintain balance.

I often think back to that moment, when the wilderness reminded me of its presence. This allows me to contemplate the juxtaposition of self-imposed suffering to strive towards a human-contrived goal, and my mind's relationship with nature. I have learned now that I need to take time to re-establish that bond after difficult running challenges, before my focus and ambition can move on, regardless of how quickly physical recovery is achieved. Only then can I start to dream again, to wonder what I might still be capable of.

As you move through this book, you'll encounter many extraordinary women and their inspirational achievements in the mountains. With each story, you will uncover not only the physical attributes but also the mental qualities that allowed these women to climb as they did. From Junko Tabei's first female ascent of Everest – completed days after being avalanched and left unable to walk – to Sharon Wood's journey of self-discovery on Huascarán Sur, these accounts reveal how the human spirit, paired with wild places, can bring about the incredible. Each story is a reminder of what can emerge from resilience, courage and the humbling connection between climber and mountain.

Prior to this year, many people claimed a woman could never complete the Barkley Marathons. I was delighted to prove those doubters wrong. Nevertheless, as a full-time vet with two young children, I could not have done so without the incredible support I received from my family and friends. The pioneering women described in this book were mountaineering at a time when such support was rarer than it is now, when the high places were even more dominated by men. These women defied beliefs and expectations, often treading exceedingly lonely paths and ultimately leading the way for generations to experience the mountains on a more equal footing. In doing so, they showed us that passion, self-belief and endurance can change the world.

Page 2: Sarah Hueniken starting up the crux pillar of Pomme d'Or in Quebec.
Page 4: Lynn Hill free-climbing the Nose, El Capitan, Yosemite National Park.
Opposite: Jasmin Paris journeying through Wales on the six-day, 380-km (236-mile) Dragon's Back Race®, 2015.

THE ASCENT OF WOMAN: "THE CLIMBER"—NOT BY E. F. BENSON.
THE WORLD'S MOST FAMOUS LADY MOUNTAINEERS.

1. MRS. BULLOCK WORKMAN.
2. MISS ANNIE PECK.
3. MLLE. ROSE FRIEDMAN.
4. MLLE. VINITA MAYER.
5. MLLE. MARVINGT.
6. MLLE. ELÉONORE HASENCLEVER.
7. MRS. AUBREY LE BLOND.
8. MISS DORA KEEN.
9. MLLE. MARGUERITE GRÖSSE.
10. MLLE. ELIZABETH GRÖSSE.
11. MME. CATHERINE BROSKE.
12. MME. LA GÉNÉRALE VON REPERT.
13. MME. JULIEN GRANDE.
14. MME. PAUL PRANTZ NAMUR.
15. MLLE. LÉONTINE RICHARD.

There is no sphere of sport, in its more serious and perilous aspects, in which women have more distinguished themselves than in mountaineering. Woman, in fact, seems to have an aptitude for climbing, not only in a social sense, as exemplified in Mr. E. F. Benson's novel, "The Climber," but in the actual and literal meaning of the word. In the above picture are seen, on an imaginary peak, fifteen of the most famous women climbers in the world, from Mrs. Bullock Workman, who holds the record for altitude, at the top, downward in the order of the heights they have severally attained. On another page will be found an article giving further details of some of their exploits.

INTRODUCTION

Nandini Purandare

In the nineteenth century, women throughout the Western world were subject to severe restrictions. Their clothing and behaviour were straitjacketed, marked by firm dos and don'ts. Women were allowed to amuse themselves with drawing or writing poetry, but riding in a hansom cab alone? Hitching up their cumbersome skirts? Allowing a peek of their knee-length bloomers? Absolutely not.

It is all the more remarkable, then, that the first women to explore the European Alps belong to this era. They paved the way for mountaineering *because they wanted to*. In a world where women were expected to bear children, look after the needs of men and run the home, climbing can be seen as a metaphor for, and physical embodiment of, breaking free. But climbing was a struggle, with a range of pressures to navigate and barriers to overcome – social, psychological, practical and structural. Many of these obstacles still affect female mountaineers today, albeit in different ways.

The stories in the pages that follow, of extraordinary women and the paths they forged, pay homage to those who decided to go their own way.

The women in this book are extraordinary not only because of their ascents, but because of the journeys that led them up. They differ from previous generations in that they have frequently reinvented ways to get to the top. In 2011, Gerlinde Kaltenbrunner became the first woman to summit all the world's 8,000-metre (26,247-foot) peaks without using supplementary oxygen; Pasang Lhamu Sherpa became the first Nepalese woman to stand atop Mount Everest in 1993; Catherine Destivelle, the first woman to receive the Piolet d'Or for lifetime achievement (2020); and Alison Hargreaves, the first woman to summit Everest and K2 in a single season (1995). The list goes on. Their stories are all here.

Human presence in the mountains didn't start with Victorian men and women scaling the Alps. Mountain communities have appeared in recorded history for centuries. During the Inca Empire (1438–1533), people travelled and lived in the Andes, at heights of 6,000 metres (19,685 feet) and more. They grazed cattle, crossing peaks and passes as part of their routine. The Amazigh (Berbers) of the Atlas Mountains are believed to be the oldest pastoralists, first mentioned in Ancient Egyptian texts. Central Asian steppes and mountain ranges, including the Altai and the Tien Shan mountains, the Tibetan Plateau and even the Alps and Himalaya have been home to communities herding yaks, sheep, goats, cows and horses across the high-altitude grasslands for thousands of years.

Mountaineering as a sporting activity began in the late eighteenth and early nineteenth century, when the Alps captured the European imagination. This was the Romantic Era, when humanity was celebrating newness, individualism and the wonders of nature. Mont Blanc (4,809 metres/15,777 feet), the highest mountain in the Alps, was first climbed in 1786. By the early nineteenth century, Grossglockner, Ortler and the Jungfrau had all been summited, along with many other high Alpine peaks. The appeal of climbing soon caught the fancy of the elite across Europe and North America.

One of the earliest and most dramatic events in climbing history was the spectacular ascent of the Matterhorn (4,478 metres/14,692 feet) in 1865 by a team led by Edward Whymper. Until then, the sixth highest mountain in the Alps had been a technically terrifying enigma. By this point, mountaineering as a sport had largely reached its modern form, with a large body of professional guides, equipment and a distinct methodology. Once mountaineers 'conquered' the Alps, they began to look further afield for challenges – to Norway, Alaska, the Andes

'The Ascent of Woman: "The Climber" – Not by E. F. Benson: The World's Most Famous Lady Mountaineers', published in The Sketch, 1911. The illustration shows Fanny Bullock Workman, Annie Peck Smith and Elizabeth Le Blond, among others.

and finally the Himalaya. Climbing, like many other activities of this age, was marked by one key feature: it was almost completely dominated by men. But there were exceptions.

In 1808, 185 years before Alison Hargreaves completed the first female solo ascent of all six great north faces in the Alps (see page 150), Maria Paradis broke every rule in the book to climb the highest of them, Mont Blanc. Her climb was dismissed as a 'publicity stunt'[1] for the tea shop she ran at the base of the mountain, and Maria was disregarded as not a lady but a lowly maid. But derisive men could not wish these brave women away. In 1838, a well-heeled woman named Mademoiselle Henriette d'Angeville launched a highly publicized trip, also tackling Mont Blanc. Her detailed planning, including luggage lists and instructions for her funeral in case she did not return, filled several pages. She took legs of mutton, tongue, dozens of fowl, eighteen bottles of good wine, a cask of vin ordinaire for the porters, a large wardrobe of men's clothing, several hats and a feather boa. While she certainly imbued her climb with a flair no man had managed, d'Angeville accomplished a great feat. She completed her first ascent at age forty-four; her twenty-first summit, and her last, was that of the Oldenhorn. She was sixty-nine. Yet despite her perseverance, d'Angeville too was dismissed as a 'supposedly repressed forty-four year-old spinster'.[2] In 1871, when Lucy Walker made the first female ascent of the dreaded Matterhorn, just six years after it was first climbed by Whymper's team, chronicler W. A. B. Coolidge did not even mention it. Mountaineering was a man's world. One small but revealing incident records a female climber, after a successful ascent, remarking to a male counterpart,

Top: Henriette d'Angeville, 1838.
Above: Henriette d'Angeville, her guides and porters depart for Mont Blanc. Drawing by Jules Hébert, mid-19th century.
Below: Lucy Walker and her family with Swiss guide Melchior Anderegg, 1864.

'You said no woman could manage it.' His answer was, 'I said no *lady*!'[3]

Lucy Walker began climbing in the Alps with her father and brother in around 1858, and later with her guide Melchior Anderegg – with whom she was always chaperoned. Three women, climbing in the late nineteenth and early twentieth centuries, who approached expeditions differently in the way that they used male help, were Annie Peck Smith (1850–1935), who climbed in the Andes, setting records in Mexico and Peru, Fanny Bullock Workman (1859–1925) in the Karakoram and Dora Keen (1871–1963) in Alaska. Annie Peck Smith would plan and mount her expeditions, enlisting male help as required, but struggled at a time when men were not accustomed to accepting female instruction. Fanny Bullock Workman sought adventure alongside her husband. Though they were equal partners, he was always the face of authority. Dora Keen, on the other hand, would locate the best local leader and allow him to find the right support. Uncompromising and pragmatic, these strong figures proved that women could climb alongside men – or even ahead of them. Gender norms, subtle or overt, continue to hold great sway in the climbing world

INTRODUCTION

Above: Annie Smith Peck, 1911.
Below: Elizabeth Le Blond on Piz Corvatsch, Switzerland, July 1889.

today. These early pioneers, and the women who followed, represent those shifting the narrative. Not necessarily as activists, just by following their hearts.

Throughout history, climbing women have had very little organizational assistance. The Alpine Club was formed in 1857, but predictably, it was only open to elite men. Enter Ms Elizabeth Le Blond, who came to be known as Mrs Aubrey Le Blond after her third marriage. She was an Irish climber who went on to make twenty first ascents and write seven books. In 1900 she achieved the first 'manless' climb of Piz Palü (3,900 metres/12,795 feet) on the Swiss–Italian border.

Realizing that women needed official recognition and support, Elizabeth Le Blond took the lead in forming the Ladies' Alpine Club in London in 1907, and became its first president. Lucy Walker was one of the founding members and succeeded Elizabeth as president in 1913. A rival organization, the Pinnacle Club, was created in 1921. Gwen Moffat became a member of the latter in the 1950s; she was also invited to join the Alpine Climbing Group (which later merged with the Alpine Club). This gave her the validation and motivation she needed to train as the first female British-certified mountain guide (see page 30). Establishing structures and institutions by which women could access support, encouragement, a like-minded community and possible expedition partners was invaluable.

There were many others who forged the way for women. Isabella Charlet-Straton (1838–1918) and Emmeline Lewis Lloyd (1827–1913) join our Victorian

Above: Elizabeth Le Blond ascending the Drei Blumen, February 1896.
Below: Elizabeth Le Blond climbing an arête near St Moritz with her guide, March 1896.

trailblazers, whose achievements allowed modern women to up the game with bold, technical routes. It would have been hard for these women to anticipate Wasfia Nazreen's accomplishment as she became the first Bangladeshi and Bengali to stand on the summit of K2 on 22 July 2022. Not always recognized as a mountaineer in the conventional sense, Nazreen climbed the Seven Summits before adding K2 to her cap, inspiring Bangladeshi youth to dream the impossible (see page 48). It was here, too, that Kaltenbrunner's quest for the world's 8,000-ers reached its finale in 2011. But it was Polish mountaineer Wanda Rutkiewicz who was the first woman to climb this notoriously deadly and difficult mountain, back in 1986 (see page 56).

K2 lies in the Karakoram mountains, which extend into Pakistan, China and India, as well as Afghanistan and Tajikistan. This range contains four peaks above 8,000 metres (26,247 feet), including Gasherbrum II (8,035 metres/ 26,362 feet) – the first 8,000-er to be scaled by an all-woman team. The Karakoram mountains are part of the same mountain system as the Himalaya, home to the world's highest peak. Some four hundred women have now reached the summit of Mount Everest. Over many decades, women have continued to claim more space in the Himalaya and the forbidding Karakoram range. But before them, it was Fanny Bullock Workman who truly blazed this trail.

Although Fanny Bullock Workman doesn't feature in many chronicles dedicated to women climbers of the 1800s–1900s, she is an important figure. She came from

INTRODUCTION

a background of wealth and privilege. The Alps provided a nursery, preparing her for a life of climbing. In a style similar to that of her contemporaries, Bullock Workman always wore a long tweed skirt and jacket. Having climbed the Jungfrau, the Matterhorn and Mont Blanc, she took her bags and husband, William Hunter Workman, to the Himalaya, Karakoram and Hindu Kush to access the youngest and tallest mountains in the world. In 1898–99, they discovered that mountaineering in the Himalaya was far more complex than the alpine climbing they had done so far.[4] Here, they were required to carry what they needed for months at a time, compared to a couple of days in the Alps. Besides, there were no professional guides in these mountains.

Between 1898 and 1912, the Workmans launched six great expeditions in the region, each lasting several months. Each adventure demanded a few hundred people – porters, cooks, interpreters, guides, scientists – as well as herds of goats and several hundred chickens to eat and yaks to carry the load. William collected geological specimens and kept records while Fanny managed the mind-boggling logistics. In 1899, Fanny christened a 6,000-metre (19,685-foot) peak with their name – Mount Bullock Workman – and then set the women's world altitude record with an ascent of Mount Koser Gunge (6,400 metres/20,997 feet) in the Shigar Valley of Baltistan, Pakistan. She then broke this record by climbing above 6,858 metres (22,500 feet) to reach the summit of Lungma, also in Baltistan. In 1906, Fanny and William explored the Nun Kun massif in Kashmir, reaching 7,100 metres (23,294 feet) on Pinnacle Peak.

Above: Fanny Bullock Workman on the summit of Tawiz Peak, 6,400 m/20,997 ft.
Below: Fanny Bullock Workman standing on Silver Throne plateau, Karakoram, Kashmir, holding a newspaper with a 'Votes for Women' headline.

The Workmans' final journey in 1912 was one of their finest. Fanny led the expedition to the 80-kilometre-long (50-mile) Siachen Glacier, now a disputed area between India and Pakistan. She was a staunch advocate for women's rights, and was keenly aware that her achievements would be important for inspiring others. She wrote in her book, *Two Summers in the Ice-Wilds of the Eastern Karakoram*:

> *The object of placing my full name in connection with the expedition on the map, is not because I wish in any way to thrust myself forward but solely that in the accomplishments of women, now and in the future, it should be known to them and stated in print that a woman was the initiator and special leader of this expedition. When later a woman occupies her acknowledged position as an individual worker in all fields, as well as those of exploration, no such emphasis of her work will be needed; but that day has not fully arrived, and at present it behooves women, for the benefit of their sex, to put at least what they do on record.*[5]

Elizabeth Le Blond in her climbing skirt.

While that day has still not fully arrived, this book is an attempt to further Fanny's cause and recognize the accomplishments of women in the mountains.

This recognition must reach beyond those women, traditionally from the West, who self-identified as 'climbers' or 'mountaineers'. The simple act of journeying in the mountains dates back to the birth of civilization. Curiosity took our ancestors to mounds above land, where sky met earth. As we've heard, female cattle herders played an important role in the economic, social and cultural fabric of the Inca Empire in the fifteenth century. The Incas were a nomadic people, moving their large herds of llama and alpaca – which needed to graze at elevations between 3,500 metres (11,483 feet) and 5,000 metres (16,404 feet) – with the seasons. Inca women, just as their counterparts in later Victorian society, had fixed roles; they herded the cattle in a patriarchal world where they had no ownership rights or decision-making power. They provided labour at a time when there were no measurements of height or latitude, no man-made boundaries. The only borders were those marked by nature and the need for grass or god.[6]

There were many reasons why women climbed throughout history. Rebecca Solnit writes of the Christian pilgrim, Egeria, who lived in the fourth century a.d. Almost no trace of Egeria survives, aside from her pilgrimage diary, but it is known that she and her unnamed companions scaled the nearly 2,732-metre (8,963-foot) peak of Mount Sinai on foot – 'straight up, as if scaling a wall'. Egeria noted that 'this seems to be a single mountain all around; however, once you enter the area you see there are many, but the whole range is called the Mountain of God'.

Mount Fuji was revered as a pilgrimage site too, though women were prohibited from climbing it until the late nineteenth century. Seen as ritually unclean due to menstruation and childbirth, it was believed that their presence on the sacred mountain could defile its purity.

'The simple act of journeying in the mountains dates back to the birth of civilization. Curiosity took our ancestors to mounds above land, where sky met earth.'

In the highlands of the Himalaya, women also trudged to great heights, travelling up and down over passes and peaks to graze their herds, meet monks or make pilgrimages. In fact, Sherpa Tenzing Norgay, one of the first two people to reach the top of Mount Everest in 1953, was born somewhere in the Kharta region in Tibet – where the mountains start at a height of 6,849 metres (22,470 feet) – when his mother and sisters were on just such a pilgrimage. These pastoral women, wearing *bakus*, similar to the skirts of Victorian Western women, were not 'mountaineers' as such. The very act of 'mountaineering' implies that one climbs out of choice for the pleasure it affords. These herders climbed *because they had to*, and didn't need a new word to describe it.

So, when women in the West were rightfully fighting for shared space in a man's world, hiking up their skirts and shattering glass ceilings, unknown women on the subcontinent were achieving great heights with their yaks and cows, and babies on their backs. Their voices were unheard. While we celebrate the stories that have been reported, we must quietly acknowledge those that were not, for various reasons – a lack of education, literacy and record-keeping being important ones. These were women who lived in nations closest to the highest mountains on Earth, but their stories are lost forever.

Pasang Lhamu Sherpa became the first Nepalese woman to summit Everest on 23 April 1993 (see page 180). It was her third attempt. The earlier two had been widely publicized and critiqued; huge amounts of money had been spent and the world was watching. Pressure like this creates the perfect recipe for making wrong decisions on high mountains. She sadly died on her descent, exhausted and with no oxygen to revive her. Nevertheless, she had seen her dream through.

Sherpani carrying a heavy load on the 1953 Mount Everest expedition, Nepal.

The Sherpa people are highly esteemed as elite mountaineers. An ethnic group native to the most mountainous regions of Nepal and Tibet, Sherpas have joined expeditions as guides and porters since the earliest Western explorers came to their peaks. In many cases, triumphant European heroes would not have summited or returned home without their help. Despite this, the stories and achievements of local Sherpas have traditionally been omitted from the narrative.

Ani Daku Sherpa was born in 1925 and grew up herding yaks and trading handmade paper for salt across the Nangpa La mountain pass (5,716 metres/18,753 feet) in Tibet. It was a hard life, crossing high passes regularly. In the 1940s she ran away from home to Darjeeling to carry loads for expeditions. She was a coin carrier on a number of early projects, toting boxes of porters' wages up the mountains. 'We used canvas bags made out of old tents and [they] were very heavy, maybe forty kilos,' she said. 'The sacks were too heavy to be carried by one person so we took turns.'[7] Ani Daku was a carrier with the triumphant 1953 Everest team and recalled the event fondly. 'When we arrived in Nepal, there were many people and flowers to celebrate. We rode an elephant. We queued to meet the king.' She spoke of Edmund Hillary wistfully. 'Hillary was very tall, very fair and had a long face. He was very handsome. And he used to put his arm around my shoulder when I was tired.

Sherpas and Sherpanis with tents, boxes and equipment at Everest basecamp, Nepal, March 1953.

He loved us.'[8] Ani Daku was one of several early women climbers on Everest. They were load bearers who climbed, once more, because they needed to. They climbed for wages, helping famous white men to achieve glory.

In Tibet, the highest mountain on Earth – Mount Everest – is known as Chomolungma, Goddess Mother of the Earth. She was Pasang and Daku's mountain; they grew up in her lap. In most of these lands, it was believed that spirits and gods lived on the top of the mountain, so stepping on a summit was strictly forbidden. But then came the arrival of the white man, with his desire to conquer. Even here, he asserted his gender. Chomolungma was given a number, Peak XV, and then named Everest after a surveyor general who had not even noticed her existence. The mountain was stripped of her womanhood, of her fertility and spirituality, renamed after a powerful white man from a distant land. When reading Pasang Lhamu Sherpa's story (see page 180), we must acknowledge both Ani Daku Sherpa and the Goddess Mother.

I hope that someday, the female climbers who have charted new routes in less familiar areas are recognized alongside the ones represented in this book. That more women from the vast subcontinent, home to the Himalaya and the Karakoram, will find a way to break trail on the mountains at their doorstep. And that, eventually, we won't need to create unique spaces for women to be celebrated separately.

Until then, as Ani Daku said of her climbing days, 'What's there in staying in one place?'[9] Keep going.

Climber Stories

Junko Tabei and the First Women's Ascent of Everest

In the early hours of 4 May 1975, the members of the Japanese Women's Everest Expedition were packed tightly into a small tent at Camp 2 when they were jolted awake by a loud crack and a deep, fast-approaching rumbling sound. Unbeknown to them, they were in the direct line of an avalanche. House-sized chunks of snow and ice were released 1,000 metres (3,281 feet) above them and thundered relentlessly down the mountainside. In the inky black of night, an enormous wall of icy debris hit their camp and sent the climbers, and their tent, tumbling into the darkness.

JUNKO TABEI

Nationality:
Japanese

Born:
22 September 1939

Died:
20 October 2016 (age 77)

Active:
1949-2016

Opposite: Junko Tabei, Tokyo, Japan, 2016.
Below: Tabei family, 1974.

Weeks before, as part of its summit bid, the team had placed its camp at an altitude of 6,400 metres (20,997 feet) in what it considered to be a relatively safe place, on a wide flat bench away from the hangfire of corniced snow that had been known to tumble off the neighbouring Himayalan giant of Nuptse. As part of its expedition preparations, the team had researched the position of its camps diligently, consulting with all parties who had been successful on Everest before. The team members had also spent time at Camp 2 on several previous occasions. It seemed a relatively comfortable waypoint to work from as the team and accompanying Sherpas fixed ropes and settled other higher camps over many days and weeks, slowly trudging their way up the peak, establishing one camp at a time – a common climbing strategy known as 'siege-style' tactics. This technique greatly improves the odds of summiteers, allowing them to rest as they become accustomed to the lack of oxygen. For large national expeditions in the Himalaya, this methodical approach has one goal: to get to the top by team effort and cooperation, for the honour of a nation. On this expedition alone, six hundred porters had carried more than fifteen tonnes of food and equipment to base-camp, a significant investment of time, effort and finances. The team leaders were driven and intent on success.

Between the first ascent of Everest in 1953 and 1974, climbers from only six other nations had ascended the 8,849-metre (29,032-foot) peak. All the summiteers had been male and, at a time of rising awareness about women's equality around the world, these strong, experienced Japanese climbers were set to change the course of history. For Junko Tabei and her fellow team members, putting the first woman on the top of the world was what they had trained four years for and travelled so far to do. Tabei had left her three-year-old daughter Noriko in the capable hands of her eldest sister's family and her supportive husband Masanobu. Others on the team had made similar sacrifices before arriving in Kathmandu en route to Everest basecamp. There was no room for failure and the pressure from their climbing community back home in Japan weighed heavily upon each of them. So far, their expedition had been mostly executed to plan, and while they slept eagerly at Camp 2 after many weeks of hard work, nothing could have prepared them for the chaos and confusion that was about to ensue.

Tabei had climbed in the Himalaya before. In 1970, along with her teammate Hiroko Hirakawa, she had summited Annapurna III (7,555 metres/24,787 feet) via the difficult south face. The mountain had tested her and her companions on many levels, wreaking havoc on their mental, physical and intra-personal skills. When jealousy and ego entered their team dynamics and soured their eventual summit bid of Annapurna, Tabei was forced to garner every bit of her experience to get to the top. All her years of climbing in her beloved Tanigawa region of Japan, where she had made her first life-altering ascents, would finally pay off. Innately aware of her own physical capability, tiny 165-centimetre (five-foot-four-inches) tall Tabei reached the summit of Annapurna III and became a heroine in climbing circles upon her return home.

Tabei was no stranger to accidents and tragedy. Just three years before her trip to Annapurna, she had lost her closest climbing partner in a horrific fall from a rocky ridge in Tanigawa. Her husband had also recently suffered painful frostbite after an ascent of the north face of the Matterhorn. Several of his toes were eventually amputated and Tabei supported him through his rehabilitation.

But now here she was, high on Mount Everest, where a massive avalanche had rushed through their camp. Disoriented after the wave of snow, not only did she feel the mass of ice and snow pressing on her chest, making it difficult to breathe, she felt the heavy burden of leaving her family behind. She wanted to return home to them. Tabei forced herself back into reality, set the pain aside and began to take inventory of the situation at Camp 2.

As the avalanche threw the tent – with all its occupants and equipment – downward, Tabei and her five companions had been tossed around in every which way imaginable. The force of the slide had sent them somersaulting more than 10 metres (33 feet) from their original site. Luckily Tabei was able to orientate herself quickly and realized that, in addition to being trapped under the snow, all four of her other tentmates were on top of her. She recalled the accident in her memoir:

> 'The entire camp was frozen in place, crushed between unyielding chunks of ice blocks, myself included. I was unable to move an inch. Any attempt to flex a muscle or shift my position was met with defeat. All effort was in vain while our tent, with my teammates inside, was buried in a mound of avalanche debris.'

As her companions' weight and the snow continued to press down on her lungs, Tabei temporarily fell into unconsciousness. Moments later, she was shocked awake by several of the expedition's Sherpa team members, who yanked her from the tent.

A few of the Sherpa guides had respectfully pitched their tent away from the others, a gesture offering privacy for the women. This turned out to be just enough to miss

---

INFO

EVEREST: A CORNUCOPIA OF FIRSTS

FIRST ASCENT:
Tenzing Norgay (Nepal) and Sir Edmund Hillary (New Zealand), 1953

FIRST FEMALE ASCENT:
Junko Tabei (Japan), 1975

FIRST ALL WOMEN'S ASCENT:
Japanese Women's Everest Expedition, 1975

FIRST ASCENT BY A NORTH AMERICAN WOMAN:
Sharon Wood (Canada), 1986

MOST ASCENTS OF EVEREST – MALE:
Kami Rita Sherpa (Nepal), 24

MOST ASCENTS OF EVEREST – FEMALE:
Lhakpa Sherpa (Nepal), 10 ascents

FIRST ASCENT BY AN AFRICAN AMERICAN WOMAN:
Sophia Danenberg, 2006

FIRST ASCENT BY THREE SIBLINGS:
Dawa Futi Sherpa, Tshering Namgya Sherpa and Nima Jangmu Sherpa (Nepal), 2003

FIRST ASCENT BY A FEMALE AMPUTEE:
Arunima Sinha (India), 2013

MOUNT EVEREST (CHOMOLUNGMA) SOUTH COL ROUTE

The South Col route on Mount Everest was first climbed in 1953 and is the most common route up the mountain today.

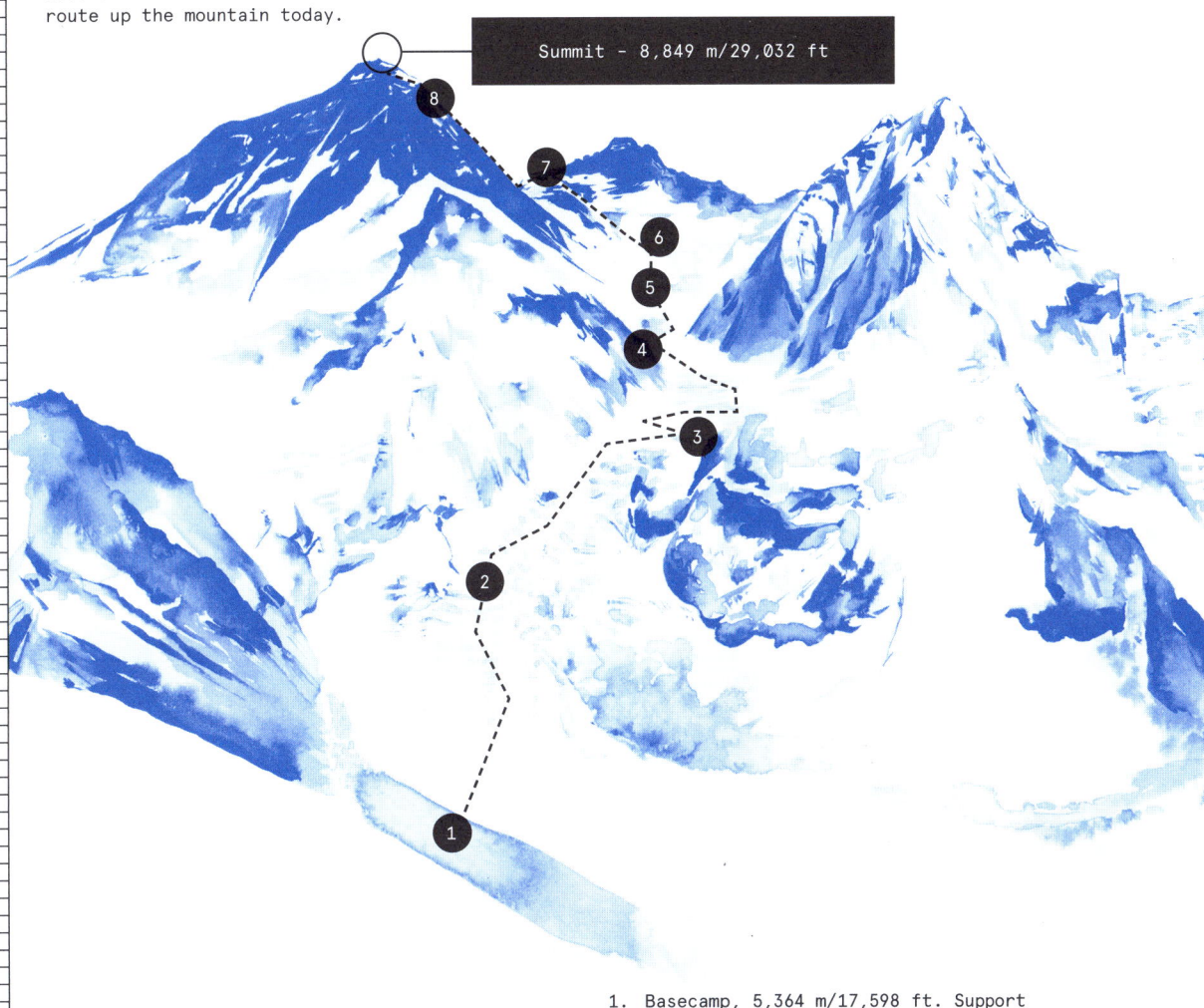

Summit - 8,849 m/29,032 ft

1. Basecamp, 5,364 m/17,598 ft. Support staff remain here. Climbers train and acclimatize.
2. The Khumbu Icefall is one of the most dangerous sections of the South Col Route on Chomolungma.
3. Camp 1, 6,035 m/19,800 ft.
4. Camp 2, 6,400 m/20,997 ft.
5. The Lhotse Face, a steep, shiny ice wall.
6. Camp 3, 7,158 m/23,484 ft.
7. Camp 4, 7,900 m/25,919 ft. First camp within the Death Zone. Most climbers at this elevation can no longer acclimatize.
8. Hillary Step, 8,790 m/28,839 ft. This steep wall is one of the only technical rock-climbing sections on the route.

JUNKO TABEI

CLIMBER STORIES

the main path of the avalanche. They set about rescuing the climbers and the valuable equipment that had been scattered in the mayhem.

Tabei was placed in an intact neighbouring tent, assessed for injury and given supplemental oxygen to ward off hypothermia – a danger to many of the survivors who had been submerged in snow. As she slowly began to comprehend what had happened, ever the group leader, she ran through the team members in her head and called out to the rescuers to ensure all the climbers were accounted for. Against all odds, everyone was found and nobody suffered severe injury.

As the hours progressed, Tabei was acutely aware that her body was not functioning normally. In fact, she could barely move. Somehow the trauma of the accident had rendered her immobile. Sherpa porters had been sent down to Camp 1 and up to Camp 3 to ask for help from other team members, but no one was able to descend further to basecamp, where the team's logistical members were located. A critical part of the team's route had been rendered impassable when a secured ladder had been jostled free and fallen into a crevasse. The dangerous ice chasms of the Khumbu Icefall are often crossed by ladders placed horizontally across these crevasses. Only climbers from below would be able to repair the route now. Communication with basecamp would have to wait until the daily radio call at 6 a.m.; it was only then, six hours after the avalanche, that the expedition's leader learned of the accident.

Despite pleas from those at basecamp, Tabei insisted on remaining at Camp 2, trying to convince everyone that she would heal with time. Journalists who were at Camp 2 and had witnessed the avalanche declared that the expedition couldn't possibly go on. As tempers flared, Tabei reiterated her desire to continue on to the summit with the team. Much to the dismay of the team's doctor, several team members stuck by Tabei's side and refused to abandon the summit bid. In the days that followed, Tabei's companions began to slowly repair tents by hand and re-establish the ropes that had been swept away. Tabei's instinct turned out to be correct and within four days she was able to walk on her own. They would remain on course and push for the summit of Mount Everest.

Boxes of precious food had been lost in the avalanche, among other equipment, and the team was also robbed of valuable time as its members recovered from the disaster. The spring climbing season is notoriously short, with many expeditions scrambling to make their ascent while good weather holds before the impending monsoons. But because of the rapid improvement to her physical condition, Tabei was selected as the team's best chance of achieving its goal.

'As the hours progressed, Tabei was acutely aware that her body was not functioning normally. In fact, she could barely move. Somehow the trauma of the accident had rendered her immobile.'

Opposite: Junko Tabei on the summit of Mount Everest, 16 May 1976.

At 5.30 a.m. on 16 May, Tabei and climbing Sherpa Ang Tsering turned on their head torches, departed their final camp and headed for the summit. They fought their way through newly fallen snow, climbed expertly through the Hillary Step, a steep wall of rock steps named after first ascensionist Sir Edmund Hillary, and made their way onto the final snowy ridge. At 12.30 p.m., Tabei and Ang Tsering reached the top, making them the thirty-eighth and thirty-ninth people to set foot on to this coveted summit. The pair called down to basecamp exclaiming their news and they were met with a hearty 'Otsu-karesama deshit!'[2] – congratulations on a job well done!

Serendipitously, 1975 had been declared International Women's Year by the United Nations. Junko Tabei was immediately recognized by the global climbing community, and indeed by popular media around the world, as one of the most influential women of the twentieth century.

Junko Tabei went on to summit many more peaks, several of which were technically more difficult than Mount Everest. She climbed to the top of the highest peaks on all seven continents, becoming the first woman to achieve the 'Seven Summits'. Years later she hosted a Mount Everest Women's Summit, eager to learn about other women's experiences on the mountain. She also continued to mentor young women climbers who followed in her footsteps and led clean-up efforts in the Himalaya. Tabei and other climbers of her era recognized decades later the impact that their expeditions had on the fragile alpine environment. She died in 2016 at the age of seventy-eight, four years after being diagnosed with cancer. Her spirit and humble nature remain tangible today in her memoirs and the accounts of those who knew her. Perhaps most importantly, her impact on the history of mountaineering is indisputable, and she remains an inspiration for anyone who sets foot in the mountains.

INFO

JAPANESE WOMEN'S EVEREST EXPEDITION

NUMBER OF TEAM MEMBERS:
22, including
7 journalists

TOTAL WEIGHT OF EXPEDITION SUPPLIES:
15 tonnes

NUMBER OF PORTERS:
600

TOTAL COST
OF EXPEDITION:
US$406,383

AGE RANGE
OF TEAM MEMBERS:
25-42

FULL TEAM ROSTER:
Eiko Hisano
Junko Tabei
Michiko Manita
Fumie Nasu
Yuriko Watanabe
Masako Naganuma
Yumi Taneya
Setsuko Kitamura
Sumiko Fujiwara
Reiko Shioura
Fumiko Arayama
Sachiko Naka
Yoko Mihara
Teruyo Hirashima
Dr Masako Sakaguchi

On the Everest summit attack morning at Camp 6, 8,500 m (27,887 ft). Standing beside the tent is Ang Tsering.

Gwen Moffat, the UK's First Female Mountain Guide

When Gwen Moffat was twenty-one, she deserted the British Army. All that structure, discipline and obedience was getting her down. It was 1946 in post-war Britain and Moffat was working with the Auxiliary Territorial Service branch. In an impulsive move to take control of her life, she packed up and left, putting her on a course she never could have imagined.

GWEN MOFFAT

Nationality:
British

Born:
3 July 1924

Active:
1946-2006

While working as an army driver, Moffat had been rolling over the countryside, rather enjoying the landscape, when she happened upon a handsome young man who seemed like he might need a lift. He refused the ride but spent some time chatting with Moffat about the war and his disapproval of it, eventually inviting her to a nearby cottage to spend the evening with him and his friends. Moffat, being rather proper at the time, declined his offer and drove away. She had never met any conscientious objectors before and, in the weeks that followed the encounter, Moffat became fascinated by the idea.

Months later, when she had some leave arranged, she sent him a letter suggesting a meet-up – and her new friend Tom took her on her first real adventure. They spent ten days camping in a barn, climbing nearby cliffs and discussing politics in the evenings by the fire. This exciting new way of life was all the convincing she needed to leave the army. She returned to her station, gathered her things and quietly slipped away from the post without anyone noticing.

Until that three-week leave in 1946, Moffat hadn't even the slightest clue that rock climbing or mountain climbing existed in Britain. In her memoir, *Space Below My Feet*, she describes her experience of leaving the army:

> 'My life as a deserter was completely strange and rather wild. I took to it like a duck to water. I was twenty-one and it was my first taste of freedom. At eighteen I had joined the ATS, where any spark of initiative and individualist [sic] had been ruthlessly suppressed. For four years I had been ruled by convention and employers who, on the whole, exercised more authority than sense.'[1]

Her first days on the run were spent trying to keep a low profile with nights spent in barns, working here and there in exchange for a few pounds. Along the way, she met a similarly free-spirited stray border collie, whom she named Thomas, and he immediately became her travelling companion.

Over the next few months, she wandered across beautiful mountain ridges with Thomas, living each day as it came. Eventually she met back up with Tom and his group of bohemian friends, with whom she climbed during the days and discussed poetry, literature, painting and philosophy in the evenings. This artistic troupe of climbing vegetarians holed up in decrepit cottages, claiming squatters' rights, living simply off the land and sometimes doing paid forestry work.

Moffat's life had changed abruptly from following a structured, conventional career path to an undecided, aimless one that was based on maintaining a connection

Opposite: Gwen Moffat, Penrith, Cumbria, England, 2015.

to the outdoors through climbing. She quickly fell in love with mountains and the climbing way of life, and spent all of her free time tackling local rock-climbing classics, eventually improving her technique enough to begin leading VS-graded (Very Severe) rock climbs. Moffat spent much of her time in North Wales and the Lake District, where she did several test pieces, such as Holly Tree Wall, Belle Vue Bastion and Gibson's Chimney on Glyder Fach in Snowdonia. She stayed at hostels, often acting as custodian or doing daily chores to pay for her room and board. When it wasn't raining, she climbed. Moffat was beginning to understand the philosophy of climbing too. She relished her self-sufficiency: she alone was the master of her destiny, on the rock and off.

Little did she know at the time, but Moffat was likely the first woman to complete many of the routes she did with her male companions. She was remarkably complacent about recording her climbs, and they appear only as casual mentions in her autobiography. Had a comprehensive 'ticklist' been of interest to her, it would have helped future generations recognize the scope of her achievements.

Moffat became accustomed to a life of discomfort too. She could be found sleeping in barns or camping wild in a mountain meadow, washing in cold mountain lakes. Moffat also climbed barefoot, realizing that having direct contact between her skin and the rock made her understand the surface better. She was unconcerned about what others might think of her lifestyle. Being homeless or living in poverty didn't worry her as long as it meant she had the freedom to climb. Moffat recalls those carefree days: 'We were young and healthy and, after six years of war, we were free. Poverty? We felt more than privileged, we were rich.'[2]

In 1947, once she had accomplished many climbs in Wales and the Lake District, Moffat hitchhiked north to the Isle of Skye to satiate her need for harder, wilder routes. That summer she climbed on the Cuillin of Skye in delightful, warm weather and then returned to the mainland to scale the North East Buttress of Ben Nevis in fog and mist. She enjoyed Scotland so much that she decided to stay on and find work in Fort William, perhaps partly compelled by the fact that she had run out of money.

Moffat found work as a forester and lived in an abandoned shepherd's hut, called a bothy in Scotland, near Fort Augustus with five other women. The Scottish women didn't think much of Moffat, her climbing lifestyle, vegetarianism and predisposition to swimming nude in mountain lakes

CUILLIN RIDGE TRAVERSE

The Cuillin Ridge on the Isle of Skye is a popular climbing and scrambling ridge that stretches for 13 km (8 miles) with more than 3,000 m (9,843 ft) of height gained that usually takes two days to complete.

1. Gars-bheinn.
2. Sgùrr a' Choire Bhig.
3. Sgùrr nan Eag.
4. Sgùrr Dubh Mòr.
5. In Pinn.
6. Sgùrr a' Ghreadaidh.

GWEN MOFFAT

(never mind in Loch Ness in December!). That Christmas, Moffat planned to meet up with a climbing friend in Glencoe, but instead joined forces with a 'funny, wiry little man with sparkling eyes'[3] named Gordon Moffat.

Gwen and Gordon formed a fast friendship and she introduced him to some of the climbs nearby. They eventually rented a shabby cottage together on Skye, where for four months they set up something of a domestic household – albeit with fleas and rats as companions. The pair spent their days fishing and scouring tidal pools for mussels, crabs and shrimps. In the evenings, they read voraciously. They made a long but fine traverse of the 13-kilometre (8-mile) Cuillin Ridge in June. They were determined not to rush it, but to take their time and soak it all in. When an electrical storm caught them on the climb eleven hours in, they became drenched and hungry. The rain confirmed that taking thirty-nine hours to complete the route may not have been the best tactic after all.

After the Cuillin, they travelled to Chamonix to explore the French Alps, despite having no money or experience on the snow and ice of higher-altitude peaks. Moffat was mesmerized at the first glimpse of Mont Blanc. She made a few ascents to get a flavour of Chamonix's climbing world and the high alpine huts of the region. When she and Gordon returned to the UK, she knew she would be back.

Moffat and Gordon were married soon after and, in 1949, she became pregnant with their daughter, Sheena. In the years of poverty that followed, the couple had various unusual living arrangements – for example, living on a boat – where Moffat struggled to find the balance between motherhood and her desire to maintain her active, climbing life. She eventually sought help from her mother and friends so that she could spend the occasional weekend climbing or a summer in the Alps. Faced with so many domestic and financial challenges, she and Gordon went their separate ways a few years after Sheena's birth.

Moffat returned to the high peaks of mainland Europe, with another successful trip to the Alps and the Italian Dolomites, where she made many first female ascents. She realized that she had a talent for climbing, and by making a career out of her love for the mountains, she could feed and care for Sheena without a husband's salary. Moffat became a member of the women's Pinnacle Club and was invited to join the Alpine Climbing Group; others recognized her potential and provided valuable encouragement. With this boost to her confidence, Moffat decided to become a mountain guide. She and Sheena lived in various climbing clubhouses and hostels as she trained hard to meet the British Mountaineering Council's qualification criteria.

'In that exquisite moment before the hard move, when one looks and understands, may lie an answer to the question why one climbs. You are doing something hard, so hard that failure could mean death but because of knowledge and experience you are doing it safely. This safety depends on yourself, there is no other factor, no horse or piece of machinery to let you down. What you accomplish is by your own efforts and the measure of your success is the width of your margin of safety.'[5]

– Gwen Moffat

Pages 34–35: The Cuillin Ridge, Isle of Skye, Scotland.

INFO

THE LADIES' ALPINE CLUB

In December 1907 a group of ladies who were climbers in the Alps met in London and agreed to form a new club, similar to the long-established Alpine Club, which at the time did not accept women members because of their supposed 'physical and moral deficiencies in the matter of mountain climbing'. It was the first club founded specifically for women mountaineers.

The club's first president was the Bishop of Bristol, then in 1908 Elizabeth Le Blond (see page 11) became the second president. She was an experienced mountaineer who climbed Mont Blanc twice in her career and made more than one hundred climbs in the Alps over two decades.

As well as arranging climbing expeditions, the Ladies' Alpine Club organized a monthly lecture and provided rooms where members could meet for tea. The club had its base at the Great Central Hotel, Marylebone, now the Landmark London. It wasn't until 1975 that the club merged with its male counterpart, the Alpine Club.

Moffat recalls, 'With a guide's certificate behind me I could work full-time at what was, to me, a fabulous salary. Sheena, who needed the company of other children, could go to a boarding school. Or I could stay at the hostel and augment my wages by private guiding in Snowdonia.'[4]

In 1953, after years of hard work, Gwen Moffat became the first certified woman mountain guide in Britain. She had done it against all odds. Although Moffat was qualified to guide others, there was still rampant discrimination against women in the men's world of climbing, and she faced further prejudice as a single mother. Moffat decided to ignore all the social conventions and simply do what she loved. She was ahead of her time, a true champion of British climbing. She set an adventurous blueprint for other women guides to follow, allowing them to realize their dreams and confidently commit to an unconventional lifestyle.

After establishing herself as a guide, Moffat finally set up home more permanently in North Wales, where she launched a successful writing career. In 1961, her memoir Space Below My Feet was published. She would eventually write thirty-five books, including her memoir and more than thirty crime novels. In the 1970s and 1980s she travelled to the US, where she explored the Rockies and the deserts of the American Southwest, once again writing about her experiences. In her seventies, Moffat moved to the Lake District, where she bought her first washing machine after realizing that she quite liked the idea of settling down.

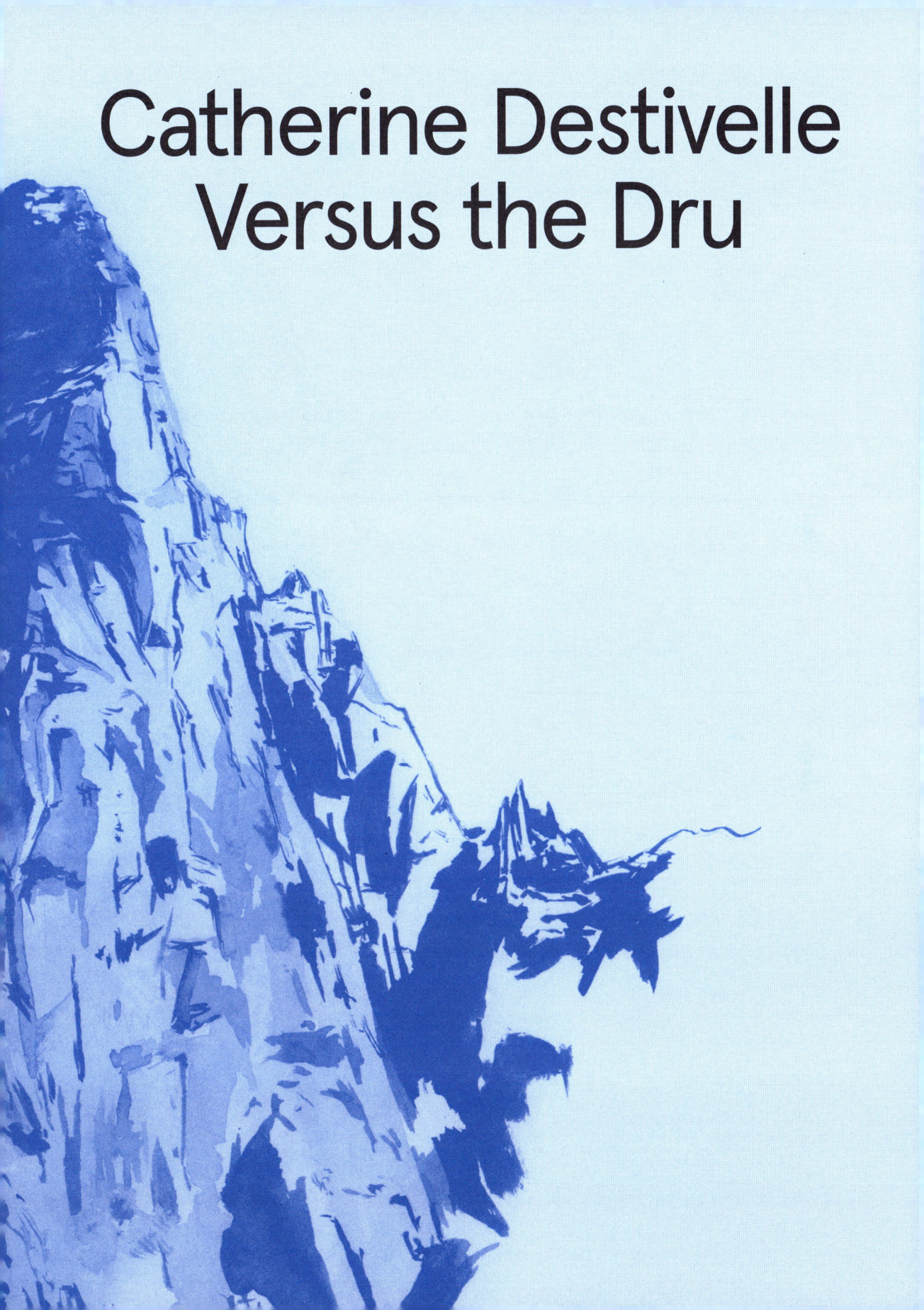

Catherine Destivelle Versus the Dru

The forest of Fontainebleau, located about an hour's drive southeast of Paris, has long been the training ground for French climbers. Like many families, the Destivelles would escape Paris on the weekends, exchanging traffic jams for adventure and fresh air at Fontainebleau. The wooded areas there contain some of the best bouldering in the world; ancient sandstone boulders are scattered throughout the forest and the sandy floor makes for soft, comfortable landing zones. It was here that Catherine Destivelle began her journey to becoming one of France's most celebrated climbers and alpinists.

CATHERINE DESTIVELLE

Nationality:
French

Born:
24 July 1960

Active:
1972-present

Opposite: Catherine Destivelle.
Below: Catherine Destivelle climbing on the Italian side of the Matterhorn.

Destivelle's parents soon recognized her natural affinity for climbing. She was scampering up difficult boulders from an early age and when she turned twelve, she joined Sunday climbing excursions organized by the Club Alpin Français (CAF). Destivelle speedily advanced through some tough boulder problems and her instructors realized that she grew bored quickly, so they eventually left her to explore nearby boulders on her own. In the evenings she would read, lapping up the stories of the many great French forefathers of climbing: men like René Desmaison, Pierre Allain and Gaston Rébuffat.

Just a year later, in bouts of teenage rebellion, Destivelle began escaping to Fontainebleau and even further afield to the foothills of the Alps on her own. She would board a train from the suburbs of Paris and meet a guide friend to climb mountains, her parents believing she was still joining the CAF group.

The summer when Destivelle turned fourteen, her parents allowed her to circumnavigate the Oisans, near the town of La Grave. She carried everything she needed for a strenuous ten-day hike through the mountainous area alone: a thrilling adventure that instilled confidence in her and affirmed her desire to make a life in the mountains.

By the time she was sixteen, Destivelle had come under the mentorship of several Fontainebleau regulars, all men ten to fifteen years her senior. It was around this time that she was first introduced to the climbs of the Verdon Gorge, a steep limestone canyon that is one of France's most famous climbing areas. Known for its sustained, difficult routes, it is considered the birthplace of modern sport climbing. On the long, vertical walls of the Verdon, Destivelle honed her technique on tiny, invisible holds and learned about conserving energy and building endurance. She soaked up the technical expertise of her elders, watching their every move, hanging on every word they said.

Destivelle's natural ability and willingness to learn eventually drew her to the bigger mountains in the Alps and soon thereafter she had the opportunity to climb the Aiguille du Dru, part of the Mont Blanc massif. The sharp granite peak of the Dru is intimidating as it rises impossibly out of the Mer de Glace (Sea of Ice) glacier. It would capture Destivelle's imagination for decades to come, and she would perform some of her most celebrated climbs on this peak. On this trip in 1977, she and her companion Pierre managed the 'American Direct' route on the Dru in a record seven hours. 'I felt as if I had wings and I wanted to soar,'[1] she said when they returned to the valley floor.

In the decade that followed, there was a lull of four years when Destivelle pursued a career in physiotherapy. But the pull of the mountains proved too strong, and she followed the outstanding achievements of some of her countrymen – climbers like Patrick Edlinger and Christophe Profit – who were at the forefront of the new free-climbing movement. Determined to get back in shape, Destivelle agreed to be part of a film project that would have her return to the Verdon. This launched her back into the French climbing limelight, with media acclaim that drew sponsors and allowed her to quit her job and become a full-time climber.

Like many climbers in the 1980s, Destivelle joined the newly formed competition climbing scene and was very successful at mastering the manmade walls. She came up against several outstanding women climbers like Lynn Hill (see page 100), whom the French media played up gleefully as her adversary. Although her victories were many, Destivelle felt that climbing on artificial routes was too distant from the original feeling of being on real rock. The competitions lost their allure, and she commited once again to the mountains as an alpinist.

For her first big challenge, Destivelle chose to return to the mighty Dru. This time, she would solo the classic Bonatti Pillar on the southwest face, a formation named for the Italian alpinist Walter Bonatti, who established the route in 1955. Bonatti was considered a visionary: using equipment and techniques of the day, it took him six days to solo the pillar.

Destivelle's first planned attempt at a solo on the Dru was stymied by poor weather. Not one to rest on her laurels, she eagerly accepted an invitation to join an otherwise all-male expedition to the Great Trango Tower in Pakistan, organized by US alpinist Jeff Lowe. The expedition was rife with financial and logistical challenges from the start, but the trip proved to be a vital cog in the development of Destivelle's career as an alpinist. The team was successful on the tower, and this gave her experience in the realm of remote mountain ranges, as well as credibility among her peers. A highly acclaimed documentary of the expedition followed, which was shown at mountain film festivals worldwide, spreading the news of her talent and likeable personality.

When Destivelle returned to France, the Dru beckoned once more. A French filmmaker had got wind of her plans and Destivelle agreed to document her ascent. On 10 October 1990, she made her way up the snowy couloir, which brought her to the bivouac at the base of the climb. After a good night's rest, she started up the granite monolith in the brilliant autumn sunshine. Destivelle soon found the rhythm and flow that is coveted by so many climbers. She danced quickly up the rock, resting only

'Every now and then pieces of protection that she placed in cracks and seams would fail, sending her down several metres until the next piece held and the rope caught her fall.'

Summit – 3,733 m/12,247 ft

THE PETIT DRU SOUTHWEST FACE

Both the Bonatti Pillar and Destivelle's route, la Voie Destivelle, have succumbed to serious rockfall and no longer exist.

1. Bonatti Pillar route (see page 45).
2. Arête des Flammes de Pierres.
3. Grand Dru.

occasionally to drink and rest. After only a few hours she was greeted on the summit by the film crew. Once news of her climb spread, the French media once again pounced on the opportunity to celebrate 'la belle Catherine' and her mountain exploits, attention she has never been comfortable with. Comparisons were made between her ascent and Bonatti's, but this frustrated Destivelle, who believed her speedy ascent was the result of improved equipment and an already established route. Although she became the first woman to solo the route, she downplayed her achievement in her autobiography but admitted the comparison had inspired her to attempt a new route of her own, which became her next goal.

Since the expedition to Trango Tower, Destivelle had maintained a close connection with Jeff Lowe. Knowing she would have to spend several days and nights on the blank walls of the Dru while setting up a new route, she went to Utah with him to learn about the nuances of living in a hanging tent called a portaledge and how to aid climb, which would be crucial to her success. After her solo, she had been accused of taking too many risks, criticism that was unlikely to befall her male counterparts. Nothing could have been further from the truth as she sought out knowledge and skills that would make her next ascent as safe as possible.

When the day came to establish her new route, Destivelle felt all the cards were in place. She was physically and mentally prepared, new sponsors had been secured and she had friends ready to both support her and document the climb. At 5 a.m. on 24 June 1991, Destivelle stepped on to the granite of the Dru, unknowingly committing to what would become eleven days of intense climbing made more difficult by almost impassable rock features combined with several days of unpredicted, atrocious weather.

From day one, Destivelle encountered blank sections of rock that took exceptional amounts of physical and mental energy to overcome. Every now and then the pieces of protection that she placed in cracks and seams would fail, sending her down several metres until the next piece held and the rope caught her fall. Unnerving as it must have been, Destivelle was determined to continue and managed three pitches on the first day.

The next few days brought dismal weather. The Dru was covered with light rain and fog, making progress difficult. Destivelle inched her way up the wall between tiny storms, maintaining positivity as best she could. In the evenings, she would return to her hanging camp, soaked to the bone, to prepare a humble meal of soup or dehydrated vegetables and try to sleep.

Catherine Destivelle climbs the Clocher de Planpraz in Chamonix, France.

> **INFO**
>
> **THE COLLAPSE OF THE BONATTI PILLAR**
>
> In June 2005, the Bonatti Pillar disappeared from the face when more than 300,000 cubic metres (10,594,400 cubic feet) of rock collapsed on the Dru. Two years before, part of the pillar had already fallen off, likely due to frost heave, or melting and freezing of ice. Walter Bonatti's original 1955 route and Catherine Destivelle's are now lost.

On the fifth day she awoke to fresh snow, which made it impossible to climb until midday. Ever vigilant, she pressed on inch by inch, seeking out imperfections in the smooth rock face that would allow her to protect her climb. Sometimes the crack she was following would get smaller and smaller, then disappear entirely, forcing her to the left or right in search of new passages. When the seams were tiny, she could only sink the pitons partially into the crack, and when she weighted them with her body, they would sometimes fail. On her sixth day she experienced one such failure. Five other pieces failed in succession, sending her down 12 metres (39 feet) until she finally landed upside down, caught by the rope.

After so many days on the sharp granite walls, Destivelle's hands had been butchered by the rock. As part of her evening routine, she would cover them tightly with medical tape to temper infection and preserve the little skin she had left. By day nine, she could barely flex her fingers because they were so swollen, but she persevered nonetheless.

Destivelle continued to encounter difficult obstacles throughout her ascent. Sometimes she would have to perform delicate sections of free climbing or set up pendulums where she swung sideways on the rope looking for a new line to access. Ultimately, after eleven days, she emerged on the summit. She had established a new route, from the ground up, under her own steam, emulating the great climbers she had so admired as a child. In the months and years that followed, Destivelle would receive many accolades but her new route on the Dru holds its place in history as one of the great first ascents.

Destivelle would go on to climb many more peaks and achieve many more outrageous ascents including a triple crown of soloing three great north faces of the Alps in winter: the Eiger, Grandes Jorasses and the Matterhorn. She also ventured into the Himalaya several times and successfully climbed Shishapangma, although it was her climbs in the Alps that give her the most pride. More recently, she established a publishing company, Éditions du Mont Blanc, which is dedicated to publishing mountain literature. In 2020, she was awarded a Piolet d'Or Lifetime Achievement Award, the Oscars of mountaineering, and she is the only woman so far to be recognized for her life's work in alpinism.

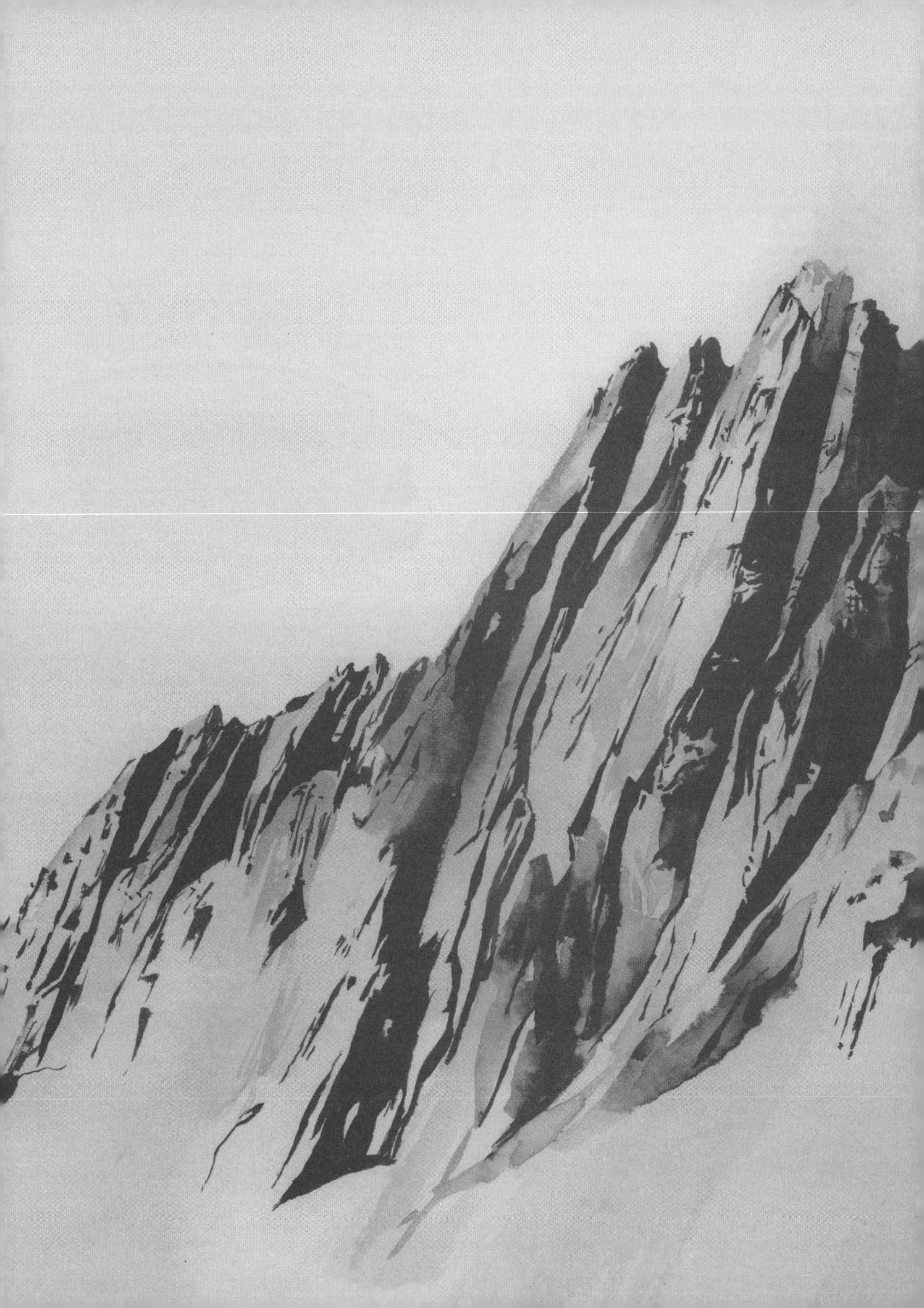

Wasfia Nazreen and the Seven Summits

Wasfia Nazreen doesn't look like a climber. At least, that's what most people say when she tells them she's climbed the Seven Summits, the highest mountain on each continent, as well as K2. They can't understand how a Bengali woman from Bangladesh, one of the poorest countries in the world, who didn't grow up surrounded by snow-capped peaks, could summit the tallest mountains on the planet. Nazreen has experienced discrimination throughout her life – it's the driving force that sent her on a path of self-discovery while climbing the world's highest peaks.

WASFIA NAZREEN

Nationality:
Bangladeshi

Born:
27 October 1982

Active:
2002-present

Opposite: Wasfia Nazreen canoeing in British Columbia.
Below: Wasfia Nazreen with mentor Pat Morrow, the first to ascend the Seven Summits.

When she was twelve years old, Nazreen's parents divorced, an unusual occurrence in the conservative nation of Bangladesh, where marriage is the pillar of society. Young women are encouraged to marry early, a practice rooted in centuries-old patriarchy.

Raised in the tradition of Islam, Nazreen recognized at an early age the unfairness of others dictating her future – and that of so many Bangladeshi women like her. As a teenager, she refused to conform to society's expectations and, as soon as she was able, left for the US, with less than two hundred dollars in her pocket. Desperate to find a higher calling, she decided that pursuing a college education abroad would lift her out of the cycle of repression in Bangladesh.

Nazreen focused her studies on art and social psychology, and she received a grant to go back to Asia and research how women were using art as therapy. She travelled to northern India, where she started working with female Tibetan refugees who had been tortured in Chinese prisons. She then moved to Dharamsala, the home of His Holiness the Dalai Lama, a lively community in the foothills of the Himalaya. Nazreen soon found purpose in the Free Tibet movement. She could relate to the struggle of others and was determined to help them in their fight against injustice.

Not long after her arrival in Dharamsala, the Dalai Lama heard about Nazreen and sent a formal request asking her to meet with him. She was surprised, honoured and terrified. She had no idea what to expect.

Nervous and still a little confused, Nazreen listened intently to His Holiness until suddenly the Dalai Lama pressed his thumb to her forehead (the place between the eyes often referred to as the 'third eye' in Buddhist tradition). He empathically told her that she needed to stop doubting herself and recognize the power that she had within. She was speechless as the Dalai Lama followed this gesture with his signature belly laugh. And so began their friendship, a relationship that deepened during the years that followed, as the Dalai Lama guided Nazreen's healing and spiritual journey. He later told her that while he was grateful for her involvement in the Free Tibet movement, it was the young women of Bangladesh who really needed her help – and that she was destined to be the inspiration for an entire nation.

Learning from the Buddhist teachings of mindfulness and respect for the earth, Nazreen began her journey of freedom and forgiveness through meditation and self-realization practices. She began to visit and revere the 5,000–6,000-metre (16,404–19,685-foot) peaks in India. This naturally led to a number of visits to mountain communities in neighbouring Nepal, where she immersed herself in the culture of the high Himalaya.

Summit - 4,884 m/16,023 ft

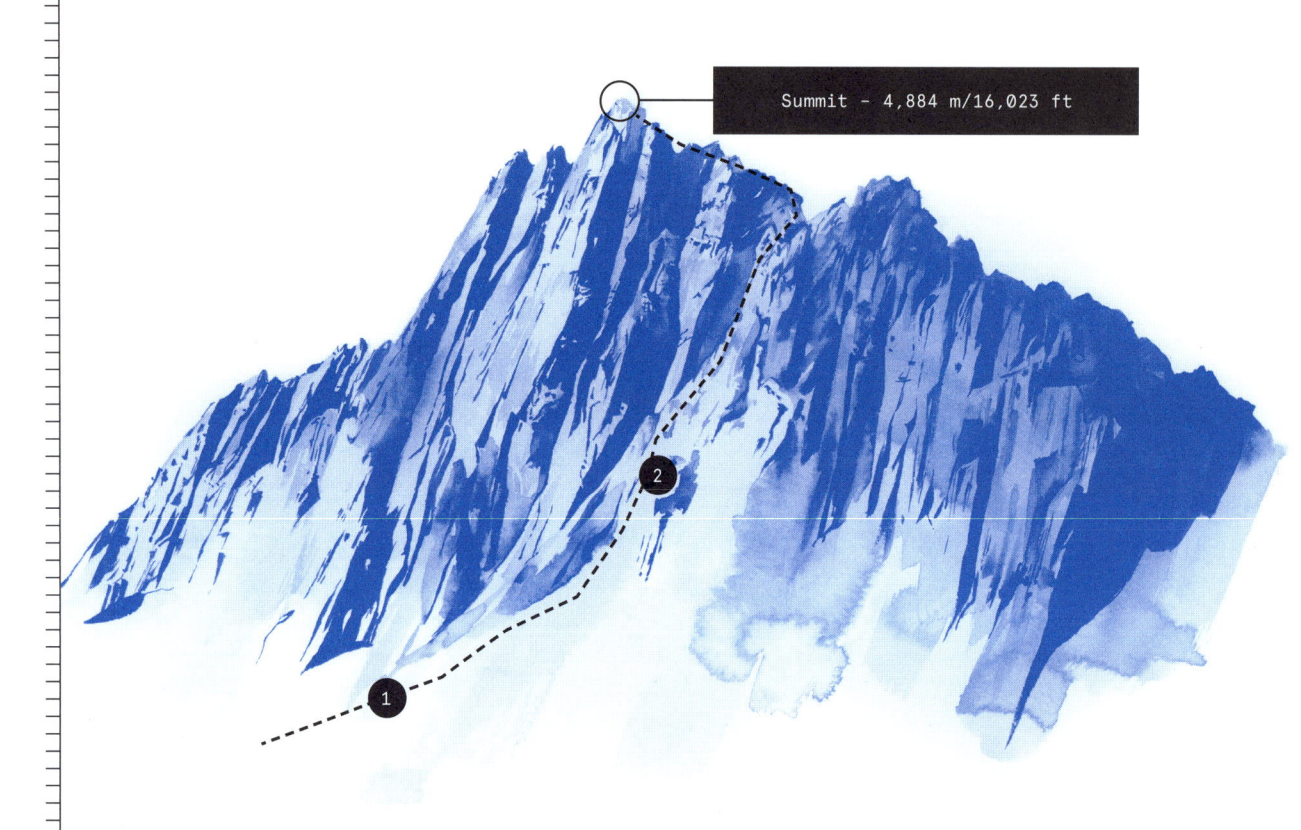

CARSTENSZ PYRAMID (PUNCAK JAYA) STANDARD ROUTE

Located on the island of New Guinea in Indonesia, Carstensz Pyramid is the highest island peak in the world and one of the Seven Summits. The Standard Route on Carstensz Pyramid requires moderate technical rock climbing but can be summited in one day.

1. Basecamp - 4,200 m/13,780 ft.
2. Standard Route.

INFO

THE SEVEN SUMMITS
– THE HIGHEST
PEAKS ON EACH
CONTINENT

AFRICA:
Kilimanjaro, Tanzania
5,895 m (19,341 ft)

ANTARCTICA:
Mount Vinson
4,892 m (16,050 ft)

ASIA:
Chomolungma (Mount Everest), Nepal/Tibet
8,849 m (29,032 ft)

EUROPE:
Mount Elbrus, Russia
5,642 m (18,510 ft)

NORTH AMERICA:
Denali, USA
6,194 m (20,321 ft)

OCEANIA:
Puncak Jaya (Carstenz Pyramid), Indonesia
4,884 m (16,024 ft)

SOUTH AMERICA:
Aconcagua, Argentina
6,961 m (22,838 ft)

Nazreen immediately found connection and friendship with the Sherpa people in Nepal, whose ancestors had also hailed from Tibet centuries before. With each trip, she honed her climbing skills and learned about the Sherpas' deep respect for nature and reverence for the deities that live among the Himalayan peaks. She began to understand what it meant to be emotionally and spiritually connected to the land, learning how to perform the puja, a ceremony conducted before each climb to seek permission from the mountain, and the importance of seeking blessings from Lamas and other spiritual advisors before ascending the peaks.

Encouraged by His Holiness, Nazreen's love of climbing and the Himalaya eventually led to the goal of climbing the Seven Summits to inspire her fellow Bangladeshis. In 2011, in recognition of forty years of Bangladesh's independence, she announced her Seven Summits plan to raise awareness of the plight of young women in her country. Nazreen found herself once again fighting against a generational mindset intent on discrediting her and her achievements, but she refused to let any obstacles stand in her way. In 2015, when she summited Carstensz Pyramid in Indonesia, she became the first Bangladeshi to complete the challenge. Finally, an entire nation, if not the whole planet, was paying attention to her message of hope.

When Nazreen returned to Dhaka, Bangladesh's capital city, she was met by a media circus and thousands of fans. She had succeeded in shifting the mindset of many Bangladeshis, men and women alike. Having become a national hero, brand endorsements, modelling offers and acting proposals – as well as marriage proposals – began to roll in. This newfound fame overwhelmed her. While she could have stopped seeking new heights, and used the attention to uplift her women's rights foundation, Nazreen wasn't done with climbing yet. One mountain still lingered in the back of her mind: K2.

K2 is known as Chogori, the 'King of Mountains', in the Balti language. No Bengali had yet set foot on its top when, in 2012, Nazreen began dreaming of a trip to the Karakoram. Since Bangladesh's independence movement of the 1970s, diplomatic relations between Bangladesh, India and Pakistan have remained tense. Many Bangladeshis still feel a strong cultural connection to their Bengali brothers and sisters in Pakistan but are also proud of their own nationhood.

Nazreen would spend countless hours over the next decade trying to obtain a visa for Pakistan and secure a permit for her climb. Political tensions between India and Pakistan were always threatening to boil over. Frustrated by red tape, and needing affirmation that her desire to climb K2 was the right thing to do, Nazreen sought guidance from a Rinpoche (a reincarnated holy man or teacher of Buddhism). He advised her which team would suit her while cryptically divining that all her expectations would be upended.

With the help of Nazir Sabir, former President of the Pakistani Alpine Club and one of Pakistan's most celebrated mountaineers, Nazreen's visa and climbing permit were finally granted at the end of 2021, allowing her to enter the country in the spring of 2022. As the Rinpoche had predicted, her expedition to Pakistan was nothing like she expected, starting with her arrival in Islamabad. Pakistanis welcomed her with open arms, declaring that their Bengali sister had arrived home. Unbeknown to Nazreen, the Pakistani press had widely publicized her expedition and the local climbing community supported her bid to climb K2. They saw the potential of having a Bengali woman summit: if she achieved the ascent, it could act as a bridge between their two countries.

The 70-kilometre (43-mile) approach to K2 was gruelling. Nazreen was used to the well-trodden trails of Nepal, not the harsh landscape of the Baltoro Glacier. She also worried about the lack of rescue services in Pakistan, where the army is largely responsible for attending to climbers in distress. High-altitude rescues are complex and take time, and money, to organize. Nazreen would have to summon all her physical and mental strength to ensure success.

Wasfia Nazreen arriving at the airport in Bangladesh after achieving the Seven Summits.

Nazreen and her climbing partner, Mingma Sherpa, were part of a larger expedition that included women from other countries and Sherpa team members from Nepal, plus a team of local Balti porters and camp staff, who provided vital support. Sharing basecamp is common practice with remote expeditions where permits are complex and logistics are difficult. This allows resources and manpower to be used by everyone, both those climbing independently and as guided clients.

As part of their two-and-a-half-month acclimatization process, Nazreen and Mingma climbed to various high camps on nearby Broad Peak. Acclimatizing is a strategy where climbers move up the mountain slowly, sleeping in higher-altitude camps so their bodies gradually adjust to having less oxygen in this harsh environment. Nazreen and Mingma returned to basecamp regularly to rest and to wait for the ideal weather window for their final summit bid on K2.

The year 2022 was an interesting one at K2 basecamp. More climbers were awaiting their turn on Chogori than ever before, as the COVID-19 pandemic had prevented most expeditions from entering Pakistan in 2020 and 2021. Nazreen and Mingma would have to fight to secure their place in line on the Abruzzi Ridge when their summit bid began in earnest. Once at the higher camps, they would also find crowded conditions, and that some underprepared groups were taking advantage of their expedition's equipment – for example, using their tents at high camps, something normally considered unacceptable except in a life-or-death situation.

After many weeks of alternating between training, moving to higher camps and resting at basecamp, Nazreen and Mingma found their weather window and decided to make an attempt on the peak. They left K2 Advanced Base Camp at 5,303 metres (17,398 feet) and climbed directly to Camp 2 (6,700 metres/21,982 feet), where they spent an uncomfortable night with five climbers crammed into a two-person tent. The following day they progressed up the steep rock of the Abruzzi Spur to Camp 3, at 7,250 metres (23,786 feet). From here, Nazreen and Mingma felt strong enough to tackle the Shoulder and the Bottleneck in one push to the summit. These are two of the most difficult parts of the climb and would prove to be a real challenge without overnighting at the higher Camp 4. They reasoned that the less time they spent above 8,000 metres (26,247 feet), in the 'Death Zone', the better their chances of reaching the summit and completing the difficult descent off the mountain.

In the early hours of 22 July, Nazreen and Mingma left their tiny tent and crept into the darkness, their path lit only by the tiny beams from their headlamps. Slowly, they worked their way up the fixed lines that brought them below the ominous serac that looms over climbers as they approach the notorious pinch of the Bottleneck. Nazreen was grateful for the cover of night. Not seeing the huge chunk of ice somehow made her feel better, even though she knew that should the serac come tumbling down, it would take out everything and everyone in its path. On the ascent and in her training climbs, Nazreen had sadly observed other climbers who had not been so lucky: along the route there are several bodies that have been left to the elements, too difficult to bring down for proper burial. Passing these corpses was a harsh reminder that the mountain could take whomever it wanted, at any moment. Nazreen waited patiently as slower climbers moved on the lines ahead of her. In the confusion of the night, she was separated from Mingma.

As daylight began to break over the Karakoram range, Nazreen was dumbfounded by the glorious peaks that surrounded her. After reuniting with Mingma, she topped out at 8.55 a.m. The realization of a life-long dream, Nazreen broke down and wept, releasing all the emotion that had built up over years. Only months before, her father, who had supported her mission to empower young Bangladeshis, had passed away. As joy and sorrow poured over her, she placed a precious ring of her father's on the summit. It was overwhelming to be atop K2. Forging her own path, she had proved everyone wrong, ignoring the forces that told her she wasn't capable.

Since 2015, Nazreen has led the Ösel Foundation, an educational institute set on empowering Bangladeshi youth through outdoor adventures. In addition to her involvement in the Free Tibet movement, she continues to be an active voice for many international causes, including environmental groups and animal rights organizations. She has many accolades and is a former National Geographic Adventurer of the year and National Geographic Explorer. She was named by Outside magazine as one of forty women in the last forty years who have advanced the outdoor world through their leadership, innovation and athletic feats.

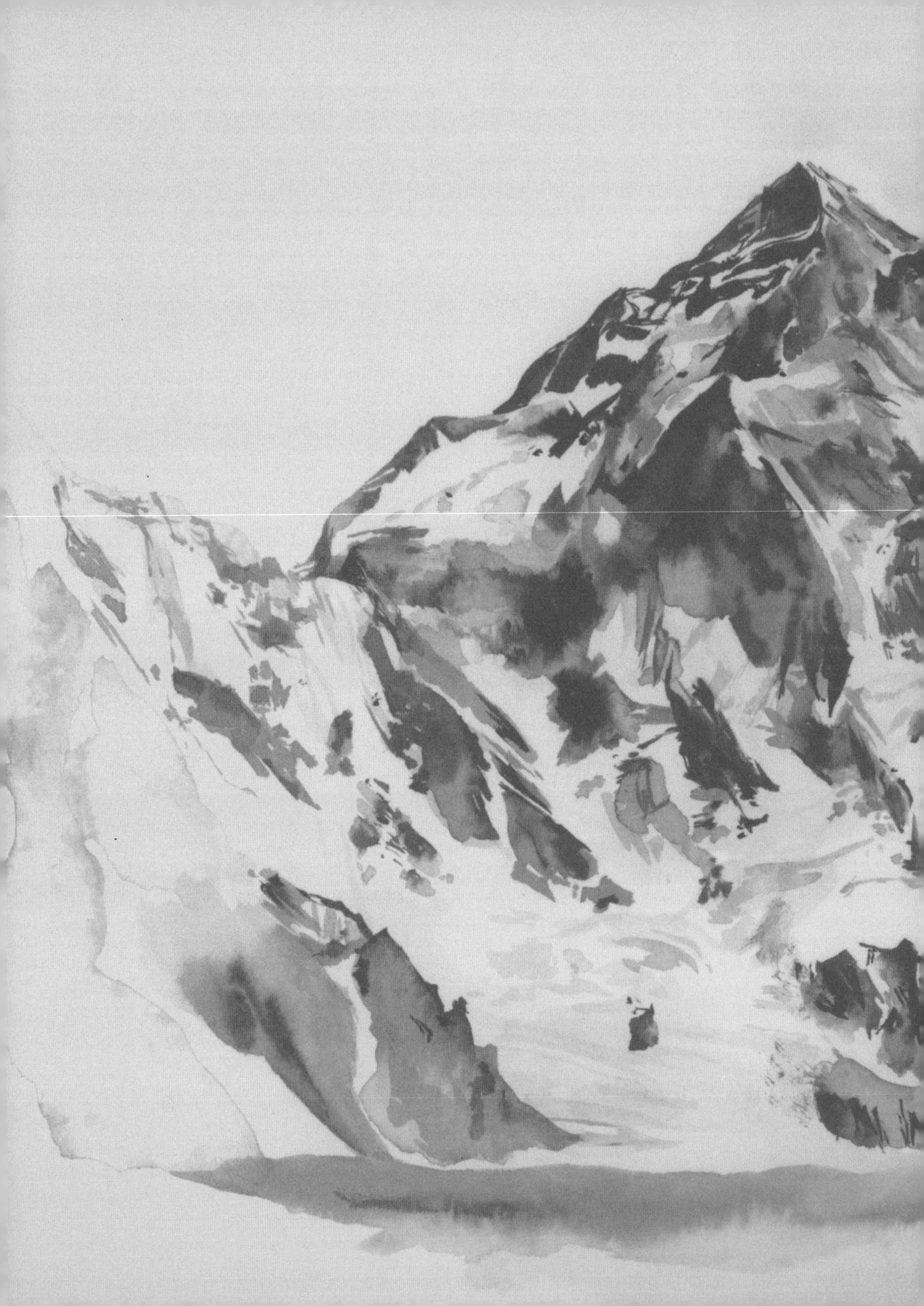

Wanda Rutkiewicz and Her Obsession with K2

Polish climbing celebrity Wanda Rutkiewicz had never worked so hard for a summit. She couldn't quite believe she had made it to the top. She had already been successful on five 8,000-metre (26,247-foot) peaks, but K2 had remained elusive. In 1986, this was her third attempt on the world's second highest mountain. With her successful climb of Everest eight years earlier, Rutkiewicz had become the third woman and the first Polish climber to reach the top of the world. She was on a roll and the media loved her, but standing atop K2 was not the time to celebrate. She still had to come down off the mountain, a journey that would prove more challenging than anyone on her team expected.

WANDA RUTKIEWICZ

Nationality:
Polish

Born:
4 February 1943

Died:
13 May 1992 (age 49)

Active:
1964-1992

Opposite: Wanda Rutkiewicz ascends a glacier.
Below: Wanda Rutkiewicz climbs in Sokoliki, near Wrocław, Poland, in the 1960s.

Rutkiewicz glanced ahead, through the raging wind and driving snow near the top of the Bottleneck, a narrow icy pinch and one of the steepest sections of K2's Abruzzi Spur. She froze. Her climbing partner, French journalist Michel Parmentier, descending quickly in front of her, had slipped. He was now sliding down the precarious icy slope. Rutkiewicz was sure he would be severely injured and she would be forced to organize a complex high-altitude rescue – or worse still, he might plummet to his death. Remarkably, Parmentier hit a firm snowbank, breaking his fall. He stood up, dusted himself off and continued downwards without so much as a glance in her direction. Rutkiewicz could hardly believe her eyes, but she had no time to wonder at his luck. Getting back to camp had to be her primary goal and she would let nothing distract her.

Rutkiewicz's early life had equipped her well to respond to desperate situations in the mountains. She grew up in post-war Poland, where life was not easy under Soviet occupation. Millions of Poles had been dispossessed of their properties under communism. Cities were in ruins and food was scarce. When she was very young, her brother had been killed while playing near an unexploded landmine, a horrific episode in her family history that would have a lasting emotional impact. When Rutkiewicz was an adult, her father was brutally murdered and dismembered by his assailants. She was sent to the morgue to identify the body. These traumatic incidents shaped Rutkiewicz's character, building the strength and mental fortitude that distinguished her climbing career.

Rutkiewicz had been working towards her successful summit of K2 for decades. Early in the 1960s, she discovered climbing through friends at university and took every opportunity to meet with other climbers between her studies in mathematics and engineering. She began climbing at the small local crags of Góry Sokole near Katowice before making her first forays into the higher and more challenging Tatra Mountains. From the outset, Rutkiewicz built a special relationship with other women climbers, though there were very few in the Polish climbing community at the time. These friendships would become an important aspect of her life once she started organizing large expeditions in the decades that followed.

By 1967, Rutkiewicz had completed four trips to the Alps, all on a shoestring budget. In 1968, along with fellow climber and countrywoman Halina Krüger-Syrokomska, she took on the intimidating Trollryggen – a huge vertical wall in Norway. She had met Krüger-Syrokomska the year before in the Alps. They proved to be a formidable rope team and became the first all-women's team to ascend the

East Buttress of Trollryggen. They returned to Poland to a rapturous reception. Climbing was a national sport and they were the darlings of the communist party.

Following her success in Norway, Rutkiewicz was invited to join several large mixed-gender expeditions to Central Asia, but she never felt she was treated as an equal. Her best moments came when she was climbing with like-minded women. Never been one to conform to societal expectations, she made it her mission to plan and execute women-only expeditions. After a particularly tumultuous trip, Rutkiewicz confided in a friend, 'Climbing with all-women teams gives me the most satisfaction because even the presence of a man on a rope sometimes sub-consciously frees one from taking responsibility for a climbing action.'[1]

Before 1974, no woman had summitted any of the 8,000-metre (26,247-foot) peaks in the Himalaya. This did not escape Wanda's notice. With lofty goals in mind, she systematically began to hone her technical skills in preparation. In 1973, she turned her attention to the Alps and – along with Danuta Wach and Stefania Egierszdorff – made a notable first female ascent of the North Pillar of the Eiger in Switzerland, despite almost losing her toes to frostbite. The climb was the second ascent overall and was widely celebrated by the Polish media. Rutkiewicz rode the momentum of this victorious climb and organized many all-women's expeditions in the decade and a half that followed.

After the Eiger, Rutkiewicz made a first ascent on Gasherbrum III (the highest unclimbed peak at the time) and the first all-women's ascent of the North Face of the Matterhorn. She also became the first Pole to reach the summit of Everest. In 1981, Rutkiewicz applied for a permit to climb K2 the following season. To prepare, she planned a training expedition to the highest mountain in Europe, Mount Elbrus in the Caucasus. This proved to be a mistake when one of her companions above her fell, knocking her more than 200 metres (656 feet) down the slope. When she came to, Rutkiewicz realized that she had badly broken her leg; her trip to K2 was in jeopardy.

Rutkiewicz underwent multiple surgeries and a long recovery period. But she refused to let the injury deter her; as a Pole with little access to currency beyond the Iron Curtain, she was acutely aware that her Pakistani climbing permit fee was non-refundable. So, in the spring of 1982, as planned, she managed the arduous multi-day trek to basecamp on crutches so that she might support the other women – who would now attempt the summit without her. In her book *Savage Summit*, author Jennifer Jordan describes the trip:

'Gritting her teeth against the pain, Wanda wore through several pairs of crutches on the onerous eleven-day journey but was nonetheless nonchalant. She was determined not to slow the team down and not to feel sorry for herself... she used her crutches to propel herself from rock to rock and over to the increasingly wild floodwaters of the Baltoro and Godwin-Austen Glaciers.' [2]

As the rest of the women worked hard to set up higher camps, Wanda managed to hobble along and reach the team's advanced basecamp at 5,400 metres (17,716 feet), where she acted as expedition leader. After weeks of relentless effort, the team established their Camp 2. Erected below the daunting Black Pyramid, it put them in a promising position for establishing two more high camps that would enable a summit bid in the days that followed. One of the hardest-working members of the team was Rutkiewicz's former climbing partner Halina Krüger-Syrokomska. Sadly, the night after establishing Camp 2, Krüger-Syrokomska fell unconscious and suddenly died. All the team members were shocked. She had been an extremely valuable team member, a lively, inspiring personality and dear friend. The decision of whether to proceed with the summit bid or pack up and go home weighed heavily on Rutkiewicz as team leader. After a few days of reflection, the women decided that Halina would have wanted them to press on and try for the summit. A small team ultimately went as high as 7,100 metres (23,294 feet) before finally retreating due to uncooperative weather. After sixty-nine days on the mountain, and a tearful goodbye to a cherished friend, the expedition abandoned their efforts.

Before leaving K2, Rutkiewicz and her teammates decided to give Krüger-Syrokomska a proper burial. Recovering bodies is not common practice in high-altitude expeditions; they are often left on the mountain, particularly at altitudes above 8,000 metres (26,247 feet), where retrieval can mean risking one's own life. Other expedition members from neighbouring peaks, including famous climbers Jerzy Kukuczka and Reinhold Messner, convened at K2 basecamp and joined the efforts to bring Halina down off the Abruzzi Spur so that she could finally be put to rest at the Gilkey Memorial.

Rutkiewicz was not yet prepared to give up on K2, but she needed time to let her leg heal properly. So, it wasn't until 1984 that she returned to the peak – with three other women climbers, including Anna Czerwinska and Krystyna Palmowska from the 1982 attempt. Poor weather hampered the expedition yet again, leaving the team no choice but to

Summit - 8,611 m/28,251 ft

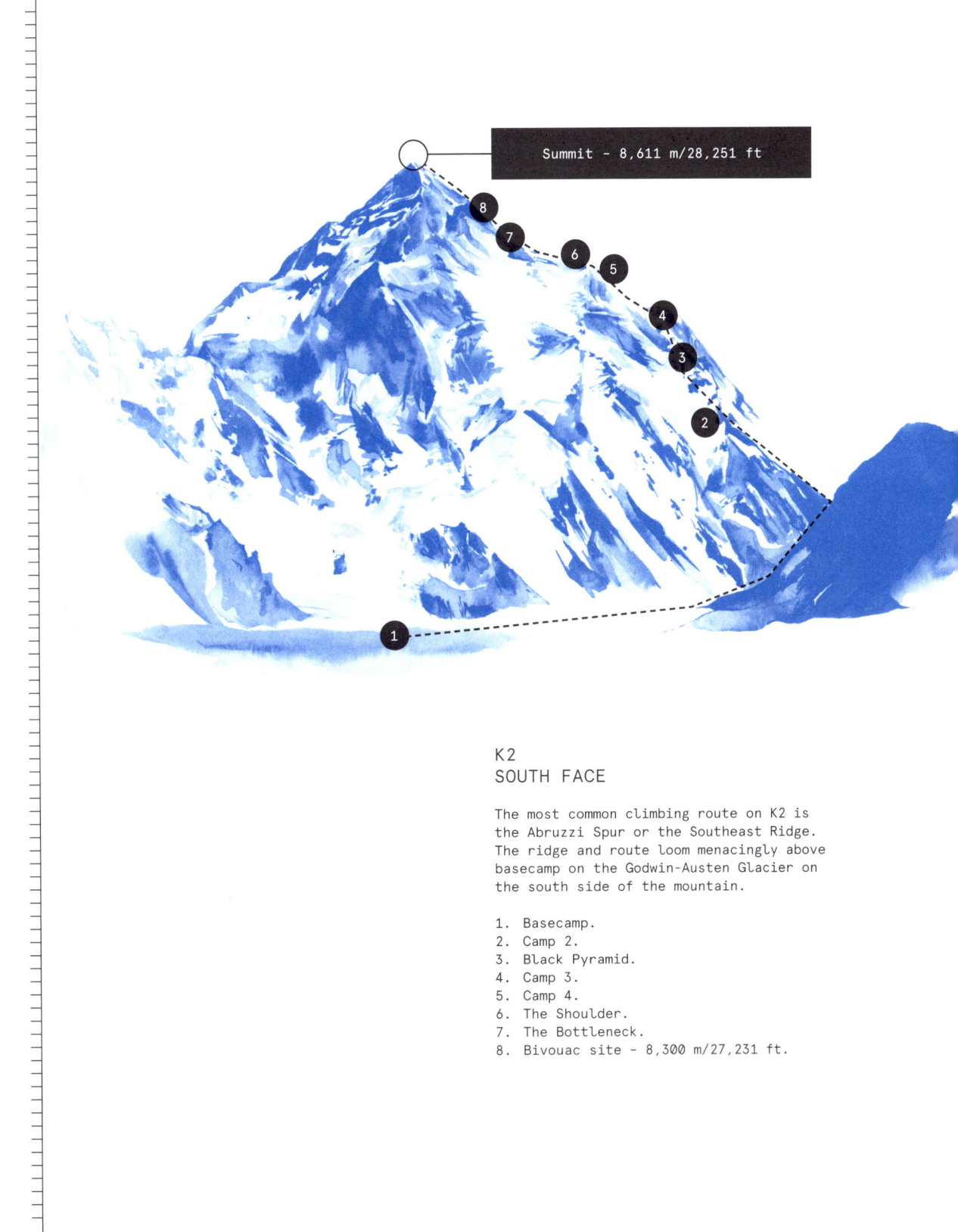

K2
SOUTH FACE

The most common climbing route on K2 is the Abruzzi Spur or the Southeast Ridge. The ridge and route loom menacingly above basecamp on the Godwin-Austen Glacier on the south side of the mountain.

1. Basecamp.
2. Camp 2.
3. Black Pyramid.
4. Camp 3.
5. Camp 4.
6. The Shoulder.
7. The Bottleneck.
8. Bivouac site - 8,300 m/27,231 ft.

WANDA RUTKIEWICZ

settle for reaching Camp 3 at 7,400 metres (24,278 feet). Still, K2 would not relent.

Rutkiewicz went on two further expeditions before her final attempt on K2 in 1986. First, she ascended Aconcagua, the highest mountain in South America. Next, she summited Nanga Parbat in Pakistan and, on the same trip, attempted an ascent of Broad Peak. Both these expeditions faced challenges involving conflicting personalities. After the trip, several climbers decided that they would never climb with Rutkiewicz again, claiming her hardheadedness and intense competitiveness were too much.

In 1986, there were a number of other expeditions planned for K2, several of which had their sights set on putting the first woman on its summit. Rutkiewicz was snubbed by former climbing partners and conspicuously not invited to join a large national Polish team, so she was forced to find companions elsewhere.

She turned to French climbers Maurice and Liliane Barrard. They had high-altitude experience and Liliane had recently become the first woman on Nanga Parbat. They were planning to attempt K2 that spring in alpine style – moving lighter and faster than larger expeditions, establishing smaller camps only as needed and stashing supplies along the way rather than spending weeks establishing camps in set locations on the Abruzzi Spur. Rutkiewicz joined their expedition, along with journalist Michel Parmentier. The two butted heads almost from the outset when it was decided that they would be partners, while Liliane and Maurice would be the second rope team. Rutkiewicz refused to share a tent with Parmentier on the lower parts of the ridge, which meant additional weight for her to carry on the climb. Parmentier had a tendency to abandon his teammates and proceed on his own, increasing the risk for himself and others.

All differences aside, the small team managed to summit K2 in a six-day push from basecamp and Rutkiewicz became the first woman to stand on top of the second highest peak in the world. The group had moved slowly but steadily on their ascent, making the climb without the use of supplemental oxygen, and she had beaten the Barrards and Parmentier to the summit. They finally arrived an hour after her and spent some time enjoying the view.

After almost two hours on the summit, Rutkiewicz became bitterly cold and realized she had to start descending, so she moved ahead of her companions and waited for them at 8,300 metres (27,230 feet) at a flat spot where they had bivouacked the night before. When Maurice arrived, looking haggard and exhausted, he declared they would go no further that day. Rutkiewicz reluctantly agreed to spend the night, knowing that staying so high would affect their

---

INFO

ALL-WOMEN'S EXPEDITIONS ORGANIZED BY WANDA RUTKIEWICZ

1968
Trollryggen, Norway

1973
North Pillar of the Eiger, Switzerland

1975
Gasherbrum III, Pakistan

1978
North Face of the Matterhorn, Switzerland

1982
K2, Pakistan - unsuccessful, reached 7,100 m/23,294 ft)

1984
K2, Pakistan - unsuccessful, reached 7,400 m/24,278 ft)

1985
South Face of Aconcagua, Argentina

1989
Gasherbrum II, Pakistan

Opposite: Wanda Rutkiewicz with K2 in the background.

'My life doesn't have any meaning until it's the way I want it to be. I'd rather not waste my life, I prefer to risk it.'

– Wanda Rutkiewicz

bodies even more than the physical effort of descending lower. The four climbers spent a horribly uncomfortable night crammed into a two-person tent.

It was on the technical descent the next day that Rutkiewicz witnessed Parmentier tumbling down the Bottleneck. The incident highlighted just how exhausted they all were, and the team couldn't afford to make mistakes. They were gambling with their lives. Rutkiewicz continued downwards, marking each step carefully until she finally rejoined Parmentier at 7,700 metres (25,262 feet) on a feature called the Shoulder. They rested and prepared some meltwater in their tiny tent.

By the time they had fired up their small stove, the Barrards had not yet arrived. A storm was moving in and the next morning, the couple were still nowhere in sight. Rutkiewicz and Parmentier now faced the difficult choice of whether to go back up – in their fatigued state – and try to locate the French climbers, or to descend to a lower camp for their own safety. Parmentier decided he would wait for the Barrards but convinced Rutkiewicz to descend alone.

Climbers from other expeditions had spent the night nearby, at 7,700 metres (25,262 feet), and had also decided to climb down from the Shoulder because of the storm. Rutkiewicz managed to stick with them for a while, but

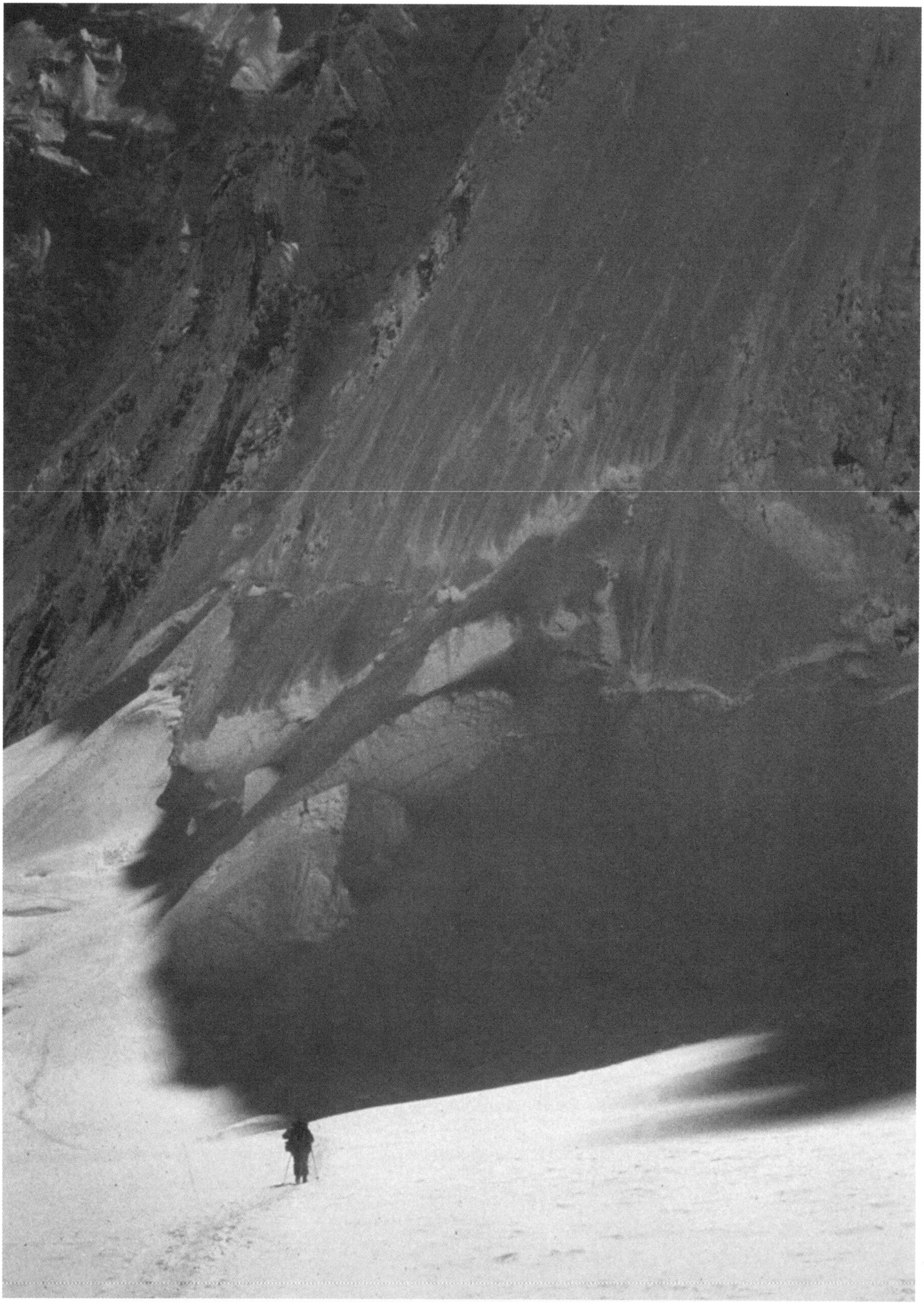

INFO

K2: A GLOSSARY

ABRUZZI SPUR
The Abruzzi Spur is named after Prince Luigi Amedeo, Duke of the Abruzzi. In 1909, Prince Luigi attempted one of the first ascents of the mountain; his high point was 6,250 m (20,505 ft) on the ridge that now bears his name.

GILKEY MEMORIAL
The Gilkey Memorial is named after American climber Art Gilkey, who died on an American expedition to K2 in 1953. A short walk from basecamp, it has become the collective memorial for the many climbers who have been lost on K2 since.

THE BOTTLENECK
The Bottleneck is a narrow couloir that is overhung by seracs, located about 400 m (1,312 ft) below the summit. Climbers must traverse about 100 m (328 ft) while below the seracs to pass it. Due to the height and steepness, this stretch is the most dangerous part of the route.

Opposite: Wanda Rutkiewicz on her 1978 expedition to Mount Everest.

---

visibility was poor and she eventually lost their tracks in the snow. Her world became an indistinguishable palette of white. Straining to see features that would confirm she was on the correct route, she miraculously spotted two ski poles that must have been left for her by the climbers ahead. They sat at the top of the fixed ropes that would guide her safely all the way down the ridge.

Rutkiewicz clipped herself to the fixed lines and continued descending, bringing the ski poles with her. Sometime over the course of the next few hours, she realized her mistake. The poles weren't left for her specifically. They marked the top of the fixed lines so that every climber on the route would be able to easily find them while descending. She was mortified that this would put Parmentier and the Barrards in further jeopardy, but she had no choice but to continue. Going back up was suicide.

Rutkiewicz made it to Camp 2 that night and eventually, after a gruelling effort, arrived at Advanced Base Camp. During the descent, she had lost her gloves. She had found a replacement pair at one of the camps, but her hands were badly frostbitten and she needed medical attention. When the other expedition members saw her approaching, they were both amazed and delighted. Some had started to climb up to search for her. Others had assumed she was dead.

In the days that followed, Parmentier returned to basecamp but the Barrards did not. The storm continued to rage and all hope was lost for those who had spent several nights in higher camps. Maurice and Liliane became numbers in the gruesome statistics – two of the thirteen people who died on the peak that year, many of them Rutkiewicz's friends. It was one of the worst seasons in the mountain's history.

Rutkiewicz's achievement was overshadowed by tragedy, and it wasn't until years later that she could truly celebrate her climb. As she said, 'Sorrow at the death of so many friends far outweighed any triumph I might have felt.'[3]

Wanda Rutkiewicz went on to climb many more peaks after her ascent of K2 in 1986. She amassed copious accolades during her career, particularly for her visionary establishment of all-women's expeditions. As she approached the age of fifty, she became increasingly obsessed with becoming the first woman to ascend all fourteen 8,000-metre (26,247-foot) peaks, a project she called her 'Caravan of Dreams'. By 1991, she had climbed eight of the fourteen. Sadly, as she attempted Kanchenjunga, the world's third highest peak, she died, leaving the Caravan of Dreams unrealized.

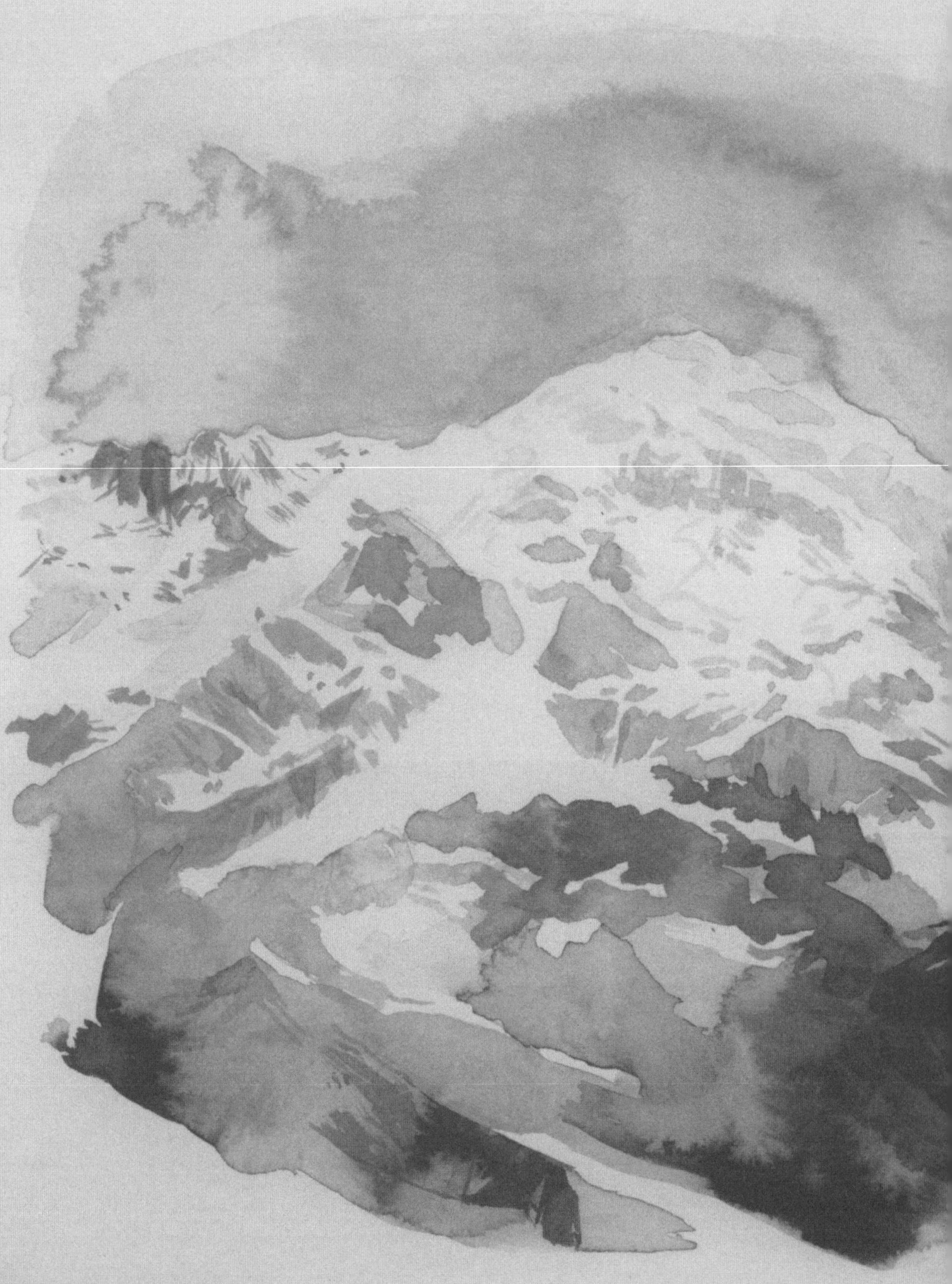

Pat Deavoll
Faces Karim Sar

Looking up at the enormous south face of Karim Sar, New Zealand climber Pat Deavoll scanned the mountain for a safe route to the top. The face was wrought with steep snow gullies, overhanging seracs and sections of complex rockbands, all culminating in an impressive, snowy summit pyramid. Navigating the multi-day trip to their basecamp in the Shilinbar Glacier valley from Islamabad had been nerve-wracking enough. With 2,600 metres (8,530 feet) of vertical gain between her and the summit, it would be the largest face she had ever climbed.

PAT DEAVOLL

Nationality:
New Zealand

Born:
12 June 1959

Active:
1973-present

In October 2007, Taliban militants began operations to seize control of the Swat Valley in Pakistan, threatening to kill anyone who didn't conform to strict Sharia law. Fighting had erupted in the Hindu Kush mountains in the region, as the Pakistani army tried to tease the Taliban out of their high-altitude hideouts. For two years the insurgency continued, with the Taliban securing the region and ruling with a heavy hand, denying education for women and issuing death threats to those who played music or made their living as barbers. Swat Valley residents fled to more stable regions of Pakistan.

Deavoll had been to Pakistan and remote regions of Asia before but in 2009, her team had noticed heightened security right from their arrival in Islamabad. She and her climbing partner Paul Hersey encountered swathes of Swat Valley refugees along the Karakoram Highway as they made for the village of Gilgit, the sending-off point for their journey to Karim Sar (6,180 metres/20,275 feet). The original plan had been to attempt the Kampire Dior, but it was dangerously close to the Afghani border, so the expedition focused its attention on the unclimbed massif of Karim Sar.

The Karakoram range stretches from the Afghanistan border through northern Pakistan into India and is home to the largest number of high-altitude peaks in the world, even trumping Nepal in the number of peaks between 6,000 and 8,000 metres (19,685 and 26,247 feet).[1] Unlike the lush foothills of the Nepali Himalaya, the Karakoram is arid, making farming extremely challenging for the local Balti people. Expeditions to the area support Balti communities financially, offering the men off-season work as porters or cooks. Many families have come to rely on the annual pilgrimage of Westerners. Without the support of the Balti people, climbing in the Karakoram over the centuries would have been close to impossible; their knowledge of the region is invaluable.

With assistance from porters from the town of Budelas, Deavoll's team made its way up the seldom-visited valley to the Shilinbar Glacier, where they established their basecamp. Even though the weather was unsettled during their first days on the glacier, Deavoll and Hersey conducted an acclimatizing reconnaissance mission, hoping to gain more knowledge of Karim Sar from other parts of the valley. Deavoll secretly passed her fiftieth birthday at the remote basecamp, not wanting anyone to make a fuss over the milestone. After a few days back in camp, Hersey became ill and announced that he wouldn't be participating in the climb. If Deavoll wanted to climb Karim Sar, she would have to do it alone. She would need all the skills and experience she had gained over the course of her climbing career.

Opposite: Pat Deavoll on an expedition to Pakistan in 2007.

Deavoll had begun climbing in her early teens as part of her high school 'tramping' club. She was recognized early on for having a good head for adventuring and moving swiftly and efficiently through mountain terrain. She became hooked and sought out climbs in the New Zealand Alps, including many difficult '10,000ers' (3,048 metres) and an ascent of the country's highest peak, Aoraki.

Deavoll also honed her ice-climbing skills by spending several winters climbing frozen waterfalls in the Canadian Rockies. She completed some of the world's hardest test pieces, including a successful ascent of Sea of Vapors. It was on that climb, high on Mount Rundle in Banff National Park, located on the aptly named Trophy Wall, that Deavoll entered what many extreme athletes refer to as the 'flow state', a calm yet highly focused mindset when faced with an extremely difficult task. She found herself unable to place ice screws for protection high on the climb, where a fall meant certain death for her and her partner. Instead of panicking, she mindfully channelled her emotions, pushing all fear aside and harnessing the physical energy she needed to complete the intricate moves and reach safety above.

This experience gave Deavoll the confidence to seek out even more difficult alpine climbs in the more remote mountain ranges of the world. She climbed on Mount Huntington and Mount Hunter in Alaska, attempted peaks in the Indian Himalaya and made two expeditions to the Tibetan plateau in China. After the incomparable highs of each successful expedition, however, she would often fall into a deep depression. Without a mountain goal to focus on, she found the day-to-day grind overwhelming and became a recluse.

Deavoll had started experiencing these feelings early in life. After her first joyful forays in the New Zealand Alps in her early twenties, she would often feel a lack of purpose after she returned to the valley bottom and would beat herself up about climbs she had failed on. After one of her expeditions to Alaska, her depression reached a critical state, leading her to seek professional help. She checked herself into the local hospital for mental-health treatment.

After emerging from treatment, still following a strict regime of medication, Deavoll proved to herself that she could function normally when she wasn't climbing mountains. However, no medicine could replicate the happiness she felt while climbing. The Karakoram, in particular, beckoned. She had felt its pull on an overland trip through Asia in the mid-1980s, and thirty years later, she knew she had to return to its spectacular landscape, so she began seeking sponsorship and funding for her next expedition.

In 2007, Deavoll joined fellow New Zealand climber Lydia Bradey for an all-women's attempt on an unclimbed

INFO

THE KARAKORAM HIGHWAY

This 1,200-km (746-mile) highway starts in the Punjab province in Pakistan, where it crosses the Khunjerab Pass in Gilgit-Baltistan. From there it continues into China, connecting with the ancient silk routes frequented by Genghis Khan and Alexander the Great. The KKH - as it's known locally - has been the access road to the high mountains of the Karakoram since the 1970s, used by climbers and trekkers in the region, who take the road from Islamabad directly to the climbing towns of Skardu and Gilgit, launching points for K2 and Nanga Parbat. Annual risk of flooding makes it susceptible to landslides, causing erosion. A busy transportation corridor, the KKH has been identified as one of the most dangerous roads in the world.

Summit - 6,180 m/20,276 ft

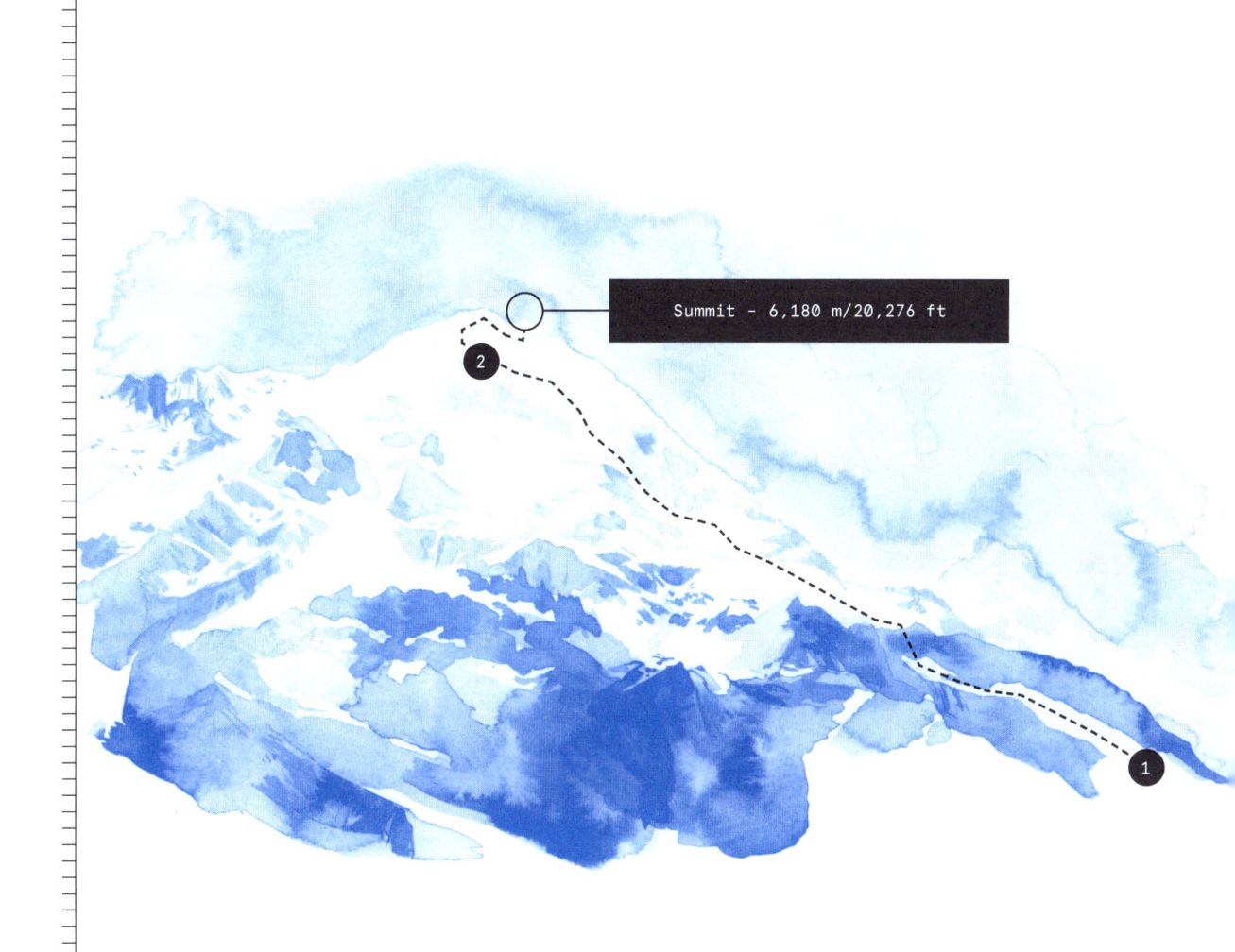

KARIM SAR
SOUTH FACE

Karim Sar is located in the seldom visited, remote Shilinbar Glacier valley in the Karakoram, Pakistan. The peak rises an impressive 2,600 m/8,530 ft above basecamp.

1. Shilinbar Glacier.
2. Route of ascent. The line of ascent follows a hidden gully until the top third.

peak called Beka Brakai Chhok (7,012 metres/23,005 feet). Unfortunately, Deavoll suffered from altitude sickness, and they had to descend to lower altitudes without completing the climb.

Deavoll returned to the peak again in 2008, this time hoping to stand on its elusive summit. She and her partner Malcolm Bass made steady progress, establishing camps as they went, until they were trapped and tent-bound for more than a week in a fierce snowstorm. When the storm finally broke, they made a dash for the top, only to be turned back by volatile snow mushrooms that lined the way to the summit. Seeing no way to navigate these delicate cornices safely, they abandoned their effort only hundreds of metres from the top.

Friends and family thought Deavoll was mad when she decided to return to Pakistan the following year, this time for a shot at Karim Sar. After Hersey fell ill, she wasn't sure that she had the ability to climb the mountain alone. But she had come so far and invested so much already; her sponsors were relying on her and it seemed crazy to abandon all efforts without even setting foot on the face. She had just turned fifty and had her knee replaced – both factors that made her question, and thus want to prove, her ability. It was at that moment Deavoll decided she would set her uncertainties aside and try the south face alone.

When the morning of her departure arrived, Hersey announced he would join her on the bottom half of the climb, offering invaluable moral support. The duo made their way up the icefall to an advanced basecamp, a place to rest before tackling the real challenges of the climb. The view of the face from this temporary camp gave Deavoll another chance to scope a route with her binoculars. She imagined moving through the various obstacles of the face, memorizing a proposed route. The next day, in the darkness of the early morning, she and Hersey set out.

The first part of the climb involved a steep snow gully that brought them to a rockband threatened by exposure from overhanging ice cliffs. Instead of gaining the rockband, as Deavoll had planned when first scouting the route, she would have to adapt her plan. In the name of safety, instead she would carry on up the gully to a small col. There, she would cut out a snowy ledge for their tent and have another look at the face to reassess her options.

The duo passed a sleepless night on their icy perch. Deavoll knew that if she couldn't sleep, it would be best for her mental state if she continued upwards, so she stepped away from the tent, leaving their only sleeping bag with Hersey so at least one of them could rest. She was immediately met with challenges: rockbands that had seemed accessible proved very precarious, forcing her to make constant adjustments as she gained ground. Although in some ways she dreaded the unknown on peaks like Karim Sar, it was in this environment that she truly excelled.

Tackling notorious, previously climbed 8,000-metre (26,247-feet) peaks had never held charm for Deavoll; she much preferred the pursuit of first ascents. If she could successfully work her way through all the obstacles Karim Sar posed, she would be thrilled. Mindful of the ice hazards above, she gingerly set her crampons on precarious rock steps and climbed in narrow ice runnels, slowly progressing up the mixed terrain and through terrifyingly large crevasses towards the summit pyramid above.

When the exposure became too much and doubt seized her, Deavoll reminded herself to take a deep breath. 'Don't think about where you are,' she wrote in her accounts of the climb. 'You can't make the first ascent of a mountain solo without exposing yourself to some risk.'[2] A seventy-degree ice slope brought her close to the top and all the doubts dissipated. She walked the easy 100-metre (328-foot) ridge to the top, where she fell to the ground in joy and exhaustion. It had taken her all day; the vastness of the mountain range lay before her, a wonderful gift for all her efforts.

Realizing that the warmth of the sun was now hitting snow and ice on the route, making conditions dangerous as the snow softened, Deavoll spent little time on the summit before beginning her descent. The unreliable surface threatened a fall and she had to make a conscious effort not to break down in tears. Nevertheless, with each step, Deavoll began to realize the scope of her achievement.

Just as she was getting low on water and the snow was becoming slushier, she spotted the tent on its tiny perch, and Hersey waving at her from below. With spirits raised, she reached the bivouac and embraced him. Despite her doubts, she had done it.

The next morning, still in a state of disbelief, Deavoll arrived at basecamp, exhausted after many days of physical exertion at altitude. Local visitors offered congratulations when they learned she had climbed the peak alone. When she returned home, her climb was celebrated internationally by the climbing community.

Pat Deavoll is recognized as one of the most talented alpine climbers of her generation. After her solo climb of Karim Sar, she went on to attempt the west face of Vasuki Parbat in the Indian Himalaya and in 2012, the peak of Koch-e-Rank in the Wakhan Corridor of Afghanistan. In 2011, with her sister Christine Byrch, she reached the 6,800-metre (22,310-foot) summit of Koh-e-Baba Tangi, also in the Wakhan Corridor, via the northwest ridge. Deavoll continues to climb to this day, including ascents such as Langua-tai-Barfi (DNS), Pakistan, in 2014, Karl Marx Peak and Engels Peak, Tajikistan, in 2017, Koh-e-Shakawr, Afghanistan, in 2017 and the infamous Cassin Ridge on Denali in 2022.

Opposite: Paul Hersey coming up towards Camp 1 on Karim Sar.

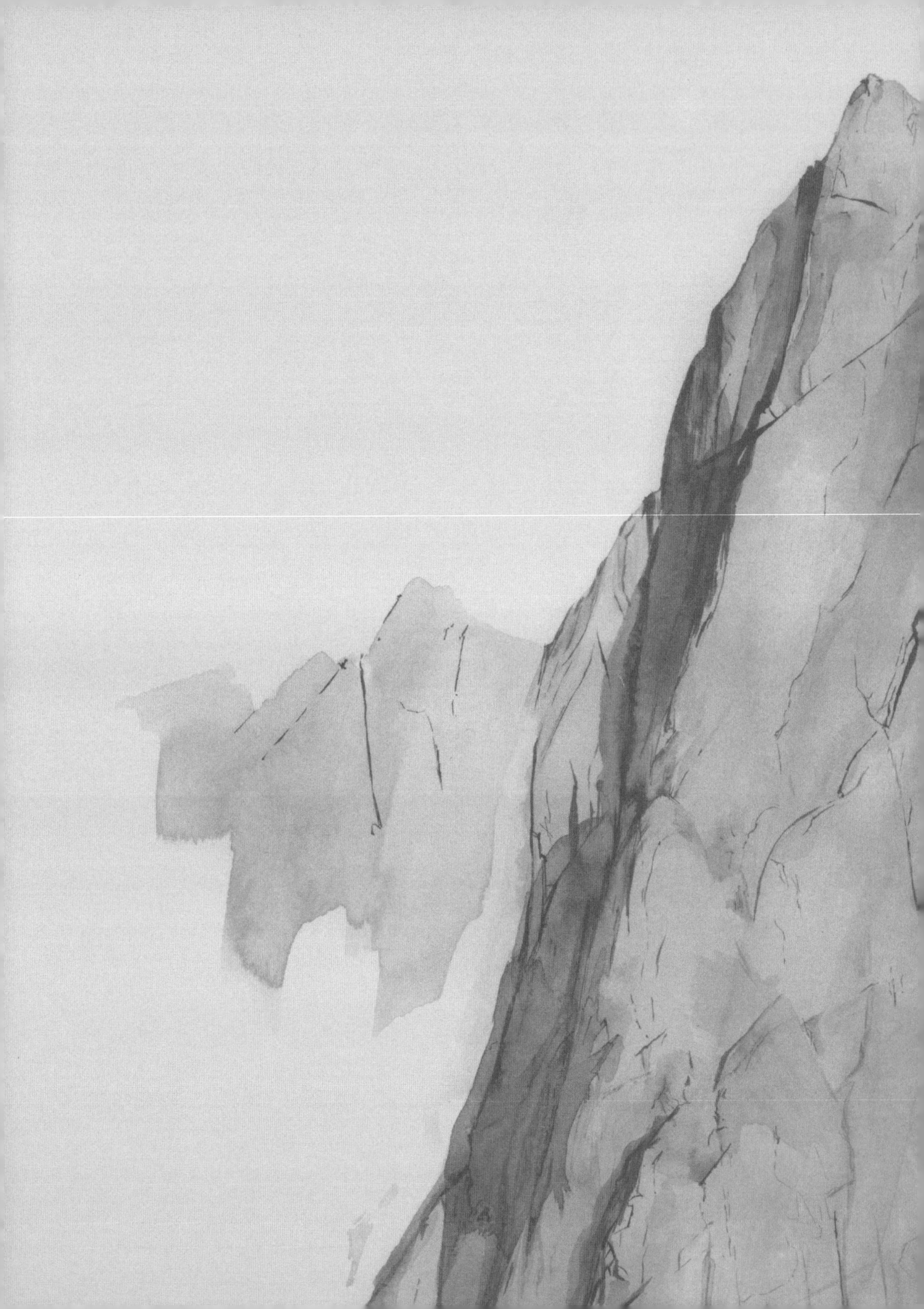

Brette Harrington and Her Free-Solo of Chiaro di Luna

Patagonia is known for two things: wind and magnificent granite towers that stretch sharply upwards from the inhospitable landscape below. These piercing pinnacles of amber rock burst out of the surrounding glaciers. Seeming to defy gravity, they are both a climber's dream and nightmare. If a rare weather window permits passage on to the continuous cracks that weave endlessly towards snow-capped summits, climbers can have the best days of their lives here. But if the relentless Patagonian wind kicks up and rages across the largest contiguous non-polar icecap in the world, the storms send most scrambling down into the valley as they desperately seek shelter. If caught out too long on the wall, you might just be blown off the rock itself. Patagonian storms can last for days, sometimes weeks, and the unpredictability of the weather makes it even more challenging.

BRETTE HARRINGTON

Nationality:
American

Born:
1 January 1992

Active:
2006-present

Opposite: Brette Harrington surrounded by equipment.

US climber Brette Harrington has a special love for the harsh and beautiful vertical world of Patagonia. Born in Lake Tahoe, California, Harrington inherited her love of skiing from her parents. She also had a natural affinity for climbing trees but it wasn't until she was introduced to rock climbing through a programme at her boarding school that she realized it was what truly made her heart sing. She bluffed her way on to the school's climbing team (knowing very little about safety and ropework) and gradually garnered the experience that would prepare her for the difficult climbs she would tackle in her twenties.

After school, Harrington enrolled at the University of British Columbia. Just an hour's drive away from the campus in Vancouver were the sheer imposing cliffs of Squamish, one of Canada's most famous rock-climbing havens. Here, Harrington cut her teeth in big-wall granite climbing and free soloing. Her natural talent and eagerness to learn made her fun to have around, and she soon joined a posse of local Squamish climbers who would become friends and mentors. Among the most influential was a young, socially awkward climber named Marc-André Leclerc.

Harrington and Leclerc hit it off almost immediately. They climbed together often and eventually became more than just climbing partners. They had similar mindsets: both wanted to climb as much as possible, to move as freely as they could while on the rock. On easier climbs they would solo-climb routes together, one following the other without a rope between them. On harder routes in the alpine, they would often simul-climb, a technique where climbers move quickly together while roped, placing minimal gear for protection and stopping infrequently, only belaying in the most difficult sections of the route. Although they climbed with other partners, there was something special about their relationship – a mutual understanding and full trust in the other's ability. Harrington once wrote about their relationship: 'Together, our energy seemed to double, whisking us along in an unconscious dance.'[1]

Harrington's 2014 climbing season was an exceptional one. In addition to regular forays on the walls of Squamish and the nearby Tantalus Range, Canada's formidable Waddington Range offered endless opportunities for the pair to explore the alpine. For days on end, they would ascend crisp granite ridges and stepped walls, often soloing for efficiency of movement without the hindrance of a rope. It was the ultimate training ground to obtain glacier skills and to perfect soloing techniques in alpine conditions, an experience that would serve Harrington well when she made her first trip to Patagonia with Leclerc later that same year.

In December of 2014, the tiny Argentinian mountain town of El Chaltén was in full summer mode, bustling with

AGUJA SAINT-EXUPÉRY NORTH FACE

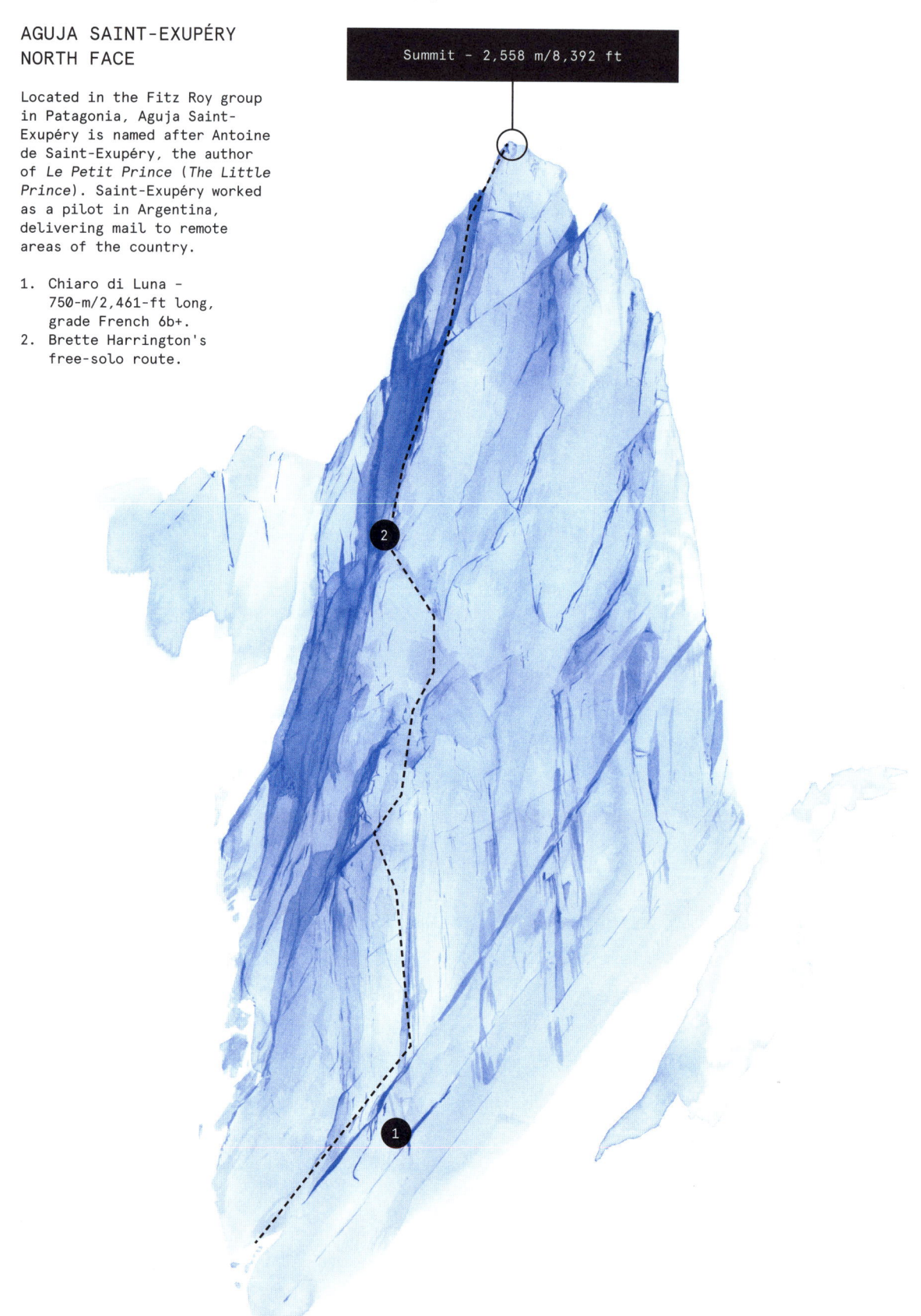

Located in the Fitz Roy group in Patagonia, Aguja Saint-Exupéry is named after Antoine de Saint-Exupéry, the author of *Le Petit Prince* (*The Little Prince*). Saint-Exupéry worked as a pilot in Argentina, delivering mail to remote areas of the country.

1. Chiaro di Luna – 750-m/2,461-ft long, grade French 6b+.
2. Brette Harrington's free-solo route.

Summit – 2,558 m/8,392 ft

CLIMBER STORIES

foreign climbers, when Harrington and Leclerc arrived for the season. They fell into the jovial chatter at their local hostel, exchanging climbing stories and hearing about other climbers' plans. Leclerc had aspirations for two climbs on Cerro Torre: one with alpinist Colin Haley, and a first solo ascent of a difficult route called the Corkscrew. While he prepared for these attempts, Harrington climbed with various partners she met in town between weather windows.

As the season rolled on, she added more and more mileage to her Patagonian experience. It was from a climb on the sharp needle of Aguja Rafael Juárez that she first spotted a golden buttress named Chiaro di Luna on the neighbouring tower of Aguja Saint-Exupéry. Mesmerized by the route, the wheels in her mind began turning, and she wondered if it would be possible to solo it.

Chiaro di Luna (Italian for moonlight) was first ascended by an Italian team in 1987, their night-time descent prompting the naming of the route. It haunted Harrington over the next week. She asked friends about the route, collected information and finally told Leclerc about her ambitions. She learned that famous German climber Alex Huber had made a rope solo of the route a few years prior, protecting his climbing with a rope as he ascended, a very different approach from the free climb that she envisaged.

The more Harrington learned, the more she became convinced that it was possible. She and Leclerc climbed the route together as a reconnaissance mission, soloing as many of the pitches as they could. It was only on the cruxes that they pulled out the rope and worked the hard moves with the security of a belay. Harrington learned that she would have to change some of her standard techniques to make the cruxes feel more secure. She would have to be precise and focused in her movements on these pitches. There was very little margin for error. After this practice climb, she prepared mentally for her solo as she waited for the winds to subside and the weather to clear.

A few days later, Harrington and Leclerc hiked into the Torre Valley, where they spent the night at a bivouac camp. The next morning, they set out in different directions: Harrington towards Aguja Saint-Exupéry and Leclerc towards Cerro Torre. It must have been difficult for the two to separate in that moment, but both felt each other's support over the days that followed, each working towards achieving a personal best.

Harrington made her way over the ice of the Torre Glacier and then navigated through the loose rock of the moraines below Aguja Saint-Exupéry. She made camp in a tiny cave at the base of the route, and was grateful for the small overhanging roof when clouds enshrouded the tower and it began to

'For days on end, they would ascend crisp granite ridges and stepped walls, often soloing for efficiency of movement without the hinderance of a rope.'

rain. Pulling further back into the cave and nestling into her sleeping bag, Harrington pondered the route for hours as she listened to the storm outside, visualizing herself working through all the moves and successfully reaching the top. She climbed the spire no less than three times in her mind, committing each difficult section and move to memory. As soon as the weather cooperated, she would be ready to go.

Once the rain subsided later the next morning, Harrington waited a few hours for the rock to dry and finally set out just after noon. A scramble up a low-angled rock ramp made of basalt led her to the first crux on the route. She was confident on this first difficult crack. It was wedged into an inward-facing corner, known as a dihedral. By spanning her feet on each side wall in a technique known as stemming, and working her fingers into the crack, Harrington moved upwards, locking her fingers in and placing each foot with absolute precision on the next small feature on the walls. These were familiar climbing moves and even though the exposure to the ice and rocks below was enormous, Harrington danced through the seemingly smooth lower pitches with a kind of 'sacred stillness'.[2]

The more difficult sections of the 750-metre (2,461-feet) route are interspersed with easier climbing, allowing a few moments of physical and mental recovery. Harrington moved efficiently through these sections. She worked her way up towards the part of the climb that she feared the most: an awkward layback crux. She had brought along a few pieces of protection just in case her head wasn't prepared for the difficulty, so, if necessary, she could rappel the route.

But Harrington wouldn't need the gear she had clipped to her harness. Summoning inner strength and focus, she completed the difficult layback moves quickly and perfectly, although she confessed that she never felt completely secure with her foot placements. She acknowledged the fears, but kept them in check – a vital skill when free-soloing. Once on the other side, Harrington realized her goal was well within reach. She flowed joyfully up perfectly symmetrical cracks and was soon on the summit taking a photograph of herself, glowing and smiling.

Harrington took in the beauty of the windless day. The clouds had dissipated and the expanse of sapphire sky contrasted with the golden glow from the granite towers. It was a glorious moment for the twenty-three year old. Harrington strained her eyes against the bright sun, hoping for a glimpse of a dot in the distance that would be Leclerc on nearby Cerro Torre.

Harrington found the rappel route that she and Leclerc had used days before. She pulled out the lightweight small-diameter rope she had brought for emergencies and began the dozens of abseils that would bring her back to her camp in the tiny cave. The amber light of the sunset warmed her as she made the last few rappels, and she was back at the base by 8 p.m. There was no time to relax or reflect on her climb. The winds started to pick up and Harrington realized she needed to head further down quickly; a storm was approaching.

Once back in the Torre Valley, Harrington set up camp and then heard of Leclerc's success on the Corkscrew route from other climbers passing through. By the time he arrived, the storm had descended on their camp, and they decided to wait out the weather. Their tent strained against the wind, and the seams began to split.

When Harrington and Leclerc made it back to El Chaltén, word had spread of their two epic solo successes. Once the news of her climb hit Europe and North America, she was invited to write about her experiences in magazines and offered sponsorship that would make it more comfortable to commit to a life of climbing full time.

After their solos in Patagonia, Harrington and Leclerc continued to climb at the top level, both together and alone, all over North and South America. In 2018, just three years later, Leclerc tragically died while climbing with a partner in Alaska. Harrington was devastated. As part of her mourning process, she sought solace in the mountains. She soloed difficult alpine routes, often in winter, some so challenging that friends began to worry about her motives.

In 2019, Harrington returned to Patagonia with friend and climber Quentin Roberts. They revisited the granite spires in the hope of completing the Vision, one of Leclerc's uncompleted projects, on the intimidating tower of Torre Egger. Although he had only ever conceived of the climb, she felt his presence as they battled through small weather windows. Eventually the harsh Patagonian winds subsided to allow them to reach the summit. They completed the route in Leclerc's honour, renaming it MA's (Marc-André's) Vision.

Harrington continues to make regular visits to Patagonia and to push the boundaries of climbing and cutting-edge alpine ascents. She has gone on to complete many difficult first ascents in the Canadian Rockies since Leclerc's passing, including Life Compass on Mount Blane and Sound of Silence on the east face of Mount Fay. Lately, she has combined her winter climbing skills with steep skiing, completing outrageous first ski descents with Canadian pro-skier Christina Lustenberger.

Brette Harrington, Torre Egger, Patagonia, 2019.

INFO

AN INCOMPLETE HISTORY OF WOMEN CLIMBERS IN PATAGONIA

SILVIA METZELIN
Participated in sixteen expeditions to Patagonia and co-authored two guidebooks to the region. She also made the first ascent of the Italian Route on Aguja Saint-Exupéry with Gino Buscaini, Lino Candot, Walter Romano and Silvano Sinigoi in 1968.

ROSANNA MANFRINI
First ascent of Chiaro di Luna on Aguja Saint-Exupéry with Maurizio Giordani and Sergio Valentini. Completed the first female ascent of the Compressor Route on Cerro Torre in 1987.

SILVIA FITZPATRICK
First traverse of Las Adelas (from the north) with Eduardo Brenner, 1988.

SUE HARRINGTON
First ascent of the Kearney-Harrington route on Aguja Saint-Exupéry with Alan Kearney, 1988.

LAURENCE MONNOYEUR
First female ascent of the south face of Cerro Torre, 1997.

MONIKA KAMBIČ AND TANJA GRMOVŠEK
First all-female ascent of Cerro Torre, 2005. Monika also completed the first ascent of the Eslovena route on Aguja Guillaumet with Klemen Mali in 1998.

STEPH DAVIS
First ascent of the Potter-Davis route on Aguja Poincenot, 2001. First ascent of the Potter-Davis route on Aguja Standhardt, 2006.

CRYSTAL DAVIS-ROBBINS
First ascent of La Suerte Sangrienta on Cerro Domo Blanco with Chris Brazeau and Jon Walsh, 2007. First ascent of Fingerlicious on Cuatro Dedos, 2007. First ascent of The Art of War on Aguja de l'S, 2007. First ascent of El Flaco con Domingo with Max Hasson, 2008. First ascent of Witches Brew on the Gran Gendarme del Pollone, 2011.

DÖRTE PIETRON
First female ascent of the Compressor Route on Cerro Torre without using the controversial bolt ladder installed by Cesare Maestri. First female ascent of Ensueño on Cerro Fitz Roy, 2011.

KATE RUTHERFORD
First ascent of Hard Saying, Not Knowing on Aguja Guillaumet, 2009. First ascent of The Washington Route on Cerro Fitz Roy, 2011. First ascent of Astro Choss on Aguja Saint-Exupéry, 2012.

CAROLINE NORTH AND CHRISTINA HUBER
First female free ascent of Cerro Torre, 2015.

WHITNEY CLARK AND NICOLE LAWTON
First link-up of Thaw's Not Houlding Wright on Aguja de l'S and Chiaro di Luna on Aguja Saint-Exupéry, 2022.

Opposite: Early morning sun on Karim Sar high camp. Paul Hersey waited here while Pat Deavoll continued to the summit.

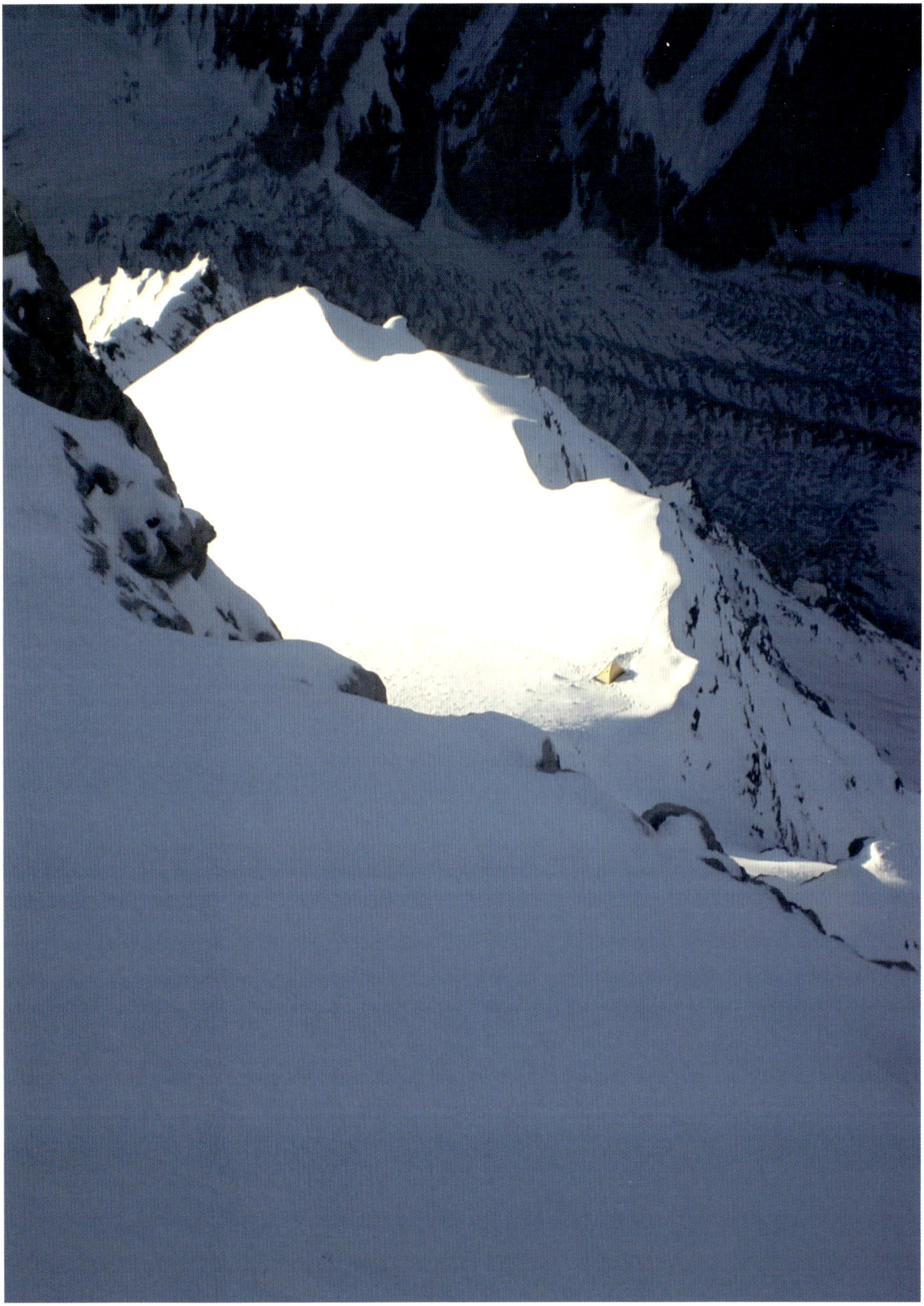

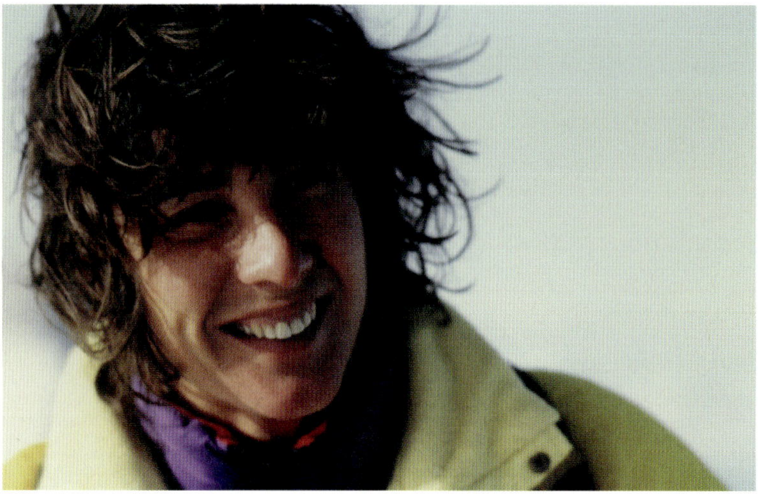

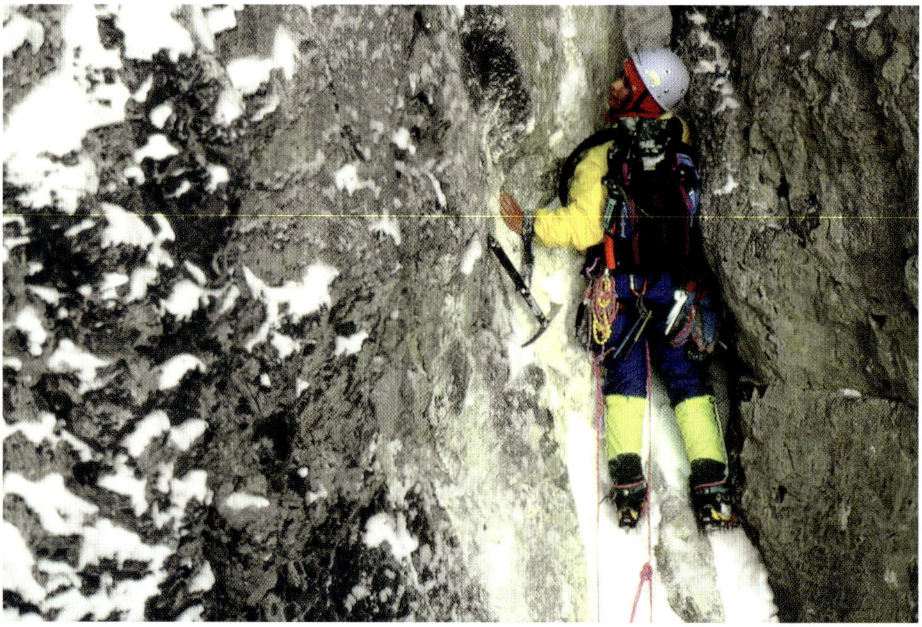

Opposite above: French climber Catherine Destivelle.
Opposite below: Destivelle on the north face of the Eiger.

Above: Destivelle after her ascent of the north face of the Matterhorn, 1993.
Pages 84–85: The dark pyramid of Mount Everest (Chomolungma) is centre left, Cholatse the sharp peak on the right.

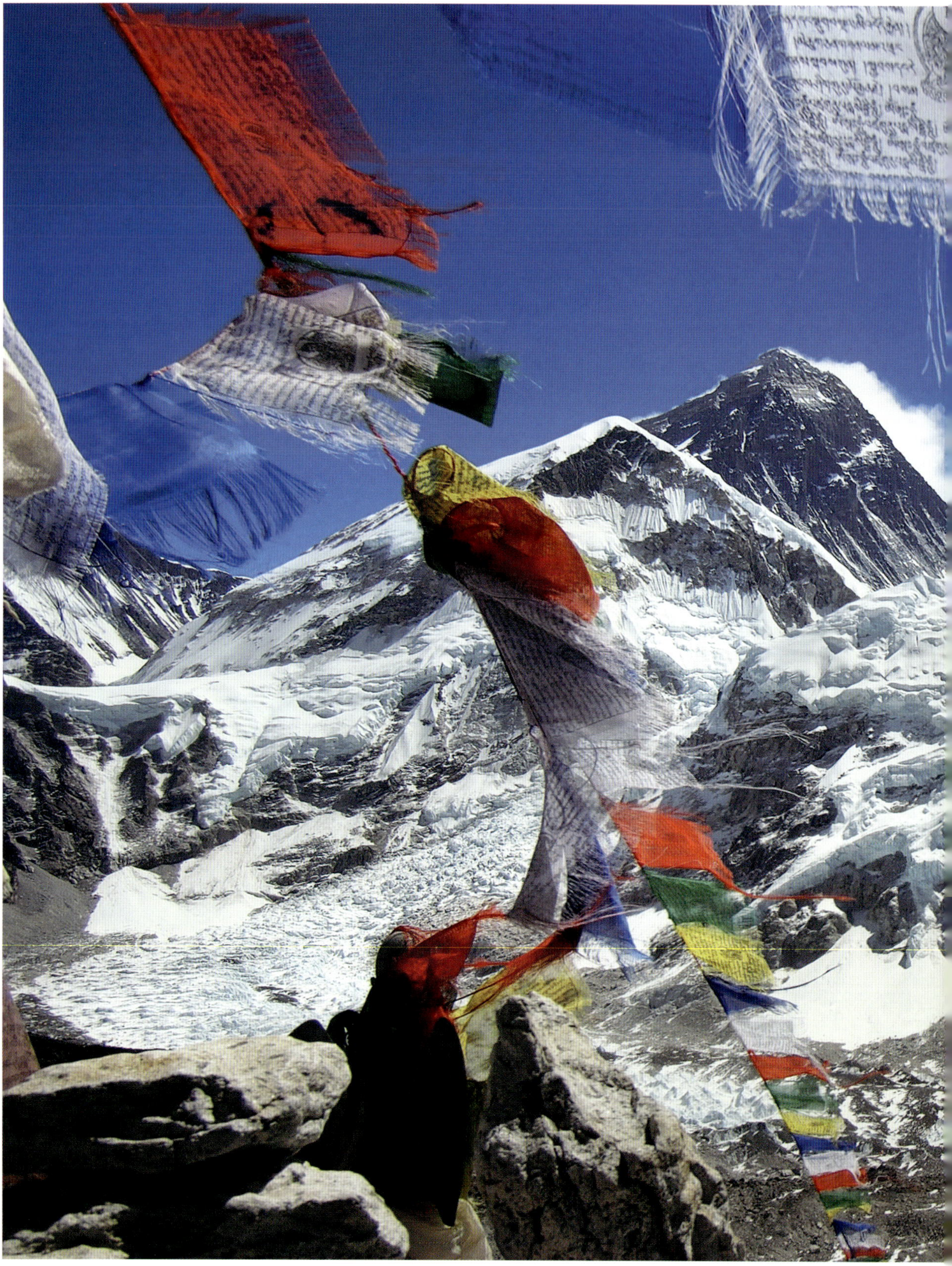

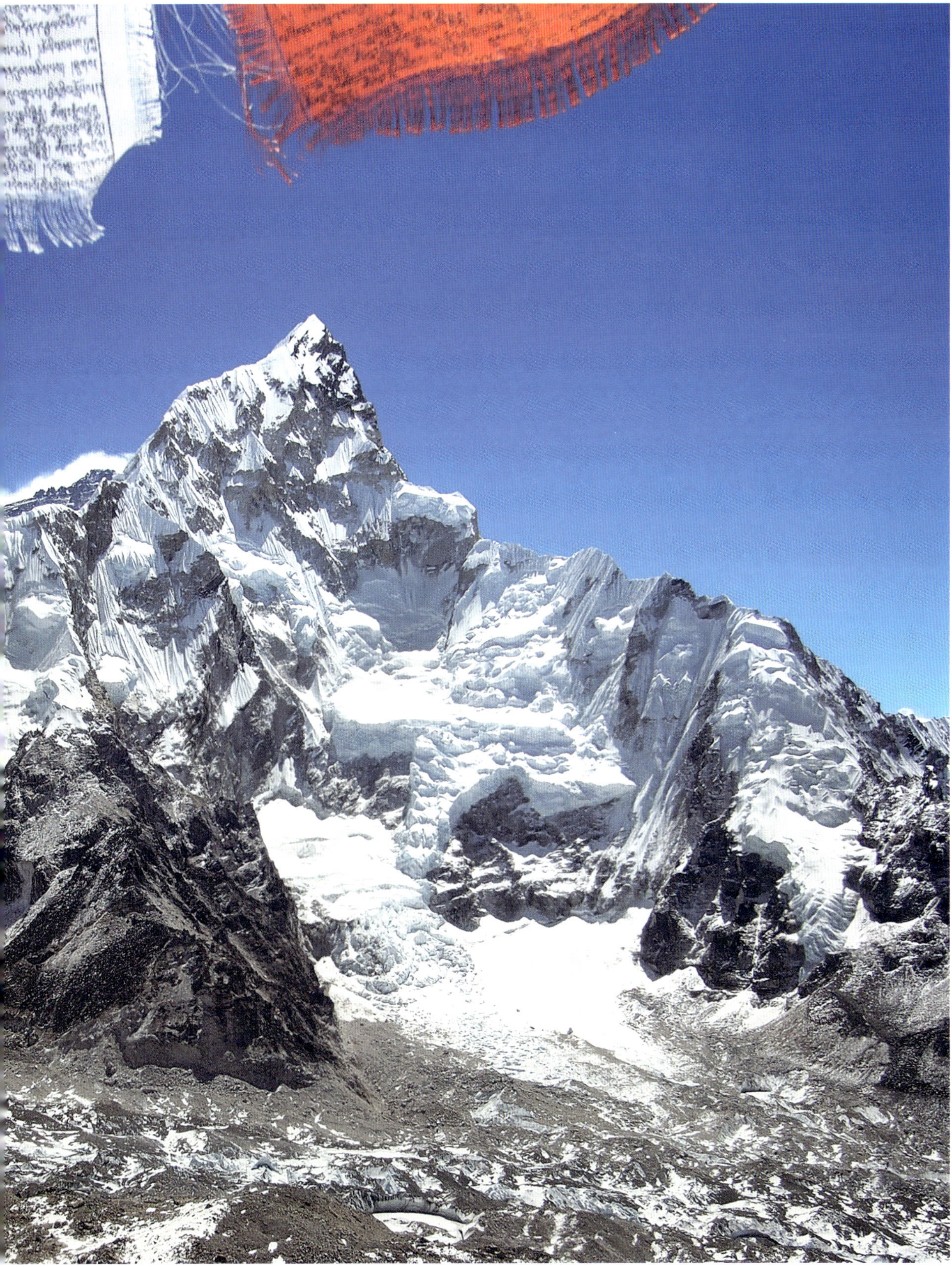

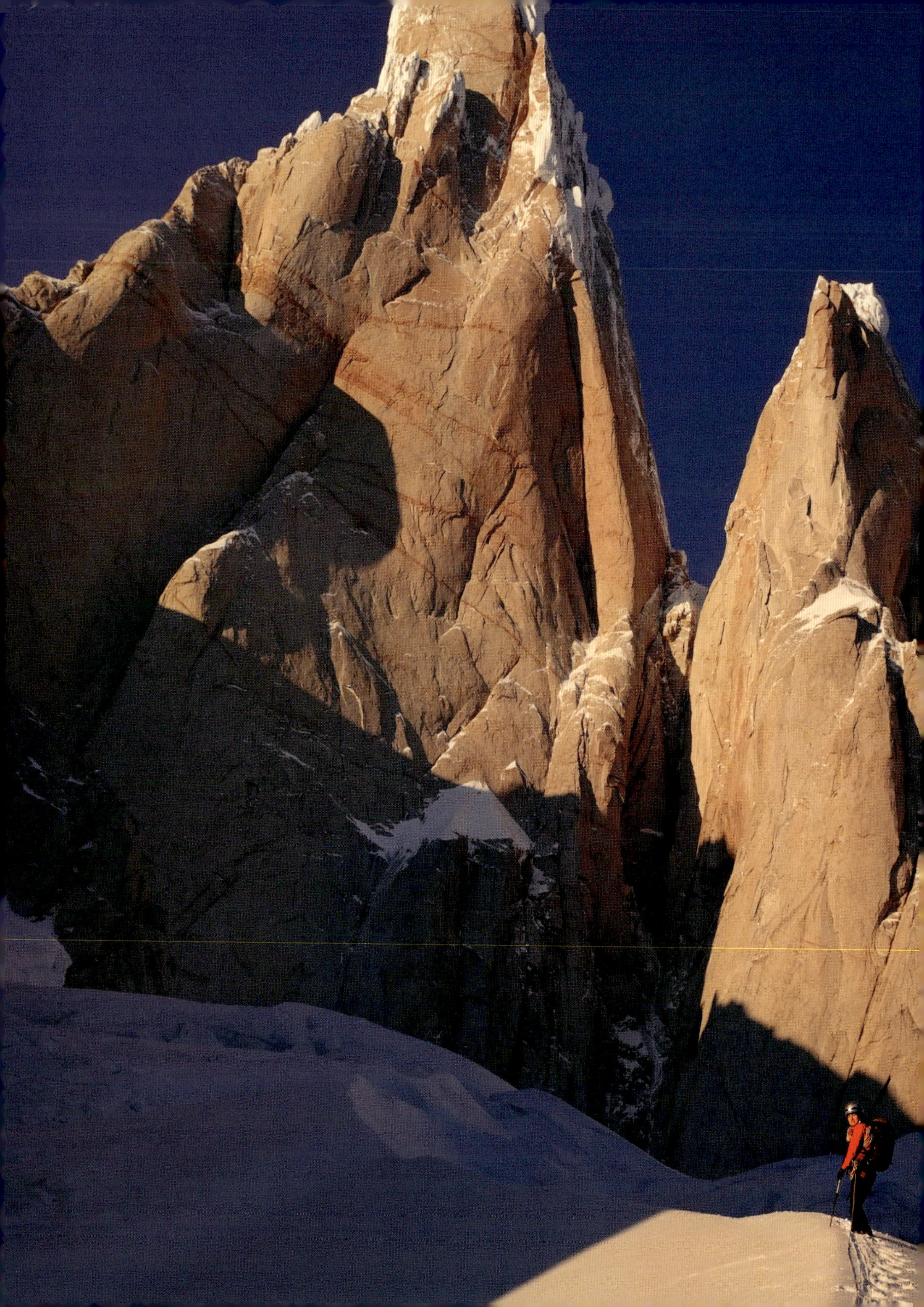

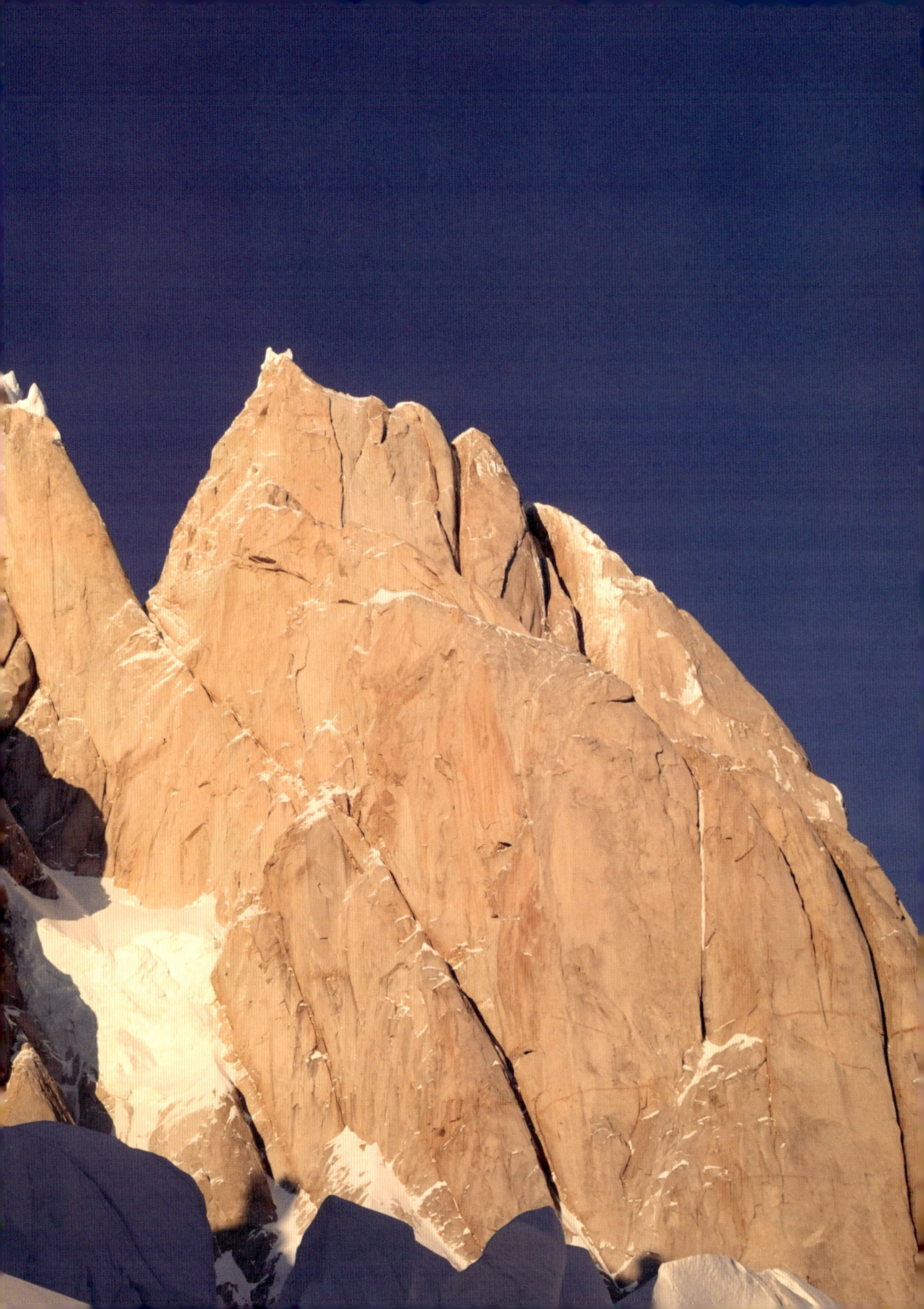

Pages 86–87: Brette Harrington, Torre Egger, Patagonia, 2019.

Above: Setting up Karim Sar basecamp on the grass; the porters getting ready to leave.
Opposite: From the Wanda Rutkiewicz Collection.

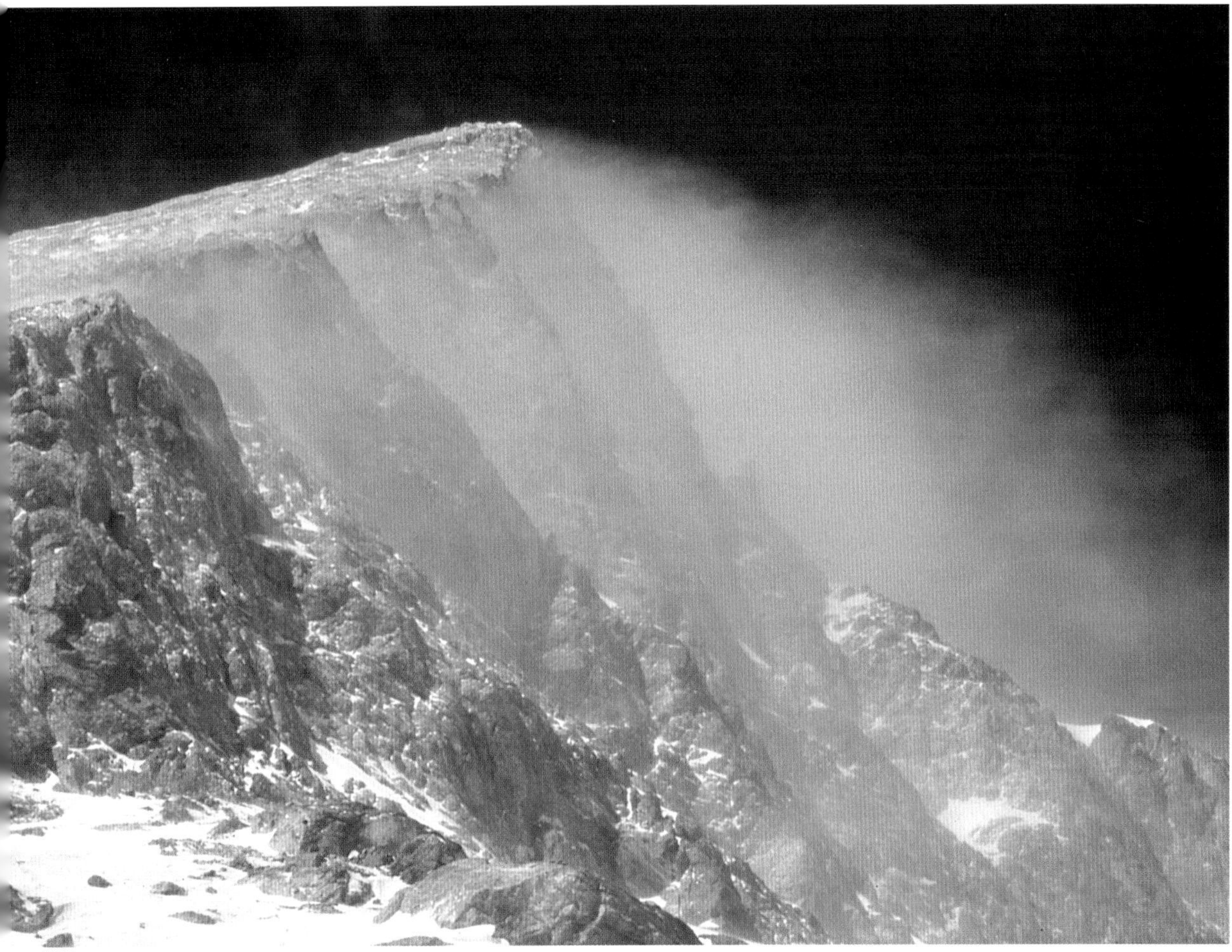

Above: Wanda Rutkiewicz on her Shishapangma expedition. She reached the top on 18 September 1987.
Opposite: Kei Taniguchi (in green jacket) and Junko Tabei (in purple jacket) with expedition team members at Manaslu basecamp, 2006.

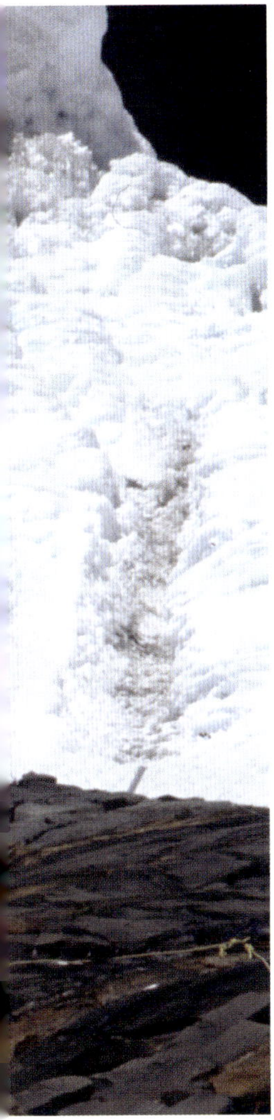

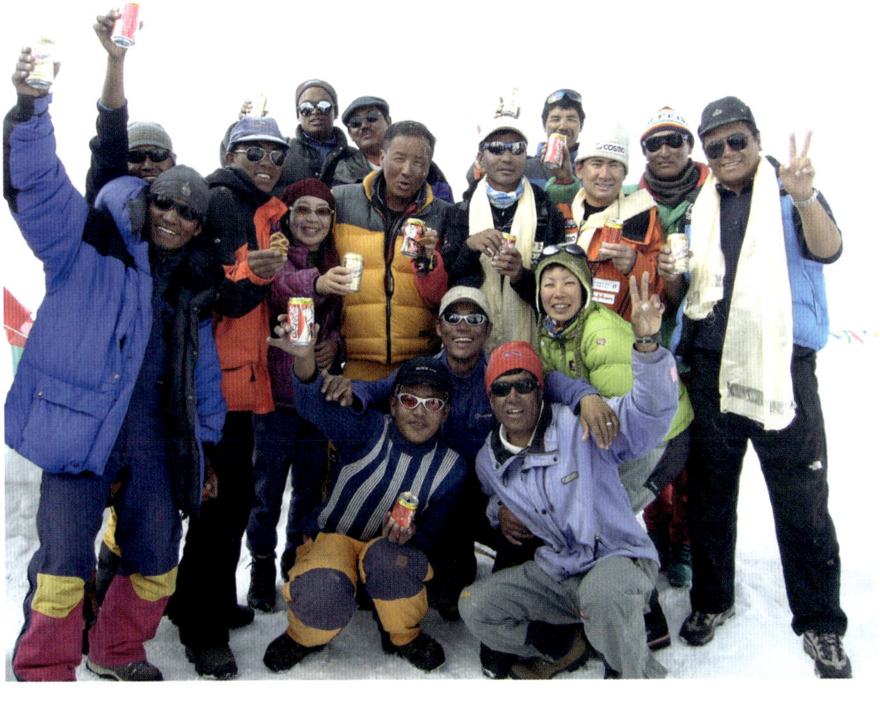

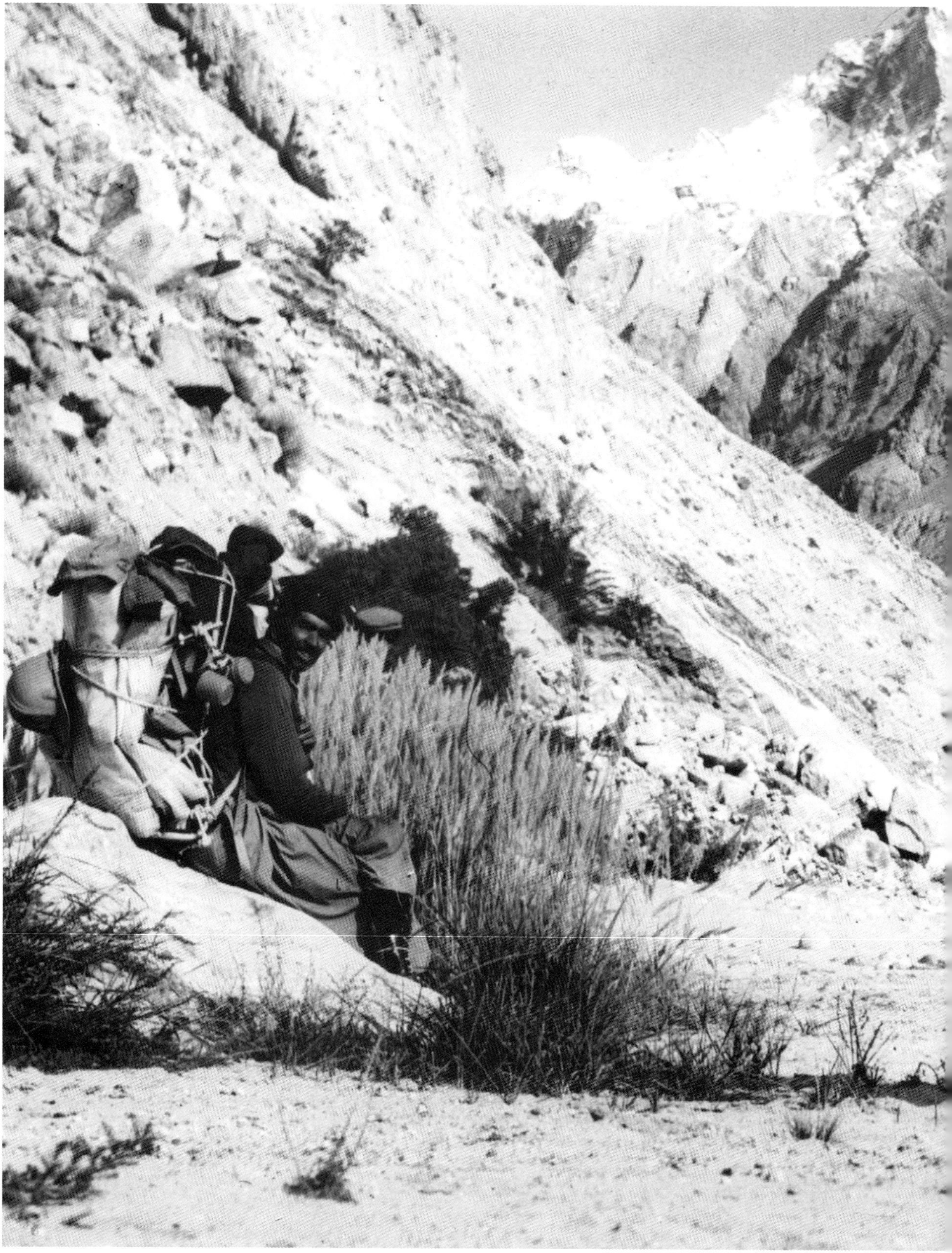

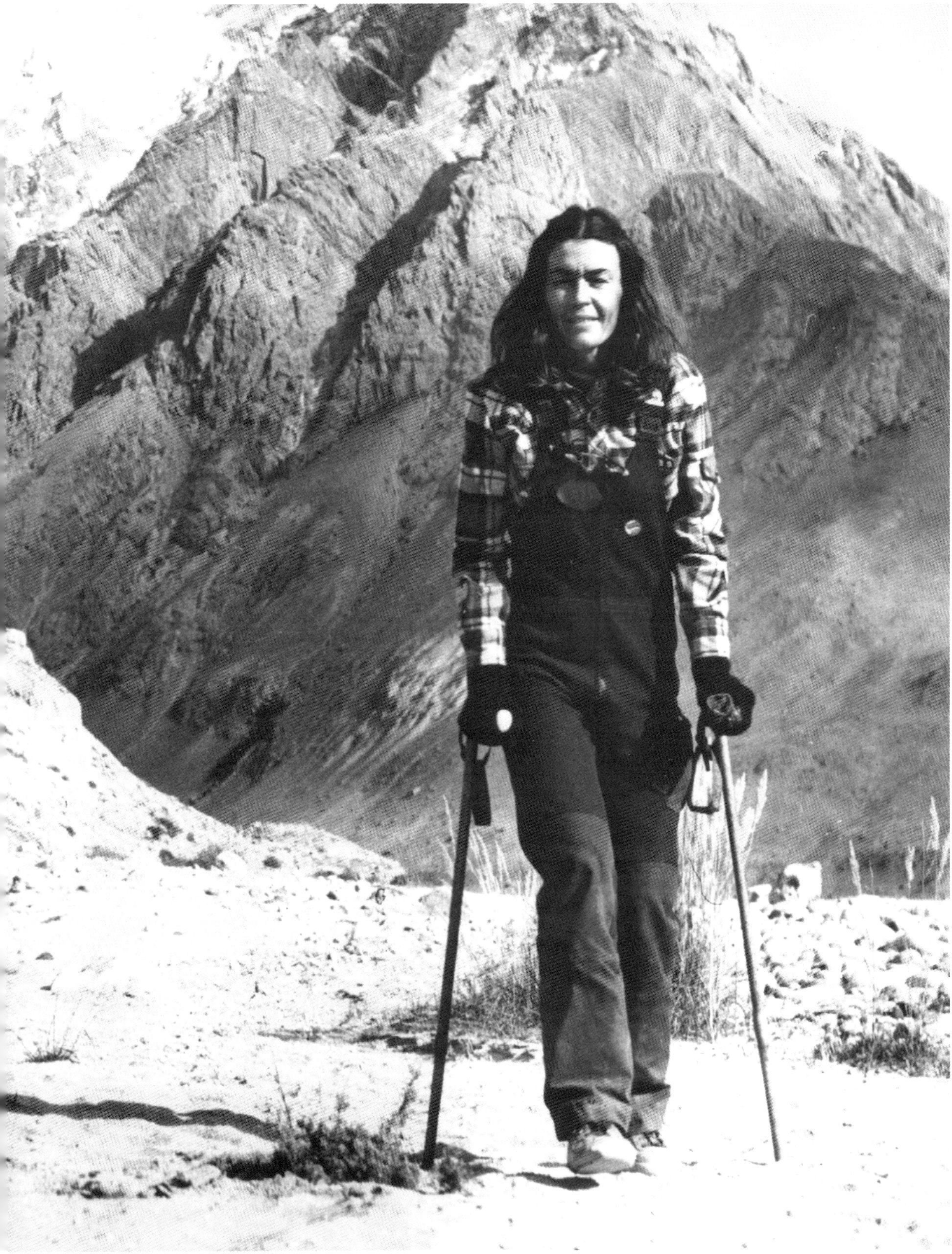

Pages 92-93: Wanda Rutkiewicz on her way to K2 basecamp on crutches.
Above: Wanda Rutkiewicz in her element.

Opposite: Catherine Destivelle climbs near Chamonix, France.
Page 96: Wanda Rutkiewicz on the summit of Everest, 1978.
Page 97: Mountains in the Karakoram. northwest of Karim Sar.

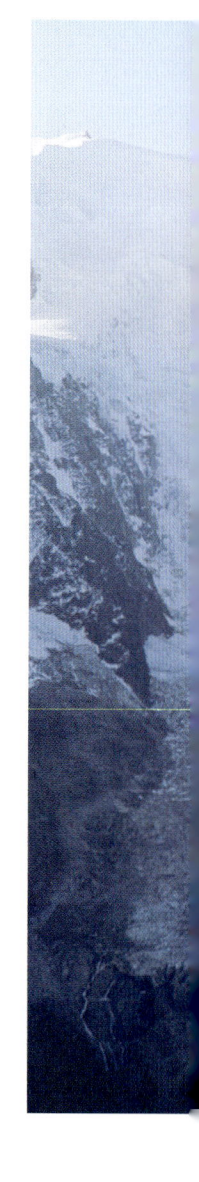

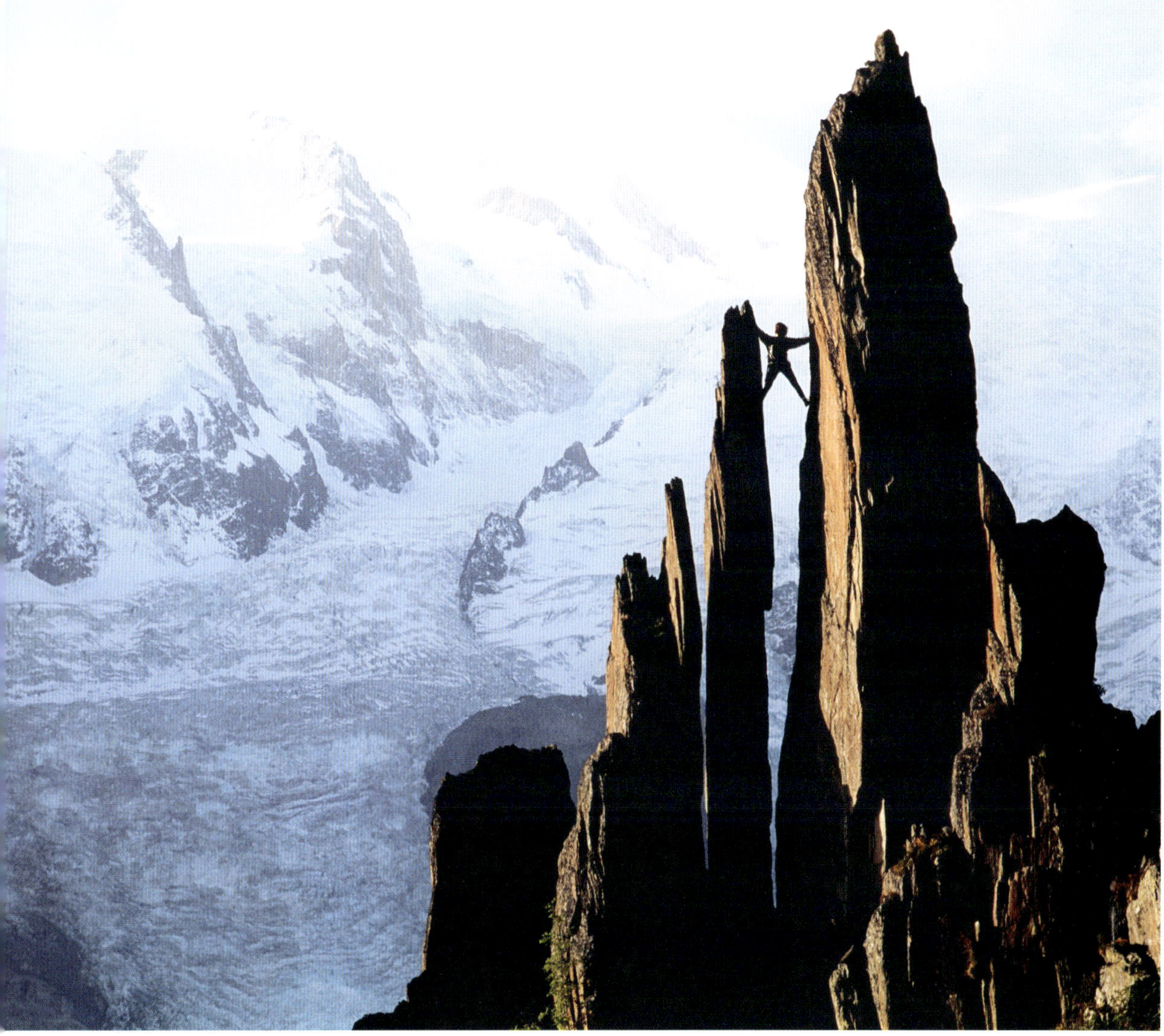

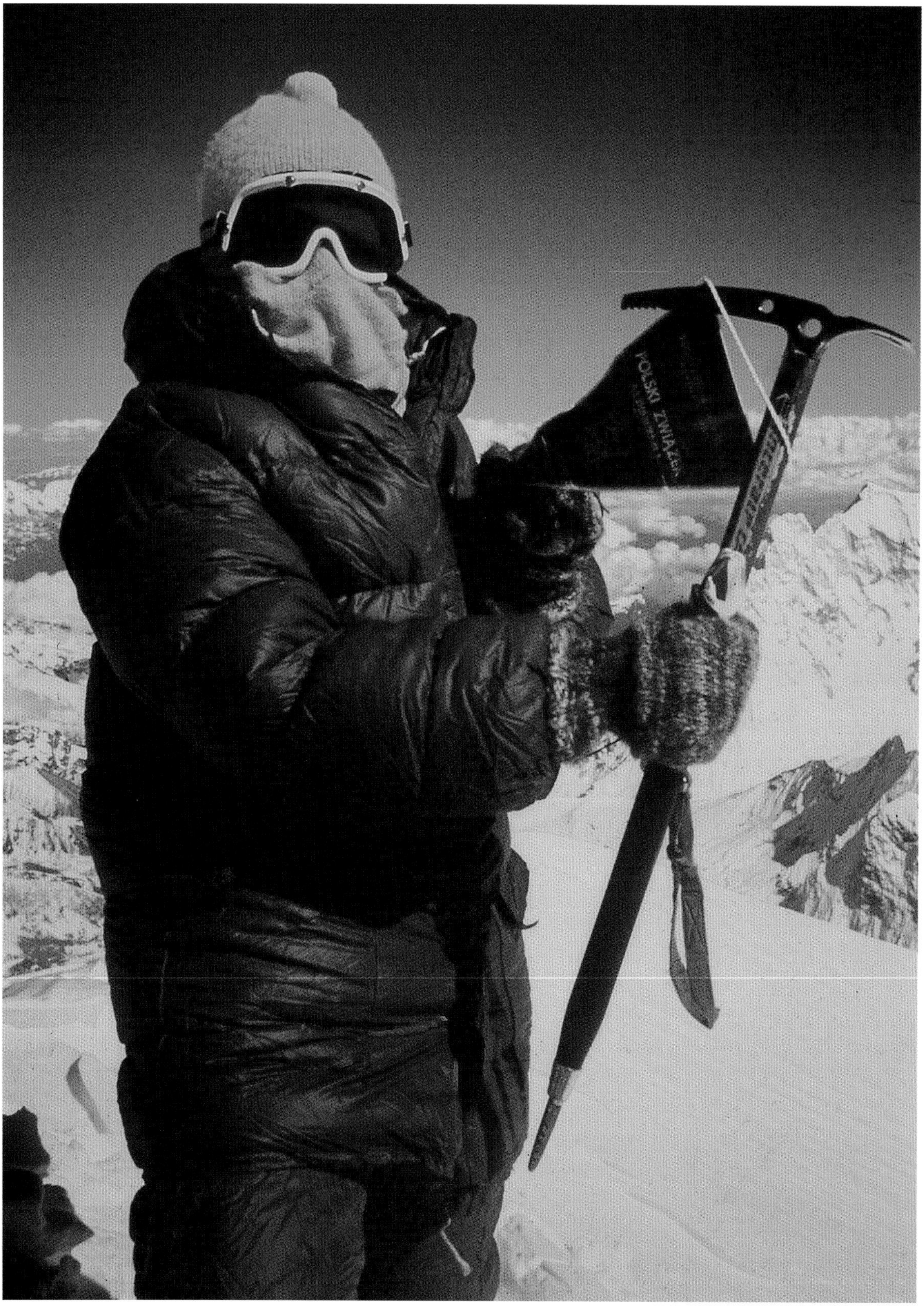
POLSKI

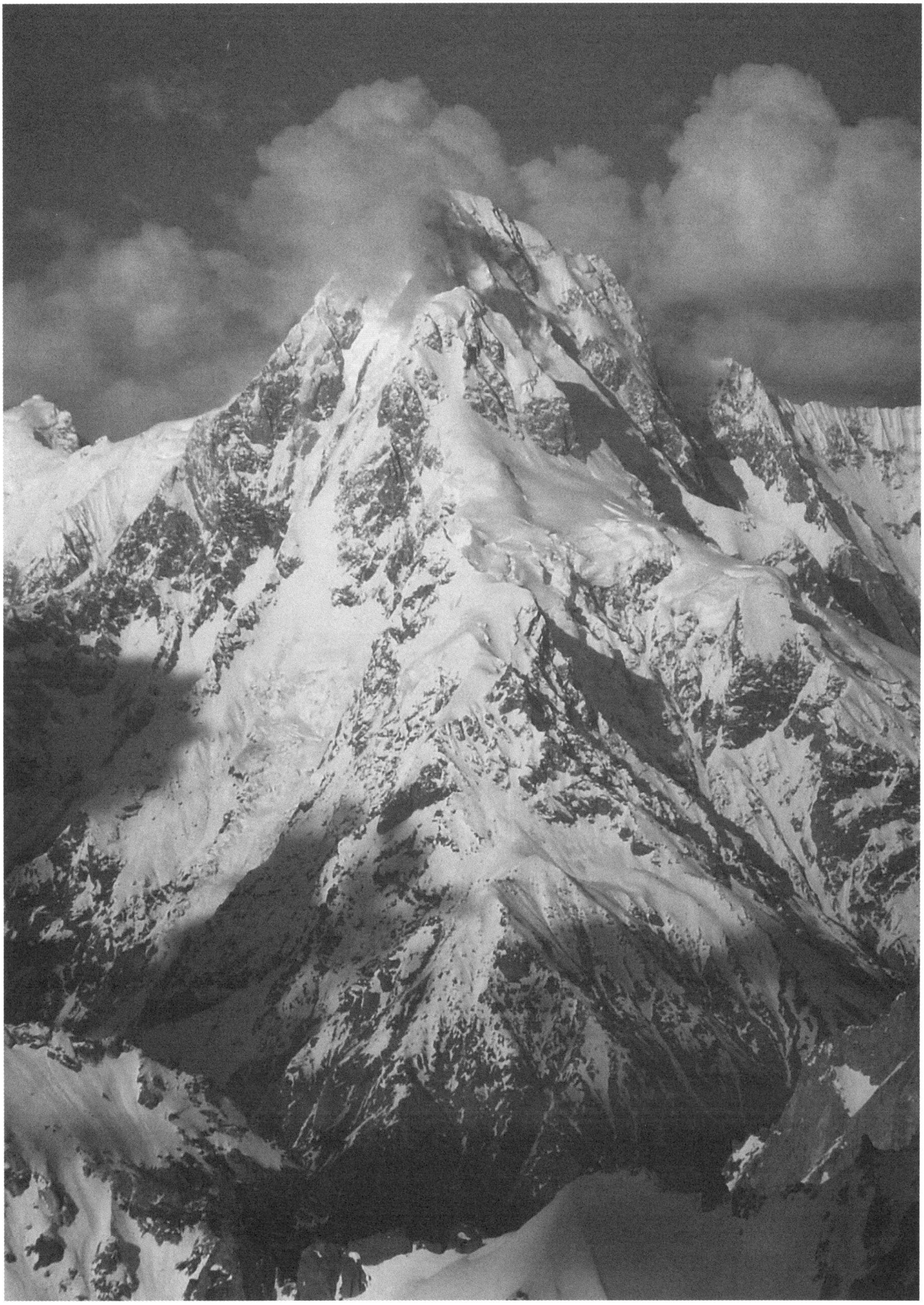

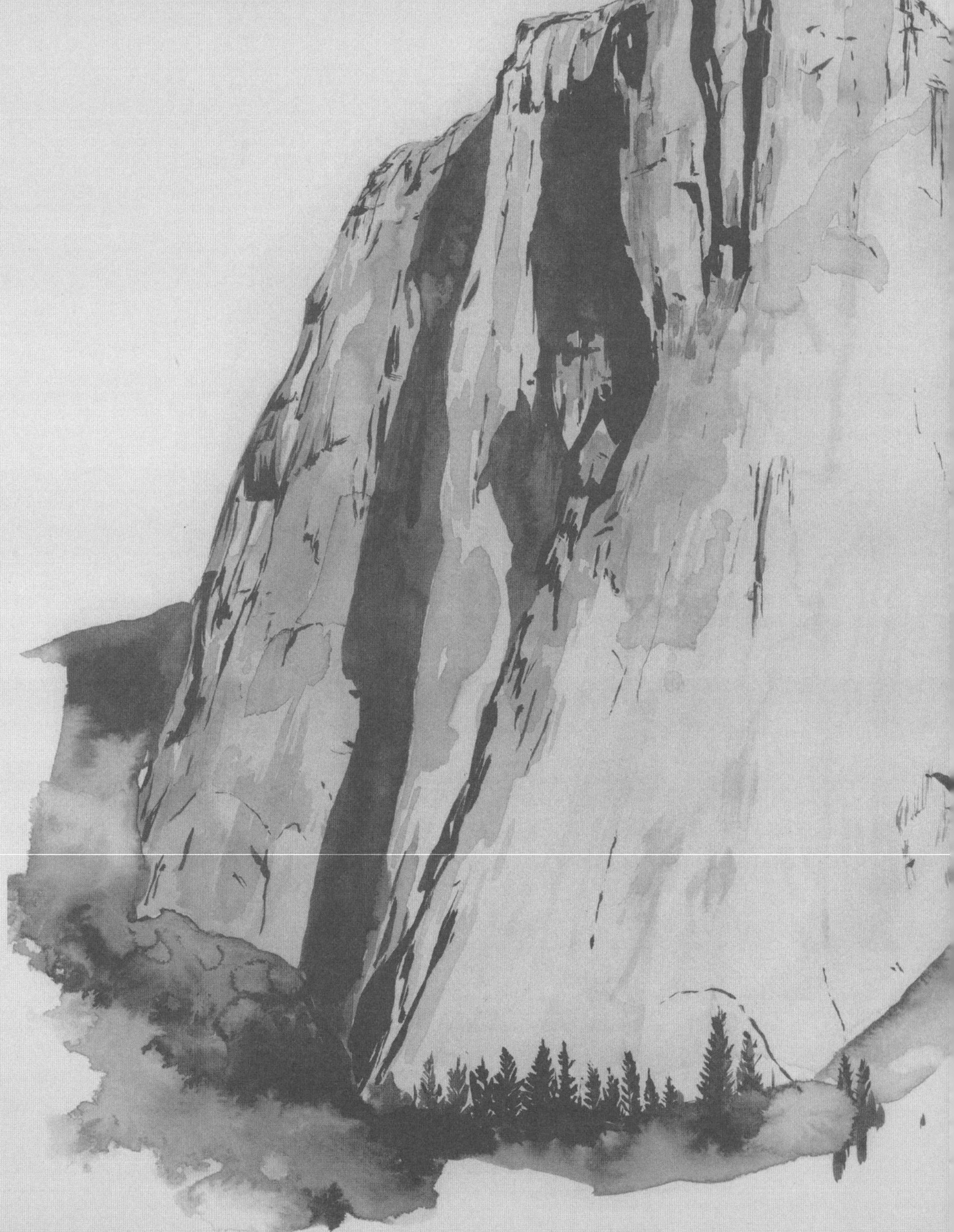

Lynn Hill and the First Free Ascent of the Nose

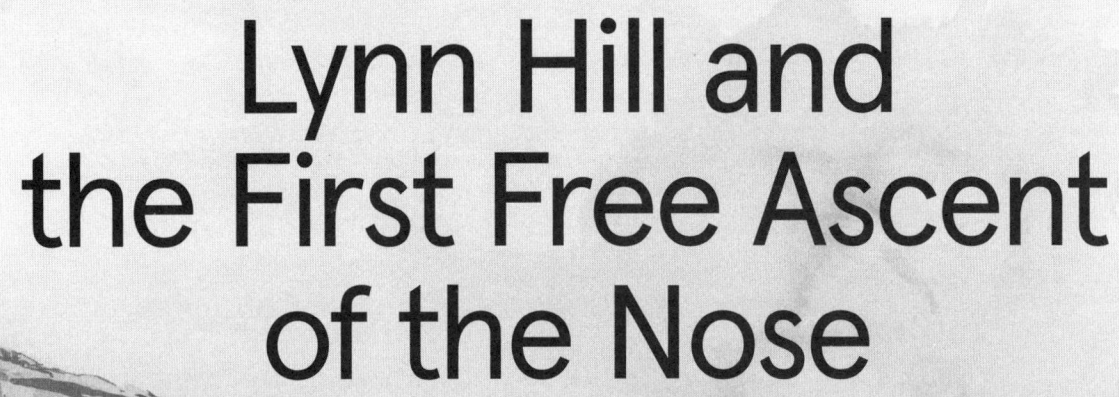

As you wind your way through Yosemite National Park, one of the most famous and beautiful in the world, all of a sudden, the 'tunnel view' appears. A lush, vast carpet of enormous trees stretches out below and the intimidating granite walls of El Capitan rise on one side of the valley, while to the east, the magnificent Bridalveil waterfall tumbles down from the alpine. In the distance, the iconic rock formation of Half Dome lingers, inviting you to drive on and explore the valley.

LYNN HILL

Nationality:
American

Born:
3 January 1961

Active:
1975-present

As it was with the Indigenous Ahwahneechee tribe, whose traditional lands are here, this miraculous valley was so valued by early Western settlers and pioneers that Abraham Lincoln placed it under federal protection in 1864, saving the land from falling into the hands of lumber or mining companies until it was formally established as a national park in 1890 by President Benjamin Harrison.

When thirteen-year-old Lynn Hill went to Yosemite for the first time on a family trip from Los Angeles, she could hardly believe her eyes. She knew that rock climbing existed, and that Yosemite was a pilgrimage for climbers – her older sister's boyfriend Chuck Bludworth had told her all about it – but she couldn't imagine that humans could actually scale the mighty 2,307-metre (7,569-foot) monolith of El Capitan, 'El Cap' for short.

At first glance, El Cap seems smooth and impassable. But if you strain your eyes, you might just make out tiny human beings moving slowly but surely up its great walls, hauling huge bags of equipment along – all the water, food and supplies needed for several days on the wall. The commitment required to climb these routes cannot be underestimated and many climbers have died in the attempt.

Nestled a short distance away is the famous climber's campground known as Camp 4. Camp 4 is rich in climbing culture and history and has been used as the home base for some of the US's most prolific and innovative big-wall climbers. It is recognized around the world for its counterculture vibe, home to seriously committed, often impoverished climbers who can stretch a dollar further than anyone else in their efforts to spend an entire season here. In the late 1970s and early 1980s when Hill first began climbing in Yosemite, Camp 4 residents were known for dumpster diving or finishing off tourists' leftovers from the nearby cafeteria.

Hill began climbing as a teenager, introduced to the sport by her sister and Bludworth. Hill built on the fitness, strength and spatial awareness she had developed through gymnastics. With her tiny frame (just over 5-feet/1.52-metres tall), this would become invaluable when she was problem-solving difficult climbing moves on the sheer faces of Yosemite.

Right from the beginning, Hill led traditional routes, inserting protective gear in seams and cracks in the rock and then clipping the rope to these as she went up. Her first climb saw her leading immediately because her sister was afraid to go first. Most climbers, when learning, are held safe by a rope above them, known as a top-rope, which is placed there by a more experienced climber in advance, so that the beginner can, in the event of a fall, be caught by the rope and rest if needed. Lead climbing is usually learnt later, as a beginner first focuses on honing technique on top-rope.

Opposite: Lynn Hill.

Hill's fitness, flexibility and balance meant that she picked up the techniques quickly, and within two years she was climbing some of the hardest-graded routes. When she eventually sought longer, steeper challenges in the vertical cathedrals of Yosemite, her skill did not go unnoticed by the predominantly male posse there. Although women are part of the rich climbing history of Yosemite, at that time they were few and far between. Hill's main climbing mentors in her early career were men, with John Long being one of the most influential. Long was part of the Stonemasters, a group of talented, rough and tumble rock-climbing pioneers based in California. They recognized Hill's ability early on.

Hill's first ascent of El Capitan was at the tender age of 18, along with her friend and regular climbing partner Mari Gingery, whom she'd met at Joshua Tree, another famous climbing area close to Los Angeles. They were joined by experienced climber and photographer Dean Fidelman. Hill had already climbed some of the classic routes on other walls in Yosemite, like Sentinel Rock and Half Dome, but the Nose route on El Cap would be her and Gingery's first big-wall climb. It would be the longest route they had ever done, and they would need to use aid-climbing techniques through the most difficult sections, something neither of them had done very much of before.

The Nose follows the obvious prow of El Cap, some 880 metres (2,887 feet) in thirty-one pitches, or rope lengths. It was first climbed in 1958 by Warren Harding and has become, arguably, the most famous big-wall rock climb in the world. For the first ascent of the Nose, Harding and his companions took forty-seven days over eighteen months to complete the route. They often terrified tourists who spotted them on the wall, causing immense traffic jams and forcing park staff to demand they stop climbing until the low season started so fewer tourists would call rescue services in a panic.

Hill, Gingery and Fidelman planned to spend around three days on the route, as had become the norm decades after Harding's first ascent. Just as the time needed to climb the route had changed, so had the style in which climbers now ascended. They preferred climbing free, using physical strength and technique to gain height. With this faster, more fluid style, they would be able to bypass some of the more difficult sections where Harding used the laborious aid-climbing technique. Not all difficult sections could be easily tackled using free techniques though, so the team also used aid in some of the crux sections to gain the summit. It was not until decades later that anyone, Hill herself in fact, would free-climb the entire route.

INFO

WOMEN IN EARLY YOSEMITE CLIMBING HISTORY

1934
Marjory Bridge completes the first female ascent of Yosemite's Higher Cathedral Spire.

1950s
Meredith Ellis Little makes ascents of some Yosemite classics such as the Royal Arches route and Washington Column.

1963
Hope Morehouse Meek completes the first ascent of Great White Book on Yosemite's Pleasure Dome in Tuolumne Meadows.

1967
Liz Robbins completes the first female ascent of the Regular Northwest Face of Half Dome.

1973
Sibylle Hechtel completes the first all-female ascent of Washington Column with Anne-Marie Rizzi and the first all-female ascent of El Capitan via the Triple Direct route with Beverly Johnson.

1974
Molly Higgins and Barb Eastman complete the first all-female ascent of the Nose on El Capitan.

1980s
Ellie Hawkins does solo ascents of the Direct Northwest Face of Half Dome and Never Never Land on El Capitan. Hawkins was the first woman to establish a new solo big-wall route in Yosemite; her route is named Dyslexia.

1981-2
New Zealand climber Lydia Bradey makes seven first female ascents in Yosemite.

1994
Lynn Hill free-climbs the Nose on El Capitan in under twenty-four hours.

Summit - 880 m/2,887 ft

EL CAPITAN
THE NOSE

The Nose on El Capitan is one of the most coveted big-wall routes in the world. It rises 880 m/2,887 ft above Yosemite Valley and is climbed in thirty-one pitches.

1. El Cap Tower.
2. Boot Flake.
3. King Swing.
4. The Great Roof: a challenging section graded 5.13c.
5. Changing Corners: a 3-m/10-ft blank section of wall rated 5.14a, the hardest section of the climb, which is the twenty-third pitch.

LYNN HILL

Thirty-one pitches require a lot of climbing and it takes considerable effort, even if the route is easy, to complete a feat like this in the vertical world. Not only do you have to get yourself up the face, but you must also haul all your food, water and equipment with you so you can camp on the wall. Most parties spend at least two nights on the Nose. Hauling requires so much time and effort that on easier grades it often takes more physical strength than the climb itself.

Hill and Gingery realized early on in their climb that Fidelman might not be as reliable as expected. Despite his technical climbing prowess, his head was not in the big-wall game, and he suffered from fear of exposure the higher the team got. The two women alternated leads, free-climbing sections with difficulty up to 5.10, taking advantage of beautiful cracks with a consistent width that would accept perfectly placed hands inside, a technique called hand jamming. This allowed them to pull their body weight up and move quickly through the smooth granite, finding a flowing rhythm of hands and feet in constant motion. Their small team made two bivouacs on the wall. The first night they camped on the somewhat luxurious El Cap Tower, which provided ample space to spread out and lie flat on the ground – a precarious but comfortable perch.

On day two, the two women completed the now-famous sections of Boot Flake and the King Swing – a large pendulum swing where climbers reach the next useable crack system by running across the rock and swinging to a point 10 metres (33 feet) away. This eventually brought them to the Great Roof, one of the most difficult parts of the climb, which involves climbing a steep corner under a large overhanging rock in order to access the face and cracks above. Using aid techniques, climbers of Hill's era would place extra-thin pitons in tiny horizontal seams in the granite, to which they could clip a strong but lightweight foot ladder made of webbing, known as etriers, to stand on, securing them until the next piton could be placed. Using this technique, they could move sideways along the underside of the roof, attaching their rope for protection as they traversed underneath the roof.

Darkness fell shortly after they had gained the Great Roof and, since none of them owned a head torch, Hill ingeniously used a cigarette lighter to illuminate the path to their next bivouac at the ledge known as Camp 5. Except for an awkward moment the next morning where Hill accidentally dropped their food bag off the side of the ledge and sent it hurtling thousands of feet into the valley below, the remaining pitches went smoothly, and they were on top of El Cap by late afternoon. The whole Yosemite Valley lay below them.

'... on the cusp of the seventies and eighties, climbers viewed the experience of living for days on the end of a gigantic cliff as a mystical pilgrimage. These were heady times.'

– Lynn Hill

INFO

CLIMBING STYLES: A GLOSSARY

SPORT CLIMBING
Climbing where lead climbers clip the rope into pre-drilled existing bolts for protection while ascending.

TRADITIONAL CLIMBING
Climbing where lead climbers must place their own protection first, then clip the rope. The second climber removes the protection as they ascend.

COMPETITION CLIMBING
Regulated climbing, usually indoors on artificial walls. There are three disciplines: lead climbing, bouldering and speed climbing.

BOULDERING
Climbing on smaller rock formations that don't require a rope.

AID CLIMBING
Any form of climbing where mechanical devices or equipment are used for upwards momentum, not just for protecting the climber. For example, hammering a piton into a crack, attaching a sling and then standing in the sling.

FREE CLIMBING
Climbing where climbers place equipment only for protection in the event of a fall.

FREE SOLOING
Free climbing alone, without the use of a rope, often with serious repercussions should the climber fall.

'The Nose introduced Mari and me to the cult of El Capitan,' Hill wrote in her memoir. 'Back then, on the cusp of the seventies and eighties, climbers viewed the experience of living for days on end on a gigantic cliff as a mystical pilgrimage. These were heady times. We indulged in these "vertical retreats" as a means of affirming our belief in the virtue of abandoning material comforts in favour of the kind of character-building experiences that inevitably occur on these big-wall journeys.'[1]

After her first successful ascent of the Nose, Hill decided to explore other types of rock. She spent time in the eastern United States, climbing near New Platz, New York, at a crag called the Shawangunks, or 'the Gunks'. There, she learned about climbing competitions, which were just beginning in Europe. She would go on to become a highly successful competition climber, winning some of the first competitions she entered. By 1989, Hill was recognized as the best competitive sport-climbing woman in the world; during her competition years she went face to face with other celebrated climbers like Catherine Destivelle and Isabelle Patissier.

Being part of the European competition scene and experiencing rock climbs on her trips to the continent rounded out her experience. She learned that rehearsing the sequence of moves on a difficult route was not frowned upon in places like France, as it had been on the walls of Yosemite. Warren Harding and the Stonemasters of Yosemite still touted ground-up, no-falling ethics as the purist form of climbing, unlike French climbers, who thrived on new approaches and the evolution of the sport. To broaden her horizons, Hill moved to France with her competition-prize earnings, bought a house and honed her technique on the limestone walls where modern-day sport-climbing was born.

Despite her success in the world of competition climbing, Hill craved new challenges. On one of her annual trips back to California, her old friend and partner John Long suggested she would be capable of free-climbing the Nose, something that had not been done before. At a turning point in her career, having just left competition climbing, she decided this achievement would be the icing on the cake.

Unlike some of her male counterparts, Hill believed in being open to failure and embracing learning experiences without focusing too much on the end goal. Her free-climbing attempt on the Nose was not prefaced by months of training and it required surprisingly little rehearsal, perhaps three or four days, until she and her climbing partner Simon Nadin felt ready to make the first attempt in the autumn of 1993. She had met Simon while on the World Cup circuit and he eagerly joined her attempt after they coincidentally met while he was on a climbing holiday in California.

They failed on their first try, but in more than 600 metres (1,968 feet) of climbing, only a blank section of 3 metres (9.84 feet), known as the Changing Corners pitch, had stumped them. Just weeks later, Hill started up the enormous face again, this time with friend and climbing partner Brooke Sandahl. They rappelled down from the summit of El Cap to the blank pitch and tried several variations over the course of three days before making a formal attempt. With input from Sandahl, Hill recalls pulling out all the techniques she knew to complete the crux: 'I had invented a wild tango of smears with my feet, tenuous stems, back steps and cross steps, lay backs and arm bars, and pinches and palming manoeuvres.'[2] Once she had managed the section with just one fall, using this elaborate sequence of difficult moves, they decided to start from the ground up and give the entire climb a go.

Hill's second attempt to free-climb the route went perfectly: she completed all the pitches free, including the two most difficult sections of the Great Roof and the Changing Corners. With a storm fast approaching, the duo raced through the last few hundred feet to the top, where they stood, victorious. Exhausted and elated, they decided to bivouac on the summit and made a celebratory fire to keep warm. 'It goes, boys!' was a popular advertising campaign used once news of their success hit the climbing mainstream, a quote from Hill poking fun at her male peers who had failed to free the route first.

Lynn Hill's free climb of the Nose was a monumental event in the evolution of climbing. It proved to a doubtful, traditional climbing generation that anything was possible. But it was not to be the last feather in her cap. It set her mind racing as to whether she might free the Nose in a single twenty-four-hour push. In the late summer of 1994, she returned to the wall to give it a shot.

Hill's initial try at a free climb in under twenty-four hours was not to be. The heat of the day shut her down when she reached the Great Roof, where she tried, unsuccessfully, for five hours to free the technical pitch. Her foot placements felt greasy and her feet slipped out from under her. She had also run out of chalk to dry her sweaty hands, and she and her partner were dangerously low on water. There was also a film crew documenting the climb, adding another level of complexity and stress. The team retreated, analyzing what had gone wrong, and Hill adapted her plans.

On 19 September 1994, at 10 p.m., Hill began her second attempt under the light of a full moon. Climbing through the night meant that she would reach the Great Roof in the morning, when the rock was still cool and the friction under her feet would be better. Her tactics paid off and by mid-morning, she had climbed through the roof and was on her way to the second crux of the Changing Corners. The heat was once again a factor as they arrived at the glassy smooth section. Hill decided to rest and wait for the rock to cool before heading up.

After several hours, she began to climb. She fell three times before her efforts paid off. With another dream realized, Hill's achievements were recognized around the world. She had free-climbed the Nose in less than twenty-three hours, performing the impossible.

Lynn Hill's free climbs on El Capitan were pivotal points in the progression of rock climbing, securing her place as one of the most innovative rock climbers in history. Her sub-twenty-four-hour free climb of the Nose on El Capitan set the bar for how climbers viewed the big walls of Yosemite. It would be twelve years before the route was climbed free again. In 2005, Tommy Caldwell and Beth Rodden were the second team to free the route, leading all pitches during a four-day push. Hill would go on to climb many more cutting-edge routes around the world, in places like Kyrgyzstan, Morocco and Madagascar, where she led an all-women's expedition in 1999. Hill continues to climb and inspire young women climbers to this day. She is a mother, motivational speaker and professional climbing coach and consultant.

Opposite: Lynn Hill free-climbing the Nose, El Capitan.

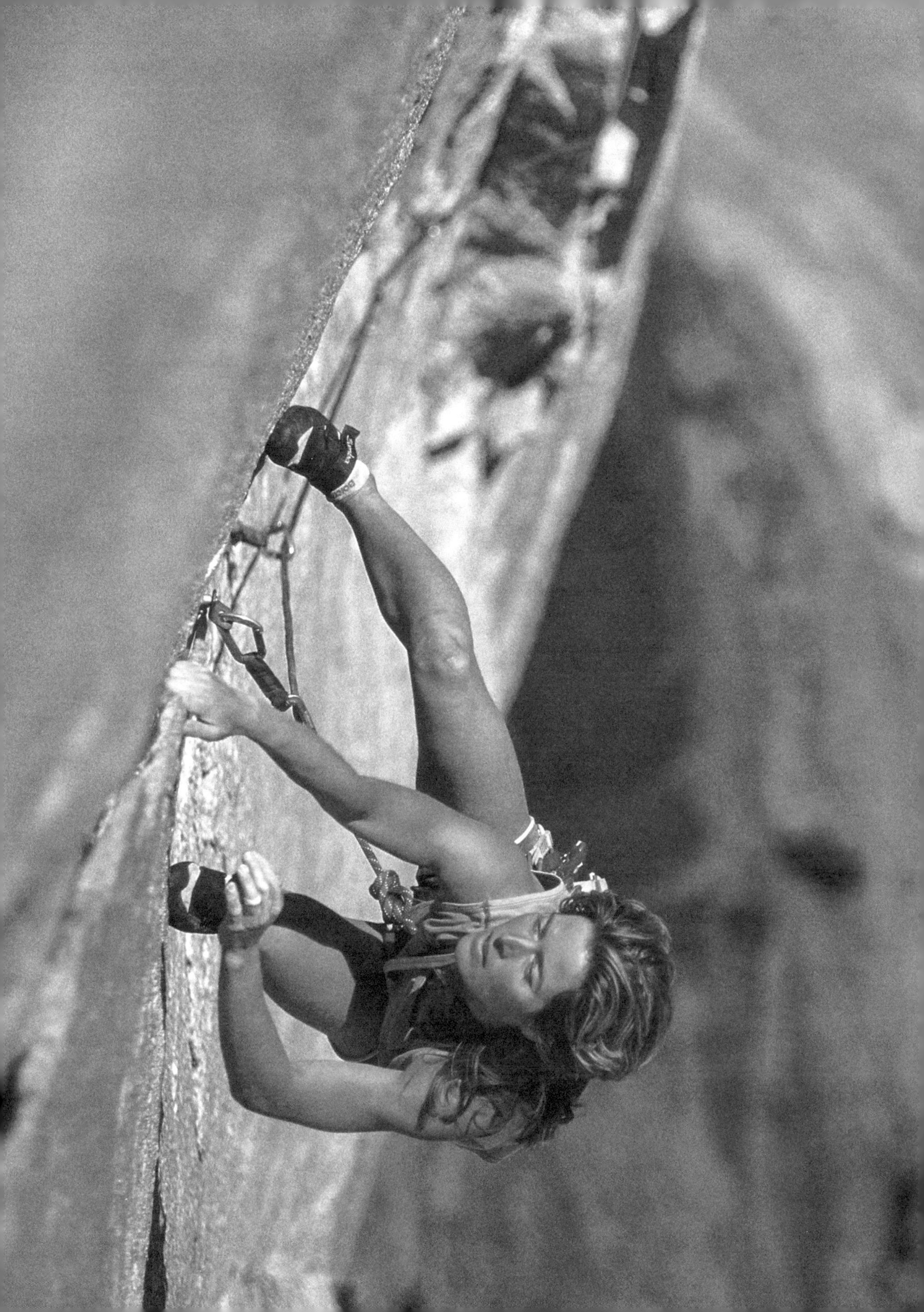

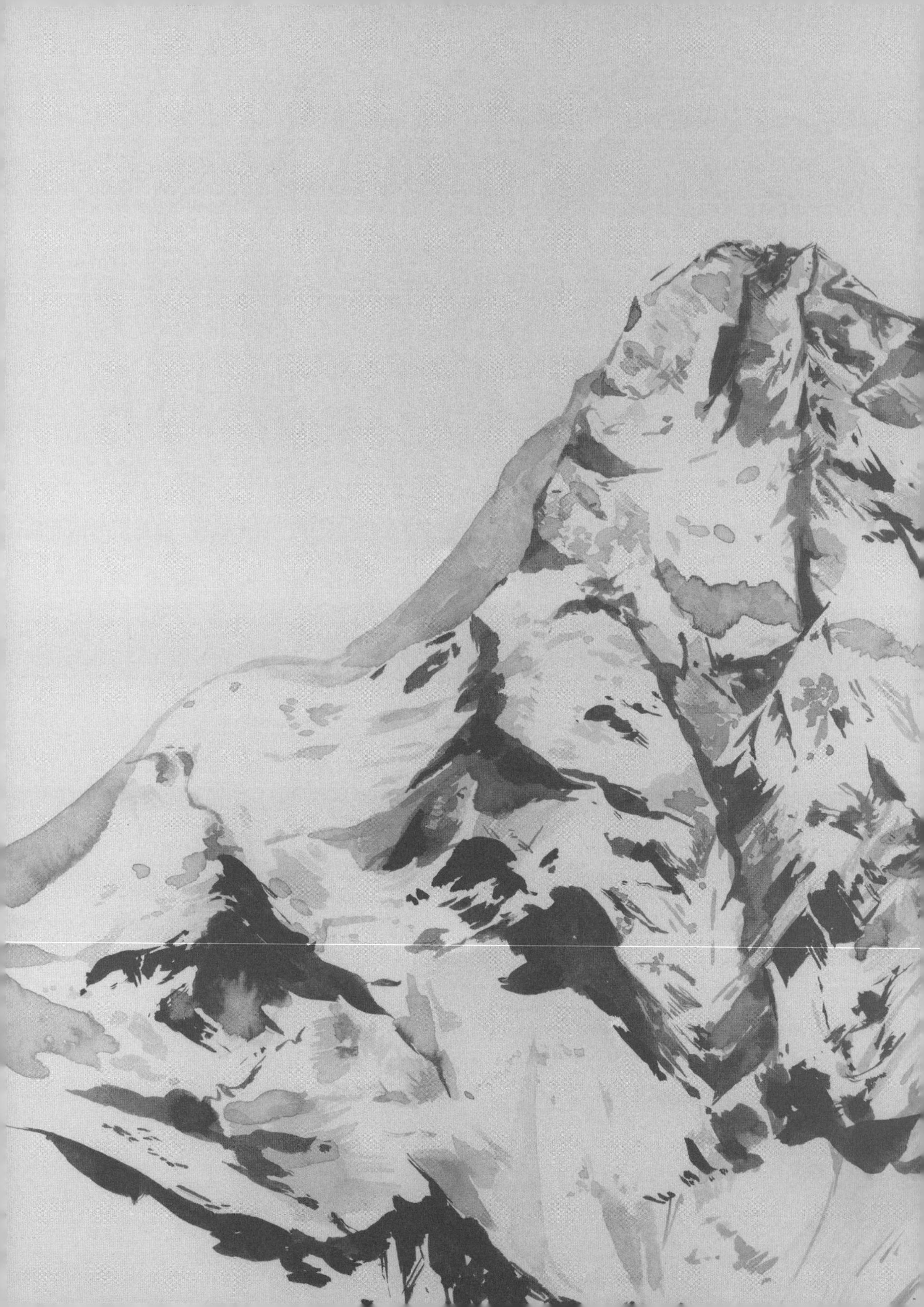

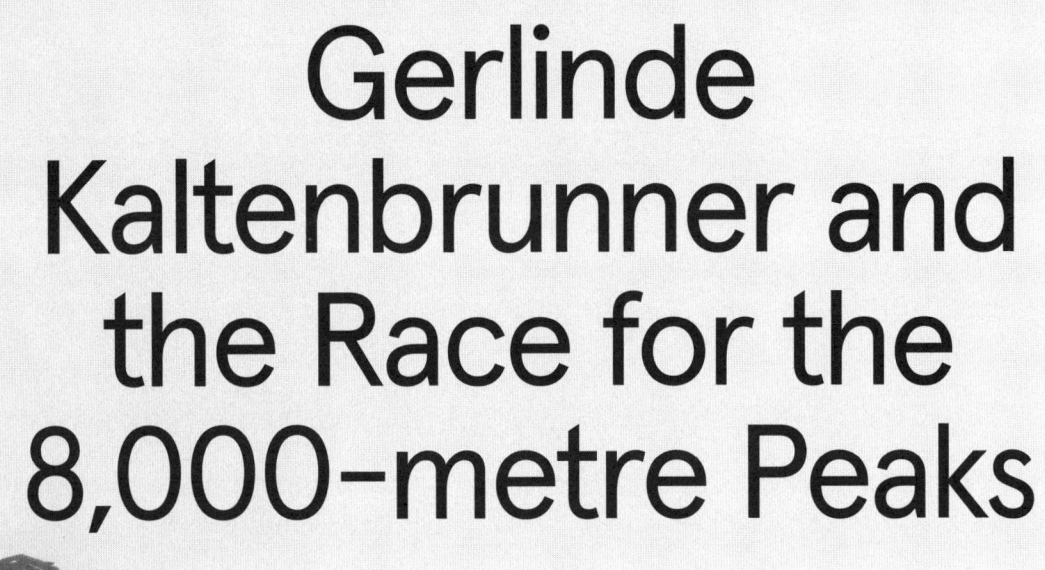

Gerlinde Kaltenbrunner and the Race for the 8,000-metre Peaks

When Austrian climber Gerlinde Kaltenbrunner finally stood atop K2 in August of 2011, she felt both joy and relief. After seven attempts to reach the summit, on four different expeditions, she had finally made it. Her choice to try the North Pillar rather than having another go on the easier Cesen route on the opposite side might have contributed to her success, but perhaps it was the simple equation of determination, strength and resilience that produced the desired result. The North Pillar is rarely accessed by teams as it involves extensive overland travel via the Chinese territory of Xinjiang. Having endured the considerable bureaucracy of securing the necessary permits and then arranged the transportation logistics, teams must contend with complex river crossings, involving camel trains carrying gear to basecamp, rather than traditional porter assistance. Whatever the reason for her success, this final, difficult summit secured Kaltenbrunner a well-earned spot in the history of mountaineering as the first woman to summit all fourteen 8,000-metre (26,247-foot) peaks without the use of supplemental oxygen.

GERLINDE KALTENBRUNNER

Nationality:
Austrian

Born:
13 December 1970

Active:
1993–present

Opposite: Gerlinde Kaltenbrunner on the sharp summit ridge of Nuptse in 2012.
Below: Gerlinde Kaltenbrunner.

From the beginning of her high-altitude climbing career, Kaltenbrunner had known that she wanted to climb the great peaks in her own way. For her, that meant completing the climb without supplemental oxygen and setting her own high camps without the assistance of high-altitude porters beyond basecamp.

Seventeen years before she summited K2, Kaltenbrunner had chosen Broad Peak in Pakistan for her first 8,000-metre (26,247-foot) climb. She was twenty-three years old and had never been above 4,800 metres (15,748 feet) before. Kaltenbrunner had been all heart on this first expedition, eager to learn the ropes from those with more experience. All the symptoms of high-altitude mountaineering had been new to her, but she was hooked for life. Even though the summit had remained elusive, she had gained so much from that first expedition. She had learned how to listen to her body, how to pace herself on the climb and the importance of melting snow for water at the higher camps, even if she was on the brink of exhaustion.

Before devoting her life to climbing full time, Kaltenbrunner had trained to be a nurse. She enjoyed helping others and worked hard at her local hospital, often working double shifts so she could earn extra holiday, allowing her to climb for extended periods. Her first medical emergency while climbing happened on this first trip to Pakistan when a team member from a Czech expedition, who had been trekking to basecamp with them, died suddenly from pulmonary oedema at an altitude of 5,000 metres (16,404 feet). Kaltenbrunner helped treat the climber and was shocked that something so drastic could happen before even reaching basecamp.

Like any international climbing expedition, there had been highs and lows, and ultimately Broad Peak had allowed Kaltenbrunner passage to the false summit, but not the true summit. Regardless, she was thrilled at having crossed the magical line above 8,000 metres (26,247 feet).

On that first flight home from Pakistan, Kaltenbrunner was already conspiring how to get back there as quickly as possible. She wondered if she could use her medical training by helping remote communities without proper hospitals or medical facilities, but her enquiries were rebuffed. She decided to focus on her training so she could return to the greater ranges solely as a climber.

When training for Broad Peak, Kaltenbrunner had ridden her bicycle 40 km (25 miles) daily to work and back, often leaving at 3.30 a.m. to make her morning shift. She maintained a rigorous training regime, sometimes competing as a non-professional mountain biker and ski racer.

Summit – 8,611 m/28,251 ft

To Advanced Base Camp

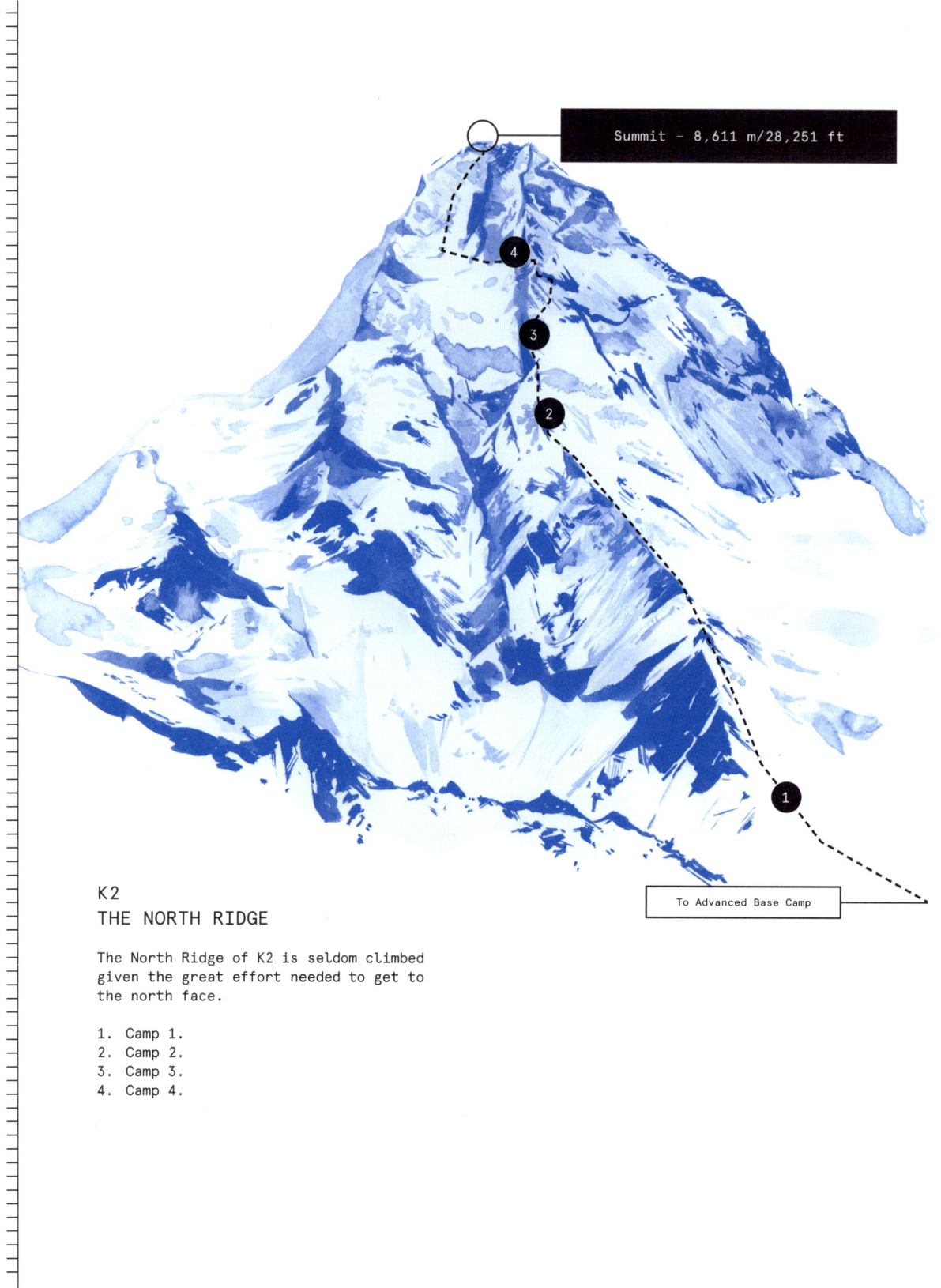

K2
THE NORTH RIDGE

The North Ridge of K2 is seldom climbed given the great effort needed to get to the north face.

1. Camp 1.
2. Camp 2.
3. Camp 3.
4. Camp 4.

Her excellent physical condition allowed her to join two more expeditions abroad before she attempted another 8,000er – one to Muztagh Ata in China and another to Ama Dablam in Nepal, where she gained more technical alpine experience.

After Muztagh Ata and Ama Dablam, Kaltenbrunner organized a trip to Cho Oyu with friends from the Austrian Alpine Club, which became officially known as the 'Upper Austria Friends of Nature' expedition. She and several other team members reached the summit at 8,201 metres (26,906 feet) but the trip turned sour when they reached basecamp. Other team members falsely accused them of forging ahead to the top without considering those lower down on the mountain. Kaltenbrunner experienced firsthand the politics that can complicate large expeditions, and she decided that she would climb in smaller groups from that day forwards.

From the summit of Cho Oyu, Kaltenbrunner had been mesmerized by the beautiful view of Shishapangma as the evening light hit its face, and decided that one day she would attempt the peak. When her dream became a reality, she decided to break with convention and use skis, which she thought would be beneficial for part of the climb up the normal route. It would also make descending much quicker. Wearing ski boots at high altitude poses a different problem than climbing boots, however. The thick, warm ski-boot liners retain perspiration on the way up the mountain when the skier is working hard and are incredibly hard to dry out at high camps. To overcome the problem, she wrapped her socked feet in a plastic bag and then stepped into her ski boots. This ensured that only her socks would get wet, while the liner would stay dry. Socks could easily be dried in her sleeping bag overnight.

Although Kaltenbrunner and her climbing partner Herbert Wolf were part of a climbing permit for Shishapangma that covered two Spaniards, two Americans and four other Austrians, the duo climbed and skied alone on the mountain. The flexibility that this gave them paid off when, after waiting out poor weather at Camp 2, they spontaneously made a dash for the summit. During a 2 a.m. toilet trip, Kaltenbrunner looked up to see a clear sky full of stars; they took advantage of clear weather and quickly got their equipment together, starting up the mountain on skis. When they could ski no further, they continued on foot for another 1,000 metres (3,281 feet) to the summit. On 17 May 2000, they reached the tiny 8,012-metre (26,286-foot) central summit, which is barely big enough for two climbers. To the north lay the endless white peaks of the Himalaya, and to the south the vast plains of the Tibetan plateau. Kaltenbrunner now had two 8,000-metre (26,247-foot) summits to her name.

In the decade or so that followed, Kaltenbrunner went on a whirlwind of Himalayan expeditions. After her success on Shishapangma, she went on to summit Makalu (8,463 m /27,766 ft) in 2001; Manaslu (8,163 m/26,782 ft) the following year; and Nanga Parbat (8,126 m/26,660 ft) via the Diamir Route in June 2003.

On Makalu, Kaltenbrunner had reached the summit alone, climbing confidently after her partner made the decision to descend. Climbing alone offered her the ability to think for herself and be free from the agendas of others. 'I no longer wanted to be subject to decisions made by an expedition leader,' Kaltenbrunner wrote in her memoir. 'I wanted to be actively involved in the discussions and to be treated as an equal.'[1] After Makalu, Kaltenbrunner would often join other international climbers on a single permit and share a basecamp, but mostly climbed alone, breaking trail, setting her own high camps and acclimatizing on her own schedule.

On many of the expeditions in the years that followed, Kaltenbrunner found herself providing medical aid. On the trip to Nanga Parbat, local villagers had asked her to assist an ailing woman in their remote settlement. She administered an IV drip, and the impoverished villagers sent eggs and fresh milk tea up to her camp as a gesture of thanks. This was likely more food than they could afford to spare, and it touched her deeply. On the same trip, she successfully treated a teammate suffering from gurgling lungs, a severe symptom of pulmonary oedema.

Kaltenbrunner had become the first Austrian woman on the summit of Nanga Parbat and was a force in the Himalayan climbing scene. Not only did she have five 8,000ers to her name, but her position as a woman in the still largely male-dominated sport of high-altitude mountaineering drew attention in media circles. She had earned the nickname 'Cinderella Caterpillar' for her ability to break trail through deep snow, slowly but surely creeping along. Up until that point, she had largely funded her shoestring expeditions by herself, whereas her male counterparts had significant financial contributions from sponsors or sporting organizations – hence 'Cinderella'. Now, she was finally ready to commit to climbing full time and decided to seek sponsorship.

In 2004, Kaltenbrunner focused her attention on Annapurna I, one of the most difficult peaks in Nepal. She had met Ralf Dujmovits, her soon-to-be husband, a few years earlier on her expedition to Manaslu. The more time they spent together, the more they realized that they had similar mindsets. Dujmovits joined her on many expeditions that followed, supporting her efforts and climbing independently, with Kaltenbrunner often in the lead. They reached the summit of Annapurna I together but faced extreme warming on their descent. With seracs collapsing all around them and snow bridges over gaping crevasses melting, their journey back to basecamp was anything but easy. Annapurna had lived up to its reputation as the most deadly mountain on Earth. For every one hundred people to summit, there are thirty-two deaths.

With sponsors now backing her and no work obligations, Kaltenbrunner went from one expedition to the next, often only spending a few weeks back in Europe before departing again. Gasherbrum I, located in the Karakoram between China and Pakistan, followed the difficult climb on Annapurna and then in 2005, Kaltenbrunner went on three expeditions to the Himalaya. First, she returned to Shishapangma, where she reached the true summit via the demanding and rarely used south face. As she descended, she also traversed the mountain, adding considerably more difficulty. She made an attempt on Mount Everest that same spring but was stopped short as she participated in a dramatic rescue, forcing her to abandon her summit bid. But as consolation, the very next month, she reached the summit of Gasherbrum II in Pakistan via the Southwest Ridge. She would pay a heavy price, however, suffering severe frostbite to her feet. Throughout these expeditions, Kaltenbrunner continued to maintain her mantra of climbing in small teams without the use of supplemental oxygen, a decision that likely contributed to her frozen toes.

With Kaltenbrunner's rush of successful summits, it now became apparent to the mountaineering world that there was a race on for the first woman to complete all fourteen 8,000-metre (26,247-foot) peaks. Since professional sponsorship now meant she could climb full time, many believed Kaltenbrunner would be the first. The German and Spanish press seized the opportunity to create a friendly rivalry between Kaltenbrunner and two other women climbers: Spanish high-altitude specialist Edurne Pasaban and Italian mountaineer Nives Meroi. When faced with life-and-death decisions high on a peak, none of the women were particularly keen on the drama of a press-induced race for the world record. Kaltenbrunner, in particular, admitted that she wanted to climb them all, but it wasn't important to her to be the first to do it.

Kanchenjunga, the world's third highest peak, was Kaltenbrunner's next successful summit in 2006. That same spring, she abandoned an attempt on Lhotse and the next she failed to reach the summit of Dhaulagiri. None of these unsuccessful attempts seemed to deter her, however, and her persistence paid off when she reached the true summit of Broad Peak, finally returning to the mountain where her climbing career had begun. By the summer of 2007, only Everest, K2, Dhaulagiri and Lhotse remained.

Dhaulagiri and Lhotse where the next to be crossed off. A month after Lhotse, Kaltenbrunner made another attempt on K2's Cesen Ridge, where she reached a highpoint of 8,300 metres (27,231 feet), but still the summit eluded her. In spring 2010, she reached the highest point on earth, summiting Everest via the Odell Route. At last there was just one summit left to complete.

After three previous expeditions to K2 and a total of six summit attempts, Kaltenbrunner was unsure if the mountain would concede. She and Dujmovits decided that they needed a new strategy and began researching the route up the mountain from the north through Xinjiang. It soon became apparent that a trip from this side of the mountain would be considerably more expensive than from the Pakistani side, but Kaltenbrunner managed to secure expedition funds from the National Geographic Society in the United States in exchange for an exclusive on the story. While this didn't cover all the costs, it made the expedition feasible. Kaltenbrunner invited four other climbers to join their expedition: two Kazakh climbers she had met on Nanga Parbat in 2003, Maxut Zhumayev and Vassiliy Pivtsov (who had given her the Cinderella Caterpillar nickname); Polish high-altitude cameraman Darek Zaluski; and Dujmovits's friend Tommy Heinrich, who acted as expedition photographer.

After five days of marching, with an elaborate train of camels and numerous stressful river crossings, the team reached a lush, green basecamp. Once higher up at Advanced Base Camp, they realized the pillar they would climb was much steeper than expected. After many days of climbing up and down, acclimatizing in the high camps and waiting out poor weather at Advanced Base Camp, the group made an exhausting eight-day push to reach the top. There was never any real certainty that they would make it, but on the evening of 23 August 2011, they finally reached the summit. Kaltenbrunner had done it, becoming the first woman to complete all fourteen 8,000-metre (26,247-foot) peaks without the use of supplemental oxygen and high-altitude guides.

Kaltenbrunner's website reached seventeen million clicks on the day of her summit of K2 and subsequently crashed. It seemed as though the whole globe was rooting for her

INFO

8,000-METRE
(26,247-FOOT) PEAKS

Listed in order of
highest to lowest:

MOUNT EVEREST
(Chomolungma,
Sagarmāthā)
China/Nepal,
8,849 m/29,032 ft

K2
Pakistan
8,611 m/28,251 ft

KANCHENJUNGA
Nepal
8,586 m/28,169 ft

LHOTSE
Nepal
8,516 m/27,940 ft

MAKALU
Nepal
8,463 m/27,766 ft

CHO OYU
Nepal
8,201 m/26,906 ft

DHAULAGIRI
Nepal
8,167 m/26,795 ft

MANASLU
Nepal
8,163 m/26,782 ft

NANGA PARBAT
Pakistan
8,126 m/26,660 ft

ANNAPURNA I
Nepal
8,091 m/26,545 ft

GASHERBRUM I
Pakistan
8,068 m/26,470 ft

BROAD PEAK
Pakistan
8,047 m/26,401 ft

GASHERBRUM II
Pakistan
8,035 m/26,362 ft

SHISHAPANGMA
Nepal
8,012 m/26,286 ft

Kaltenbrunner approaches
the North Pillar of K2, 2011.

to achieve her goal. She continued to climb afterwards, but she confesses that the summit of K2 was, perhaps, the most special to her. She had grown so much since her first Himalayan expedition in 1994 and she had now become one of the most important female mountaineers in history.

GERLINDE KALTENBRUNNER

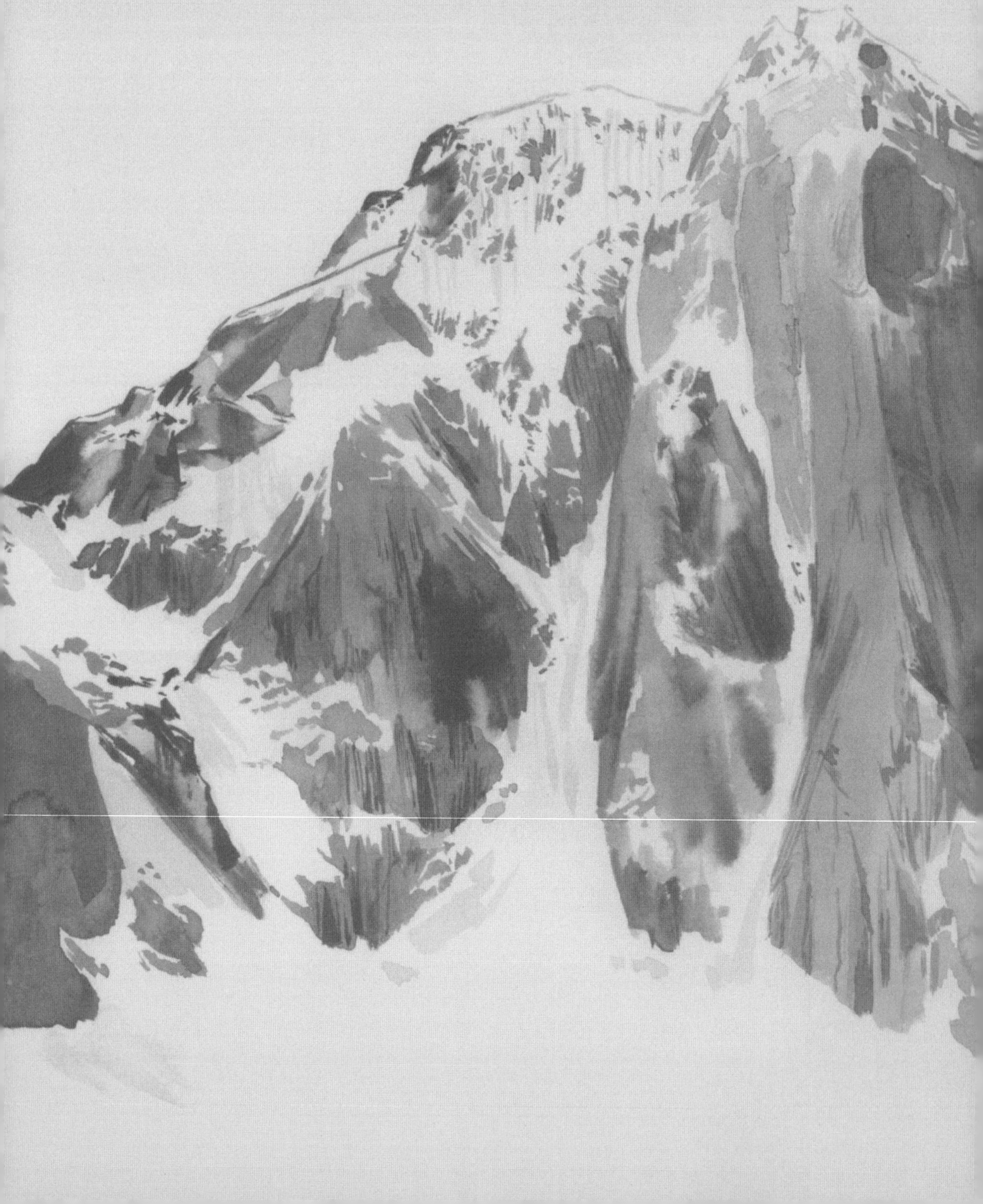

Ines Papert and the Ice Climb of Her Dreams

German climber Ines Papert kept a small, wrinkled black-and-white image of a remote peak in Kyrgyzstan in her purse for a long time. She knew very little about it, except that Kyzyl Asker was located in a distant mountain range, the Kokshaal Too, on the border of Kyrgyzstan and China. A perfect white diagonal line stretched from the base of the mountain to the summit ridge. If it was a line of pure ice, as she suspected, it could be the most magical route that she had ever set eyes on.

INES PAPERT

Nationality:
German

Born:
5 April 1974

Active:
1997-present

Opposite: Ines Papert climbing through an ice cave on a glacier.
Below: Ines Papert at home with her son.

Papert began her career as an ice climbing competition climber. She consistently won or stood on the podium at events, allowing her to abandon a regular career as a physiotherapist to spend more time climbing. In her six years as a serious ice climbing competitor, she won four World Championships, thirteen single World Cups and the overall World Cup Series three times. Papert was a young mother in those days and brought her baby Manu to competitions. Once she started winning, she found she could make a living from the prize money and sponsorship.

After Papert stepped away from the world of competitions, she started to commit to larger objectives around the globe. As one of the world's best ice climbers, she had always desired to bring this skill to the high-altitude alpine realm. She went on several major expeditions to Canada, India and Nepal, combining her love of ice and rock climbing on routes that required both skillsets. Papert also climbed regularly in the Alps, repeating difficult mixed climbs and establishing a few new ones.

When the time finally came to seek out the peak in the tattered photograph, Papert had plenty of expeditions under her belt. Kyzyl Asker, or the 'Red Soldier' in Kyrgyz, would not be easy to get to, but Papert had a friend in the area who helped with logistics, and in 2010 the trip became a reality. The thin white line embedded in her mind for so many years was an ambitious route, more than 1,200 metres (3,937 feet) of straight water-ice. A straight ice-climbing route of this length is an incredibly unusual feature to find at high altitude. At 5,842 metres (19,167 feet), Kyzyl Asker would make physical demands on the team as the oxygen levels lessened towards the summit, making it significantly more challenging than ice routes in Canada or the Alps.

After seemingly endless days of logistical drama transporting their gear to basecamp, the team eventually hiked further into the range and arrived at their next camp, where the route towered imposingly above them. There was an air of excitement at finally having arrived, but also fear. There had been a few worthy attempts at the line before theirs but all parties had been turned around by poor weather or warm temperatures that melted the ice as they went, causing extremely dangerous conditions. Papert and her team had deliberately planned their trip in autumn, hoping for cold temperatures at night and the cooperation of the sun during the day. They needed help from Mother Nature to get melting snow, which would create water that would then freeze to form a frozen waterfall – the perfect malleable climbing surface.

Winter came early to the Kokshaal Too that year, with more snow than expected. A big storm hit the team on its first try, pummelling the climbers at their bivy as they waited for daylight partway up the route. Avalanches plagued them all night as they sat tethered to the wall. With barely enough room to sit, snow ran over their heads into their clothing. It was miserably cold and they descended, hoping to save some energy for another try. At basecamp they waited more than a week for sunny skies to appear and for all the snow to flush the route clean. The team made a second effort and reached a point just 200 metres (656 feet) below the summit ridge before it once again abandoned the route. Frigid temperatures, more avalanches and a non-functioning stove made their decision for them: the expedition was over.

Despite not achieving her goal on Kyzyl Asker, Papert was mesmerized by the country and its beauty. Vast open landscapes with friendly rural farmers met them at every turn. It would be a perfect place to visit with her eleven-year-old son Manu. So, when the opportunity to return to the peak came, Papert planned a few weeks of travelling around Kyrgyzstan with him first. They rode horses, hiked in the countryside, lived in yurts and met the locals, who treated them like family. It was a transformative experience.

The second expedition saw some success, but not on the route they expected. When one of Papert's teammates fell ill with altitude sickness, she and another teammate climbed a new line on a neighbouring peak, a 600-metre (1,968-foot) route they named Quantum of Solace. It was a nice consolation prize, but the real joy of the trip had been the moments spent with her son, showing him her life as a professional climber on expeditions to remote corners of the Earth.

After the first two expeditions to Kyzyl Asker, Papert had gathered plenty of information and experience to plan for a successful expedition. However, she wanted a break from the goal and 'needed to let the idea rest' – she was worried it would become her 'sole purpose in life' and lead her to dangerous, goal-focused decisions. As important as climbing has always been for Papert, her first commitment is to her son. The climbs that she has achieved over her life are certainly difficult, but her strategy is calculated. She will not attempt anything without being fully prepared. This means intensive physical and mental training, along with unwavering focus and adaptability. When Papert plans a big trip, she often has a plan B or C in her back pocket. If the original objective becomes too risky, she switches to alternate plans without disappointment. No single peak will drive her to go beyond the known limits of her ability.

It took five years to set her sights on Kyzyl Asker again. Other climbers had attempted the route during her hiatus, which sparked Papert's interest. This time, she drew on past experience and compiled all her notes from the previous two trips. Looking at them again, she concluded that part of the strain of the 2010 and 2011 trips had been the logistics in getting to the climb. Their transport truck had been stuck to the axles in mud and they had been unable to drive close enough to basecamp both times. This forced the team to schlep heavy equipment over many kilometres on several round trips – gruelling work that had taken its toll, contributing to stress, exhaustion and sickness. She decided that an approach from the Chinese side would offer a better chance for success. With a road relatively close to the peak, they could drive directly to basecamp; their advanced basecamp would be only an eight-hour walk away. From this camp, the start of the route itself was only ten minutes further.

With her concerns about transportation seemingly resolved, Papert now had to find the perfect climbing partner. She met Luka Lindič, a renowned young Slovenian climber, at a sponsor event in Chamonix. They had similar mindsets for doing difficult climbs in the alpine, so they went on a trial climb together on Triglav, the highest mountain in Slovenia. It was clear that they would make a good team, so they began planning for Kyzyl Asker.

Approaching the mountain from the Xinjiang region of China proved to be the best tactic, despite having to navigate hundreds of fee-charging checkpoints along the road. When Papert and Lindič had flown over the mountains to meet their truck rendezvous, they had spotted Kyzyl Asker from the plane. Excitement mounted as they saw their white vertical line clearly visible on the peak: the ice had formed and they would have an opportunity to climb. Everything seemed to be in their favour.

As expected, their travel to basecamp was relatively simple. They established their camp with a local Chinese cook and photographer, and then made a reconnaissance trip to set up a new advanced camp higher up. With a perfect weather window predicted, Papert and Lindič readied their equipment, knowing that time was of the essence.

When they stepped out of their tents at their new advanced basecamp in the early morning of 30 September 2016, daylight was still hours away. Kyzyl Asker was standing proud in front of a galaxy of bright stars. The white line of ice was shining in the moonlight and the climbers began making their way up the easy ice slopes at the bottom of the route.

The ice was in good form and they made huge progress once daylight appeared. There was very little mixed ground on the route that year. In her two previous attempts,

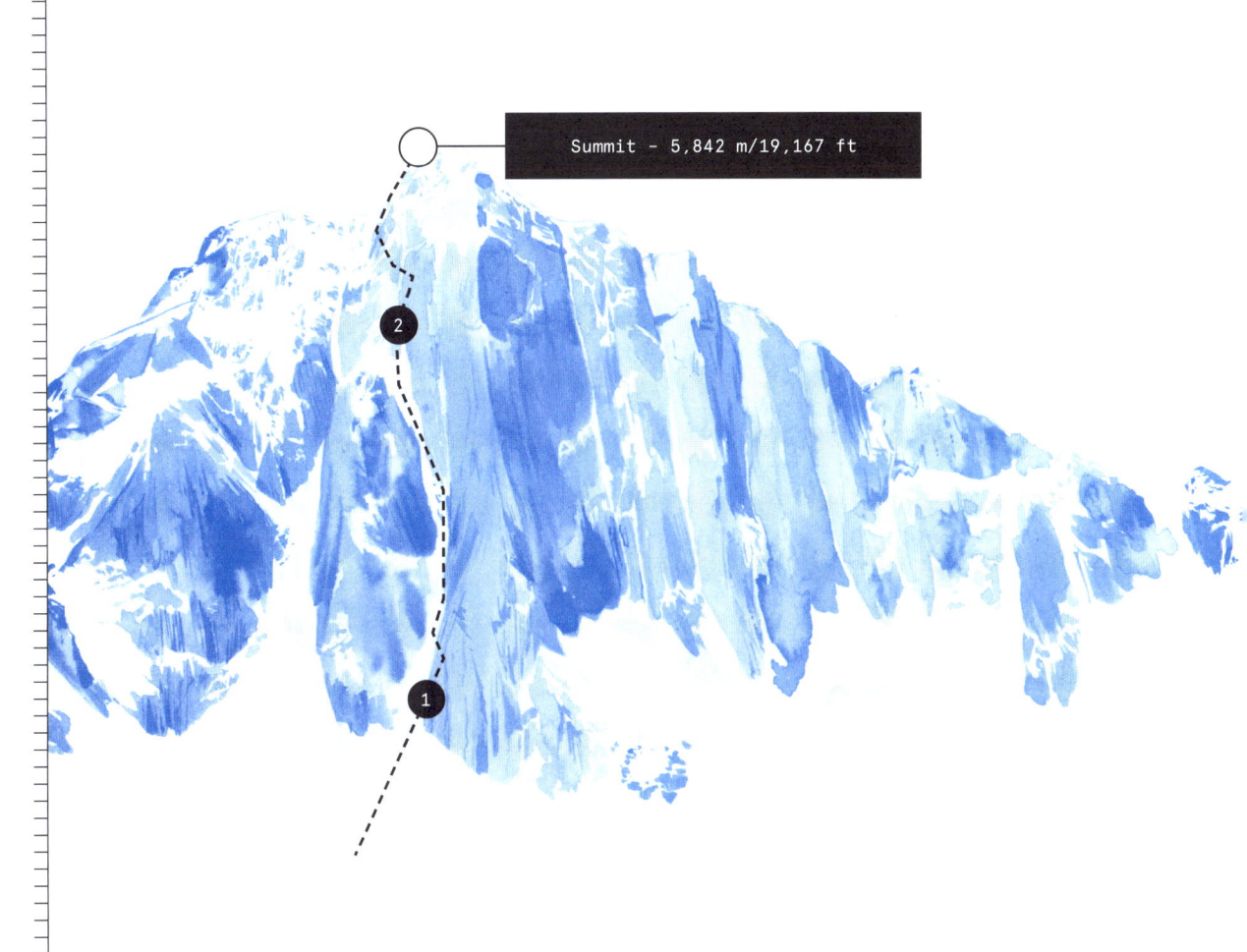

KYZYL ASKER
SOUTHEAST FACE

Kyzyl Asker, the 'Red Soldier' is a fortress of red granite straddling the border between Kyrgyzstan and China.

1. Line of ascent - the Lost in China route (1,200 m/3,937 ft, ED WI5+, M6).
2. Bivouac site.

INFO

NOTABLE CLIMBS
BY INES PAPERT

2000
Enters World Cup Ice Climbing scene and wins four World Championships, thirteen single World Cups and the overall World Cup Series three times in the six years that follow.

2003
Completes the first one-day redpoint of one of the hardest routes on the Eiger, Symphonie de Liberté (27 pitches, rated 8a/5.13b), with Hans Lochner.

2004
Free-climbs the difficult Last Exit Titlis in the Urner Alps (500 m/1,640 ft, rated 8b/5.13c) with Swiss climber Ueli Steck.

2006
Free-climbs Camilotto Pellisier's route on Cima Grande's north face in the Dolomites (500 m/1,640 ft, rated 8b/5.13c).

2007
Expedition to Arwa Tower (6,352 m/20,840 ft) in northern India.

2008
Trip to Icefall Brook Canyon in Canada, where Papert, Audrey Gariepy, Jennifer Olson and Caroline George establish ten new difficult ice-climbing routes in ten days, including Northwest Passage (600 m/1,968 ft, rated WI5), Scrambled Pancakes (600 m/1,968 ft, rated M7/WI6), Happy Hours (300 m/984 ft, rated WI6) and Into the Wild (100 m/328 ft, rated WI5, M12).

2008
Makes an on-sight ascent of the Flying Circus (rated M10), one of the world's most famous mixed routes on the Breitwangfluh in Switzerland's Bernese Oberland.

2009
First ascent of Cobra Norte (rated WI5, M8, TD & R), Kwangde Shar (6,093 m/19,990 ft), Nepal, with American climber Cory Richards.

2009
First ascent of Power of Silence (400 m/1,312 ft, rated 5.13a) on the Middle Huey Spire in the Cirque of the Unclimbables, Canada, with Lisi Steurer.

2010
First expedition to Kyzyl Asker, Kyrgyzstan.

2011
Second expedition to Kyzyl Asker, first ascent of Quantum of Solace (600 m/1,968 ft, rated M7, ABO WI7+) on the Great Walls of China, a series of walls over 5,000 m (1,6404 ft), in the Kokshaal Too range on the border of Kyrgyzstan and China.

2012
First ascent of Sensory Overload (1,200 m/3,937 ft, rated 5.11, A1) on the northwest face of the south tower of Mount Asgard on Baffin Island, Canada.

2013
First ascent of Likhu Chuli I (6,719 m/22,044 ft) in Nepal.

2015
First ascent of the Southwest Buttress of Mount Waddington's northwest summit (4,018 m/ 13,182 ft) with Paul McSorley and Mayan Smith-Gobat.

2016
Repeats Riders on the Storm (1300m/4265ft, rated 7c+, A2) on the Central Tower of the Torres del Paine in Patagonia with Mayan Smith-Gobat and Thomas Senf.

2016
First ascent of Lost in China, Kyzyl Asker, Kyrgyzstan, with Luka Lindič.

2019
Establishes the Sound of Silence (1,100 m/3,609 ft, rated M8, WI5), the only route on the east face of Mount Fay (3,234 m/ 10,610 ft) in the Alberta Rockies with Luka Lindič and Brette Harrington.

2021
First ascent of Heart of Stone (1,050 m/3,445 ft, rated M7) on Mount Huntington's west face, Central Denali Range, Alaska, with Luka Lindič.

Papert had had to navigate difficult rock and snow sections that weren't fully formed with ice, which had taken considerable time and effort. This time, because the ice was present across the entire route, she and Lindič were able to move quickly and conserve energy. They fell into an easy rhythm. Finding comfort in each other's ability, they found it unnecessary to talk; there was an unspoken understanding between them as they moved upwards.

By the time darkness fell, they had completed more than half the route, but the walls of ice were too vertical to build a bivouac to spend the night. Instead, they managed to find a small ledge and tucked themselves into their down jackets and sleeping bag, trying to stay out of the line of spindrift, the small waves of snow that regularly sloughed off the mountain.

They both knew that persevering through the night meant that the morning would provide opportunity, and as first light appeared and they readied their climbing gear, they realized they were within a few hundred metres of the summit ridge, which they reached by 10 a.m. A further two hours of climbing along the snowy spine of the ridge brought them to the summit and an amazing view, overlooking both Xinjiang in China and Kyrgyzstan.

The pair celebrated for a few moments and then began the process of setting up abseil stations. Both Papert and Lindič believed in a 'leave-no-trace' climbing ethic, so they would make Abalakov threads (named after their inventor) for each rappel – a technique where ice screws are used to create a 'V' in the ice so a rope can be fed through. Once the rappel is complete, the climbers can pull the rope without leaving any equipment behind.

When Papert and Lindič reached their advanced basecamp at 7 p.m., they were thrilled that the route had finally been sent. They named it Lost in China and gave it the grade of ED, WI5, M6, meaning: extremely difficult, waterfall ice grade 5 and mixed grade 6. They calculated the route at 1,200 metres (3,937 feet), an exceptionally long ribbon of ice. It had taken them about thirty-six hours of intense effort to complete the climb and was much celebrated once news of their achievement reached Europe.

Succeeding on Kyzyl Asker was a transformative experience for Papert. She had returned to this mountain multiple times, and there had been moments where she thought she might abandon the idea. Although she was already a determined character, Kyzyl Asker taught her that sticking with a goal – however difficult and logistically challenging it may be – was worth it. She believes that there is always valuable knowledge gained in failure and exercising patience. This third trip could have easily been a failure too. The night spent on the wall, as terrible as it was, was a pivotal moment in their decision-making. The mutual understanding between herself and Lindič was key to their success.

Papert would go on to retell her experiences on Kyzyl Asker and other climbs to a number of corporate groups, as her philosophy on decision-making has become a valuable tool not only for climbing but also for life and business. Papert and Lindič would enjoy a prolific partnership for the next seven years, establishing new routes all over Europe and North America, including a tremendous first ascent on the west face of Mount Huntington in Alaska. Papert is recognized as one of the most successful alpine climbers in the world. Even as she enters her fifties, she has no intentions of slowing down and climbs with her son Manu as often as she can.

'I really enjoy the process that leads me to achieve the goal I have in mind. That's all part of it. It's not just the moment of finally doing it, but also how you got there.' [1]

– Ines Papert

Pages 124–25: Ines Papert in Kyrgyzstan, 2016.

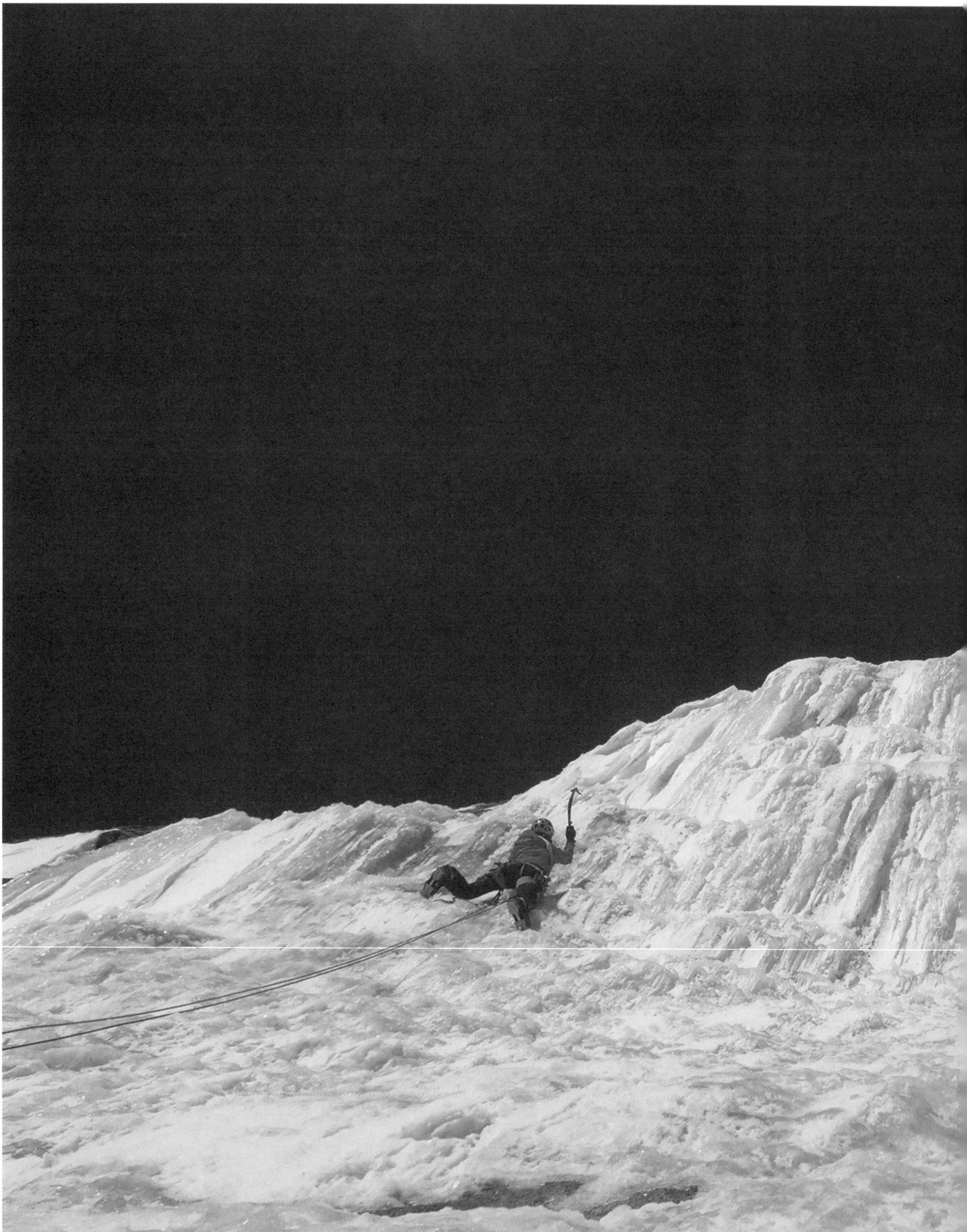

INES PAPERT

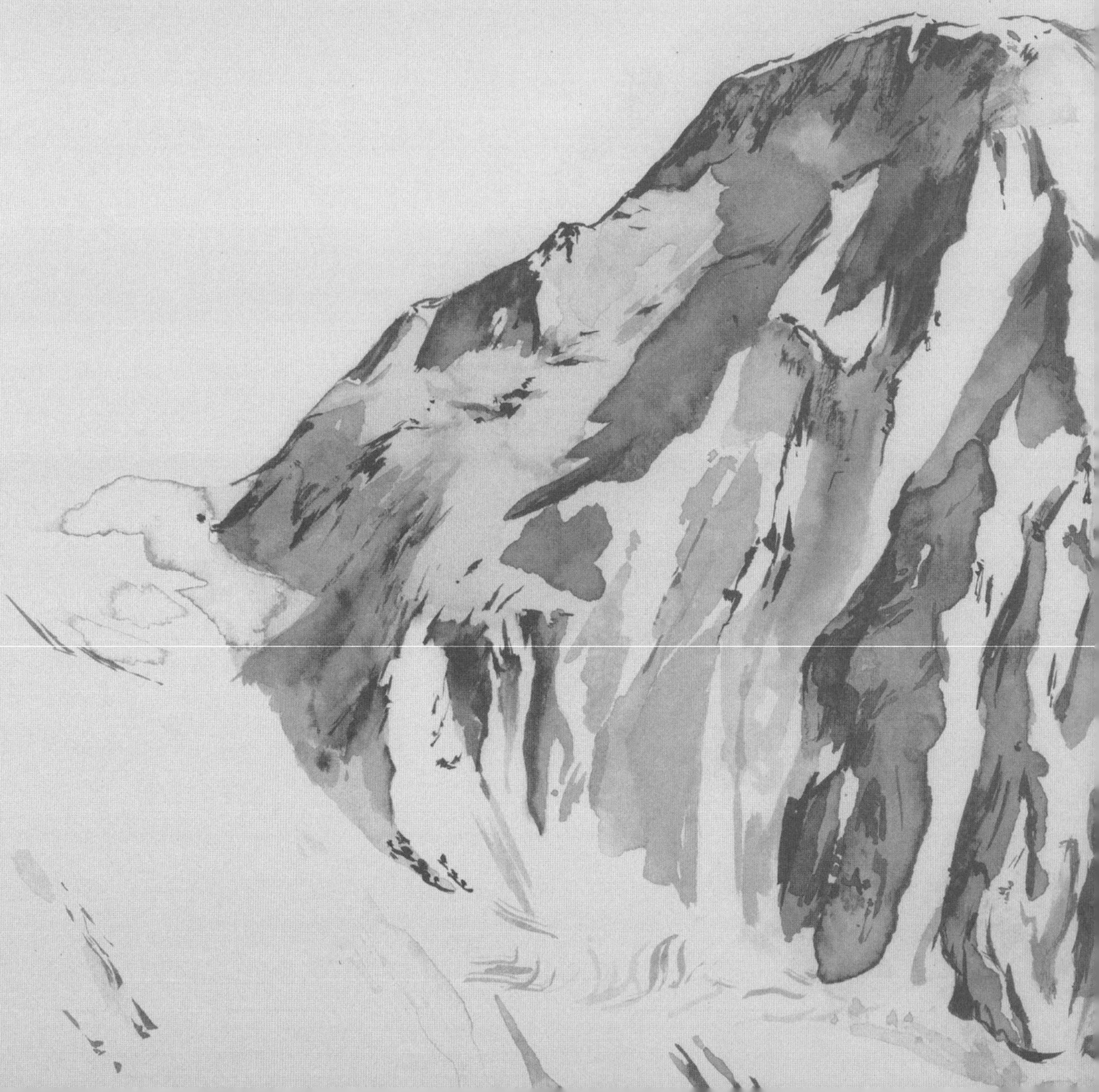

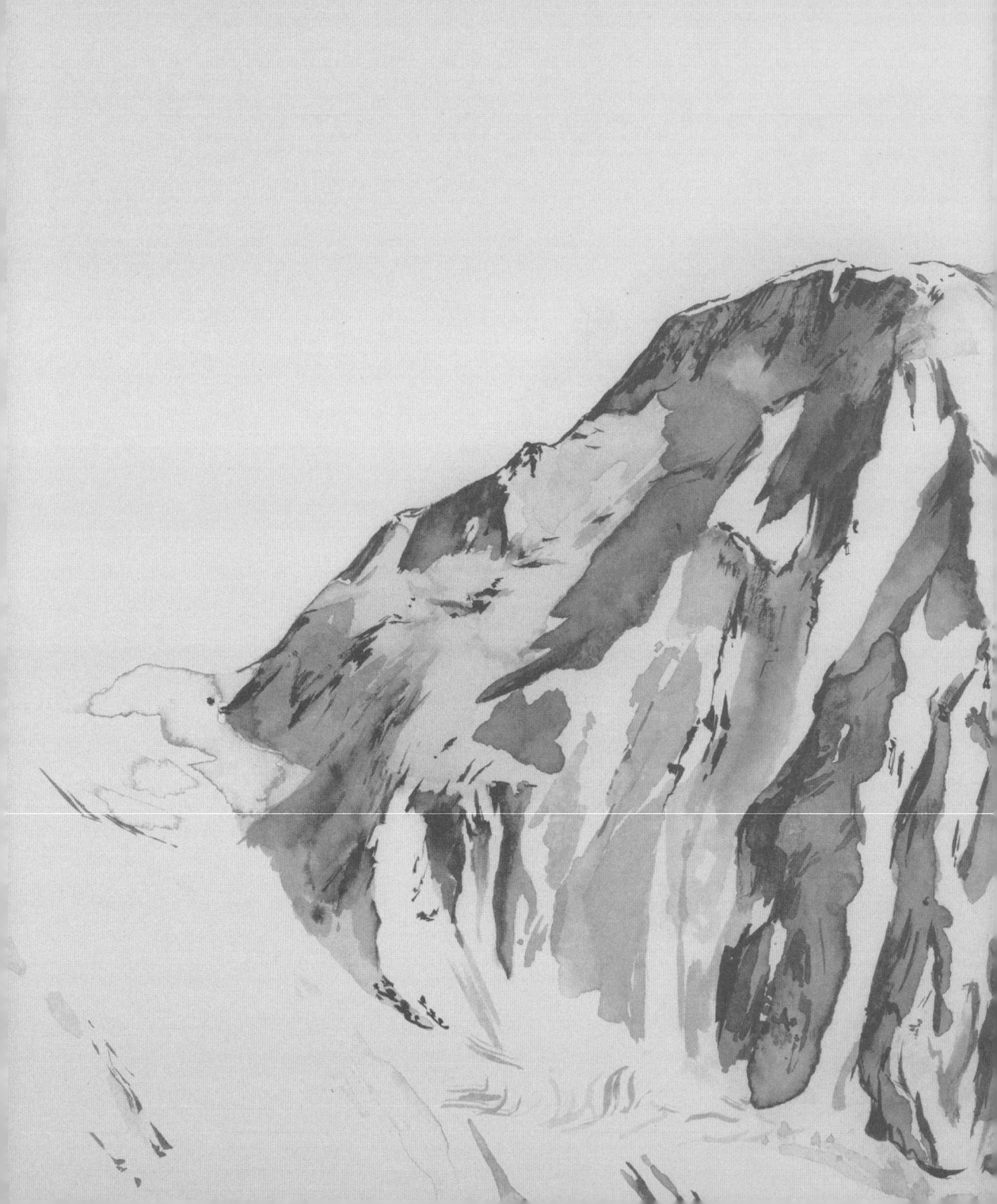

Élisabeth Revol's Fight for Survival on Nanga Parbat

Élisabeth Revol could hardly comprehend her predicament. Here she was, seeking shelter from the harsh wind in the icy depths of a crevasse high on the slopes of Nanga Parbat in Pakistan. She was trying to stay awake and keep warm in temperatures well below -40°C (-40°F). It's difficult for a non-climber to imagine finding safety and comfort in a gaping hole on a glacier, but Revol knew this frigid cave could save her life – if she could rest and collect her thoughts. It was 26 January 2018.
Only the day before, she had managed the impossible by ascending Nanga Parbat (8,126 metres/26,660 feet) – dubbed 'The Killer Mountain'– in the depths of Himalayan winter. It was a remarkable feat that had been achieved only once previously, by a team of three men. This was Revol's fourth attempt on the mountain and she had just become the first woman to scale Nanga Parbat in winter. But deep in her frozen shelter, running the risk of severe frostbite, she began to wonder why she had returned to such an inhospitable place. Curled up on a precarious snow shelf inside the crevasse, she tried to keep the core of her body as warm as possible. It was thoughts of her husband, Jean-Christophe, that pulled her through the horrific night. If she could only survive until the morning, a helicopter would arrive and she would be rescued. Or so she thought.

ÉLISABETH REVOL

Nationality:
French

Born:
29 April 1979

Active:
1998-present

Early in the morning of 25 January 2018, French climber Revol had been in fine form. She and her climbing partner Tomasz 'Tomek' Mackiewicz had left their high camp at 7,300 metres (23,950 feet) just after 7.30 a.m. and had made a strong push for the summit of Nanga Parbat. Their strategy was to climb as lightweight as possible, a tactic known as alpine style. They carried only what they needed: water, some energy bars, goggles, spare mittens and a basic first-aid kit. They were intent on returning to their camp later that night and so left their heavy rope behind. The weight would have slowed their progress and both climbers were confident in their ability to navigate the terrain without being tethered to one another. Moving more quickly would enable a dash to the summit and then back to the relative safety of Camp 4, where, along with their rope, they left their sleeping bags, mats and the most essential piece of their equipment: their stove. Both climbers had also made the decision to ascend without the use of supplementary oxygen. This would leave them at increased risk of altitude sickness, also known as pulmonary oedema, and of course frostbite that could lead to the loss of fingers and toes.

After three hours of upwards movement, the pair had gained 200 metres (656 feet) of vertical distance and the sun blessed them with a bit of warmth as they emerged from the shady slopes. Revol immediately put her goggles on – years of experience climbing at high altitude reminded her about the dangers of snow blindness, a brutally painful condition where the eyes essentially become sunburnt and are rendered useless. She reminded Mackiewicz about his goggles and he nodded, reassuring her that she need not worry about him. With a burst of energy, Revol set off again, determined that this time they would reach the summit.

Slowly but surely, they went up, pacing themselves, resting infrequently. As darkness fell, Revol took the final steps to the 8,126-metre (26,660-foot) summit under the light of her head torch, arriving somewhere between 6 and 6.30 p.m. Elated, she waited for Mackiewicz to join the celebration, his light visible through the frosty crystals of her breath. After years of previous attempts, seven expeditions to the mountain for Mackiewicz and four for Revel, they were now on top of the ninth highest mountain in the world. It was a dream come true. Little did Revol know that all the joy of reaching this wonderful goal would be sucked from her the instant Mackiewicz joined her at the rocky cairn that marked the official summit. It was there, well above the point of no return, that he revealed he could no longer see.

Opposite: Denis Urubko and Adam Bielecki rescue Élisabeth Revol.

At first, she was angry. She had reminded him to put on his goggles when they had first reached the sunny slopes above Camp 4, but he had ignored her. She pushed this anger aside and immediately began to plan their difficult descent in the dark. They were above 8,000 metres (26,247 feet), well into the 'Death Zone' – the altitude at which your body begins to shut down. Only going down in elevation would allow them both to rest and recover from the physical strain of the climb, not to mention Mackiewicz's snow blindness. Descending in his condition meant that he would need to hold her shoulder as she guided him down. Once at lower altitudes, she could use her emergency beacon to send a message back to Europe to request an immediate helicopter rescue. If she could just reach Camp 4, she could make Mackiewicz comfortable with a warm sleeping bag, melt some snow for water and put in the rescue call.

As they left the summit, Revol and Mackiewicz crept along at a snail's pace, careful not to stumble and fall down the slopes below them. Revol strayed from her normal descent strategy of moving quickly. She had no choice; she could only move as fast as Mackiewicz. Her head torch offered limited vision with its tunnel of light, and she frequently second-guessed where they were when she was unable to see their original tracks in the snow. Revol intermittently checked on her climbing partner's physical status. Shining her light on his face, she asked him how he felt. On one occasion she came to the horrific realization that his nose was pure white, frozen because, in a moment of exasperation when struggling to breathe, he had ripped the covering from his face. Revol also noticed a more ominous tell-tale sign that he was in serious trouble. Blood was flowing from the side of his mouth, a symptom of pulmonary oedema. Mackiewicz was close to death. She needed to find their camp.

After hours of gruelling descent, Revol checked her altimeter. They were at approximately 7,500 metres (24,606 feet) and the camp should have been close, but Revol found no familiar signs in the snow. The pair continued on as Revol searched in the dark vastness of the upper slopes for the safety of their shelter, but to no avail. Mackiewicz could no longer walk on his own. Revol, with her tiny 48-kilogram (7½ stone) frame, braced and supported his 80 kilograms (12½ stone) with each painful step. Exhausted, they both sat down in the snow and Revol finally took out her emergency beacon so she could communicate the desperate situation to her husband and a friend in Europe, who would be able to call the Pakistani military for a rescue.

Once the emergency message was sent, Revol could feel the support of family and friends from afar. She became

---

INFO

NOTABLE CLIMBS BY ÉLISABETH REVOL

North face of the Drus, Chamonix

North face of the Grandes Jorasses, Chamonix

Ascents of Les Droites, Aiguille Verte, Les Courtes, Chamonix

Ascent of the Eiger, Switzerland

Ascent of the Matterhorn, Switzerland

First ascent of Pharilapcha, Nepal

Link-up of two 8,000-m (26,247-ft) peaks, Gasherbrum I and II, Pakistan

New route on Annapurna East, Nepal

Lhotse, Nepal

New route on Nanga Parbat in winter with Tomek Mackiewicz

Everest, Lhotse link-up, Nepal

Manaslu, Nepal

Summit - 8,126 m/26,660 ft

NANGA PARBAT
WEST FACE

Nanga Parbat is the ninth highest mountain and is situated in the Gilgit-Baltistan region of Pakistan.

1. Revol-Mackiewicz route.
2. Camp 4.
3. Crevasse bivouac - Revol descends down to 7,280 m/23,884 ft.
4. Kinshofer route - Denis Urubko and Adam Bielecki climb up to rescue Revol as she descends down towards them.

more determined than ever not to let Mackiewicz down. She would use everything within her power to get him to safety so that others could lift him off the mountain. They continued down, down, ever downwards against the howling wind and into the inky blackness, only pausing now and then to send GPS coordinates to the rescue effort. But then, suddenly, Mackiewicz collapsed. Revol came to the awful realization that he could no longer move. She scanned their surroundings and found a hole in the glacier that they had been traversing. With more encouraging words, she guided him into the crevasse so she could re-evaluate his condition.

The crevasse was narrow and did a decent job of protecting them from the elements. They had descended almost 1,000 metres (3,281 feet) from the summit and were now in the relative safety of this hollow. Revol and Mackiewicz tried to keep each other warm as she continued to communicate with those abroad using her tiny emergency device. She couldn't know how quickly her friends had sprung into action to save them both. One friend was in constant communication with the Pakistani military as the primary logistical organizer. Another had started a crowd-funding campaign to pay for the costly rescue. Her husband, Jean-Christophe, was in her thoughts constantly. Mackiewicz's wife Anna sent messages of love and support. As Revol continued to relay Mackiewicz's deteriorating medical condition to those involved, they encouraged her to descend by herself. Rescuing two climbers from such a high altitude was nearly impossible: she would need to leave him behind to save them both. This was a horrific thought. Abandon her climbing partner? She would be breaking the unspoken oath climbers share – to ensure each other's safety.

After many hours, Revol finally took the advice of those on the outside. She was convinced that Mackiewicz would be rescued first and then the helicopter would fly to her afterwards and bring her to basecamp. She reluctantly made the decision to leave, marked the entrance of the crevasse for the rescuers and left Mackiewicz in his icy bed, having secured him to the walls of the cave with her ice axes. With only one ski pole to aid her balance during the descent, Revol continued downwards.

Now, holed up some 500 metres (1,640 feet) below Mackiewicz in another crevasse, Revol battled with the decision. Every fibre of her being told her she should have stayed to help. When another communication from the outside world reached her and conveyed that the helicopter had been delayed, for a moment she believed that her friends had tricked her and had no intention of rescuing Mackiewicz. Her thoughts turned sour. Revol reviewed every

'...all the joy of reaching [the top] would be sucked from her the instant Mackiewicz joined her at the rocky cairn that marked the official summit. It was there, well above the point of no return, that he revealed he could no longer see.'

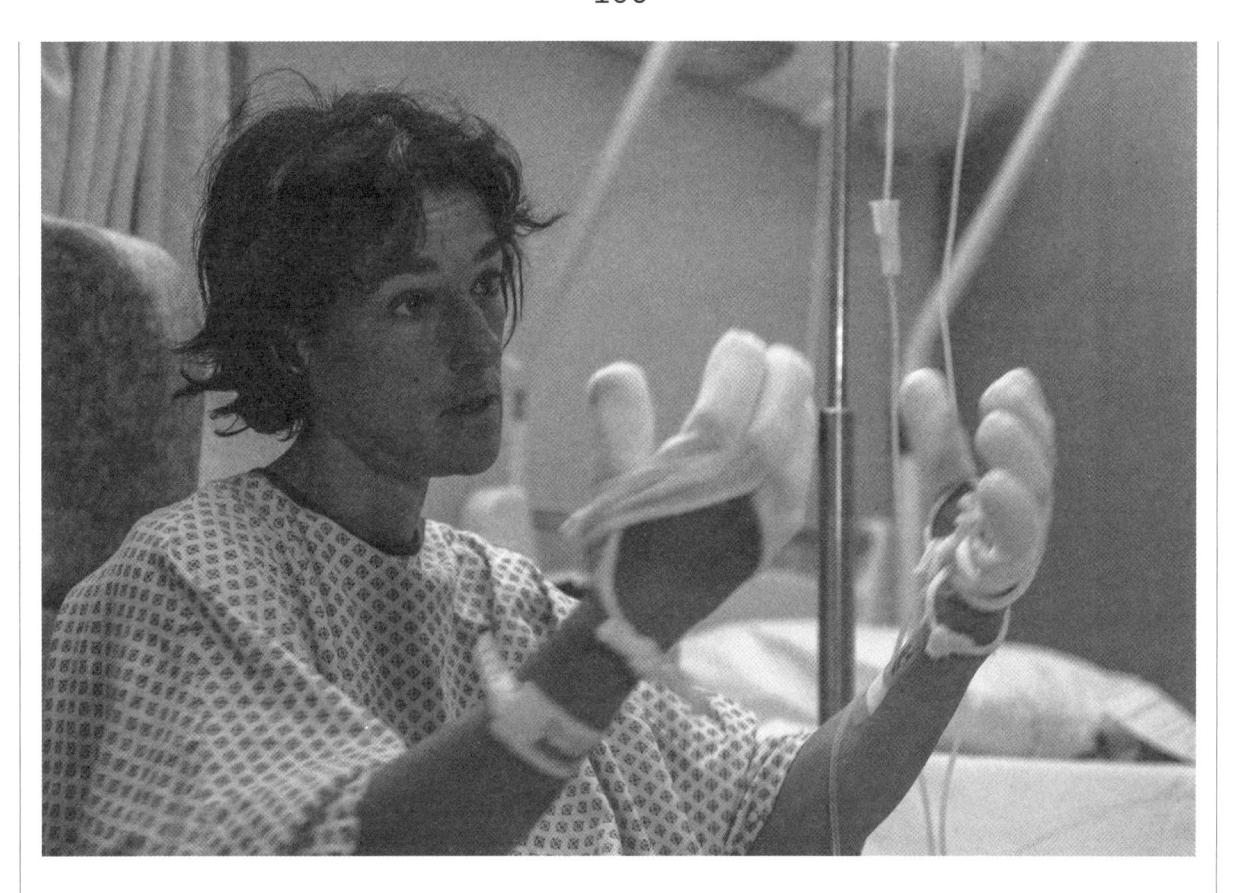

inch of their expedition, every decision that they had made. In that agonizing period of waiting alone, her back against the snowy wall of the crevasse, she searched for the answers that wouldn't come until many years later. Revol tried to sleep and succumbed to the involuntary ritual of constant shivering, which kept her warm in spurts. At one point, she awoke in a panic, only to discover that she had knocked her boot off the icy shelf. She had removed it hours before in an effort to defrost her foot, placing it carefully beside her as she tucked her foot inside her down suit. Now not only was she alone and suffering from extreme fatigue, having gone without food and water for more than twenty-four hours, but she had also lost her boot. She had no choice but to descend deeper into the crevasse to find it. She climbed down into the frigid darkness, unsure of what lay below.

Élisabeth Revol found her lost boot, left the crevasse and eventually descended a further 800 metres (2,625 feet) via the Kinshofer route. Once the complexity of the helicopter rescue became evident, her rescue team contacted a nearby Polish expedition at K2, where four climbers – Denis Urubko, Adam Bielecki, Piotr Tomala and Jaroslaw Botor – scrambled to gear up and were flown to Camp 1 of Nanga Parbat. Urubko and Bielecki climbed up and intercepted Revol at the top of the precarious headwall of the Kinshofer route. Together, they made their way down to Camp 1, where a helicopter whisked her to hospital in Islamabad. On her return to France, doctors assured her that given Mackiewicz's symptoms, he would only have survived for a few hours after she left him, meaning even an immediate rescue was unlikely to have saved him. Revol recovered from severe frostbite to both hands and one foot and narrowly avoided amputation. The expedition and rescue were widely covered by mainstream news sources. Revol, a particularly private person, avoided all contact with media as best she could. In 2019, she returned to the Himalaya and completed a double ascent of Everest and Lhotse in one difficult push.

Élisabeth Revol talks to journalists on 31 January 2018 after she was rescued off Nanga Parbat.

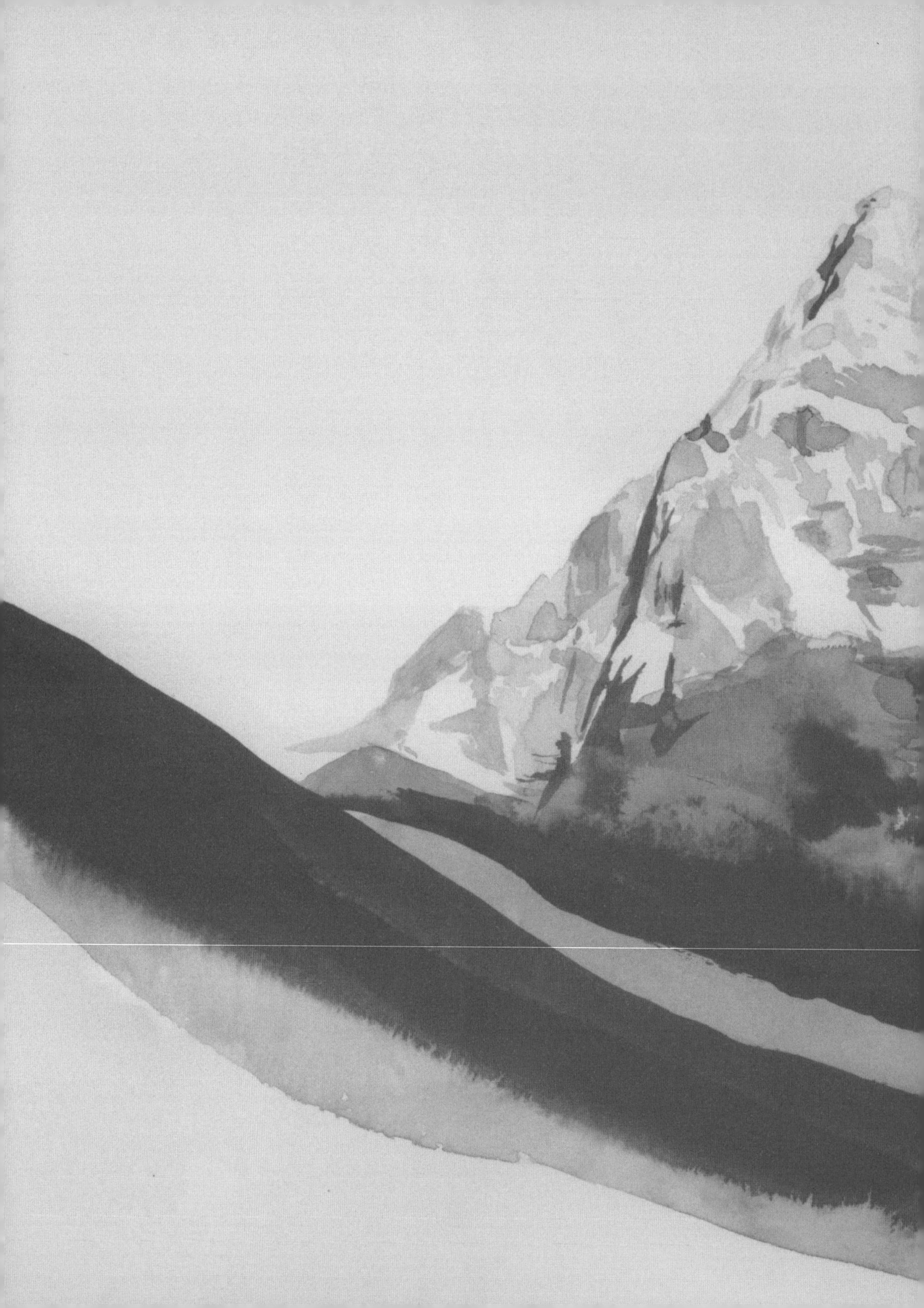

Kei Taniguchi
Climbs Kamet

When Frank Smythe and his British team reached the summit of Kamet in 1931, it was the highest mountain climbed to date, an astounding 7,756 metres (25,446 feet). Kamet is tucked into a corner of the Garhwal Himalaya, mountains that form India's border with China to the north. In the 1930s, getting to such a remote peak involved an expedition of more than 320 kilometres (199 miles), mainly bushwhacking through dense mountain forest. Smythe's team had made their climb via the Purbi Kamet Glacier, taking the obvious line up the northeast ridge. Almost eighty years later, when Japanese alpinists Kei Taniguchi and Kazuya Hiraide approached Kamet, it was with a small team and a sense of humility. Taniguchi and Hiraide had their sights set on the formidable, unclimbed southeast face. A new route on this steep face would only be achieved with permission from the mountain. They would need patience and understanding to complete the difficult climb.

KEI TANIGUCHI

Nationality:
Japanese

Born:
14 July 1972

Died:
22 December 2015 (age 43)

Active:
1992-2015

Opposite: Kei Taniguchi rests at Manaslu basecamp.

Like much of the population of Japan, Kei Taniguchi held the traditional Shinto belief that *kami* (神) permeate all natural places on the Earth. *Kami,* in Western terms, are often defined as spirits or divinities of nature that inhabit specific mountains, waterfalls, trees or geographical features like canyons. They might manifest as natural disasters such as typhoons, thunderstorms or avalanches. Shinto followers do not worship *kami* as idols, but they seek to find harmony with these spirits in a merging of humanity and the natural world.

From an early age, Taniguchi had been fascinated by the wildness of nature. She longed to escape the confines of her classroom. When it came time to study for her university entrance exams, without a word to her family, she ran away from home. The year before, she had spent a school term in the United States on a student exchange programme and now, back home in Japan, she did not want to pursue further education and an unsatisfying corporate career. The world called to her and she listened, taking matters into her own hands.

In her early adulthood, Taniguchi sought out difficult physical activities that would make her feel connected to the land. Hiking, scrambling and bicycle touring allowed her to experience the landscape with a slow-paced intimacy. Recognizing the economic realities of living in Japan, however, she did succumb to university eventually, but committed to spending every moment she could in the outdoors. At university she participated in adventure races, joined the cycling club and eventually became a member of the Keiyo Alpine Club, where she learned to climb. She felt at her best outside, doing the activities she loved. Climbing partners years later would comment that in every photo they took, she was always smiling from ear to ear.

The worship of mountains is a millennia-old practice in Japan and from the beginning of her climbing career, Taniguchi entered the hills with a desire to be accepted by the *yama no kami* (山の神), the mountain spirits. For Taniguchi, it wasn't about reaching the summit but about the journey, how she felt and what she learned along the way. In one article, she reflected, 'In severe, high places, I'm forced to see how small and powerless all humans are compared to the vastness of the wild', concluding, 'at the same time, I realize our unlimited potential.'[1]

Taniguchi made a point of forming a relationship with each peak she climbed, studying their individual temperaments. She first spent time getting to know her beloved Japanese Alps and the limitations of both her body and mind, but eventually she ventured to the greater ranges,

Summit - 7,756 m/25,446 ft

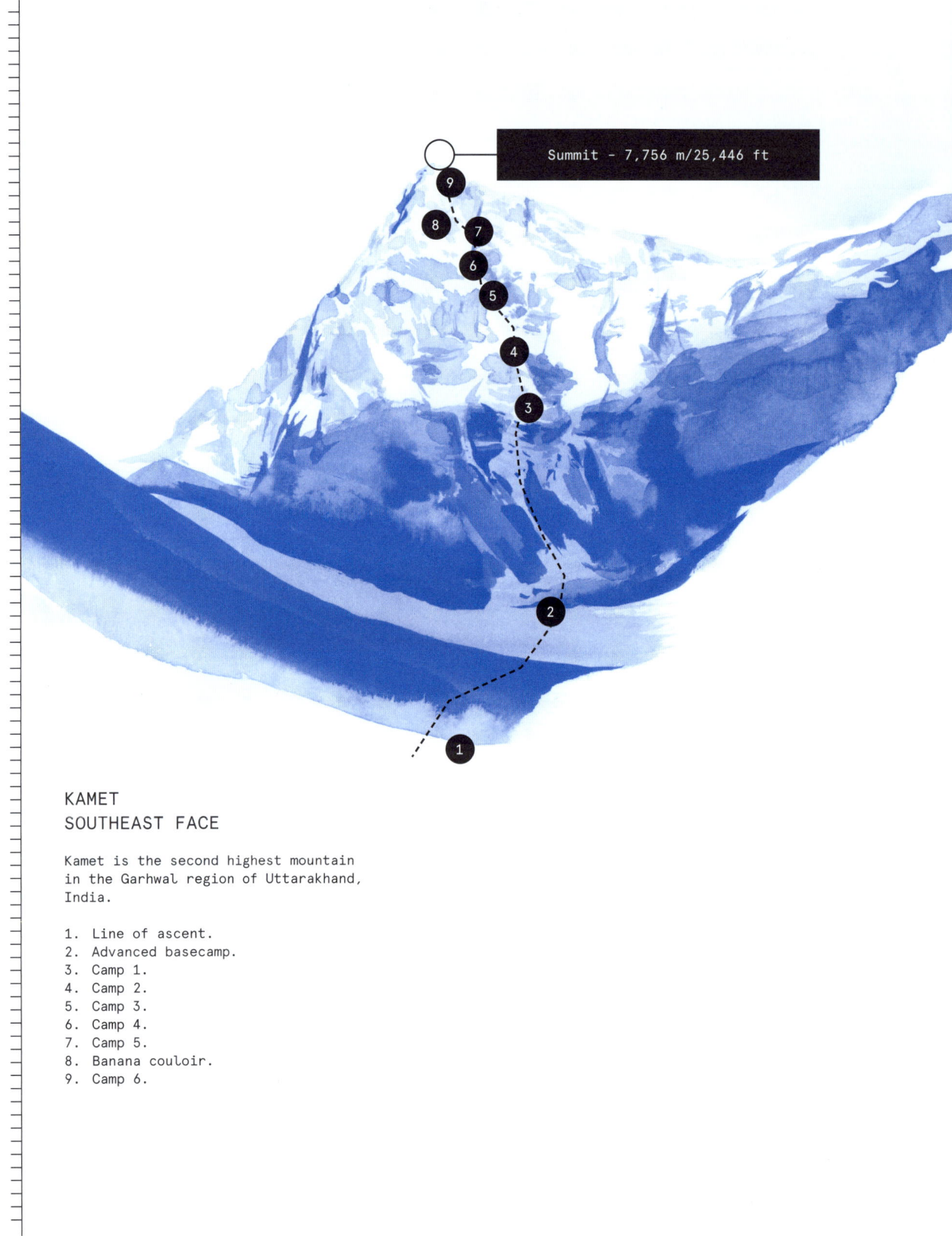

KAMET
SOUTHEAST FACE

Kamet is the second highest mountain in the Garhwal region of Uttarakhand, India.

1. Line of ascent.
2. Advanced basecamp.
3. Camp 1.
4. Camp 2.
5. Camp 3.
6. Camp 4.
7. Camp 5.
8. Banana couloir.
9. Camp 6.

INFO

NOTABLE CLIMBS BY KEI TANIGUCHI

2001
Denali, 6,190 m
(20,308 ft), Alaska

2004
Spantik, 7,028 m
(23,058 ft), Pakistan

2004
Laila Peak, 6,096 m
(20,000 ft), Pakistan

2005
Shivling, 6,543 m
(21,466 ft), India

2006
Manaslu, 8,163 m
(26,781 ft), Nepal

2007
Mount Everest/
Chomolungma 8,849 m
(29,032 ft),
Nepal/China

2008
Samurai Direct on
the southeast face
of Kamet, 7,756 m
(25,446 ft), India

2011
Naimona'nyi, 7,694 m
(25,243 ft),
Tibet/China

2013
Diran, 7,266 m
(23,839 ft), Pakistan

2014
Four new routes in
the Ruth Gorge, Alaska

2014
Mansail, 6,242 m
(20,479 ft), Nepal

---

including the Himalaya, the Karakoram and Alaska. With every climb on a steep face, Taniguchi would imagine herself drawing a beautiful line, like an artist, as simply and silently as possible. When the opportunity came to climb Kamet, she jumped at the chance. Although she had already summited higher peaks, Manaslu and Chomolungma in Nepal, for example, Kamet would provide a more technical challenge. What would the personality of Kamet be like, she wondered?

In preparation for the climb, Taniguchi and her partner Kazuya Hiraide garnered as much information as they could from past expeditions. They were both anxious about the fact that there had been no successful parties on the southeast face before them. Hiraide and Taniguchi had already proven themselves to be a formidable team, climbing Spantik (7,028 metres/23,058 feet) and the north face of Laila Peak (6,096 metres/20,000 feet) in Pakistan. The following year they drew new lines on the east ridge of Muztagh Ata (7,546 metres/24,757 feet) in China and the north face of Shivling (6,543 metres/21,466 feet) in India. Their experience on Shivling was a close call, during which Hiraide lost four toes to frostbite. The mountain had shaken them and their success was not without permanent scars. Afterwards Taniguchi reflected on the experience, recognizing that the *kami* were truly in charge as she wrote, 'I ask to return safely, to be given some experience of beauty and to be taught some good way to shape my own life.'[2]

For their ascent of Kamet, Taniguchi and Hiraide established their basecamp at the confluence of the Raikana and the Purbi Kamet glaciers and immediately began reconnaissance climbs to reach the toe of the stunning couloir that cuts the face in half. They needed to assess the danger from avalanches on this exposed route. They decided to climb Smythe's route as well, part of Taniguchi's strategy to get a feel for the mountain and familiarize themselves with their descent route.

Snowstorms ravaged basecamp for a few days before their intended departure. Because of budget constraints, Taniguchi and Hiraide hadn't subscribed to expensive foreign weather forecasts. They were forced to observe the weather and wind as it came; after several days, they began to see a pattern emerge. If the wind blew from the southwest, there were small weather windows that would allow them to attempt the climb. If it came from the north or northeast, big storms were imminent. It was after one of these storms that they made their move.

Deep snow made progress to their advanced basecamp difficult, but the following day brought blue skies and the perfect opportunity to attempt the first third of the route. By the end of the day, they had reached 6,600 metres (21,653 feet) and began the arduous task of chopping away snow to create a shelf of level ground so they could erect their small tent.

The next section of the climb proved much more challenging, with mixed ice and loose rock bands. Warming temperatures on the face sent spindrift and stones down on the duo and they were forced to bivouac after gaining only 150 metres (492 feet) of altitude.

The second third of the face proved more difficult than they had anticipated. The mountain continued to send showers of snow and loose rock down upon Taniguchi and Hiraide as they climbed on rotten ice. The effects of altitude made them slow, each move became strenuous and they had trouble navigating on the huge face. The pair climbed until midnight. When they finally settled into their tiny tent, both realized their toes were at risk of frostbite and needed attention.

A terrible sleep meant the fourth day of climbing was short, with just four-and-a-half pitches achieved. They looked upwards and the massive final third of the climb seemed too much to bear. They were incredibly cold and the thought of carrying on required more energy than they had, so they made a fourth bivouac and once again attended to their feet.

The fifth day on the face began with more mixed terrain and alpine ice. The pair finally reached the banana couloir and the snow slog began, bringing them to within 150 metres (492 feet) of the summit. They sought refuge in a crevasse and rested, knowing that the following day they would reach the summit and the relative safety of Smythe's original route, which would guide them home to basecamp.

After eight days, Taniguchi and Hiraide finally reached the summit. The *yama no kami* had smiled upon them for more than a week and they were gifted with a stupendous view of the entire Garhwal Himalaya. The rising sun washed Mount Kailash in an orange glow in the distance. Kailash, the holy peak that is sacred to Hindus, Buddhists and worshippers of the Jain faith, seemed supernatural that morning. The ascent of Kamet had been a battle for both climbers and they decided to name their new route *Samurai Direct*.

Taniguchi's diary revealed that during the most difficult section of the climb, she had felt another presence. 'I felt many times that there was someone else there with us,' her friend Akihiro Oishi translated from her journals. 'Who is it? Please don't call me there yet. I have never been strained this much before.'[3] We'll never know if it was the *yama no kami* that Taniguchi felt that day or if she succumbed to hallucinations because of altitude, also known as 'third man syndrome', a common condition of alpinists at the edge of their ability, riding the line between life and death. Taniguchi and Hiraide achieved a monumental summit that day. The pair were awarded a prestigious Piolet d'Or (Golden Ice Axe) in 2009 for their climb, making Taniguchi the first woman to receive one.

On 21 December 2015, friends and family were devastated to learn of the death of Kei Taniguchi. One of Japan's most prolific alpinists, with many first ascents to her name, she had died on Mount Kurodake in the Daisetsuzan Range of her native country, a relatively easy peak by her standards. She had simply disappeared; when her climbing companions approached the top of the peak, thinking she was ahead, she was nowhere to be seen. The next day Taniguchi was eventually found 700 metres (2,296 feet) below the summit, her last breath taken in a snowy ravine. No one knows for sure what happened, but it seems she must have fallen. Perhaps a gust of wind caught her small frame and unprepared, she was forced off the snowy ridge. It was a surprising end for such a talented climber and the Japanese climbing community mourned the loss.

Kei Taniguchi (top right) at Manaslu basecamp in 2006 with Junko Tabei (bottom right).

'I don't like rushing to a destination, reaching the base of a peak in the shortest possible time and starting to climb right away. To me, that approach would be like walking into someone's house with dirty shoes. Instead, I'd prefer to knock on the door of the mountain and say hello, to speak with it until we understand each other better, and only then to enter more deeply into its heart.' [4]

– Kei Taniguchi

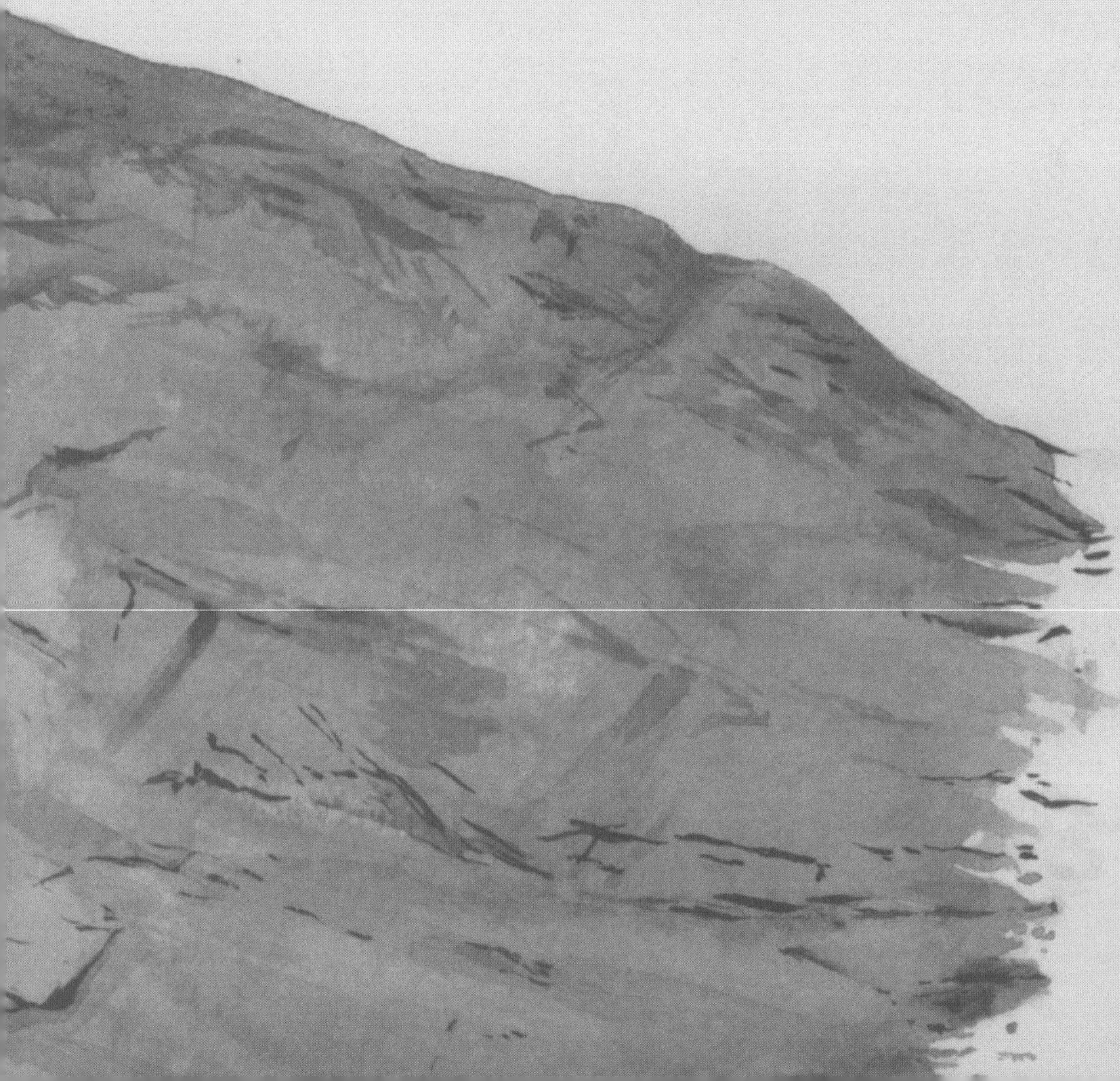

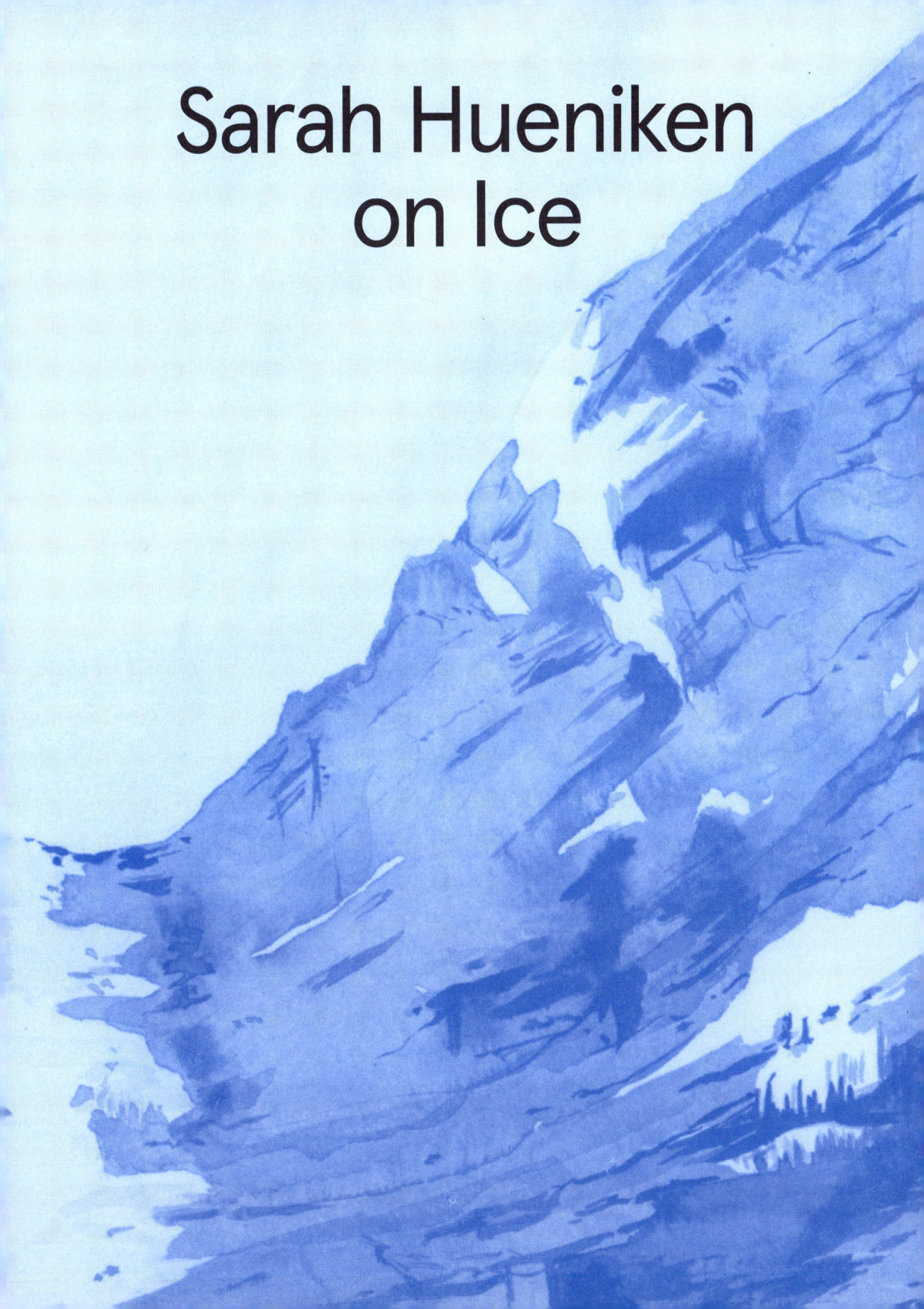

Sarah Hueniken on Ice

When Sarah Hueniken first tried climbing frozen waterfalls in winter, she didn't love it. In fact, she thought it was kind of stupid. Because of the cold, her shoulders were constantly hunched up to her ears, her muscles were tense and she was often a victim of the notorious 'screaming barfies', the excruciating moment when blood rushes back into almost frozen fingers. She much preferred the warmth of rock climbing in summer, with beautiful mountain vistas under an intense alpine sun; those were the experiences during which she discovered her love of the vertical world. There was nothing about Hueniken's first experiences that could have led her to believe that she would eventually become one of the top ice climbers in North America.

SARAH HUENIKEN

Nationality:
Canadian

Born:
10 September 1974

Active:
1995-present

Ice climbing has inherent risks as the constantly shifting surface changes from day to day. Upward progress is gained by creating your own holds using ice axes that stick if swung hard enough into the ice, and footholds created by kicking crampons into the brittle surface. On occasion, water might still be flowing under the ice, making the sport even more precarious. What if the whole piece of ice just falls off during the climb? Then there are the challenges related to body temperature. Either you are too hot from the effort of swinging your ice axes above your head or you are freezing cold while at the belay, most likely bundled in a down jacket, slowing playing out rope as you wait for your partner to complete the next pitch above. It can be a bone-chilling, miserable enterprise.

Hueniken grew up in the flatlands of Ontario, Canada, near the world-famous Niagara Falls. It wasn't until she took a three-week Onward Bound course that she realized the potential of a life in the outdoors. She was fifteen years old and had squirrelled away her own money to attend the course – which introduced her to canoe tripping, backcountry camping and rock climbing. On the first day, when she learned that she would be joining an all-girls group, Hueniken was disappointed. She had imagined meeting the boy of her dreams and spending the course alongside a cute crush. In the end, being in the all-girls group was the best thing that could have happened, helping her to recognize her natural leadership skills. Despite relentless mosquitos and physically demanding activities, her enthusiasm and excitement to learn encouraged others, and she naturally slipped into the role of group leader.

A few years later, when it came time to apply to college, Hueniken picked a degree in Outdoor Recreation at Lakehead University in Thunder Bay, Ontario. Thunder Bay is a beautiful small town nestled into a natural bay on the shore of Lake Superior, one of the largest freshwater lakes in the world. With water sports nearby and relatively easy access to surrounding granite cliffs for rock and ice climbing, she thrived in her new environment and, on completing her degree, decided on a move to the big mountains. The Rockies beckoned.

Hueniken moved with a friend to the small mountain town of Canmore, Alberta, in the picturesque Canadian Rockies. At first, they struggled to make ends meet working in a high-end outdoor fashion store in the touristy town of Banff. Hueniken eventually became a dog-sled musher (leader), a job much better suited to her personality than selling ski jackets; she worked long, gruelling days in the cold but got to spend most of her time outside.

Opposite: Sarah Hueniken on Nophobia.

Her first winter in Canmore convinced her that living and working in a mountain town was possible – and that becoming a professional climbing guide would be her ticket. She set her sights on obtaining a certification as an assistant rock-climbing guide. Hueniken headed south to the United States, working for Outward Bound and NOLS, the National Outdoor Leadership School. She began mentoring and instructing youth. This hands-on employment as an instructor, and personal rock-climbing training, prepared her for an exam with the Association of Canadian Mountain Guides. However, in the years that followed, she realized that being a rock-climbing guide was not enough. The Canadian rock-climbing season is short, and if she could expand her certification further to include mountaineering and ice climbing, she could earn a better living during the long winters in Canada. So, after a few more years spent training in the peaks, she became a certified alpine climbing guide, coming to embrace ice climbing.

Like many women guides in the male-dominated industry, Hueniken had to work hard and climb even harder than her male counterparts to prove her place in the mountains. At first her male clients would frown when they found out she would be their guide for the day. Once they hit the ice, however, they couldn't deny her talent, and in the decades that followed, she would become not only one of the most sought-after guides in the industry, but a North American Champion at ice-climbing competitions.

During her work, Hueniken noticed that her female clients performed better when they were in an environment of just women. They could freely share their concerns and fears, and they weren't intimidated by her as a leader. With the help of two close friends, she began to run all-women's ice-climbing camps, which became one of the most rewarding parts of her job. However, Hueniken's world was turned on its head when – on one seemingly perfect day in 2019 – masses of snow high above an ice climb broke free and came crashing down, burying several climbers and killing one of her best friends.

Sonja Johnson Findlater, who had founded the women's programmes with Hueniken, tragically died after the avalanche hit one of the groups at their climbing camp. Hueniken and the other guides were devastated. Findlater had been an important part of the climbing camps and her involvement was a key reason why clients felt so comfortable.

Hueniken spent the months that followed in mourning, trying to process the trauma. She felt the pain of the group's

'Once you have a horrible outcome in the mountains, your relationship changes with it. No one goes out thinking they were being dangerous that day, or putting themselves or others at risk, but after something happens, you never forget the possibility of tragedy that always exists.'

– Sarah Hueniken

HYDROPHOBIA
CANADIAN ROCKIES

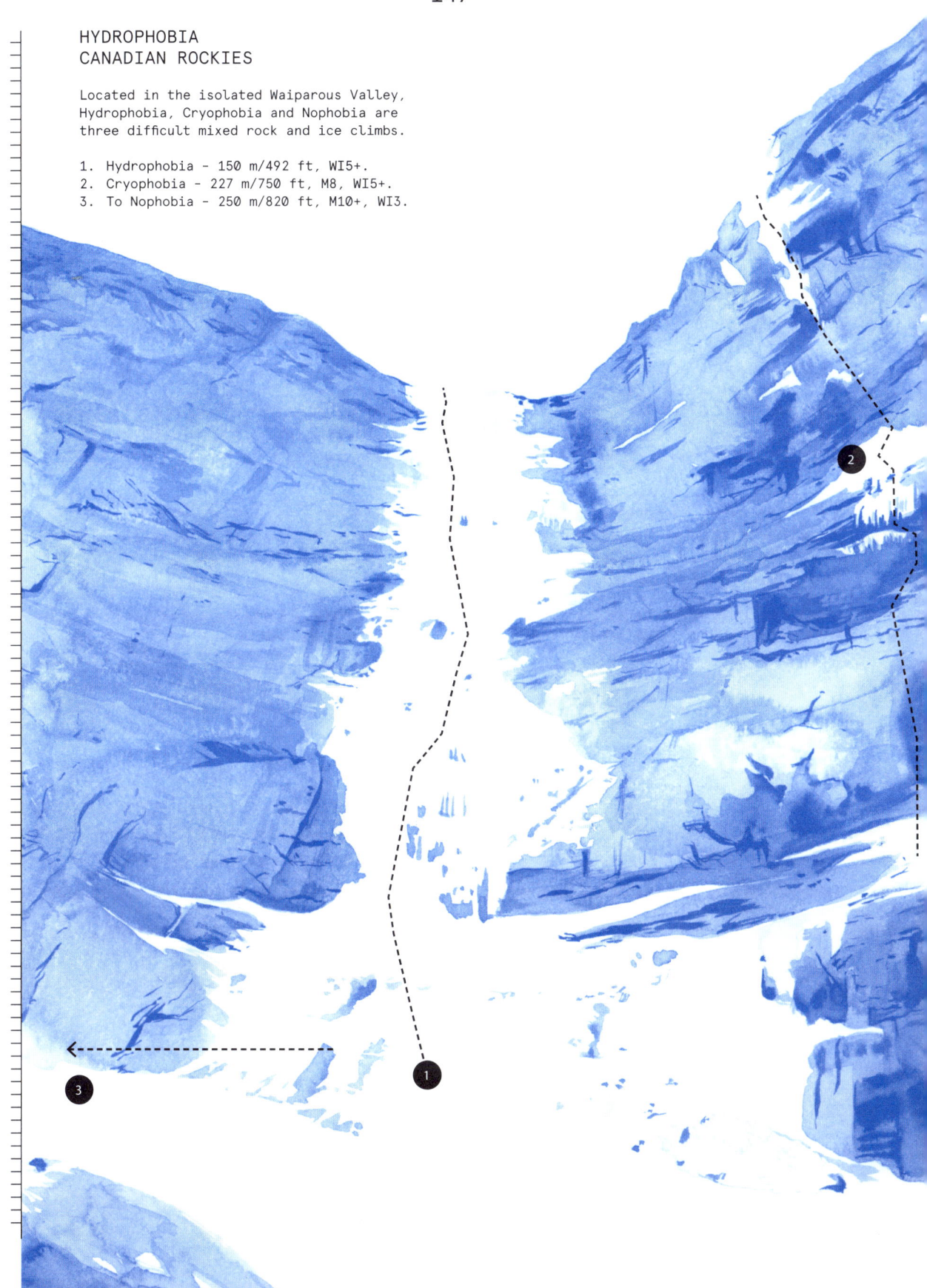

Located in the isolated Waiparous Valley, Hydrophobia, Cryophobia and Nophobia are three difficult mixed rock and ice climbs.

1. Hydrophobia - 150 m/492 ft, WI5+.
2. Cryophobia - 227 m/750 ft, M8, WI5+.
3. To Nophobia - 250 m/820 ft, M10+, WI3.

leaders and had been an active part of the rescue, running to the scene from the base of a nearby climb and digging Findlater out of the snow. She felt responsible for the accident, although she was not guiding Findlater's group that fateful day. All the guides had made educated decisions, and the avalanche danger had been rated low-moderate, an acceptable risk level to most climbers. Although there was little anyone could have done differently, Hueniken doubted her decision-making process and her ability to perform as a mountain guide. She was realizing that despite all the informed decisions mountain professionals make prior to entering an avalanche area, no one can ever really be in control in that type of terrain. She agonized over the death of her friend, and at times wondered how she would ever emerge from the darkness that surrounded her.

After months of isolation, Hueniken decided she needed a goal. She wanted a physical challenge to focus on, something that would remind her of the joy she had felt in the mountains prior to the accident. Encouraged by her husband and close friends, she began training for one of the hardest single-day link-ups of ice climbs ever achieved, taking on Hydrophobia, Nophobia and Cryophobia. She told herself she must continue with life: 'When your world falls apart, you either fall apart with it and decide that life's not worth living or you try to move forward[s] and you try to build your life back up.'[1]

Hydrophobia, Nophobia and Cryophobia are some of the most difficult and notorious ice-climbing routes in the Canadian Rockies. Hydrophobia is an incredibly aesthetic four-to-five roped pitches of pure vertical ice, graded at WI5+ (Waterfall Ice 5+). Nophobia is an altogether different climb: overhanging rock is climbed using axes and crampons in a technique called drytooling. This would be the hardest of the three routes for Hueniken, with five to six pitches rated at M10+ and WI3 (Mixed Grade 10+ and Waterfall Ice 3). The grade of the route was in her comfort zone, but she had only climbed it once before – it was sure to be a physical test. Cryophobia is also a mixed rock- and ice-climbing route, but unlike the consistent rock pitches of Nophobia, it requires crossing back and forth between rock and ice for the duration of the climb, constantly switching between the drytooling technique and pure ice-climbing style.

When Hueniken announced the project, she recalls thinking, 'Maybe I'll immerse myself in the whole notion of fear and work with it rather than against it.'[2] A successful link-up of the aptly named climbs would allow her to begin the process of overcoming her own fear – to discover whether she could ever enjoy the mountains again and feel confident guiding others in the hills or on ice.

Hueniken's friends supported her in the lead-up to the big link-up day. They joined her on long, cold reconnaissance missions to the climb sites, which are located in the remote Waiparous Valley, a two-hour drive from Canmore. The drive is followed by a two-hour approach to the base of the waterfalls on skis. In the depths of Canadian winter, during the shortest days of the year, a four-hour effort each way without even touching ice is a chore. The climbing itself would require a workout the equivalent of more than one thousand pull-ups and sit-ups, a vertical marathon of sorts, all conducted in subarctic temperatures. Rescue would be very difficult, with help hours away. The cold would add an extra element of danger should things go sideways.

After a sleepless night, Hueniken left her house in Canmore at around 3 a.m., hoping to reach the base of the first climb, Cryophobia, just as first light would be breaking in the east. The thermometer read a comfortable -10°C (14°F). Cryophobia went smoothly, and relatively fast. Hueniken reached the top by 10.30 a.m. and after a few abseils down to the base, she grabbed some food and a quick sip of tea before making for Nophobia, just a few hundred metres away, in the same cirque as her first waterfall and her final goal of the day: Hydrophobia.

Nophobia was the unknown variable. Hueniken wasn't sure she could pull off the most difficult moves. The route challenged her mentally and physically at every turn. On the incredibly difficult crux (the hardest part of the climb), the route follows an overhanging rock roof. Hueniken would have to perform many strenuous moves in sequence, including the 'figure 4', a complex, gymnastic move where the climber places one axe overhead and then wraps a leg overtop. Hueniken spent four gruelling hours on Nophobia, but finally completed the climb at 2.30 p.m., with enough daylight left to finish up with the classic and easiest route of the day, Hyrdophobia.

Hueniken didn't really expect to complete the duo of Cryophobia and Nophobia in one go, so she wasn't mentally prepared to continue climbing on that day. Even if she had chosen not to, she would have achieved something no one else had, a link-up of two notorious routes in less than 24 hours. Not one to give up without spending every last bit of energy, Hueniken composed herself and started up the vertical ice of Hydrophobia.

To a non-climber, Hydrophobia looks terrifying from below. Its sheer vertical face thrusts upwards, defying physics as the strip of icefall sticks tenuously to the rock wall behind it. It becomes even more intimidating when you add a ridiculous ten-pitch warm-up on two of the hardest mixed routes in the Rockies. Most climbers would

INFO

TEN CLASSIC ROCKIES ICE CLIMBS

HYDROPHOBIA
150 m/492 ft, WI5+

FEARFUL SYMMETRY
80 m/262 ft, WI6

POLAR CIRCUS
700 m/2,296 ft, WI5

SEA OF VAPORS
165 m/541 ft, WI6

CURTAIN CALL
100 m/328 ft, WI6

PILSNER PILLAR
215 m/705 ft, WI6

SLIPSTREAM
925 m/3,035 ft, WI4

NEMESIS
140 m/459 ft, WI6

THE SORCERER
185 m/607 ft, WI5

THE TERMINATOR
150 m/492 ft, WI6

---

never dream of beginning the climb in the late afternoon, with only a couple of hours of daylight remaining. For that, a special type of confidence is needed. So Hueniken dug deep, reminding herself of everything she had achieved in her life before this moment. She tapped all of her hidden reserves as she began the final climb with the first axe swing. It made a satisfying 'thunk' as it penetrated the ice.

As she moved steadily along, Hueniken began to revel in the joy of the perfectly formed ice. Familiar feelings seeped into her body. Climbing was what she loved; she wasn't ready to give it up. It gave her a reason to live.

Just as she was enjoying the climb and thought she might complete the link-up, circumstances shifted and tough decisions had to be made. Suddenly, water came gushing over the top. A small pool of water had burst through an ice dam on the plateau above and was now streaming down the ice wall, creating dangerous conditions for both Hueniken and her belayer below. For Hueniken, there was no discussion: they would abandon the climb and the link-up. Nothing was worth the risk of losing her own life or that of another friend. They immediately started downwards and began the long slog home. When they reached the car, Hueniken finally realized that she and her friends were safe. She had made the right decision. Even if you have all the information available and all the training possible, things can go wrong. Natural elements, out of anyone's control, are at play.

Sarah Hueniken is among Canada's leading ice climbers, male and female. She is the first North American woman to climb the difficult mixed grades of M11, M12, M13 and M14. She has completed a number of first ascents worldwide, including ice climbs in China and Japan, and, together with her husband Will Gadd, she completed the first ice ascent of Niagara Falls in winter. She was North American Ice Champion from 2014 to 2016 and placed on the podium in 2015, 2017 and 2018 at the world-famous ice-climbing competitions in Ouray, Colorado. She is a certified alpine guide in Canada and now acts as a guide-certification examiner for the Association of Canadian Mountain Guides. Following Findlater's accident, Hueniken has created the Ice Climbing Atlas Project, an online information and photographic portal for ice climbers to assess the overhead dangers of routes they hope to ascend. She is also a founder of the trauma support group Mountain Muskox, created in 2020, for anyone who has experienced loss or trauma in the mountains.

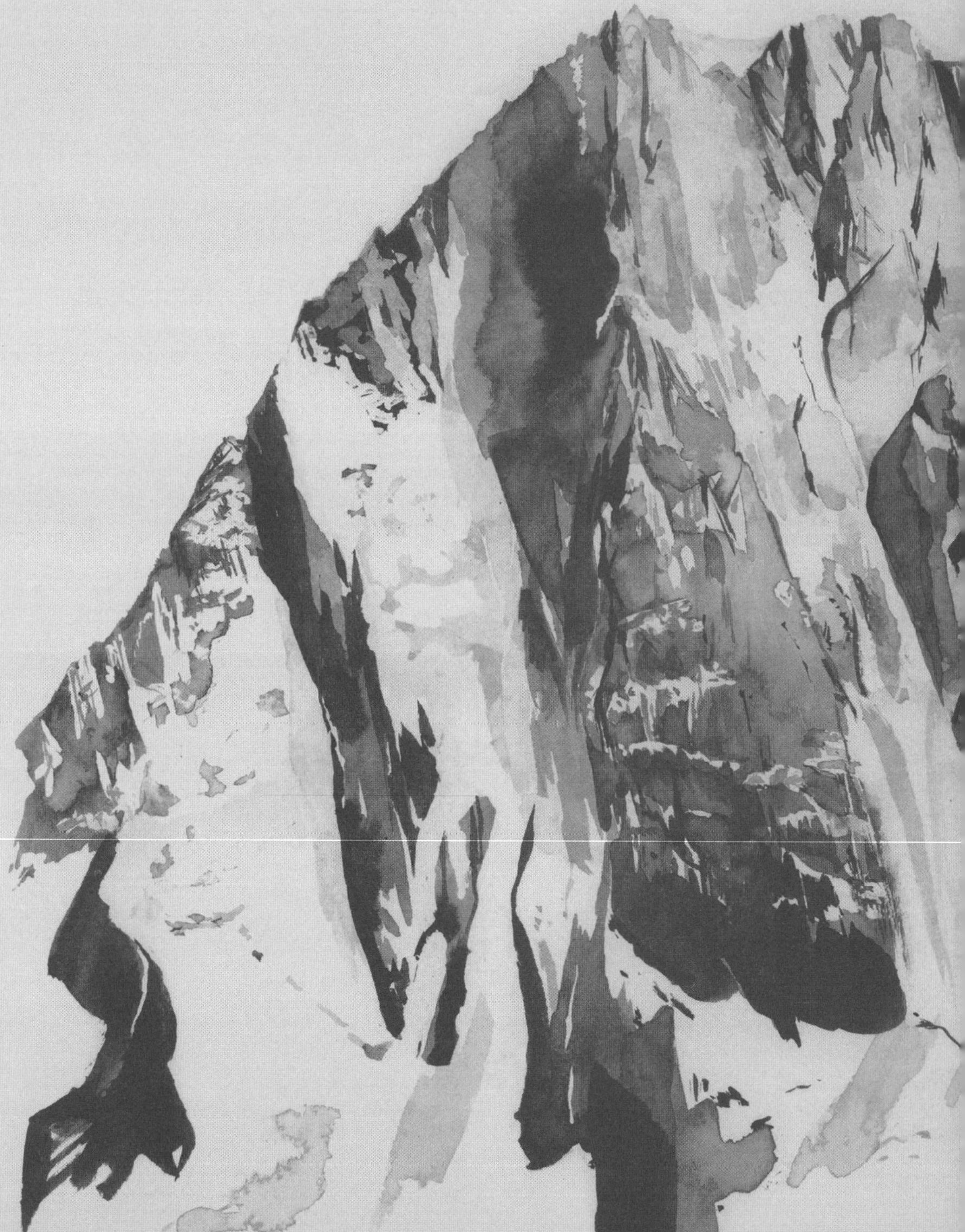

Alison Hargreaves Tackles the Alps

On the north face of the mighty Grandes Jorasses in the French Alps, caught on a featureless, blank wall with few options for retreat, Alison Hargreaves had never felt more alone. In the early morning of 17 June 1993, she had left the comfort of the Leschaux Hut in the dark. As she walked carefully on to the glacier, she was mindful of the dangerous crevasses lurking under shallow bridges of windblown snow. Her first hurdle had been crossing the icefield safely, without a partner to pull her out from the depths of the ice if things went wrong. And there were other dangers. Not long after reaching the face, she started climbing the névé (a runnel of dense consolidated snow), but the snow unexpectedly gave way and she was left scrambling on brittle ice lying on smooth rock. She had to summon all her mental fortitude to maintain her focus and pull through this tough section of climbing. There was no rope to catch her if she fell, no one to call for a rescue. As she looked at the snowy headwall above her, the wind kicked up and threw rivers of soft snow, called spindrift, on to her helmet and down the back of her jacket. The mountain jeered at her, defying her to continue her upwards progress, but Hargreaves pressed on.

ALISON HARGREAVES

Nationality:
British

Born:
17 February 1962

Died:
13 August 1995 (age 33)

Active:
1975-1995

Opposite: Alison Hargreaves during an acclimatization hike with Pumori in the background.
Below: Alison Hargreaves in Kangtega basecamp, April 1986.

The day before, she had left her husband and two young children asleep at a campsite in Chamonix, setting out by herself through the trees and meadow, then the rocky alpine, taking her first steps towards achieving her goal of climbing six north faces in the Alps – solo and in a single season. She had experienced self-doubt in the months leading up to the project. Even on the morning of her departure, during the approach to the climbing route, she had asked herself, 'Is this plan wise? Am I being reckless? Are these the actions of a good mother?' Worries rattled through her mind, but she pushed these aside to concentrate on the task at hand.

Now, well into her climb on the Grandes Jorasses, Hargreaves had never felt so invigorated. As she moved energetically upwards and breathed deeply to overcome the effects of altitude, she brushed away fresh snow from the rock to find the handholds that would lead her to the easier climbing of the Hirondelles Ridge – and ultimately the descent to the Leschaux Glacier. If she was successful, Hargreaves would become the first woman to solo the Shroud. As she reached the ridge and began her descent, she was elated. She had completed the first phase of her goal.

Alison Hargreaves was born in Mickleover, Derby, in 1962. Throughout her childhood, her family often went to the hills of the Peak District, where she completed her first real rock climb at the age of thirteen. Her parents recognized her natural talent and encouraged her to continue rock climbing despite the lack of women in the sport during the 1970s. In a largely male-dominated realm, Hargreaves was inspired by the high-profile, and widely publicized, mountaineering expeditions of famous British climbers like Chris Bonington, Doug Scott and Dougal Haston. She immersed herself in the classic climbing books of Heinrich Harrer; her admiration of these famous climbers and their summits is recorded in her personal diaries.

Hargreaves met her husband Jim when she worked at his climbing shop as a teenager. She left home at eighteen to make a life with him, much to the dismay of her parents, as Jim was almost twice her age. After a few happy years of marriage, the couple ran into financial trouble. The business collapsed, their phone was disconnected and their car repossessed. With no money to pay their fuel bill, they heated their home with wood that had been gifted by a generous neighbour. Eventually, they lost their house to the bank. Hargreaves, with her outstanding mountaineering skills and no further education, was forced to become the family's main breadwinner.

Despite plenty of public criticism and barriers, Hargreaves refused to believe that she couldn't make a life as a climber. It was what gave her joy and where she found

GRANDES JORASSES
NORTH FACE

The Grandes Jorasses and its formidable north face are located in the Mont Blanc massif, near Chamonix, France.

1. The Shroud route – Alison Hargreaves' line of ascent.
2. Pointe Walker – 4,208 m/13,806 ft.
3. Pointe Whymper – 4,184 m/13,727 ft.
4. Col des Grandes Jorasses
5. Walker Spur.

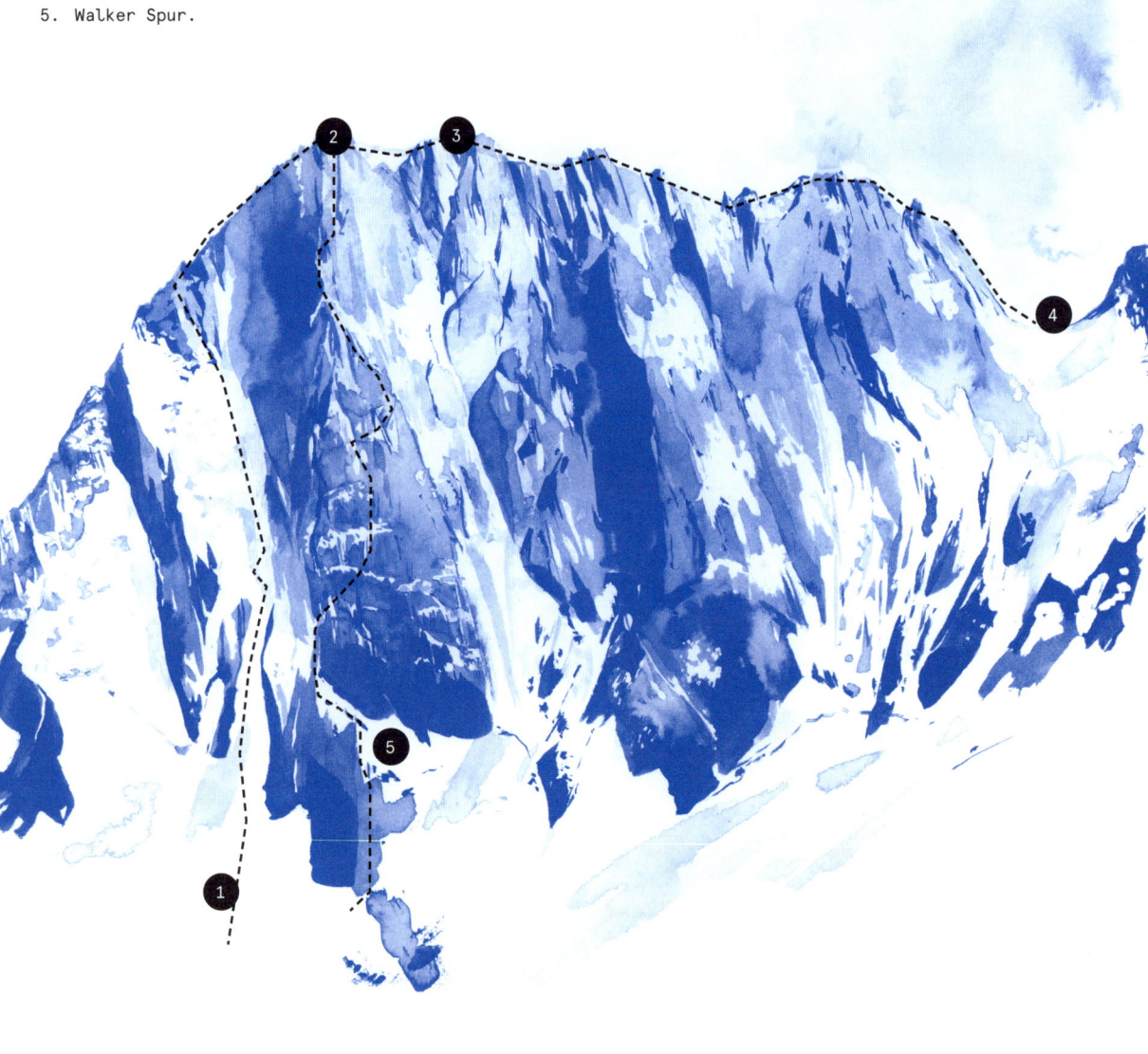

INFO

THE SIX CLASSIC NORTH FACES OF THE ALPS

EIGER
1938 route climbed by Anderl Heckmair, Heinrich Harrer, Ludwig Vörg and Fritz Kasparek

MATTERHORN
Original route, Franz and Tony Schmid

CIMA GRANDE
Comici route

PIZ BADILE
Cassin route

PETIT DRU
Pierre Allain route

GRANDES JORASSES
Walker Spur

purpose. After a few successful expeditions and recognized climbs, Hargreaves went on a reconnaissance mission to the north face of the Eiger, which she summited while five months pregnant. When the climbing community and media expressed their outrage at what they perceived as selfishness, she merely quipped, 'I think I was being quite conservative. I had planned a trip up Denali (Alaska, the highest peak in North America), but my physician said it wouldn't be wise to go above 12,000 feet, so I went to the Alps instead.'[1]

With one successful ascent of the notorious Eiger Nordwand already under her belt, the possibility of a bolder goal – six north faces, solo, in a single season – became more plausible. It would be just what she needed to convince herself, and the media, that women could excel in the high mountains. Hargreaves began to train relentlessly. With no seed money, no climbing-club support and only meagre contributions of equipment from her recently secured sponsors, all she could do was try.

From the onset, the 'Six Faces' project was wrought with unpredictable challenges. Financial and domestic issues with Jim aside, the weather in the Alps in the spring/summer of 1993 was the worst it had been in decades. There were few windows of fair weather that would allow Hargreaves to proceed with the climbs and also provide comfortable, if rustic, camping conditions for her children – who accompanied her to the Alps. Her original summit schedule was pushed back considerably, and she was forced to adapt her training regime to include uphill running instead of actual climbing. Bad luck also played a part in the delay. While awaiting better weather in the valley, the family was robbed – losing all their valuable climbing gear and precious cash reserves. Until Hargreaves made her ascent of the Shroud, the Six Faces project had been in jeopardy. Now, with the first difficult climb ticked off her list, she had unfinished business on the other Alps to attend to, and up next was the iconic Matterhorn.

French mountaineer Gaston Rébuffat once described the north face of the Matterhorn as 'the most severe, the most beautiful and the most awe-inspiring'[2] of all its faces. Over the years it has turned away many a brave climber and has haunted many others who dared to venture on to its flanks. In the summer of 1993, the north face had yet to be climbed solo by a woman, and Hargreaves was hoping to change that. Riding the momentum of her first rewarding climb, she and the family drove almost immediately from Chamonix to Zermatt in Switzerland.

Hargreaves had attempted the north face of the Matterhorn before, but poor conditions had turned her and her climbing partners away. It was only after three attempts with partner Ian Parsons that she had achieved success, becoming the first British woman to reach the top. When she arrived at the base of the peak once again, in the summer of 1993, in what looked to be perfect conditions, she wasted no time in hiking up to the Hörnli Hut to stage herself for the climb. But her first attempts proved fruitless when clouds rolled in and cloaked the summit cone. Finally on 29 June, just twelve days after climbing the Grandes Jorasses, Hargreaves ate a breakfast of hard-boiled eggs washed down with an energy drink, and by 4 a.m. she was on her way up the famous pyramid of the Matterhorn.

Having cautiously crossed the precarious bergschrund on all fours, Hargreaves ascended in the glorious light of daybreak. The middle of the wall was more nerve-wracking than she remembered. A succession of warm and dry summers had made the ice sections thinner than expected, forcing her on to the unreliable and friable rock. Scratching gently away with her ice axes and crampons, she used her small physique to her advantage and implemented a light, delicate climbing technique to gain vertical distance. As she climbed up the face to the Zmutt Ridge, Hargreaves opted for secure body movements and reliable equipment placements over speed.

By 10.30 a.m. she was on the summit, but she did not linger long. After hearing thunder and seeing lightning in the distance, she immediately headed down to the safety of the Hörnli Hut. As she moved rapidly down the long, blocky Hörnli Ridge, Hargreaves felt her hair stand on end, electrified by the coming storm. Despite her exhaustion and diminishing strength, she maintained her composure to arrive safely at the hut in time for dinner – paired with a celebratory drink offered by some friendly Slovak climbers.

When Hargreaves returned to the Zermatt Valley, she was invited by Paula Biner, the proprietor of the famous Hotel Bahnhof, to sign the Matterhorn's climbing register. Paula's brother, Bernard Biner, had been the official recordkeeper of Matterhorn ascents and she had carried on the tradition. It was a dream come true for Hargreaves to autograph the iconic ledger, signing her name alongside many of her climbing heroes.

The north face of the Eiger was next in the queue, a climb Hargreaves had completed in 1988, becoming the first British woman to scale the gruesomely nicknamed 'Mordwand' or 'murder wall'. Since climbers had first set foot on the Mordwand in the early twentieth century, it had gained a reputation for death and suffering. An ascent, even with modern-day equipment, is considered a rite of passage for serious climbers, guaranteeing a place in the mountaineering history books.

INFO

CLIMBING RECORDS SET BY ALISON HARGREAVES

1986
New route pioneered on the northwest face of Kangtega with an American team including climbers Jeff Lowe and Mark Twight.

1988
First British female ascent on the north face of the Eiger (while five months pregnant).

1993
First female solo ascents on the north face of the Petit Dru, the Cassin Route on the Cima Grande and the north face of the Matterhorn.

1995
First unassisted female ascent of Mount Everest without supplemental oxygen.

1995
First British woman to reach the summit of K2.

Alison Hargreaves climbing out of the notch between the northwest summit of Kangtega (visible behind) and the plateau beneath the main summit.

In July 1993, poor weather and snow had hammered the mountain; attempting the Mordwand in these conditions would be perilous. Hargreaves was running out of resources and was desperate to leave the Alps with her collection of north faces under her belt, so she made the decision to avoid the infamous Mordwand route, opting instead for the Lauper route. In difficult weather, she thought it would be safer and faster. As fate would have it, the sun now came out, warming the region on her selected summit day. This created more difficult conditions still, with excess meltwater and the possibility of falling cornices looming above her. Hargreaves moved quickly to avoid these dangers and made it to the top in good time, but her summit victory was short lived. Her happiness turned to shock when she discovered the body of a fellow climber on the way down, a grim reminder of the risks involved.

Unlike the wet and cold spring, August 1993 brought warm, favourable conditions for Hargreaves to complete the last three climbs on her list. She ascended the north face of the Piz Badile in Switzerland, the north face of the Petit Dru in Chamonix and finally the Comici route on the Cima Grande di Lavaredo in the Dolomites, all within a week of each other. These were difficult rock-climbing

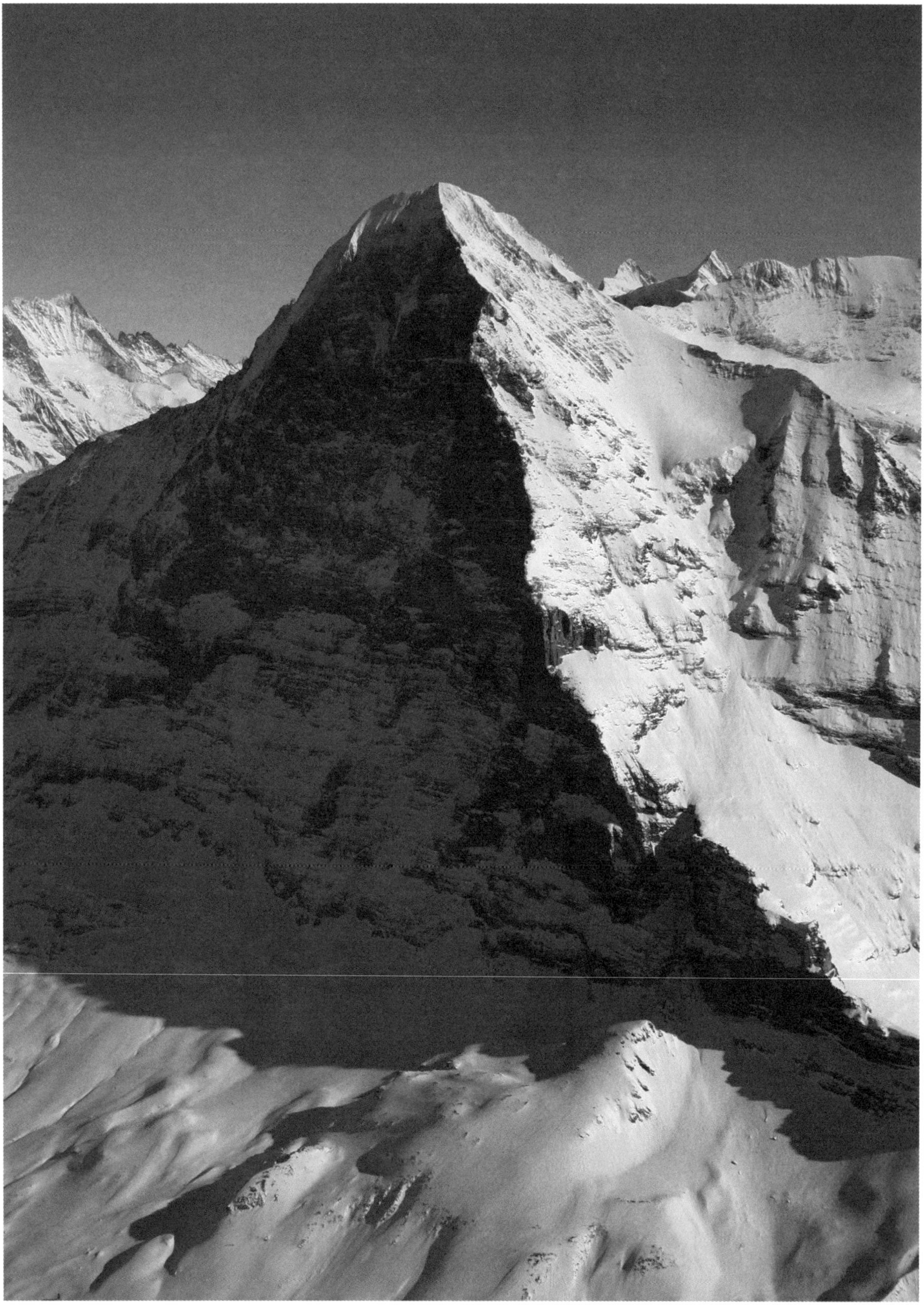

routes, and all ones she had not previously climbed. A single wrong move could send her plummeting to the ground, but she seemed to overcome each challenge almost effortlessly.

By 24 August, Hargreaves had completed her tick list. Confidence restored, she remarked in her memoir, 'I was in control and I could feel happy again.'[3] She was finally beginning to feel worthy of praise, so was stunned when some expert climbers questioned her claim to have established new speed records on a number of routes, implying she had fabricated her times. Hargreaves's opponents also argued that she had not climbed the 'classic' north faces, as proclaimed by Gaston Rébuffat decades earlier. Her ascents of the Grandes Jorasses and the Eiger were largely dismissed, despite the skill required to ascend them. In her book *Savage Summit*, Jennifer Jordan eloquently notes, 'What she had done was impressive and unprecedented, and she didn't need to exaggerate her achievement [by claiming speed records]. But she did, and the climbing world never let her forget it.'[4]

Isolated by a jealous male climbing community and still having trouble making ends meet, Hargreaves felt trapped both physically and financially. Cultural bias and societal gender expectations haunted her during her short climbing career. It was clear to her parents and sister that she loved her children and would do anything for them, but her friends criticized her for taking unnecessary risks in the field and questioned her ability as a mother. Many blamed the media controversy and the lack of acceptance from some in the climbing community on her domestic challenges. They felt Jim pressured her into climbing for financial gain. Despite much admiration for her climbing skills, they said he had pushed her too far.

Regardless, Hargreaves persevered with a new challenge, attempting the summit of Mount Everest in 1994, where her family even joined her at basecamp to cheer her on. When her first attempt at the world's highest peak failed due to inclement weather, she made plans to return in the spring of 1995 to finish the job.

In between trips to the Himalaya, she was invited to the Banff Mountain Film and Book Festival to give a presentation on her climbs and to join a panel of other high-profile climbing mothers, including Canadian Sharon Wood. The conversation led many to wonder why women with children were being criticized for putting themselves at risk, while climbing fathers were not subject to the same scrutiny. Hargreaves was not the only climber to be held to this double standard, and she left Canada empowered to begin planning her next trips to Everest and K2.

In May 1995, Hargreaves became the first British woman to ascend Everest without the aid of supplemental oxygen, and without teammates to support her. She had carried all her own equipment and set up her own high-altitude camps. News of her success reached the UK quickly and when she returned home – with only two weeks until she departed to Pakistan to tackle her next goal of K2 – she was met by a wave of reporters, photographers and TV cameramen. In a stunning reversal, she had become a media darling, celebrated as a true national hero.

Two weeks after the media circus, Hargreaves's expedition to K2 proved to be her last. Although she made it to the top, the first British woman to do so, she was trapped in a windstorm and died on the descent. The press criticized her risk-taking, claiming she had placed the mountains before motherhood. Only now, decades later, with a significant change in attitudes to gender roles, has the climbing community begun to celebrate her achievements and rightfully place her prominently in the history books. Her legacy is celebrated by a new generation of female climbers and she has become the role model that she never had. From December 2014 to March 2015, during a project known as 'Starlight and Storms', Tom Ballard, Hargreaves's son, climbed the six north faces of the Alps solo – becoming the first person to complete this feat in a single winter season without a support team. He tragically died four years later while climbing Nanga Parbat.

Opposite: The notorious north face of the Eiger, Switzerland.

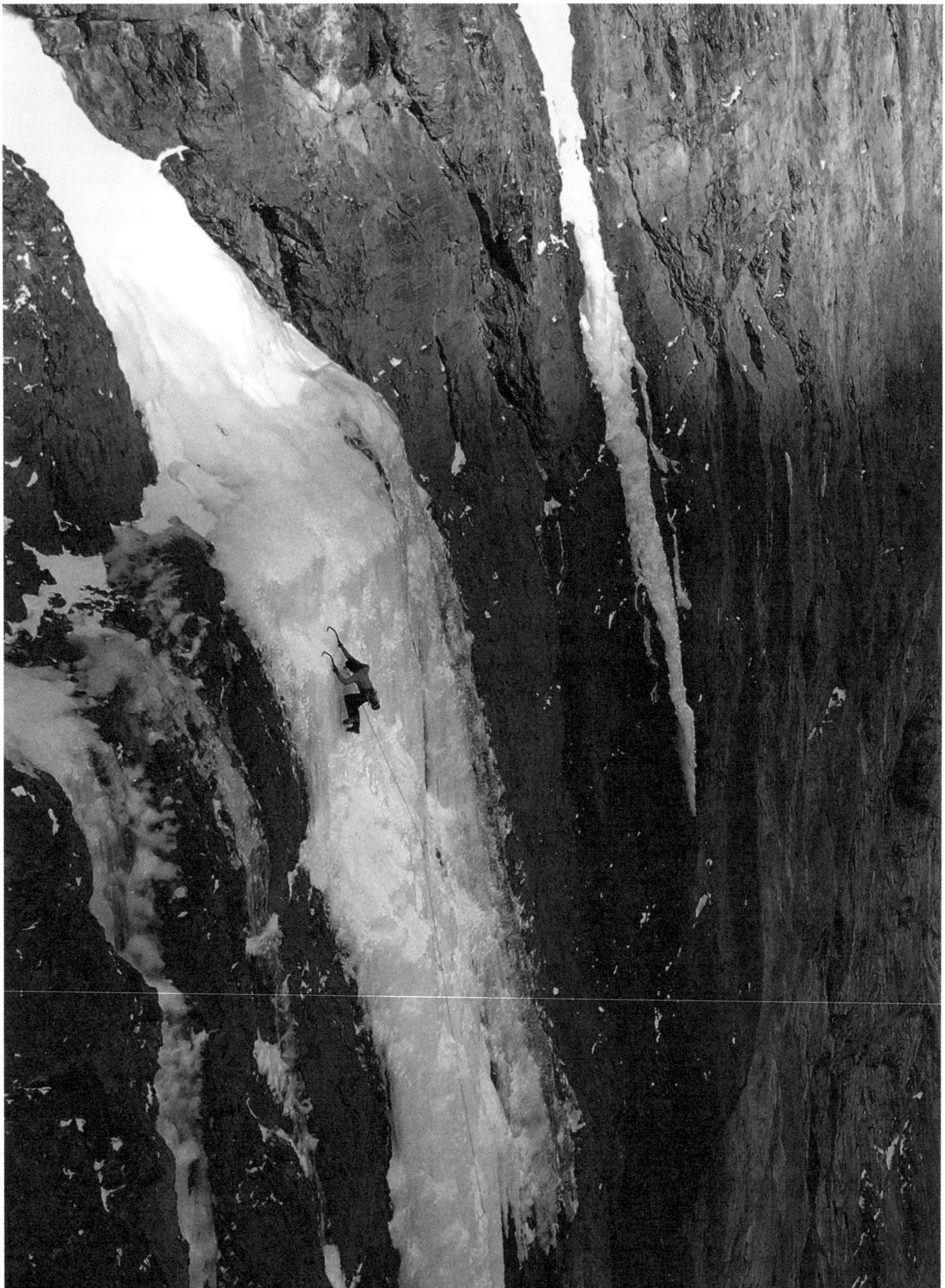

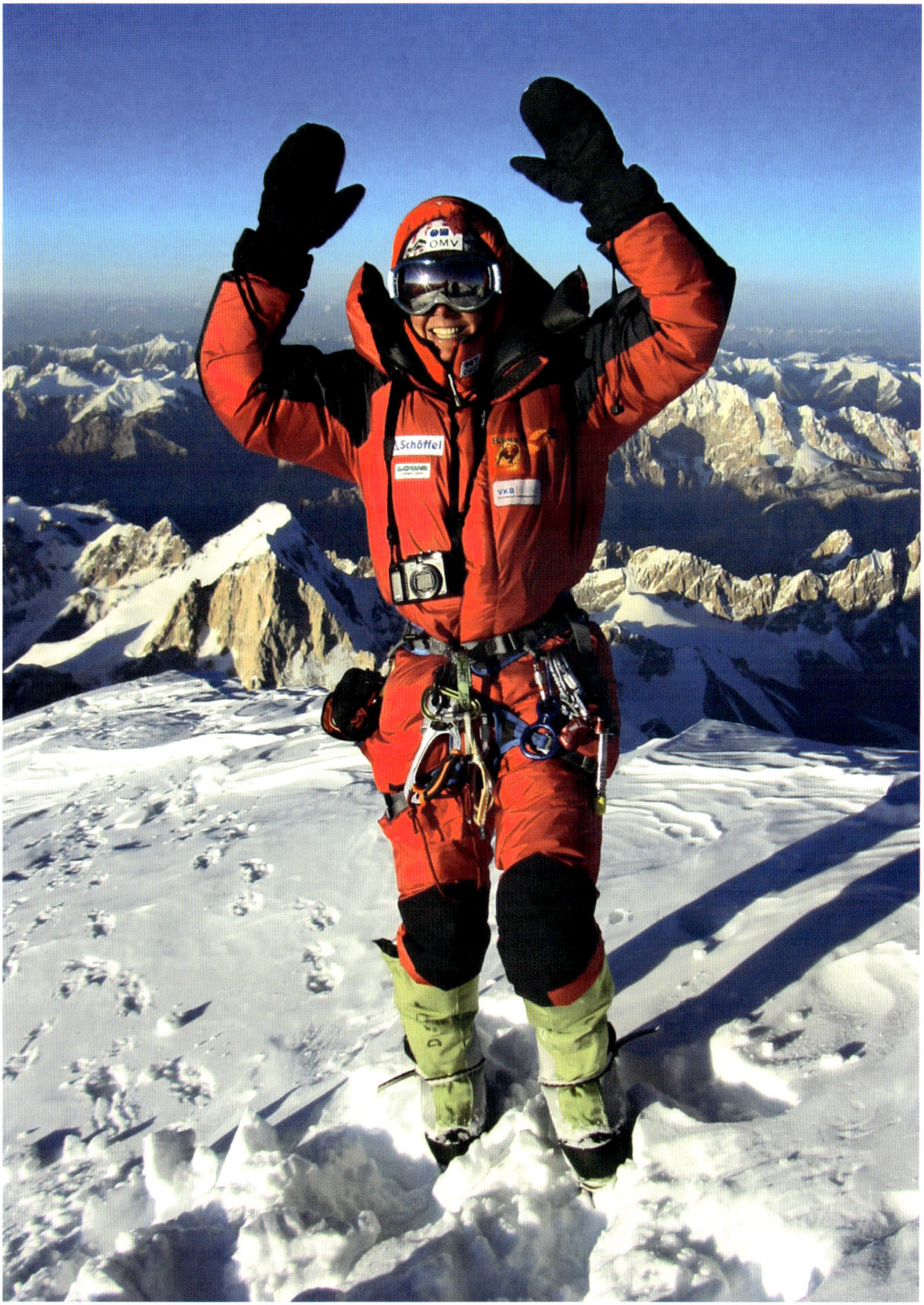
OMV
Schöffel
VKB

Page 160: Sarah Hueniken climbs on Hydrophobia, Canadian Rockies.
Page 161: Gerlinde Kaltenbrunner finally stands atop K2.

Below: Gerlinde Kaltenbrunner on the approach to Everest, 2010.
Opposite above: Alison Hargreaves on the northwest ridge of Kangtega with Cho Oyu and Gyachunkang visible behind her.
Opposite below: Ines Papert and Luka Lindič approach Kyzyl Asker.

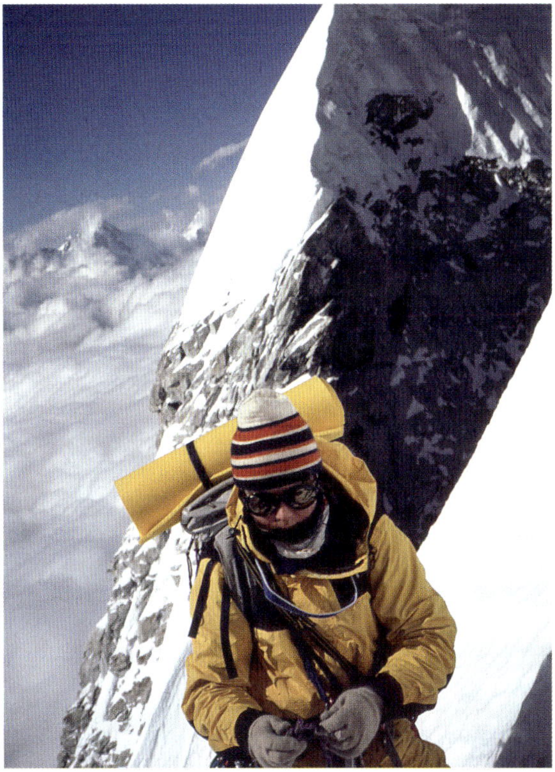

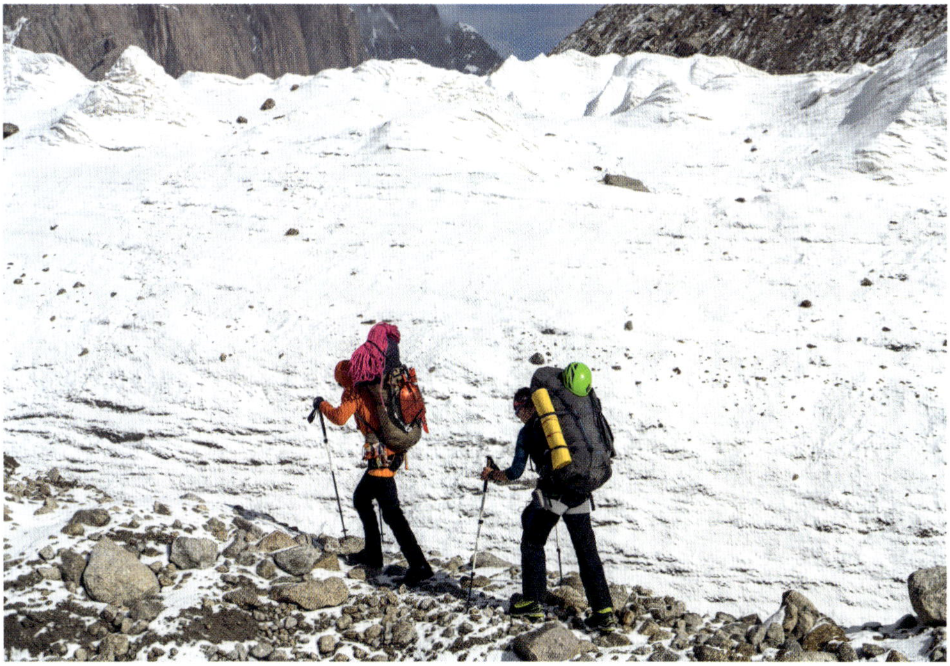

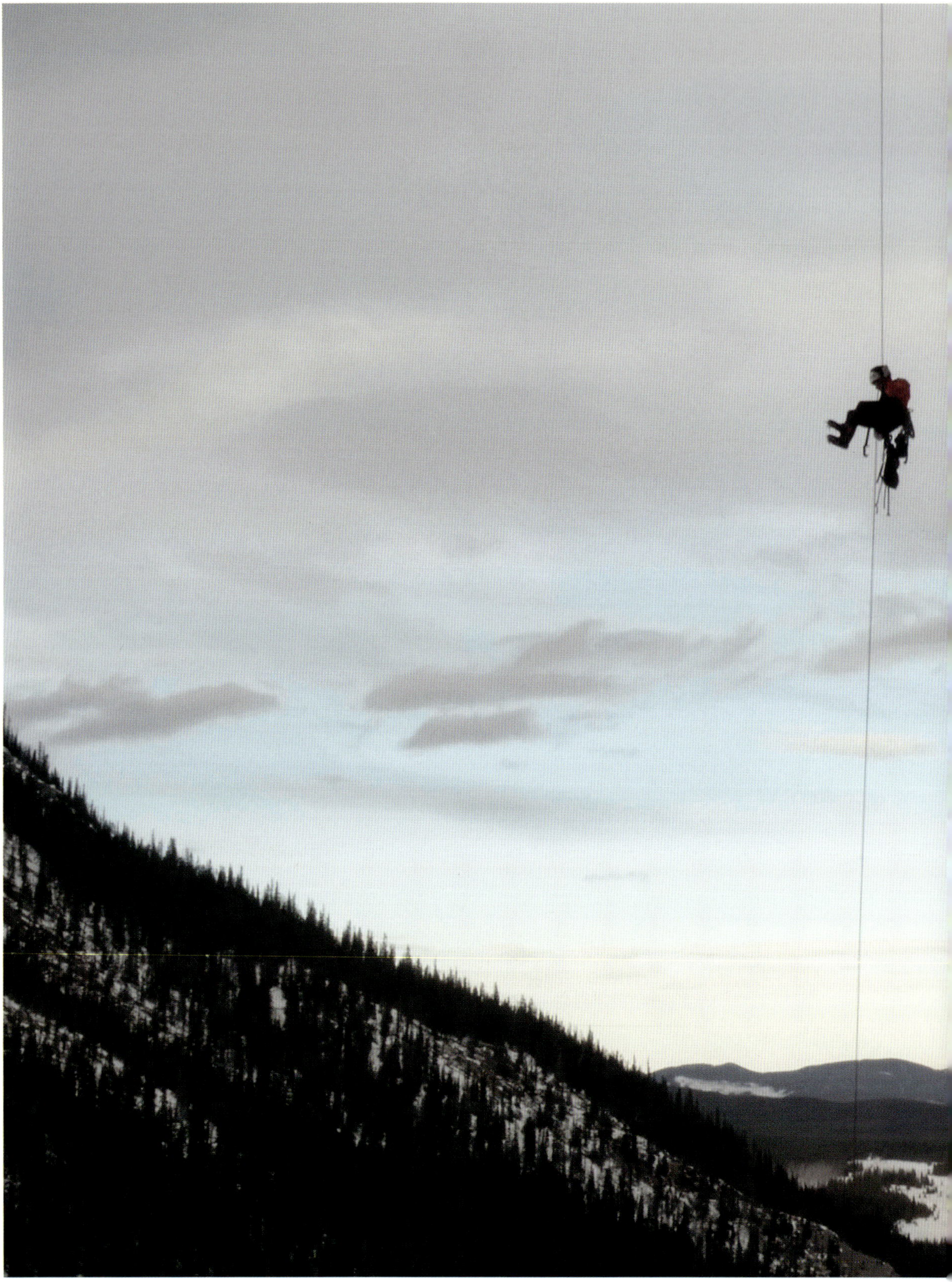

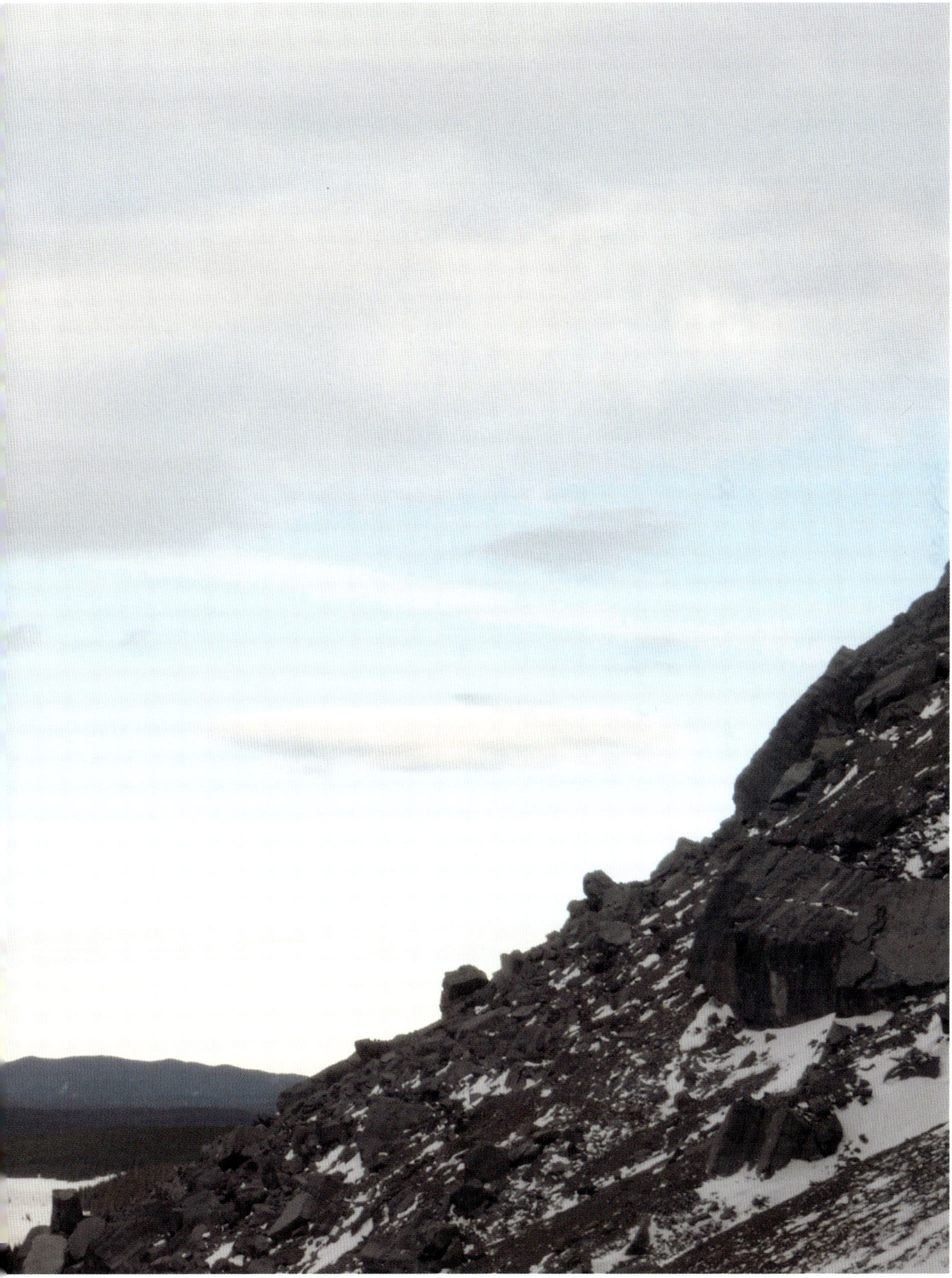

Pages 164–5: Sarah Hueniken abseils off the Hydrophobia wall, Canadian Rockies.
Above: Ines Papert's camp below Kyzyl Asker.

Opposite above: Ines Papert with her son as a baby.
Opposite below: Ines Papert, Kyrgyzstan, 2016.

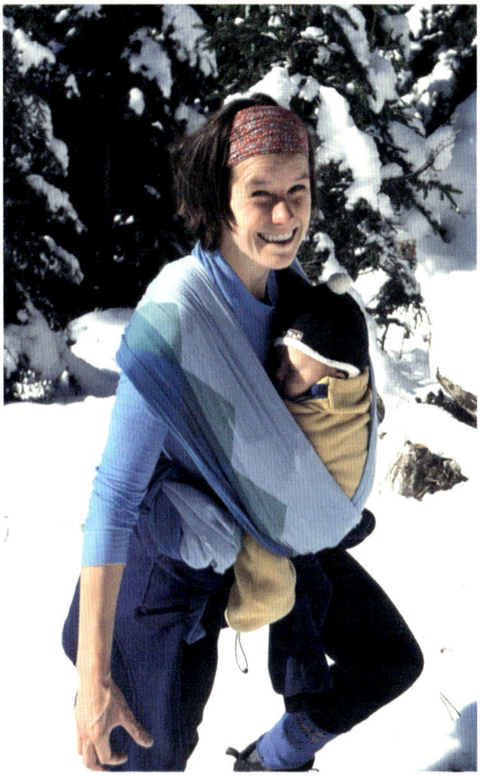

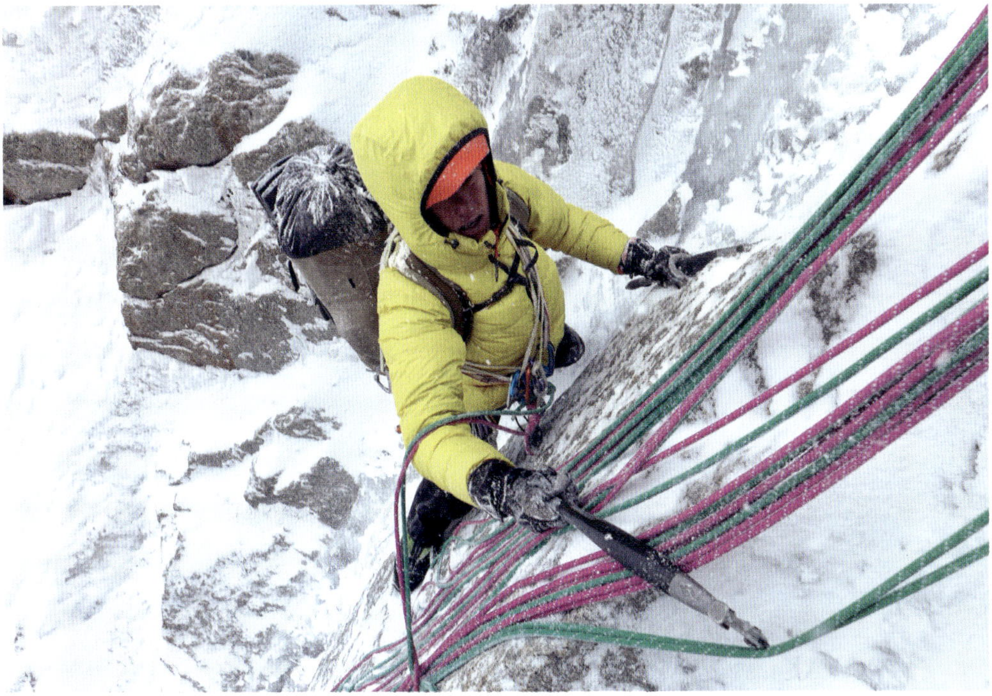

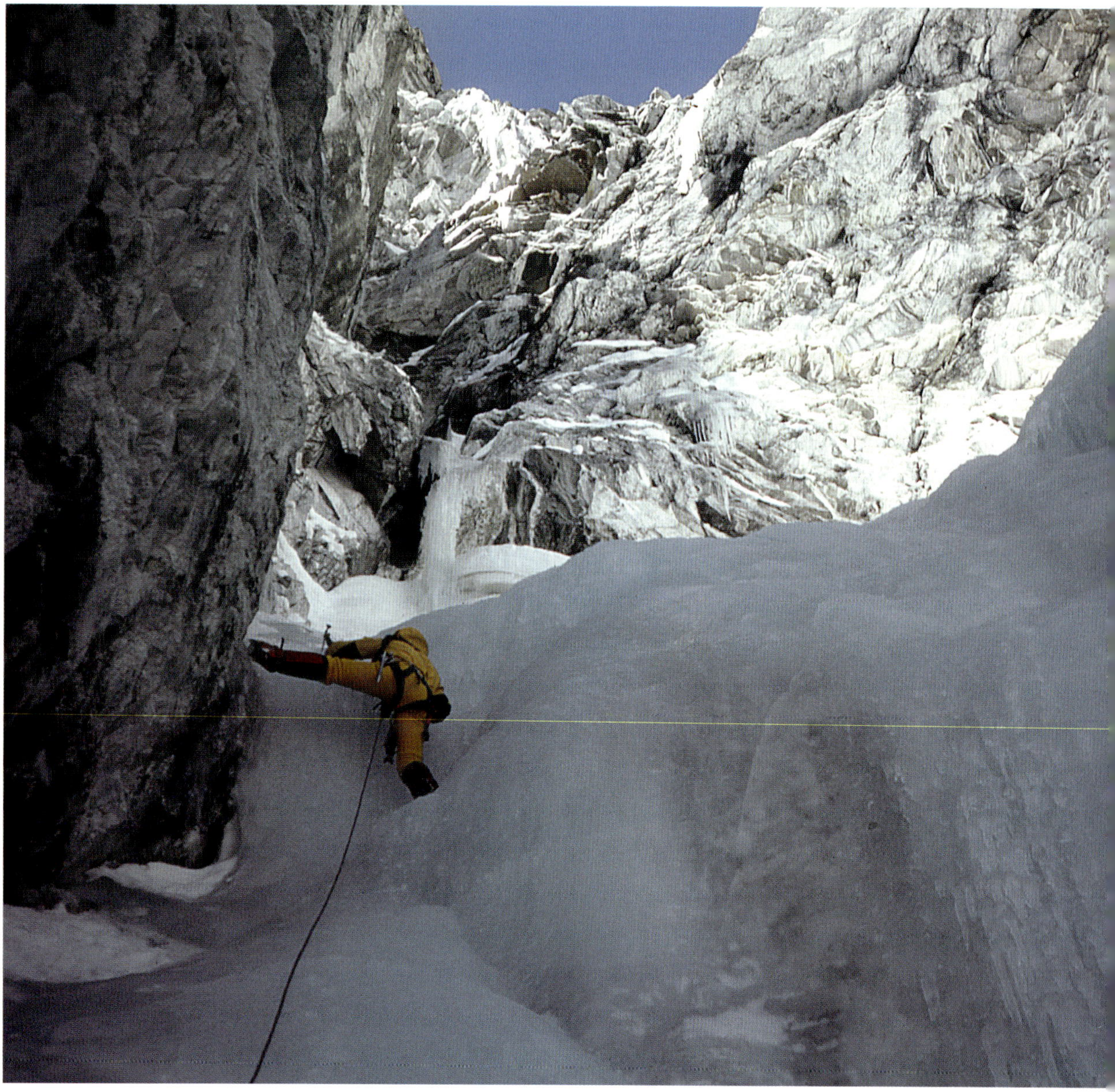

Opposite: Alison Hargreaves climbing on Lobuche, Nepal.
Above: Gerlinde Kaltenbrunner watches sunrise at the high camp of Dhaulagiri, 2008.
Below: Gerlinde Kaltenbrunner climbing the North Pillar on K2 in 2011.
Pages 170–1: Sarah Hueniken climbs Cryophobia, Canadian Rockies.

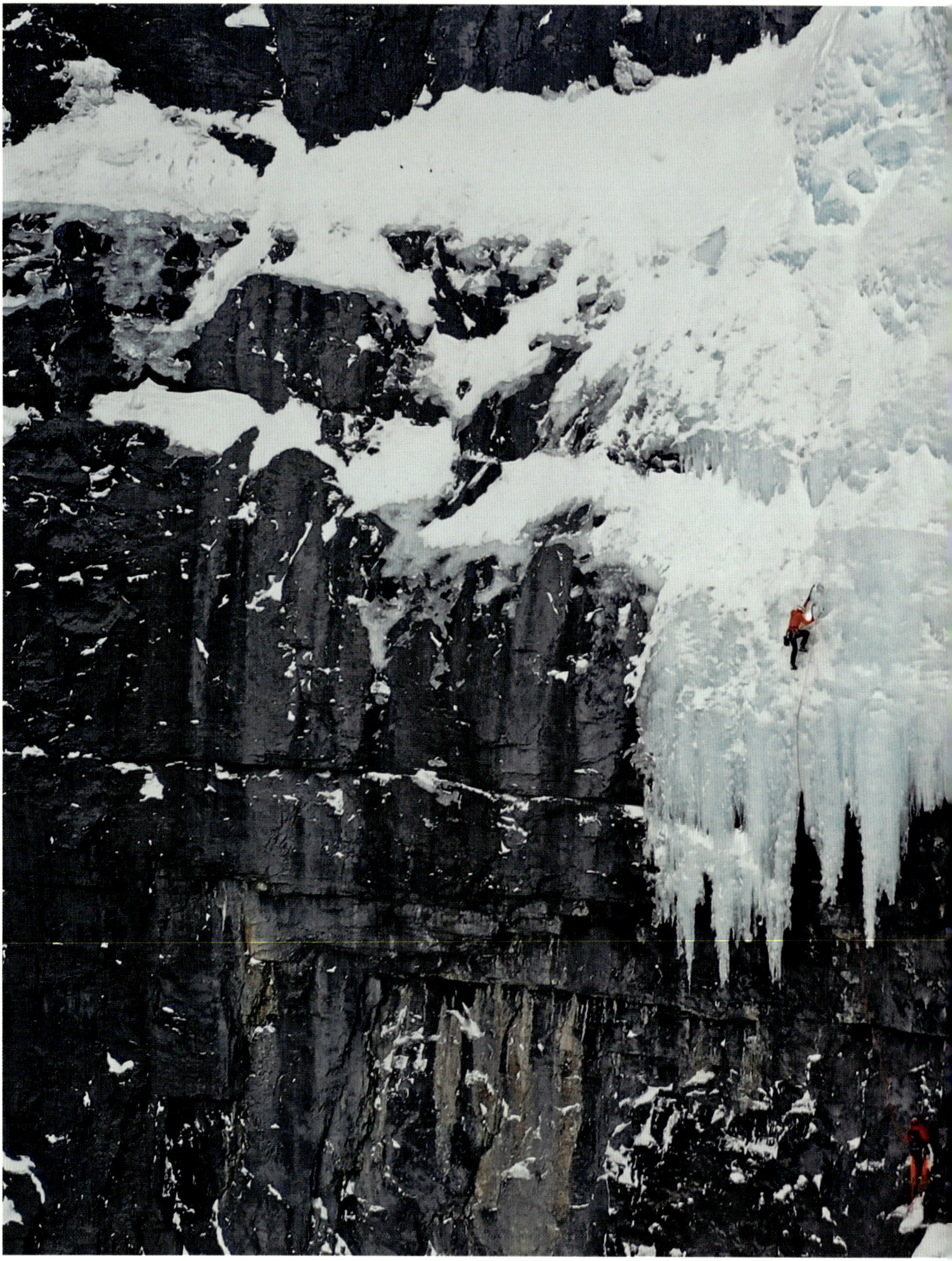

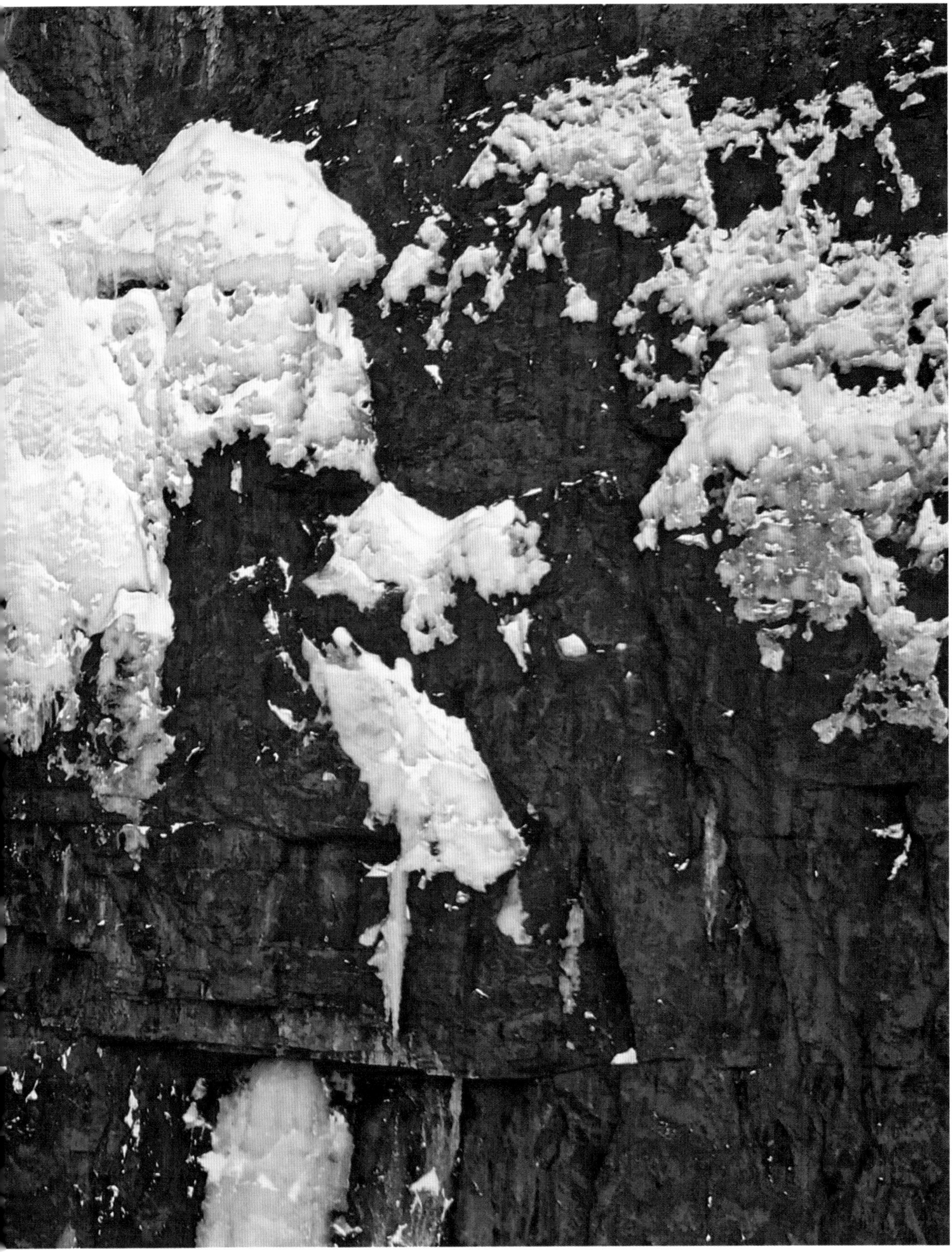

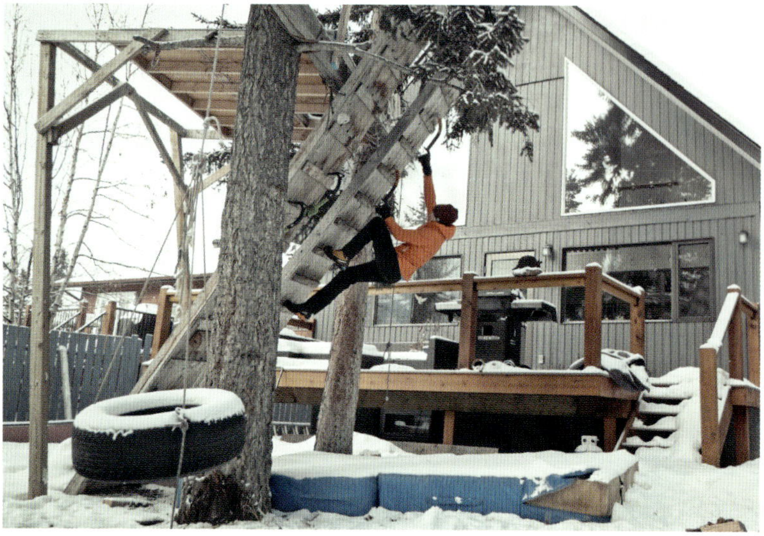

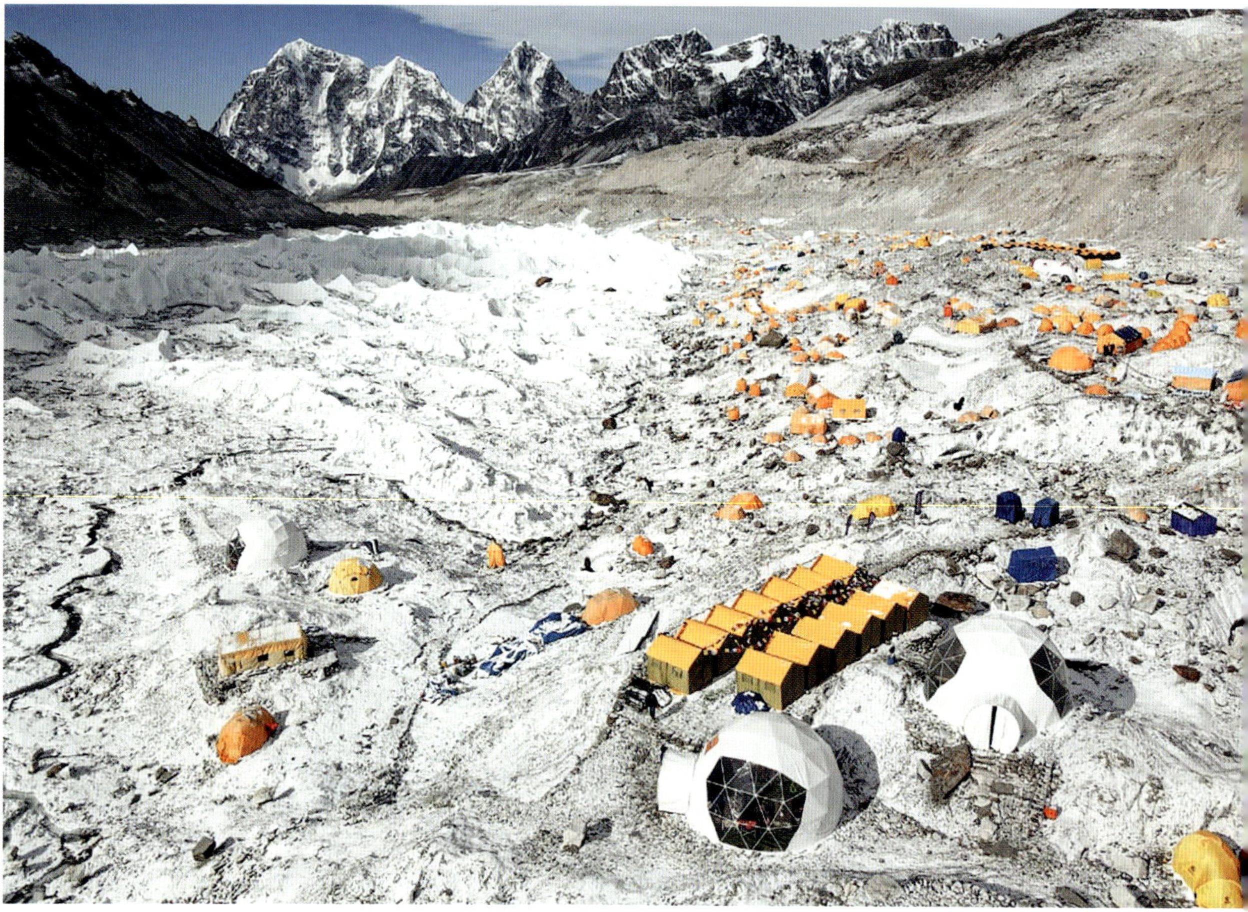

Opposite above: Sarah Hueniken training at her home.
Opposite below: Everest basecamp, April 2022.

Above: Alison Hargreaves near the summit of Lobuche, April 1986.
Pages 174–5: Kyzyl Asker.
Page 176: Alison Hargreaves approaching the summit of Kangtega, Nepal, 1986. Kusum Kanguru in the background.
Page 177: K2.

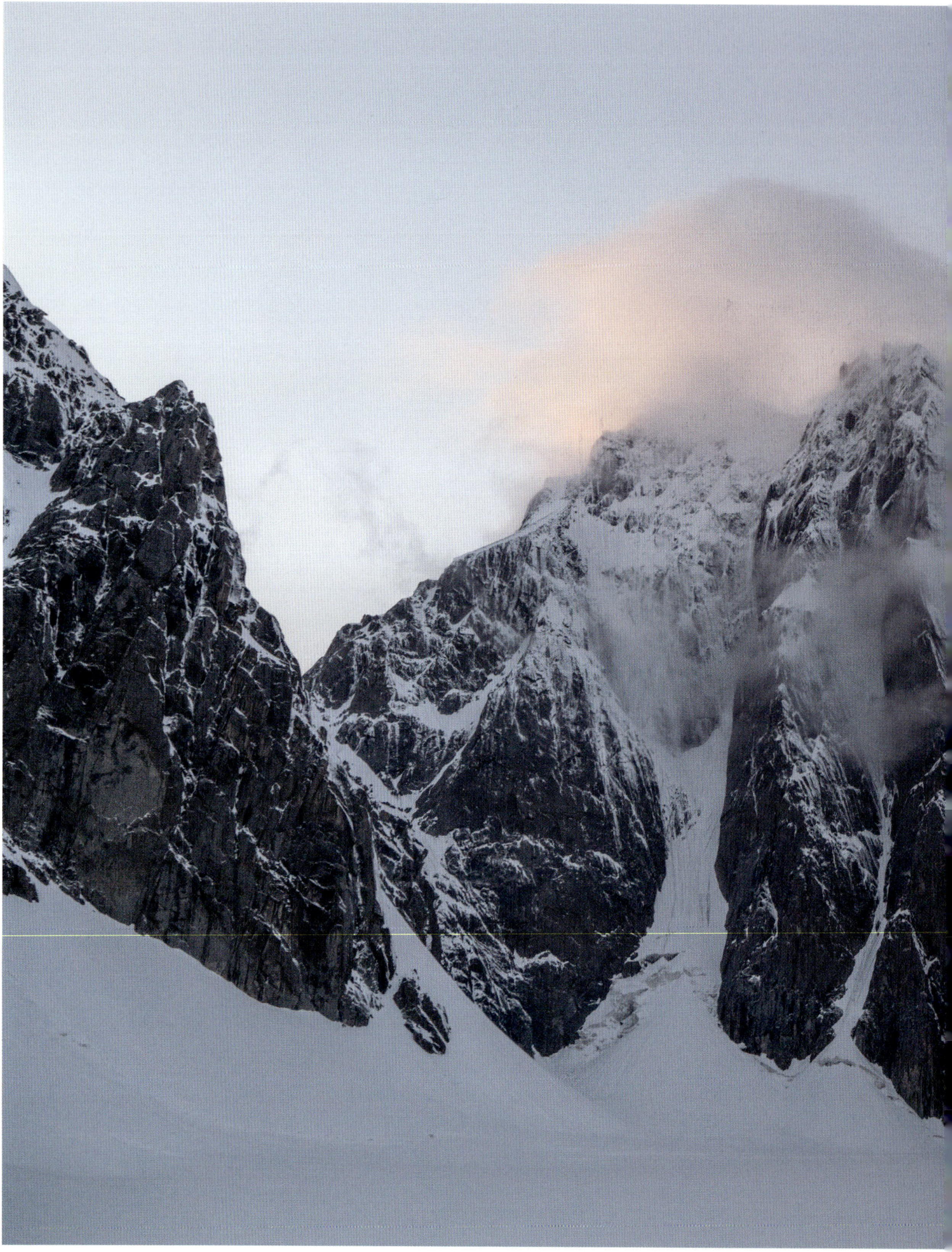

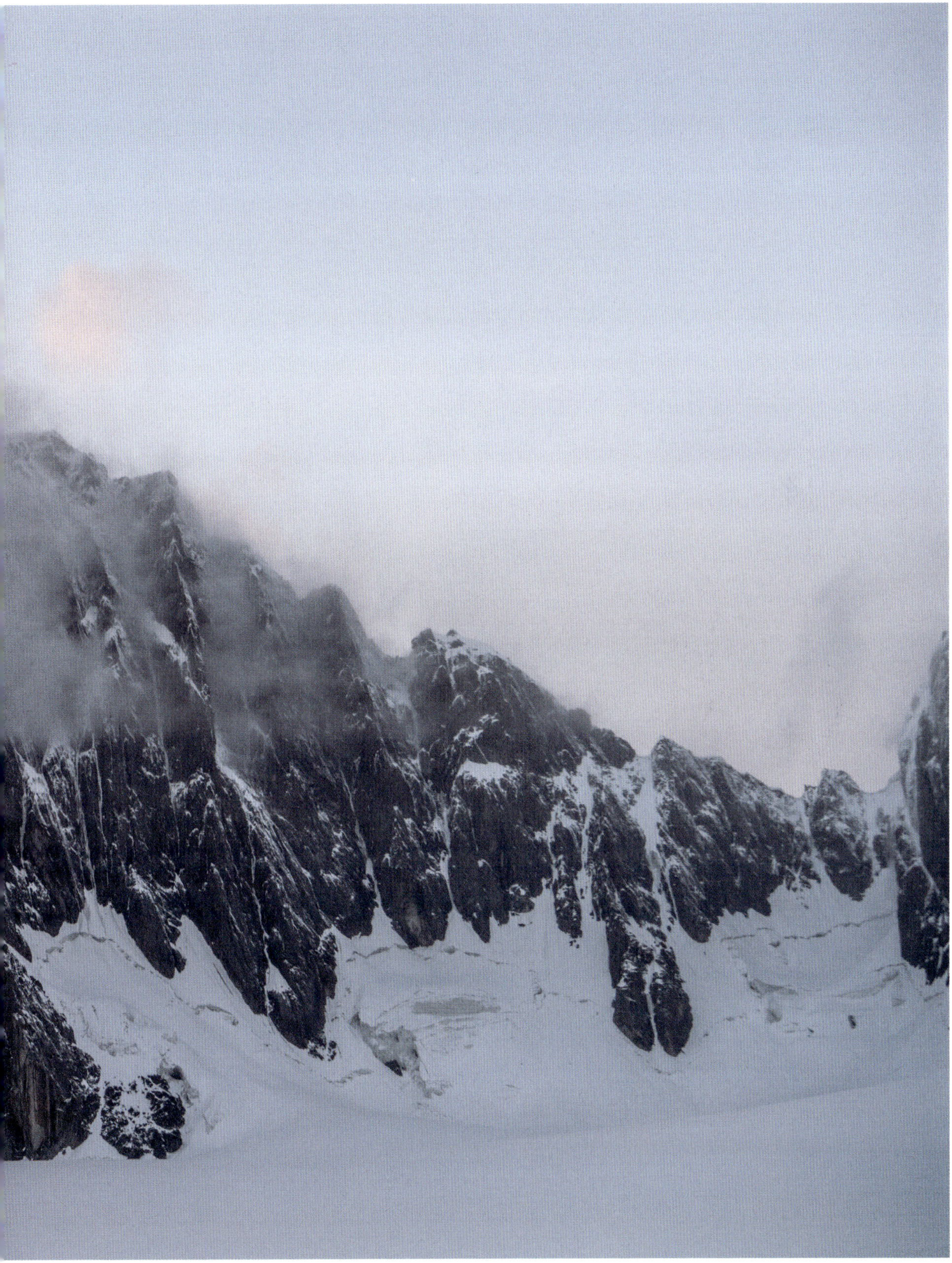

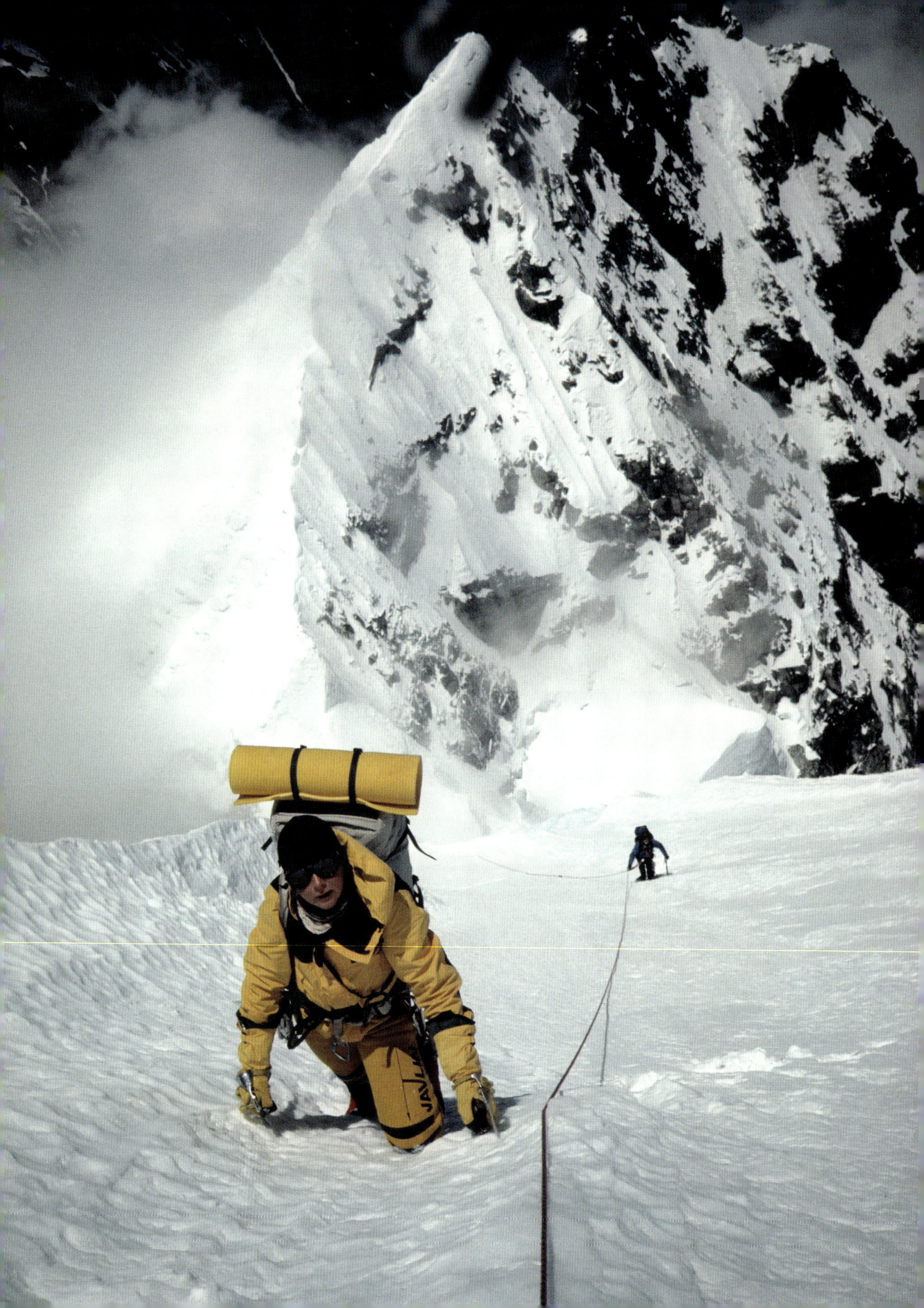

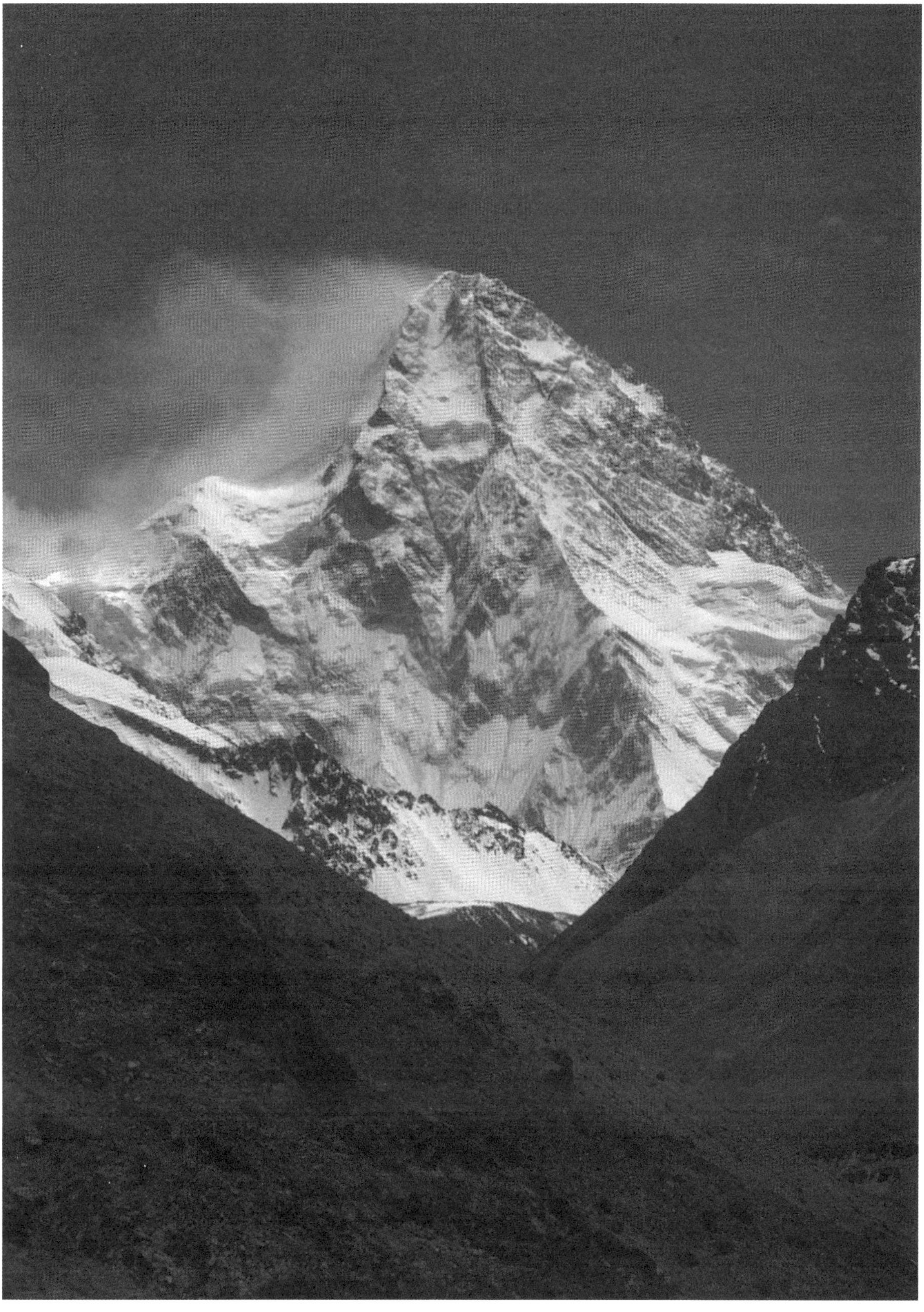

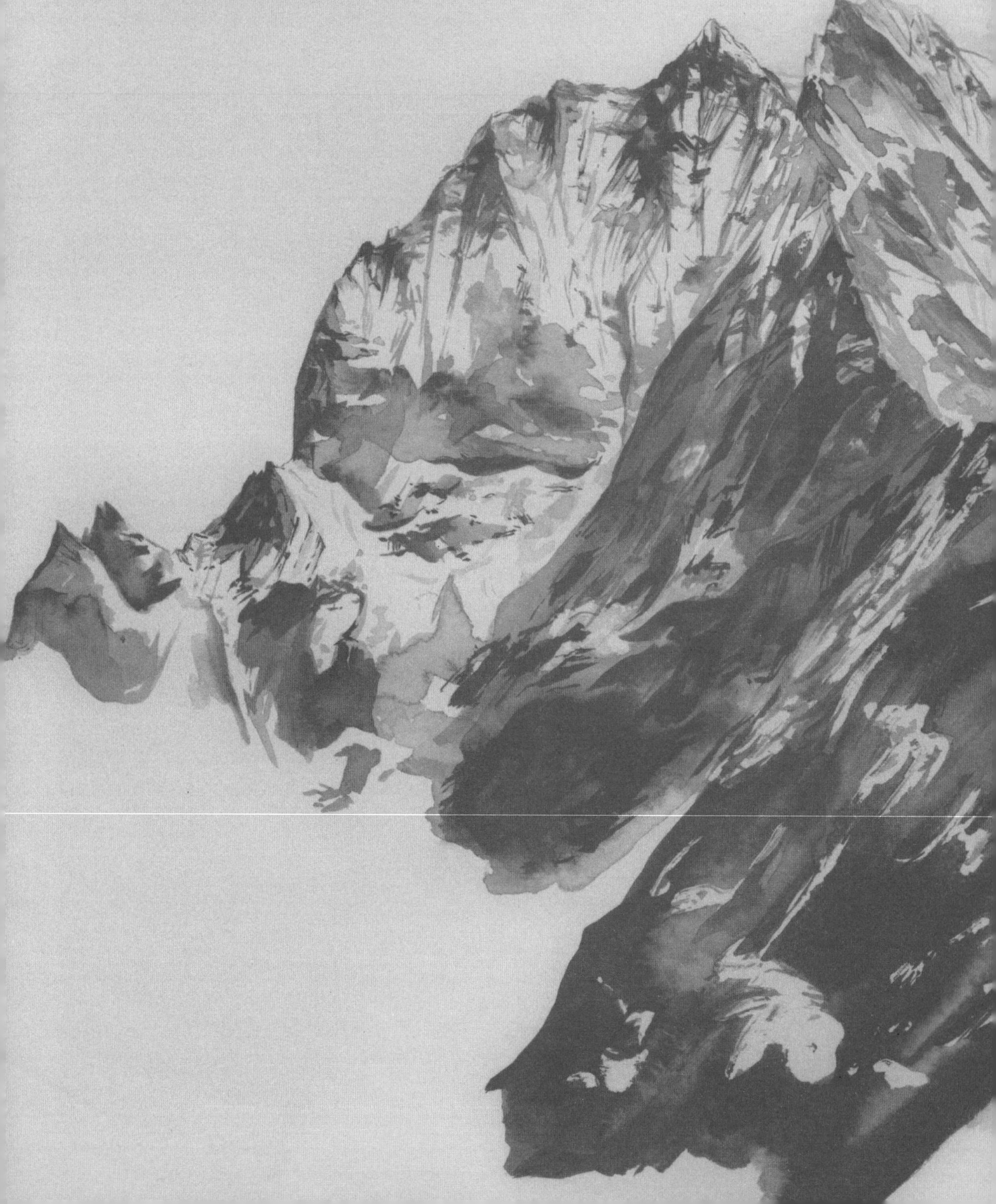

Pasang Lhamu Sherpa and the Climb of Her Life

Pasang Lhamu Sherpa may have been the first
Nepali woman to summit Mount Everest, but she
never claimed to be a great mountaineer.
In fact, she referred to herself as 'just a housewife',
but her determination transformed her into one
of the most famous Sherpa women of her time.

PASANG LHAMU SHERPA

Nationality:
Nepalese

Born:
10 December 1961

Died:
22 April 1993 (age 32)

Active:
1988-1993

Opposite: Pasang Lhamu Sherpa on the summit of Mont Blanc, France.
Below: Pasang Lhamu Sherpa in Kathmandu, Nepal.

Born in the small village of Surke in Nepal, Pasang was raised in the shadow of the imposing peaks of the Himalaya. Lukla Airport, the main jumping-off point for those travelling to the Khumbu Valley and Everest basecamp, was only a few kilometres away. Before it was built in 1964, expeditions had to make the arduous trek from the foothills on the outskirts of Kathmandu all the way to Everest, which could take several weeks.

Pasang's father, Phurba Kitar Sherpa, was a sirdar, or lead guide, and she must have regularly listened to stories from the expeditions he joined. Sirdars act as equipment and transportation leaders, often wrangling the younger, inexperienced porters, organizing carrying loads and paying wages in conjunction with foreign expedition team leaders. Pasang was the only daughter in the family with five brothers. Being the only girl, she was not permitted to attend school, but was expected to help her mother tend to the farm on their small plot of land. These cultural expectations frustrated Pasang, and around the age of sixteen, she expressed her desire to leave their family home and go trekking, a significant act of rebellion that had her family fearing for her safety.

Undeterred, Pasang left the village to work at a hotel in Lukla, where she fell in love with Lhakpa Sonam Sherpa. Sonam also refused to be bound by tradition, particularly when it came to arranged marriages, which were still very common. Pasang and Sonam defied their parents, married in secret and left Lukla for Kathmandu on foot in search of a better life.

Nepal in the 1980s was a kingdom marked by socio-economic disparity. The elite ruling families were very wealthy, while the rural communities remained impoverished. The Sherpa people are an ethnic minority, having originated from Tibet and migrated to Nepal centuries ago. From the first European contact, Sherpas were admired for their physical strength and fortitude, particularly when it came to mountaineering. However, until only a few decades ago, many Nepalis from the majority Hindu population believed that Sherpa people were backwards country folk. This attitude further ostracized their small mountain villages from the waves of urban development and technological progress that could be seen in Kathmandu during the 1980s and 1990s. Today many Sherpa people are educated and seek out various career paths, such as business, medicine or teaching, dispelling the stereotype that all Sherpas are climbers or yak herders.

Pasang and Sonam went to Kathmandu intent on starting their own trekking company, one of the first Nepali-owned in the country. They named it Thamserku Trekking after a prominent mountain on the main trekking route to Mount Everest, which greets climbers as they cross into Sagarmāthā National Park. Sagarmāthā is the Nepali name for Mount Everest, while Tibetans call the mountain Chomolungma, Mother Goddess of the Earth. Pasang acted as the business and equipment manager for the business in Kathmandu while Sonam took on the role of climbing sirdar, facilitating trips for clients to the Khumbu Valley and other major peaks.

Thamserku Trekking catered to the needs of many foreign expeditions, primarily Swiss and French teams. Because of Pasang and Sonam's exceptional generosity, many of the team members became friends and stayed with them in Kathmandu. By the time the company had achieved financial success, Pasang and Sonam had started a family of their own. Pasang was a loving mother to her children but she saw the foreign women who climbed without the burden of societal expectations and wanted to empower Nepali women to break from tradition too.

Foreign friends and clients invited Pasang to the Alps to climb with them. It was an unusual opportunity for a Nepali woman, and she grasped it. French climbing instructors taught her basic mountaineering safety, ropework and glacier travel skills in Chamonix. She thrived under their tutelage and successfully summited Mont Blanc.

Pasang returned to Nepal full of energy and ambition. She had reached the highest point in the Alps and now was set on summiting the highest peak in the world, in her own country. She and Sonam quickly put together a request to join an upcoming French expedition to Chomolungma led by Marc Batard. Thamserku Trekking had already been hired for logistics and climbing support and Batard agreed to have her come along, perhaps misinterpreting the request. Many believed that she wished to come along to see Chomolungma from basecamp but that she would go no higher. Pasang, however, had another agenda.

When Pasang reached basecamp in the spring of 1990 along with the rest of the Sherpa climbing team, she promptly proceeded to advance from camp to camp, higher and higher up the peak, without the use of supplemental oxygen, eventually spending a night sleeping at the South Col (7,906 metres/25,938 feet). Batard arrived at basecamp unaware of her intentions and was alarmed to hear that she had advanced to a high camp using team equipment without his permission. Not only had she made it to the South Col, but according to her fellow Sherpa teammates, she refused to come back down when Batard insisted she must. Enraged that she was using team resources as well as engaging other Sherpa meant to fix the route with ropes and guide foreign clients up the peak, he climbed to the higher camp himself. She agreed to come down and was forced to leave the expedition.

Despite the sour ending, Pasang's first climbing experience on Chomolungma made her even more determined to climb. She couldn't comprehend how she could be denied the experience by a foreigner, whilst in her own country, when so many women from other countries had the right to climb. Pasang vowed to return with her own locally led and supported team. She was no longer convinced that the generosity she had experienced in the Alps would be shown to her at home. She set about organizing an all-Nepali expedition for the autumn of 1991. This time, she would do it her way.

Back in Kathmandu, civil unrest seemed imminent as pro-democracy protests abounded. Social disparity had reached an apex and the people of Nepal would no longer blindly accept their predicament. With tensions rising, the Hindu monarchy dispensed the military to deal with the protesters while imposing a nightly curfew. When these authoritarian tactics failed, the King of Nepal finally succumbed and announced general elections.

Like her fellow countrymen, Pasang was tired of people controlling her life. She knew she had the mental fortitude to summit Chomolungma, even though she had less experience and training than most who attempt the mountain. Getting to the top of the world and becoming a great climber were never the main motivation. She believed that if she achieved her goals, she could inspire other Nepali women to rise up, to dream and to achieve the impossible too.

In 1991, Pasang and a small, self-supported team of Sherpa climbers set up their basecamp and made steady progress up the mountain. Chomolungma would not make their journey easy this time. When the team tried for a summit bid from their camp at the South Col, they were met with fierce winds and poor visibility along the ridge to the South Summit. A French climber who had been forced to turn around warned them of ferocious conditions ahead, suggesting they descend. His advice went unheeded and they pressed on to the South Summit (8,749 metres/ 28,704 feet) just below the true top. Pasang and her team were utterly exhausted, and the storm, rendering their descent route invisible, now forced them to bivouac at this extreme altitude for the night. The next morning, the team descended but were so physically spent by their ordeal, they no longer had the energy for another attempt.

With this failed expedition, Thamserku Trekking fell into financial trouble, as Pasang and Sonam had relied on company money to fund the team. They were forced to sell off sixty per cent of the business to stay afloat and

Summit - 6,779 m/22,241 ft — 2

1 — Summit - 6,623 m/21,729 ft

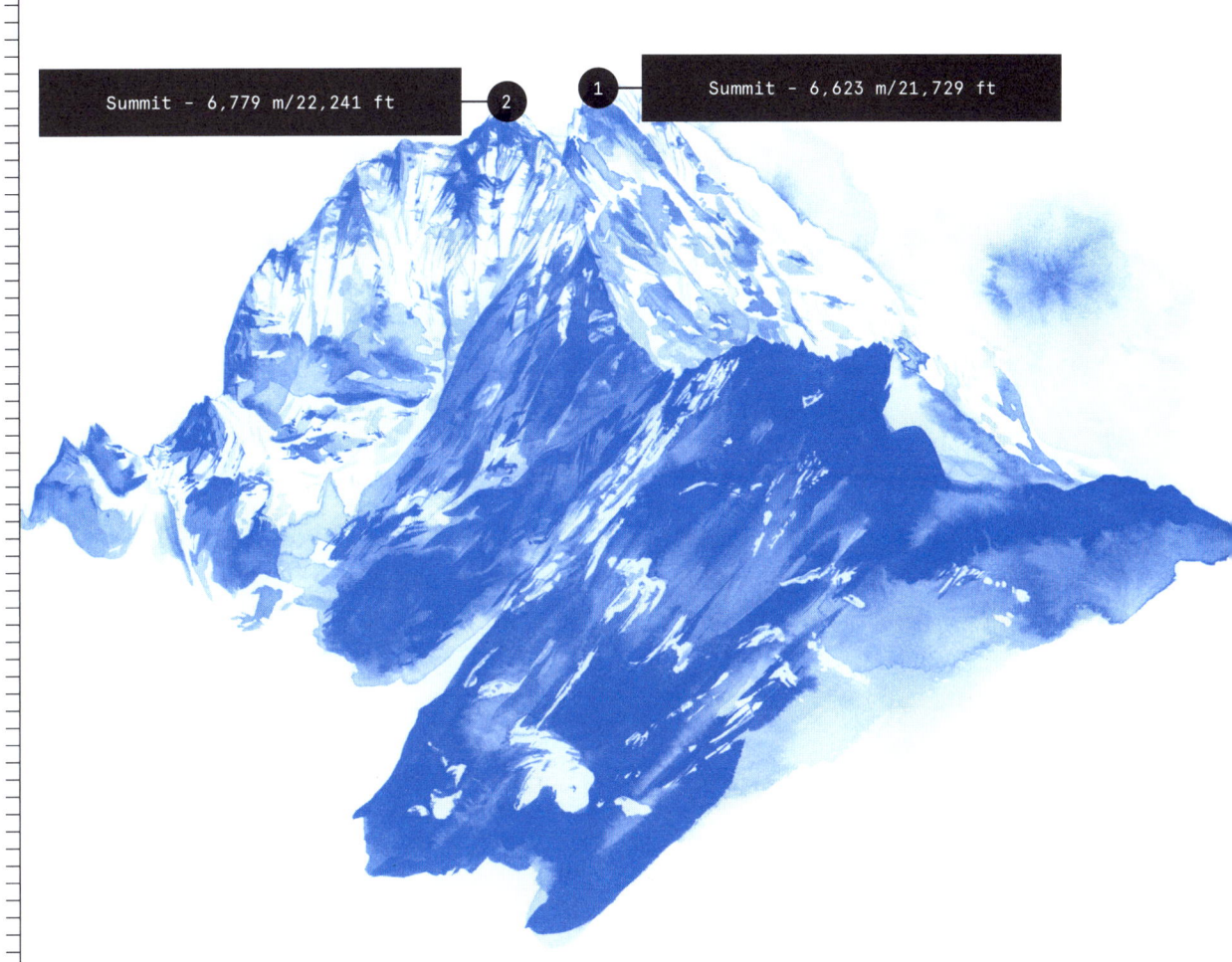

THAMSERKU
NORTH FACE

Thamserku is a prominent mountain to the east of Namche Bazaar and towers above the small village of Tangboche, famous for its Buddhist monastery.

1. Thamserku summit - 6,623 m/21,729 ft.
2. Kangtega summit - 6,779 m/22,241 ft.

Pasang went to work securing sponsors for her next attempt, with reasonable success. Pasang played the media well, exuding confidence and positivity, and the brands enjoyed the national spotlight, which shone favourably on them as supporters of this next all-Nepali attempt. Once again, however, Chomolungma would not allow Pasang passage. Outrageous winds forced her and her team to descend. After this third try, Pasang began to question if fate was intervening, and she was not meant to reach the summit. She abandoned her dream, gave away her equipment and proclaimed that she would now devote her time to raising her family and supporting the business in Kathmandu. She had suffered so much with such little reward, and was unwilling to put climbing above the other important aspects of her life.

In 1993, however, when the government announced a joint Indian–Nepali women's expedition to Chomolungma, Pasang eagerly accepted an invitation to join. She proposed she be co-team lead, but the Indian team refused to allow a Nepali as co-leader. Knowing she would not be in control of her summit chances, she decided to form her own team. Pasang recruited two other Nepali women, Lhakpa Phuti Sherpa and Nanda Rai, as teammates and worked the press for support and exposure. The nation was captivated by the idea of a Nepali women's expedition, feeling certain that the Nepalis would reach the summit before the Indian women. Pasang and her team felt the support of the entire country as they prepared for their climb.

In the lead-up to the expedition, the competition between the two teams was palpable. The Indians still had a number of Nepali women on their team, which meant that in order to become the first women from their nation to reach the top of Chomolungma, Pasang and her teammates would have to summit first. Pasang, Lhakpa Phuti, Nanda and their all-star team of Sherpa guides were the first to depart basecamp that spring. With no route established yet for the season, Pasang's Sherpa team was forced to set up ropes as they made their way up the mountain. Normally, Sherpa rope fixers, affectionately called 'Ice Doctors', place safety lines through the notoriously volatile Khumbu Icefall. Teams then make multiple trips through the icefall using these ropes, acclimatizing over weeks, gaining altitude and building camps at regular intervals. With the Indian team hot on their heels, Pasang and her team had little time – or patience – to adhere to convention.

Once Pasang and her Sherpa climbing companions reached Camp 4 at the South Col, they rested and then decided on a midnight departure the next day, allowing them time and better conditions to make a dash for the top. Under normal circumstances, this leg would take between six and nine hours. Pasang was exhausted by her trip to the South Col and her team members had to encourage her to continue to the South Summit. High winds forced the team to keep moving. Fearful that this summit attempt might be shut down by the weather too, Pasang pressed on.

On 22 April 1993 at 2.15 p.m., after fourteen hours of climbing, Pasang Lhamu Sherpa became the first Nepali woman to stand on the top of Chomolungma. When the basecamp team learned of their success, they immediately sent word to Radio Nepal, where Pasang's achievement was celebrated by the country. Pasang's Sherpa guides, however, were worried about her. It had taken her so long to reach the top and she was only halfway: the long descent loomed and the weather had suddenly turned. It was time to go down.

Wind and blowing snow slammed up the mountain from the Tibetan side, forcing the team to keep together, eyes straining because of poor visibility. Their uptrack was no longer obvious. They crept down the mountain at a snail's pace. After five hours of descent they reached the South Summit, but because of their slow ascent, everyone had now run out of supplemental oxygen. Pasang's Sherpa companions watched helplessly as she collapsed, unable to continue. Pasang remained at the South Summit with Pemba Norbu Sherpa and Sonar Tsering Sherpa, a strong climber who had participated in many previous expeditions but was now also in peril. The situation was dire: Sonar was coughing up blood, so two others descended blindly to the South Col to find help and locate oxygen to bring up to the climbers in trouble.

Meanwhile, faster members of the team had reached Camp 4 where they waited for the others. Lhakpa Phuti and Nanda were holed up even lower at Camp 3, eager to greet Pasang and congratulate her on her amazing accomplishment. Eerily, Lhakpa Phuti claims to have heard Pasang calling her name through the night; the calls were so vivid that she unzipped her tent several times and scanned the darkness with her headlight, convinced Pasang was nearby.

Sadly, Pasang and Sonar Tsering both perished high on the mountain, never to celebrate their achievement. The Sherpas who had returned to Camp 4 were unable to go back up due to deep snow and deteriorating conditions – they could not risk any more lives in a rescue attempt. Not until a week later, once the storm had cleared, was a team able to retrieve Pasang's body. Despite many Sherpa guides and climbers dying on Chomolungma, Pasang's body was the first to ever be brought down the mountain.

Pasang's family was devastated, as was a nation of supporters. The streets filled with thousands of mourners as her body was driven through Kathmandu to her funeral pyre. Pasang's final climb was bittersweet: she had achieved the

INFO

EARLY ASCENTS AND
TOTAL NUMBER OF
EVEREST ASCENTS
BY DECADE

1953:
First ascent by
Tenzing Norgay
and Edmund Hillary

1950s:
6

1960s:
18

1970s:
80

1980s:
180

1990s:
886

2000-2010:
3,969

2010-2020:
5,047

2021:
472

2022:
683

2023:
674

TOTAL NUMBER
OF ASCENTS BY 2023:
12,015

TOTAL NUMBER OF ASCENTS
BY WOMEN AS OF 2023:
887

*Statistics from the
Himalayan Database

Pasang and her husband Sonam pose in front of their business, Thamserku Trekking.

impossible but paid with her life. The government declared a national holiday in her name and a monument to her now stands proudly in the city of Kathmandu.

It's hard to measure the impact that Pasang had on the women of Nepal, but her goals and ambitions were championed by a nation and her loss was felt deeply in the decades that followed. Since her ascent, more than sixty-five Nepali women have reached the top of Chomolungma and several Sherpa women climbers have gone on to make multiple summits of the peak and break speed records. Pasang paved the way for others to dream and, in turn, achieve their goals.

PASANG LHAMU SHERPA

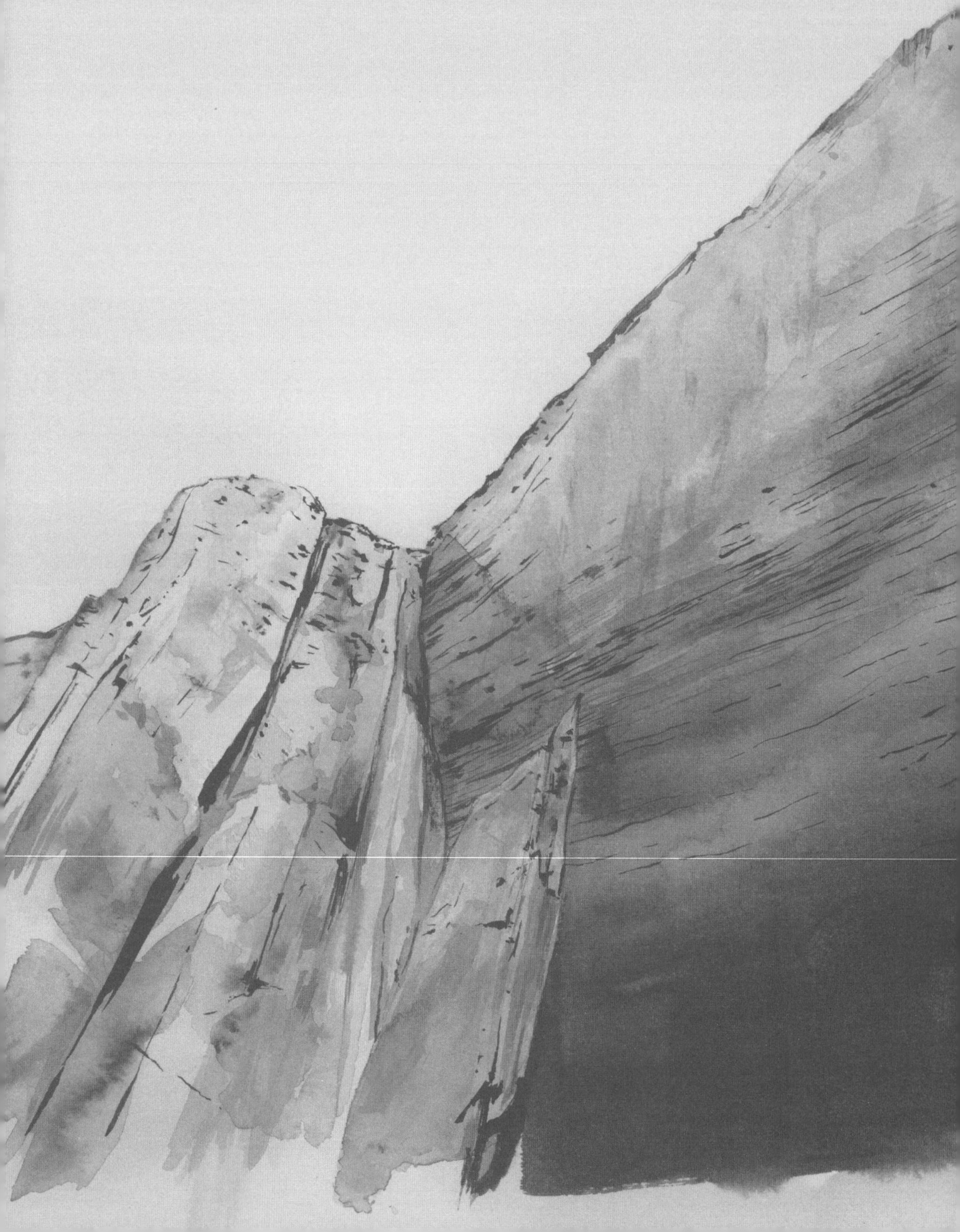

Hazel Findlay, with Strong Body and Mind

The southwest coast of England is a geological wonder. While its southern shoreline, stretching from East Devon to Dorset, is known as the Jurassic Coast because of its extensive fossil deposits, its northern neighbour (crossing the borders between North Devon and Cornwall) is called the Culm Coast. Its cliffs consist of a type of metamorphic shale, sedimentary rock composed of sandstone and slate that was compressed under the sea for millions of years before a dramatic geological event forced it skyward, creating huge vertical cliffs and steep walls of smooth rock. As the rocks thrust out of the rough seas below, the water pounds on the cliffs and the pebbles of the shoreline tumble back and forth, each wave creating a dramatic natural symphony.

HAZEL FINDLAY

Nationality:
British

Born:
3 May 1989

Active:
1995–present

Opposite: Hazel Findlay climbing in Squamish, British Columbia.
Below: Hazel Findlay.

Towards the northernmost tip of the Culm Coast, you'll find Hartland Quay and, more specifically, a climbers' crag called Dyers Lookout. This is home to more than fifty climbing routes, including one of the most notoriously difficult routes in the UK, Once Upon a Time in the South West.

As you approach from the fields of heather above, the land drops away to reveal a slab of dark stone that seems as though it might tip over in a strong gust of wind, to be reclaimed by the sea. From below, the 50-metre (164-foot) face appears completely blank. On closer inspection, a climber will catch glimpses of tiny horizontal seams with sharp edges. These cracks are barely big enough to slide in a finger or wiggle in small wires or nuts for protection. The climb is crimpy, straining on the hands, and the foot placements feel insecure on the smooth rock, requiring delicate, balancing moves to smear from one precarious hold to the next.

The climb was established in 2010 by Dave Birkett, one of the UK's most prolific route setters, known for his bold routes, often with marginal protection. Although there are a few pegs (pitons) in place from his first ascent, climbers can no longer rely on these to catch a life-threatening fall. The pegs have rusted from years of exposure to the salty air. Additional protective kit must be placed as the climber moves up, which is very difficult under the strain of the climbing moves themselves.

Dave Birkett is part of the widespread traditionalist climbing movement in the UK that adheres to strict principles: using no drilled bolts or permanent protection when creating a new route if natural features will accept removable gear, and creating all routes from the ground up, with no abseiling to review or establish the route. Practising moves in advance on top-rope is also discouraged; if a climber falls while trying to establish the route, they should return to the ground and try again. It was under these diehard rules that a young girl named Hazel Findlay learned to climb.

Findlay was born in Bristol. Her father Steve introduced her to climbing at just six years old. Like Birkett, he believed in pure, ground-up ethics. Hazel was immersed in this mantra right from the beginning, learning to trad climb and understanding that falling was risky with poor protection. Nowadays, children often start learning indoors and are encouraged to fall often so that they gain trust in the equipment. In other parts of the world, many have abandoned the traditionalist UK climbing dogma in favour of drilling bolts right into the rock, which provides better protection. Traditionalists would argue this reduces the excitement of the climb. But Findlay's early training on British trad routes would serve her well once her climbing ability advanced.

Before Findlay had even dreamed of an ascent of Once Upon a Time in the South West, she put in lots of miles, climbing with her father on the weekends and discovering the local climbing gym in Warrington, where she moved with her mother after her parents divorced. With a foot in both traditional and indoor climbing, she honed her all-round skills. During these formative years, Findlay and her father alternated between the sea cliffs of Pembrokeshire and the crags of South Wales. Early on, her father and his climbing friends were astounded by her ability on the varied rock that the UK has to offer. Findlay would eventually spend a few years climbing with the British team as a junior competitive climber, becoming the national junior champion six times.

By her teens, Findlay was seen as an exceptionally bold climber. Though she never considered herself brave or reckless, she believed that she had a good mental capacity for dealing with stress and using adrenaline in a productive way. This wasn't innate, but a skill that she worked on. She understood that while she couldn't overcome all her fear, she could manage it and recognize any internal stress triggers that might hinder her success. Her talent was undeniable, and in her early twenties, sponsors began to approach her.

With the support of sponsorship, Findlay started to climb abroad, exposing her to other climbing approaches. She witnessed how leading-edge climbers around the world top-roped difficult climbs, rehearsing the moves and pushing themselves by trying new grades. After a visit to Squamish, British Columbia, she realized the potential of using some of these techniques combined with all she had learned back home.

In 2011, when Findlay turned twenty-two, she had the opportunity to attempt Once Upon a Time in the South West. Her friend Charlie Woodburn was trying to climb the route and she decided to join him to take a look. In addition to its outlandish location, which has an 'old lost world kind of feel'[1], the climb is incredibly difficult, rated E9, 6c (5.13b R/X). The British 'E' grading system is primarily designed to give an indication of the seriousness, exposure and technical difficulty of a route, with 'E' standing for extremely severe on a scale from E1–E12 – and feasibly beyond (E12 is currently the hardest grade that has been assigned to a route). In the case of Once Upon a Time, the high E grade relates not only to the sustained difficult moves but to the notoriously poor protection available. No British woman had ever climbed an E9 route before, and once Findlay had spent a few days trying the hardest moves on the climb, she felt she might have a chance at it. Woodburn sent the route after a few days but had to return to his job before Findlay could make a successful attempt, so she called her father to see if he might join her as a belayer.

INFO

NOTABLE CLIMBS
BY HAZEL FINDLAY

1. First free ascent and third ascent of Magic Line, Yosemite, USA (5.14c R).

2. First female ascent of Once Upon a Time in the South West, UK (E9 6c/5.13b R/X).

3. First female ascent and second ascent of the PreMuir, El Capitan, Yosemite, USA (5.13+/8b).

4. First ascent of Tainted Love, Squamish, Canada (5.13d/8b R).

5. Mind Control, Oliana, Spain (5.14b/8c).

6. First ascent of Findlay-Geldard route, Aiguille de Saussure, Mont Blanc du Tacul, France (ED/E5/Scottish VI).

7. Free ascent of the Salathé Wall, Yosemite, USA (5.13b/8a).

8. First female ascent of Golden Gate, El Capitan, Yosemite, USA (5.13a/7c+).

9. First ascent of the north face of Ingmikortilaq, Greenland (5.11r).

10. First ascent of Pool Wall, Greenland (5.12).

11. Esclatamasters, Spain (9a).

Summit - 50 m/164 ft

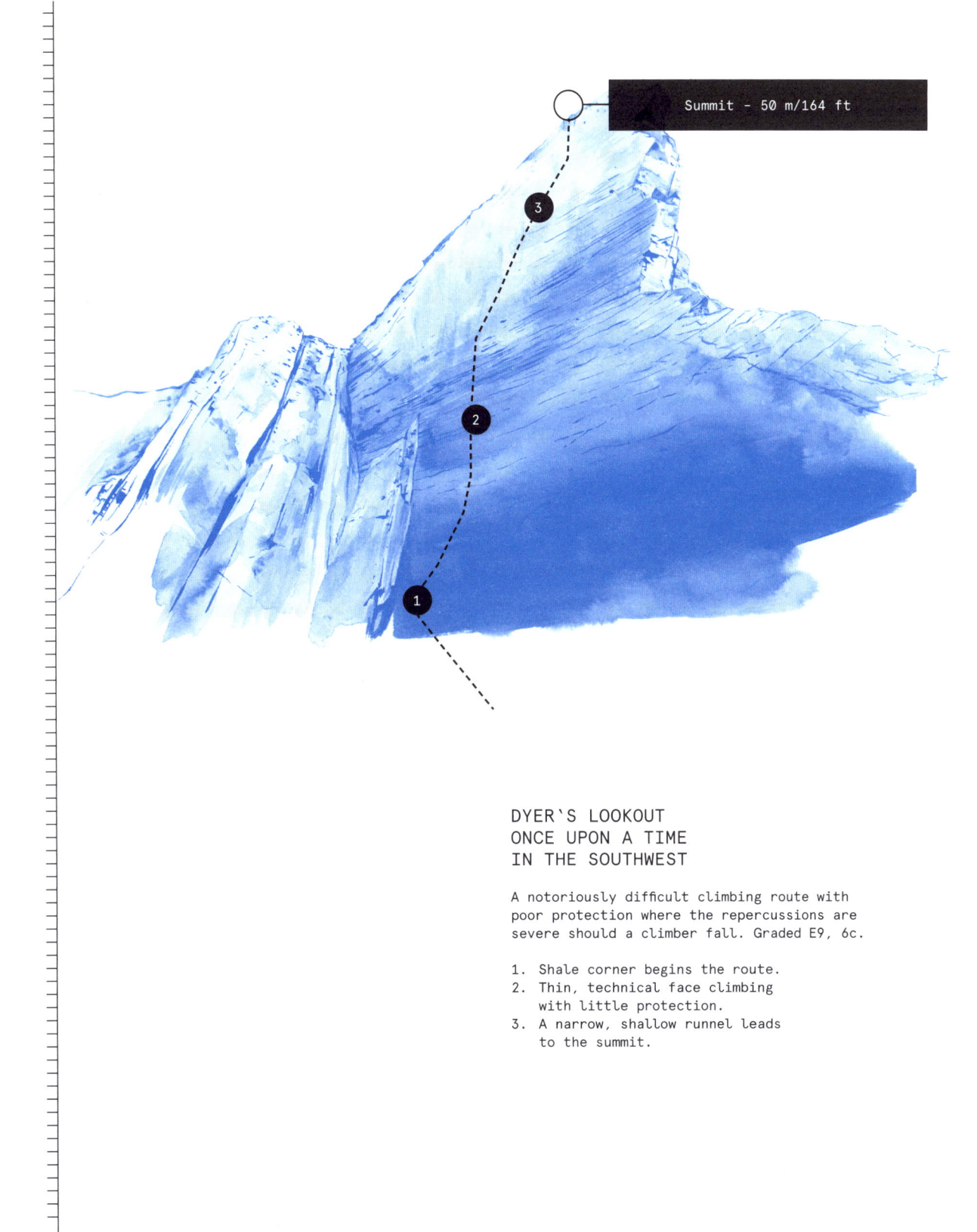

DYER'S LOOKOUT
ONCE UPON A TIME
IN THE SOUTHWEST

A notoriously difficult climbing route with poor protection where the repercussions are severe should a climber fall. Graded E9, 6c.

1. Shale corner begins the route.
2. Thin, technical face climbing with little protection.
3. A narrow, shallow runnel leads to the summit.

HAZEL FINDLAY

When Steve arrived, the two made their way down to the base of the sea cliff, next to the pounding waves. Knowing that the tide would be coming in, Findlay would have to move quickly so her father wouldn't be taken out to sea by a wave while holding the rope. With a last glance up at the slab, she began to move up the friable pillar that provides access to the wall itself.

Because Findlay is short, the first third of the climb was the most challenging. A reachy move forced her to counterbalance her outstretched arm by placing her leg awkwardly out to the side, in a move known as flagging. Luckily this section of the route has relatively good protection, so she felt more confident in pushing herself, knowing that a fall would be safe. As the route rises up, however, the seams and tiny fissures vanish and Findlay had to 'run it out' in various places, going through all the moves without protection until the next suitable crack or seam could be found.

The chance of a bad fall, risking severe injury, was real. Findlay's exceptional mental skill of working through her fear would be integral to her success on the route. Throughout the entire climb, there is no suitable ledge for the climber to properly stand on and rest, and as a result, Once Upon a Time is not only hard on the fingertips but on the calves.

Findlay's toes pressed into the rock, with her heels forced downwards for maximum friction, causing muscle fatigue. She moved quickly through the sketchy upper half of the route, reaching a small runnel that offered more reasonable holds, using speed to her advantage. With intense focus, she completed 50 metres (164 feet) of the most difficult climbing she had done to date to emerge onto the flat grasslands above, tired and relieved. Peering over the edge of the cliff, she was even happier to see that her father was still ahead of the tide.

With that climb, Findlay became the first woman in Britain to achieve the grade of E9, but was unprepared for the attention that followed. She had done the climb for herself, simply wanting to complete the hardest route she could. The climb launched her career into full swing: her sponsors were thrilled with the achievement, and the news spread around the world.

In the months that followed, Findlay completed a difficult climb in Yosemite, securing her place as one of the best free climbers in the world. Along with her climbing partner Hansjorg Auer, she successfully free-climbed Golden Gate (5.13a) on El Capitan over the course of six days in the autumn of 2011, the first British woman to free-climb the famous summit. Since then, climbing in Yosemite has become an annual ritual for Findlay, and to date, she has free-climbed El Capitan four times, each time by a different route, the most difficult being Magic Line, rated at 5.14c R.

Findlay's impressive list of achievements is in great part down to her ability to manage stress and fear on difficult climbs. Realizing early on that irrational fear can hinder progress and dampen a climber's enjoyment on the rock face, she learned to embrace it instead.

Hazel Findlay has appeared in many climbing films since her ascent of Once Upon a Time in the South West and has participated in expeditions and first ascents around the world. She recently started her own business, Strong Mind. Findlay has become a sought-after mentor and life coach and provides courses for climbers on how to take a more intentional approach to mental training.

UK Grades Comparison Table

V grade	UK technical grade	Front grade	Peak B grade
V0-	4c	3	B1
V0	5a	4	
V0+	5b	4+	B2
V1	5c	5 / 5+	B3
V2	6a	6a / 6a+	B4
V3		6b / 6b+	B5
V4	6b	6c	B6
V5		6c+	B7
V6		7a	B8
V7	6c	7a+	B9
V8		7b / 7b+	B9
V9		7c	B10
V10	7a	7c+	B11
V11		8a	B12
V12		8a+	B13
V13	7b	8b	

UK adj.	UK tech.	French	US	Aust.	UIAA	German
M		F1/2	5.2	10	I	I
D		F1	5.3	11	II	II
VD	3c	F2	5.4	12	III	III
S	4a	F3	5.5	13	IV	IV
HS	4b	F4	5.6	14	IV+	V
VS	4c	F4+	5.7	15	V-/V	VI
HVS		F5	5.8	16	V+	
	5a	F5+	5.9	17	VI-	VIIa
E1		F6a	5.10	18	VI	VIIb
	5b	F6a+	5.10+	19	VI+	VIIc
E2		F6b	5.10++	20	VII-	VIIIa
	5c	F6b+	5.11a	21	VII	VIIIb
E3		F6c	5.11b	22	VII+	VIIIc
	6a	F6c+	5.11c		VIII-	IXa
E4		F7a	5.11d	23	VIII	IXb
		F7a+	5.12a	24	VIII+	IXc
E5	6b	F7b	5.12b	25	IX-	
		F7b+	5.12c	26		Xa
E6		F7c	5.12d	27	IX	Xb
		F7c+	5.13a	28	IX+	Xc
E7	6c	F8a	5.13b	29	X-	XIa
		F9a+	5.13c	30	X	XIb
E8		F8b	5.13d	31		
		F8b+	5.14a	32	X+	XIc
E9		F8c	5.14b	33		
	7a	F8c+	5.14c	34	XI-	XIIa
E999		F9a	5.14d	35	XI	XIIb

Opposite: Hazel Findlay climbs at Indian Creek, Utah.

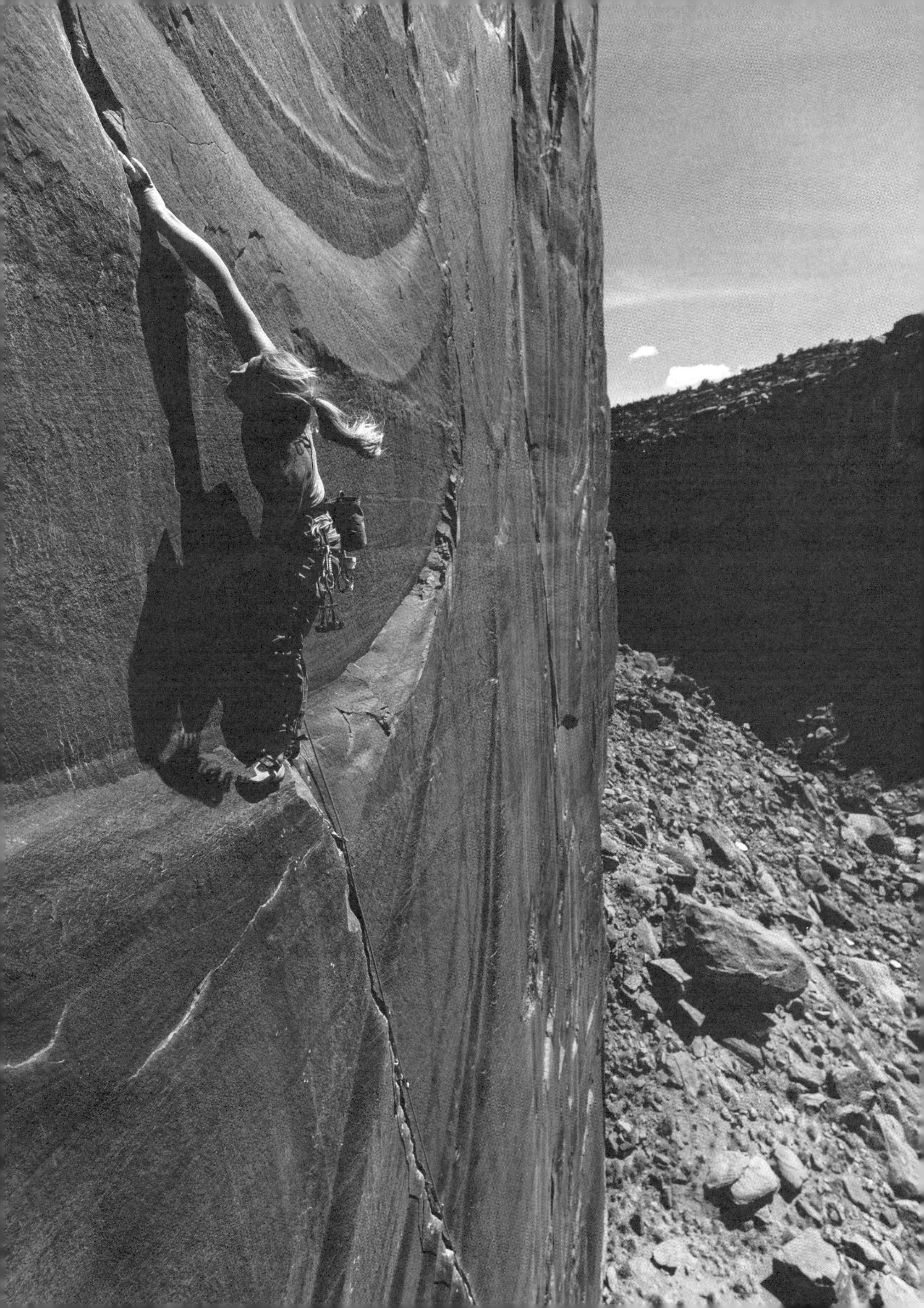

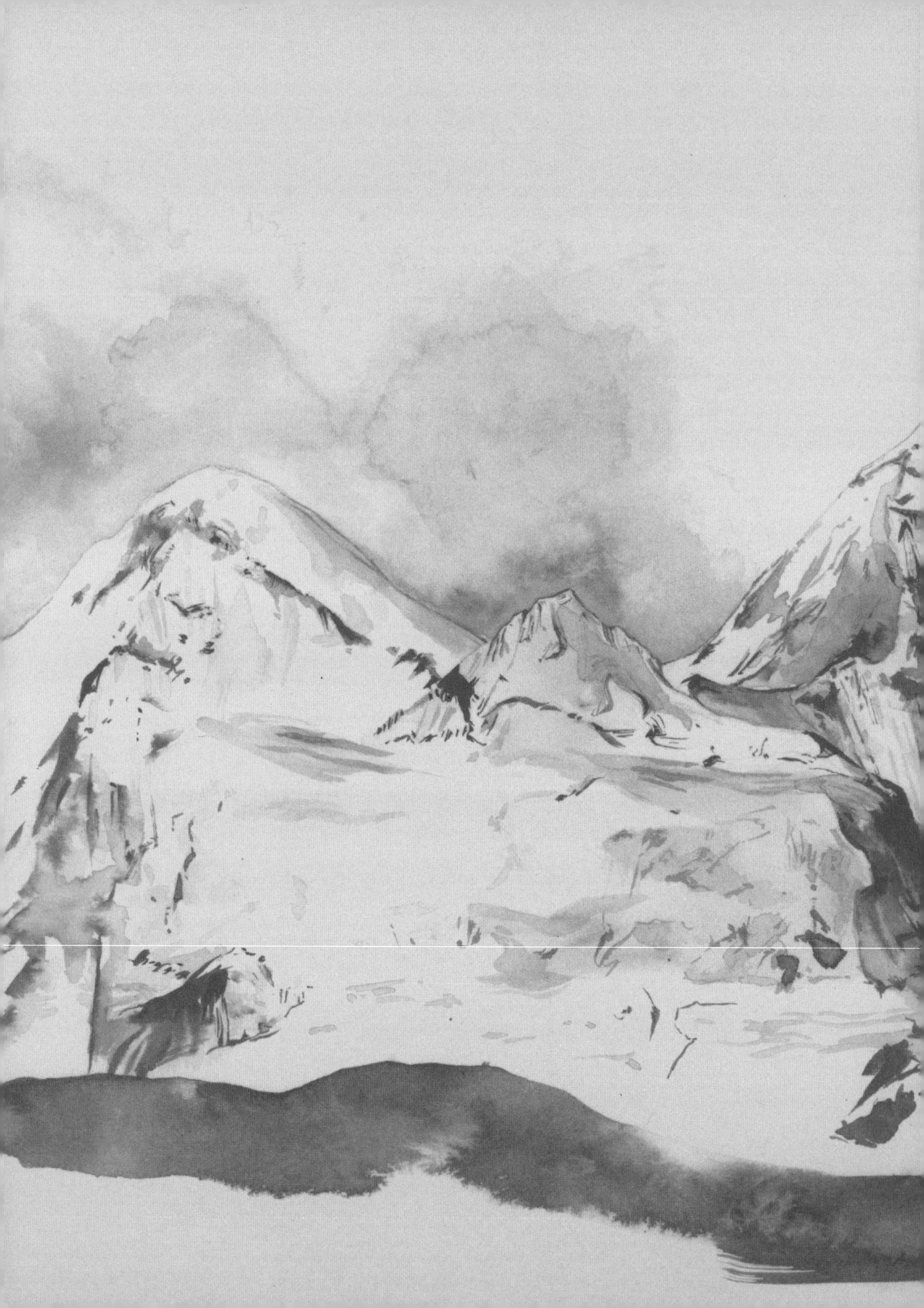

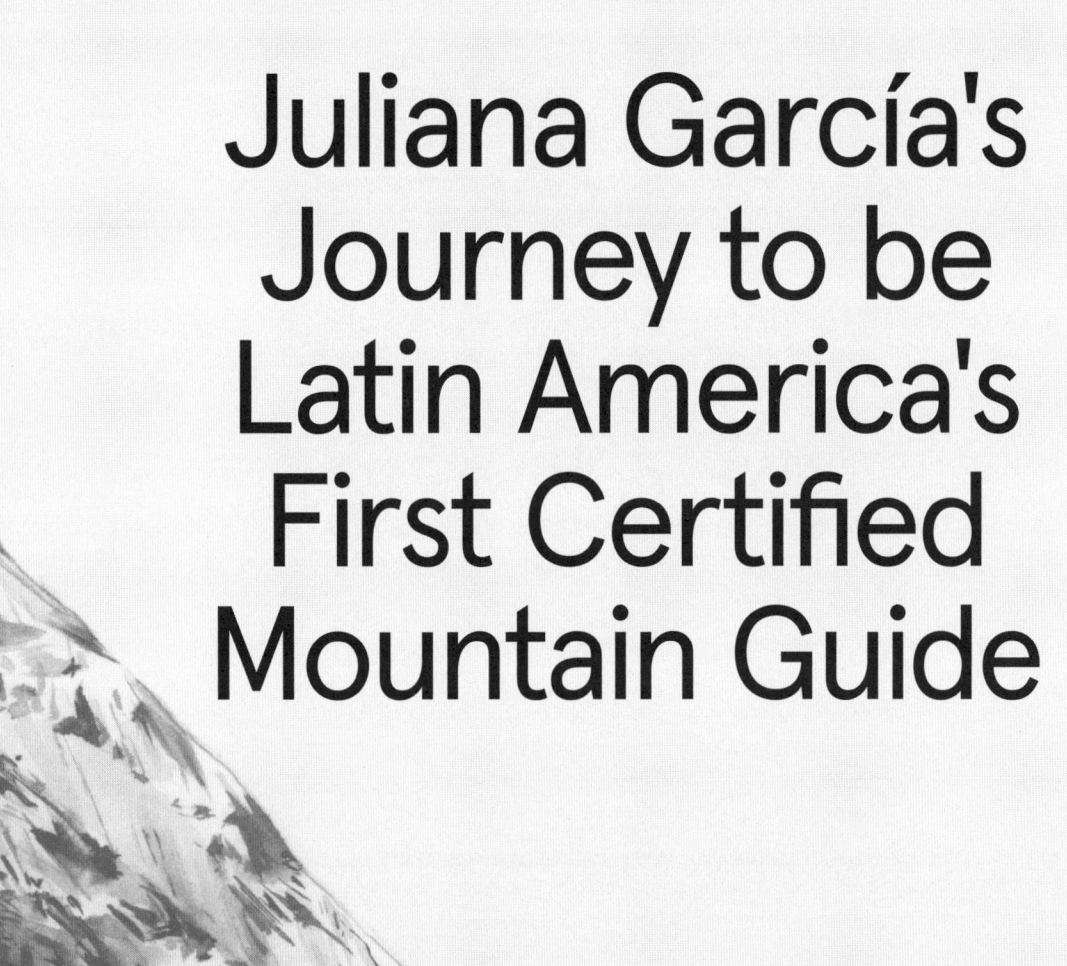

Juliana García's Journey to be Latin America's First Certified Mountain Guide

With each kick of her cramponed feet on the northwest face of Huandoy Este in the Peruvian Cordillera Blanca, Juliana García was gaining the valuable alpine experience she needed to become one of the most pivotal figures in Latin American climbing. A successful first ascent of this peak would mean another piece of valuable knowledge collected, ready to be used on another mountain at another time, to round out her already impressive list of climbs.

JULIANA GARCÍA

Nationality:
Ecuadorian

Born:
29 August 1984

Active:
1999–present

Opposite: Juliana García climbing on Huandoy Este.
Below: Juliana García during her graduation as an IFMGA high-mountain guide in Quito, Ecuador.

At that moment, however, high up in the Andes, García and her partner Joshua Jarrin were just trying to establish a new alpine route safely. They had approached the massive face of Huandoy Este the day before, working their way through complex moraines and boulder fields to reach the base of the climb at the bergschrund, where the glacier pulled away from the rock. The sustained seventy-degree slope of dense snow above, interwoven with steep rock bands, was a challenge. Most of García's previous experience was on simpler climbs on relatively easy South American volcanos. With some alpine climbing under her belt in both Peru and Ecuador, Huandoy Este was vital preparation for her official guide's training. No Latin American woman had ever attempted to become a globally certified mountain guide before, nor had they established a new climbing route.

Not one to be dissuaded by history, García pressed on. After one bivouac on the snowy slope and tackling 700 metres (2,297 feet) of mixed snow, ice and rock climbing, the duo reached the summit ridge. Huge cornices that could fall off at any moment prevented them from reaching the true summit, but their newly established route to the ridge had been aesthetically stunning, and had taken just thirty-six hours. Poco a poco, little by little, step by step, García would overcome the barriers that confronted her at every turn.

Juliana García was born in Quito, Ecuador, to parents who encouraged her adventurous spirit. When she was just thirteen, they allowed her, along with her classmates, to cycle from Ecuador to Brazil, a journey that took an astounding five months. On this first proper adventure, García learned the true meaning of hard work and that breaking down a challenge into small pieces will eventually lead to a positive outcome. She learned about camping and living in a tent for months on end, and the need to support her companions when their morale was low. These were all lessons that would prove useful later on, when she chose to make a life in the mountains.

By the time she was fourteen, García had shown interest in climbing and mountaineering, so her parents enrolled her in Aire Libre, a climbing programme led by noted Ecuadorian climber Fabian Zurita. The group's goal was to spend a year training and climbing in preparation for an ascent of Cotopaxi, a renowned volcano visible from Quito. With sessions held every other weekend, the group of ninety participants was eventually whittled down to just fifteen, and García was one of the youngest. When summit day came, the climbers found themselves at the top of the peak in terrible cloud and fog, but nothing could have been more beautiful to García. She knew, just as her parents had, that her natural talent for climbing couldn't be ignored.

García would go on to summit Cotopaxi many more times. She recognized in herself not only a natural affinity for climbing but also an ability to lead others. She felt comfortable at high altitudes in the harsh environment of the alpine, and she enjoyed learning about safety and technique. She felt a strong sense of belonging and enjoyed the peace of the alpine environment, which made her feel alive. She had found her place in the world.

When she was seventeen, García made her first trip to Peru, invited by experienced friends to hike to remote basecamps situated below some of the Andes' most famous peaks. The Cordillera Blanca captured her heart immediately and after she had taken her first steps on its majestic flanks, she returned to the mountain range consistently each season for seventeen years. It was on one of these trips to Peru that the seed for climbing Huandoy Este had been planted.

After her first expeditions to Peru, García decided to become a mountain guide. At eighteen, she trained in Ecuador with the Asociación Ecuatoriana de Guías de Montaña (ASEGUIM). To get her certification, she needed to climb lots of peaks and pass examinations. García knew that she was capable of realizing her goal, but was also intensely aware of the gender politics at play in Latin America, where an atmosphere of machismo still reigned supreme.

Once enrolled, García discovered that the rules would be different for her and her male counterparts. The instructors and examiners were unsure of how to treat García, unaware of her capabilities, as they had only had male aspirants before her. Some of her fellow guides felt that things were intentionally made more difficult for her. These episodes of chauvinism almost forced García to give up, but in the end, determined not to let her dreams be shattered by discrimination, she persevered and earned her Ecuadorian guide's certificate.

The ASEGUIM and its system of guides' training and certification was not yet internationally recognized by the IFMGA – the International Federation of Mountain Guides Associations. This meant that García couldn't be a mountain guide abroad. In order to gain globally recognized, fully certified guide status, she would have to do additional training in either Bolivia, Peru or Argentina, the only three countries in Latin America that were representatives of the IFMGA. She would also need to have more variety in her climbing experience – on peaks like Huandoy Este.

After García and Jarrin reached the summit ridge of Huandoy Este, they celebrated briefly before beginning a series of difficult abseils to return to base. Exposure to rockfall was their greatest concern as they made their way down. Only after they had retraced their steps over the

Summit - 6,070 m/19,915 ft

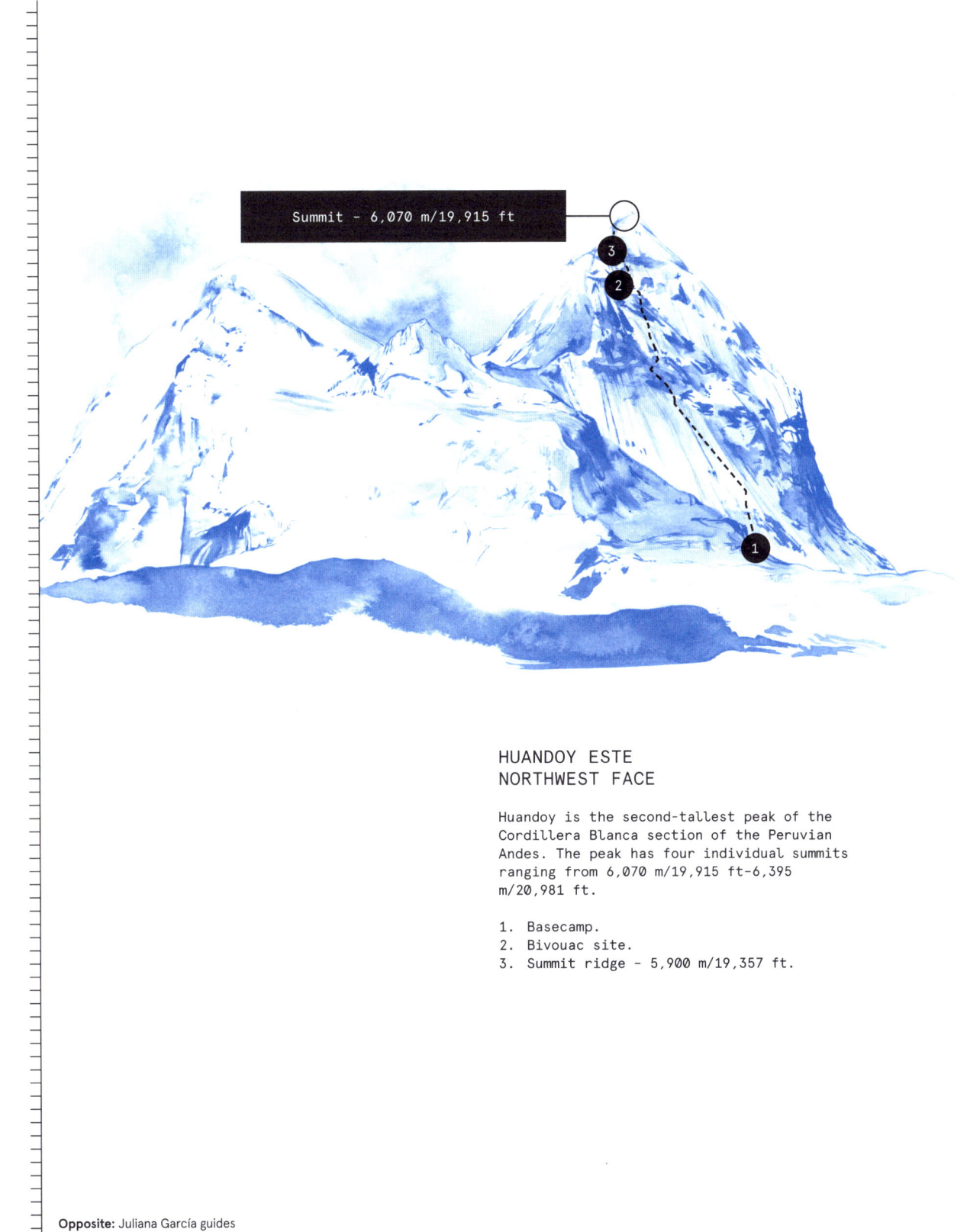

HUANDOY ESTE
NORTHWEST FACE

Huandoy is the second-tallest peak of the Cordillera Blanca section of the Peruvian Andes. The peak has four individual summits ranging from 6,070 m/19,915 ft-6,395 m/20,981 ft.

1. Basecamp.
2. Bivouac site.
3. Summit ridge - 5,900 m/19,357 ft.

Opposite: Juliana García guides a client in South America.

glacier and were finally making their way back to the village of Huarez did the success of the climb really sink in. It was a pivotal moment for García. She finally believed that she had the skills necessary to lead others and show them the magic of the mountains.

Once news of their ascent reached international climbing circles, the new route was recognized by the committee of the Piolets d'Or as a notable ascent in 2013. The Piolets d'Or (literally 'golden ice axes') is considered the Oscars for mountaineering, and it is an honour for your climb to make the longlist. Few South American climbers had been recognized before, and this was the first time a woman from the continent was given a nod by the European committee.

García set out to begin her IFMGA training in Bolivia in 2013. She was the only female aspirant during the three-month intensive training regime. She completed various skills and safety exercises daily. Her instructors didn't communicate with her well, likely due to their prejudices about women's capabilities. They had never had a woman candidate before. García thought she had performed well, but when it came time for the graduates to be announced, she was ignored and, to her dismay, realized that she had failed the training. Her IFMGA instructors gave her no indication of how close she was to passing, nor did they provide feedback on what skills she needed to work on. It was as though she had never been there. Confused but undeterred, García continued to climb and sought answers in the mountains she loved.

Two years after her success on Huandoy Este and after the disappointment of her training in Bolivia, García was elected President of ASEGUIM. With her friend Jarrin as Technical Director, they set out to make positive changes to the organization. Their first priority was to get their Ecuadorian guides' training and certification recognized by the IFMGA. Doing so would elevate the status of guides in the country and help the pair to realize their second goal: to lobby the Ecuadorian government to formalize the work of guides as an official profession. Both of these objectives would ensure standardization of safety and training protocols and would also enable ASEGUIM to purchase important insurance for its members.

García thrived in her role as ASEGUIM President and was elected to a second term. She served without pay in this role from 2015 to 2021 and huge progress was made with the IFMGA: they finally confirmed Ecuador as a member country for mountain-guiding instruction and certification standards. In 2017, the IFMGA also awarded García her official guide's pin. After years of training and hard work, she became the first Latin American IFMGA-certified mountain guide.

'Poco a Poco, little by little, step by step, García would overcome the barriers that confronted her at every turn.'

INFO

THE HIGHEST PEAKS IN SOUTH AMERICA

Listed in order of highest to lowest:

ACONCAGUA
Argentina
(6,961 m/22,838 ft)

OJOS DEL SABADO
Argentina/Chile
(6,893 m/22,615 ft)

MONTE PISSIS
Argentina
(6,793 m/22,287 ft)

HUASCARÁN
Peru
(6,768 m/22,205 ft)

CERRO BONETE
Argentina
(6,759 m/22,175 ft)

NEVADA TRES CRUCES
Argentina/Chile
(6,753 m/22,156 ft)

LLULLAILLACO
Argentina/Chile
(6,739 m/22,110 ft)

YERUPAJÁ
Peru
(6,632 m/21,759 ft)

NEVADA SAJAMA
Bolivia
(6,542 m/21,463 ft)

CHIMBORAZO
Ecuador
(6,268 m/20,564 ft)

García was finally able to work as a guide outside of Ecuador and led groups in the mountains all over South America, Greenland, the USA and Greece. When, in 2019, an opportunity came up to be part of the Board of Directors for the IFMGA, García jumped at the chance. She knew that although Ecuador was now a full member of the association, there was still a lot of work to be done to elevate the status of Ecuadorian guides in the eyes of other member nations. García was the first non-European to be elected to the Board, male or female. With her new position, she began to advocate for her small nation, and other Latin American countries. She worked with the largely European organization to embrace a less colonial view of the climbing communities there. Finally, Latin America had a voice at the table.

The intellectual work that her term on the IFMGA Board provided was gratifying to García. Alongside her career as a guide and certification instructor for ASEGUIM, she thrived in her role and improved external communication for the organization significantly. In 2023, after two terms on the Board, she was recognized as an honorary member, once again setting a new precedent for Latin American women. Little by little, García has realized her dream and set a new path, one that is wide open for other women to follow.

Juliana García overcame many barriers that still exist for Latin American women, and she has become a mentor to an entire new generation of female Ecuadorian climbers. Since the global recognition that her IFMGA certification has brought, and her gender advocacy work, many aspiring young women guides have reached out to thank her for her pioneering work in the industry. García continues to pursue a life of learning and training to this day. In addition to international guiding and certifying new Ecuadorian guides, she provides avalanche training in various countries and is rounding out her mountain skillset by improving her skiing, a sport she took up just seven years ago.

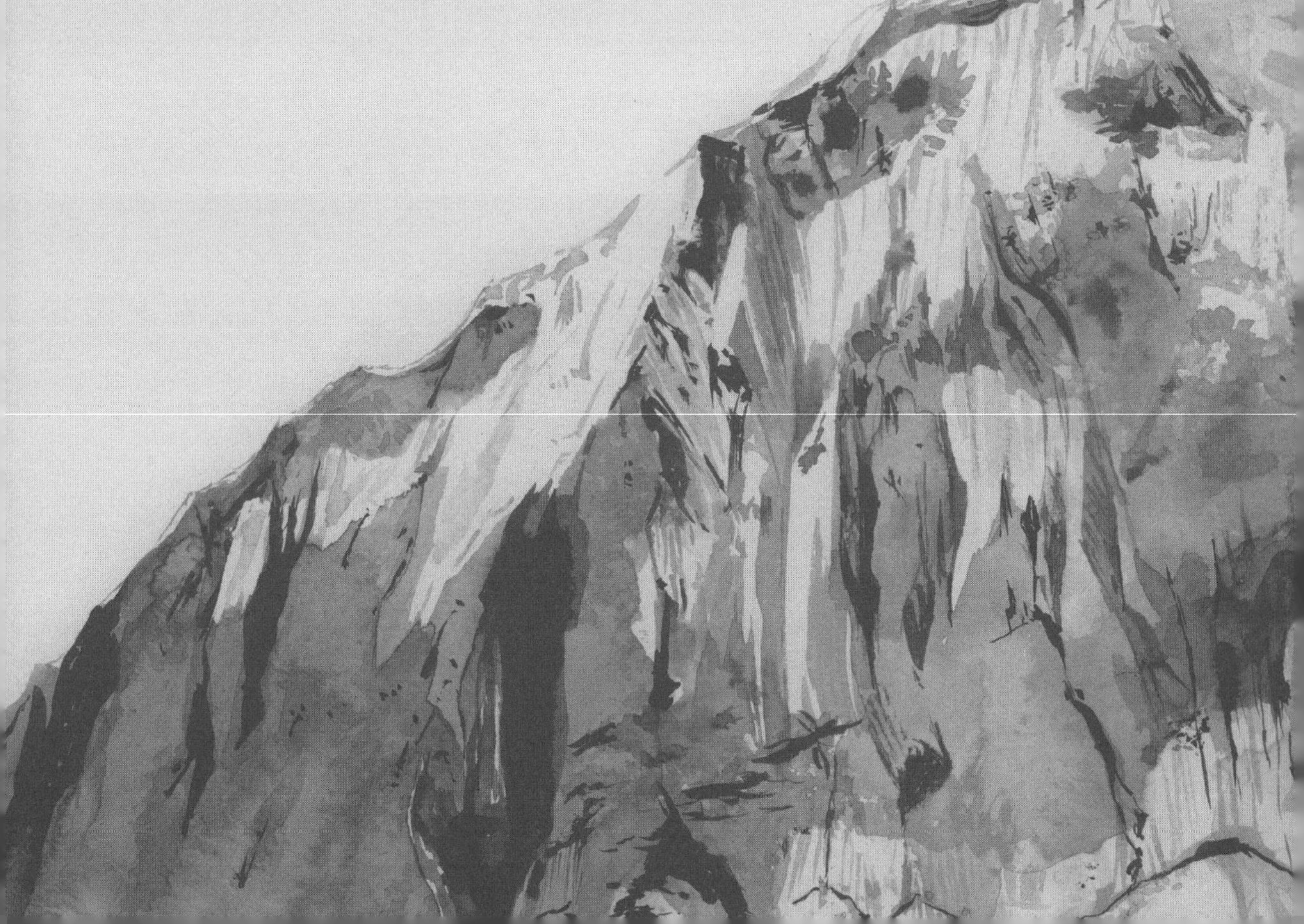

Sharon Wood's Discoveries in the Andes

For Canadian climber Sharon Wood, the important climbs in her life have always been about the process. Summits were never about fame or fortune, but about the craft and self-discovery that every moment at high altitude brings. Wood is most celebrated as the first North American woman to reach the top of Mount Everest. Although Everest changed her life, she considers Huascarán Sur in the Andes, and a climb of its northeast face, the most important in her career, which shaped her as a person.

SHARON WOOD

Nationality:
Canadian

Born:
18 May 1957

Active:
1972-present

Opposite: Last light on the upper Anqosh Face of Huascarán Sur.
Below: Huascarán Norte behind Sharon Wood on the headwall.

The Andes in the 1980s were still incredibly remote, providing climbers with some of the greatest opportunities for first ascents of 'unclimbed' high-altitude peaks. The history of Indigenous climbing in the region is largely undocumented in English-language sources, but there is archaeological evidence that Andean Indigenous cultures climbed peaks, particularly volcanos, as part of traditional rituals. Since the onset of mountaineering by Europeans, the Andes have been considered one of the more serious testing grounds for alpinists before making their entrance into the grand theatre of the Himalayas. There were not yet any large commercial expedition operations in the Andes at that time, just small, self-sufficient European and American teams, mostly intent on establishing new routes and making a name for themselves in the climbing community.

Huascarán was never on the agenda when Wood and her partner Carlos Buhler ventured down to Peru in the spring of 1985. They had their sights on other objectives, including the impossibly pointy peak of Chacraraju. But the 6,108-metre (20,039-foot) mountain eluded them. Conditions on Chacraraju were unfavourable, and there was a real risk of a cornice collapsing on them on their proposed, precarious south-face route. At the eleventh hour, with only seven days until their return flight to Canada, they abandoned their efforts on Chacraraju. After packing up their camp, the clouds parted in the distance, revealing Huascarán Sur and her mighty northeast face, also known as the Anqosh Face. Not much needed to be said. It was clear where this trip was destined to take them.

Just months earlier, before her departure to South America, Wood had been invited to be part of a small but prestigious team of Canadian climbers who would attempt the difficult west ridge of Everest in the spring of 1986. This climb from the Tibetan side, without supplemental oxygen, would be a formidable achievement. In 1963, Americans Tom Hornbein and Willi Unsoeld pioneered a route from the Nepali side, but Wood and her team would be entering new territory by attempting to ascend from the north. If they were successful, Wood would also become the first North American woman to summit Everest, and it would be in the best of climbing styles: a small team on a hard route, without supplemental oxygen. Wood questioned whether she was up for the challenge, but hoped a long season of climbing in the Andes would provide her with some answers. So she went to South America intent on gaining more high-altitude experience on hard climbs. She wanted to know how she would react both mentally and physically when the stakes were high.

Huascarán Sur is part of the Cordillera Blanca range of the Western Andes and at 6,768 metres (22,205 feet), it is the highest mountain in Peru. Its twin summits are divided by a large saddle known locally as La Garganta, translated simply as the Pass. US climber Annie Peck Smith made the first ascent of Huascarán Norte (the north summit is approximately 100 metres/328 feet lower than the south summit) in 1908, and the south summit was climbed in 1932 by a German/Austrian team. By 1950, there had been only three ascents of Huascarán Sur, all by the easiest, 'normal' route.

When Wood and Buhler made their way to the base of the mountain in 1985, no one had attempted a route on the mighty Anqosh Face that loomed above them. They would have to weave their way through ice features and rock bands to reach the summit ridge. The majority of climbing would have to be done before the heat of the day kicked in. Once the sun's rays began to melt the snow and ice above, rocks and debris could come hurtling down, increasing the danger on the route with each warming degree. Although this climb was Wood and Buhler's plan B, it was by no means a sure thing – they would have to work hard for a first ascent on this face of the mountain. The climb was a complex, multi-day challenge for any experienced alpinist, but Wood and Buhler had been in Peru for months. They were acclimatized and ready for action.

At first light, determined to get the climb underway, the duo threaded their way up through the complex icefield that led them to the base of the vertical climbing. They dodged crevasses and managed the approach so efficiently that what they thought might take a day only took hours. From the safety of the bergschrund, with the face still in shadow, Wood glanced up at their intended route and surmised that the day was still cool enough to press on. She started up the first ice pitch with her ice axes and crampons, hoping to reach a rockband some 100 metres (around 300 feet) above, where they could settle in, out of the line of fire of any potential rockfall, when the heat of the day arrived. Rhythmically, she swung her ice axes, leaving Buhler to belay her from the safety of the icy bergschrund below.

From the start of the trip to the Andes, Wood had been battling with low self-confidence, something that had plagued her most of her adult life. A decade before, she had been up Mount Logan, Canada's highest mountain, and she'd also climbed Mount Robson, a daunting peak in the Canadian Rockies. She had also completed an ascent on the difficult south face of Aconcagua, South America's highest peak, and had been to Makalu in Nepal. On this Andean trip she'd managed two solo ascents on other Peruvian peaks, but even so, Wood couldn't shake the

'The fear of failure served me well. I feared it more than the consequences of pushing on. Every experience, epic setback and conquest was an investment in getting better. Better is always possible. I thrived by that tenet. Pain and suffering were necessary precursors to the realization of my potential.'

– Sharon Wood

Summit - 6,768 m/22,205 ft

HUASCARÁN SUR
ANQOSH FACE

Huascarán is situated in the Cordillera Blanca range of the Western Andes. The southern summit, Huascarán Sur, is the highest point in Peru.

1. Line of ascent.
2. Summit.
3. Line of descent. Route down to La Garganta, the saddle leading to Huscarán Norte.

SHARON WOOD

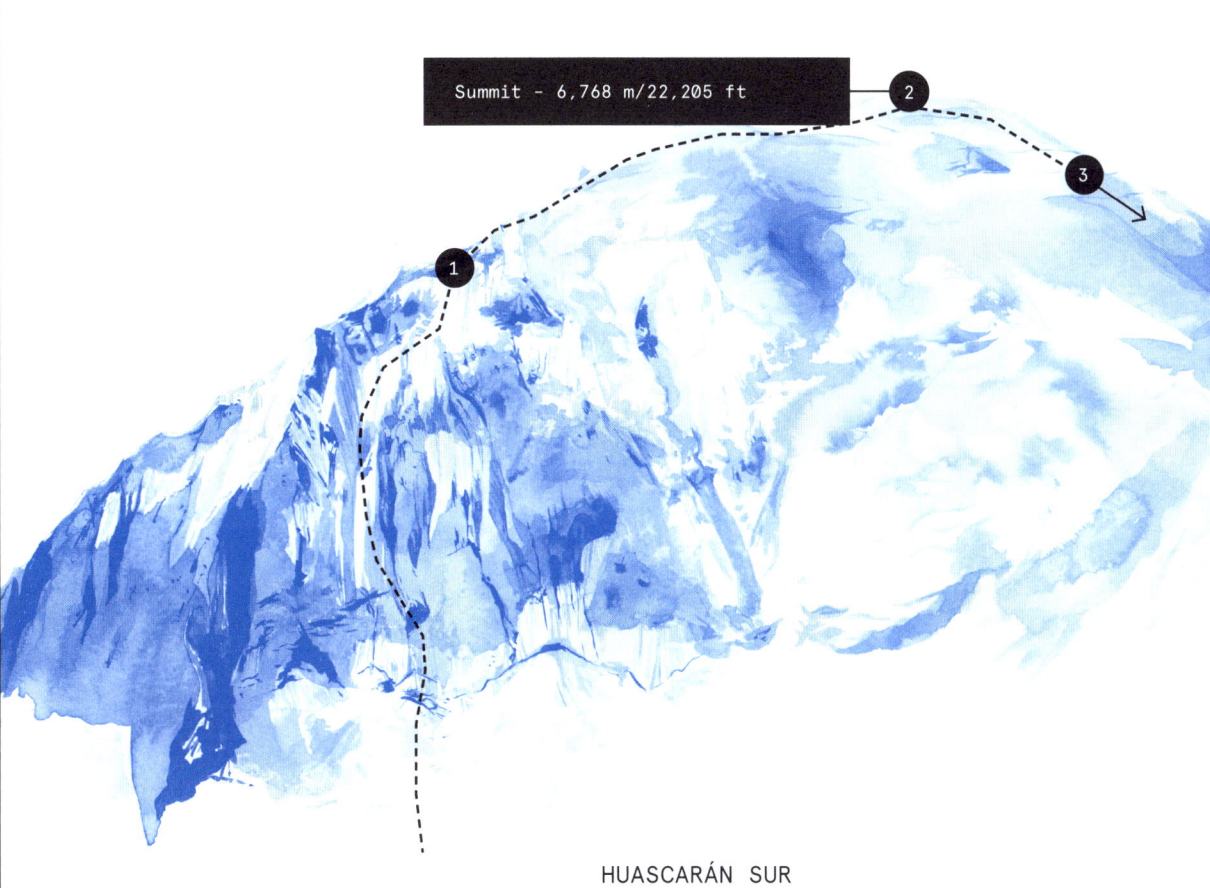

feeling that she wasn't good enough. If she found success on the technically challenging terrain of Huascarán, she would prove to herself that she was a true alpinist, ready for even bigger summits, particularly those in the Himalaya.

Just as Wood reached the end of her ropes and was placing an ice screw so she could build a belay station to bring Buhler up to her, her worst fears were realized. The sun was hitting the face and had begun to melt the terrain towering above. A flurry of rocks plummeted down, one large rock landing squarely on her right shoulder. The only thing that saved her from being raked off the face was the loop of rope she'd slipped over the head of the ice screw. The blow slammed her against the face. The crampons on her feet slipped as she scrambled for purchase. It could have meant a harrowing fall, and almost certain death, had Wood not instinctively pressed herself as flat as she could against the ice wall, allowing the torrent to pass over her. Once the rocks stopped their barrage, she quickly reviewed her body and realized her right arm was intact but rendered useless. She tried to descend quickly, avoiding more rock bombardments, as she rappelled one-handed down to Buhler in the bergschrund, where a deeper physical assessment could be made.

That night, while recovering from her injury, Wood re-evaluated her decision to move up the mountain so quickly. She obsessively reviewed the day's events in her mind. Had she been so eager to reach the summit that it had clouded her judgement? What would this injury mean to their chances of success on the peak? Had she ruined the entire trip for both of them? And what about the upcoming expedition to Everest? These questions weighed heavily on her as she tried to rest.

With the light of dawn, Wood could tell that her arm had improved but wasn't perfect. She had some increased mobility, which encouraged her enough to agree with Buhler that they could continue, despite the intense pain she felt when she reached above her head.

Buhler started up the face, regaining Wood's ground from the day before. In the shade of the morning, the pair climbed as fast as they could to reach a rock ledge where they could spend the hottest part of the day. As the sun hit them, they snoozed, and in the evening, they continued higher, once again taking advantage of cooler conditions. Wood adapted her climbing style, using her right arm mostly in a mid-to-lower range of motion, stabbing at the ice from her waist and employing only her left arm when reaching high above her head. After a few hours, she felt strong enough to take her turn to lead the climb again, with Buhler following behind.

'Just as Wood reached the end of her ropes and was placing an ice screw so she could build a belay station to bring Buhler up to her, her worst fears were realized. The sun was hitting the face and had begun to melt the terrain towering above.'

'This climb, I reasoned, was a practice joust, which diminished the gravity of our circumstances. Everest loomed. Huascarán was essential to earning my worth on the team. There was no one I needed to prove that to more than myself. Only Huascarán could resolve my doubt.'[1]

Pretty soon, Wood and Buhler passed the point of no return. They were now fully committed to the peak – retreating now would be more problematic than continuing up. The possibility of rescue was minuscule and the only choice was to press on. The duo spent several uncomfortable nights at inadequate bivouacs, some only big enough to allow them a cold seated perch. Wood's arm continued to give her trouble. She distracted herself from the pain by focusing on the precarious climbing moves she needed to perform. By now her head was throbbing too, most likely a result of her injury, in combination with dehydration and the effects of altitude.

After four days and nights on the vertical face, Wood and Buhler finally reached the snowy summit ridge. After tunnelling through the meringue-like cornice that blocked their passage and marked the final obstacle on the route, they emerged exhausted. Out of water and food, they were discouraged by what they saw. The summit was shrouded in mist and clouds, and still looked far away – not to mention that the pinnacle only represented the halfway point. The descent via the normal route towards La Garganta still remained. Feeling defeated, they hunkered down, setting up another precarious bivouac on the platform they had carved out in the snow. With nothing to eat or drink, they could do little but rest.

Wood continually processed the pain in her arm and shoulder. 'Pain is just information,' she told herself, testing her ability to withstand discomfort. Aware that she would need to know how much she could endure if she was to attempt Everest, failure on Huascarán was not acceptable. It was all or nothing.

At first light, they left their perilous bivouac and made short work of the summit ridge, which turned out to be less daunting than they'd anticipated. But just as they summited, the clouds rolled in, rendering them effectively blind. Although the descent path they were seeking was relatively easy, they could not find the beginning of the route in the whiteout. Instead, they were forced to spend another waterless and fuel-less night high on the mountain.

Weakened from lack of food, the pair rose early the next morning and in their dehydrated state moved slowly, stumbling often, inching their way down. After some hours, they eventually found the well-used mountaineering track up the 'normal route' they had been seeking. It brought them directly to the safety of La Garganta and a climbers' camp, where they were offered food and water. Already putting the worst parts of their epic journey behind them, they stuffed themselves and recounted the climb with pride.

Three days later, Wood and Buhler were back in Canada reflecting on what must have felt like a dream. A new route, in alpine style, on the northeast face of Huascarán Sur was quite an achievement and the climb was recognized in the community as a symbol of indomitable spirit, especially when Wood learned that she had, in fact, fractured her shoulder. In the eyes of the media, this made for an even better story. In Wood's mind, it meant she was, finally, ready for Everest.

At 9 p.m. on 20 May 1986, Wood and Canadian climber Dwayne Congdon reached the summit of Everest via the west ridge from Tibet. The climb was challenging, just as Wood had expected, and the team did end up using supplemental oxygen at their highest camp. The politics at basecamp had not been easy. Another woman, US climber Annie Whitehouse, was poised to try to reach the top as well. She was supported by a US expedition that was comprised of several climbers, including none other than Buhler, Wood's former partner. Despite the drama, Wood was successful, and when she returned to Canada, she was celebrated as the first North American woman to reach the top of the world. In the years that followed, Wood shared her experiences on Everest as a motivational speaker and for four decades she continued to guide others up the peaks in her own backyard. She founded an alternative educational school in the Canadian Rockies, is a recipient of the Governor General's Award and continues to climb to this day.

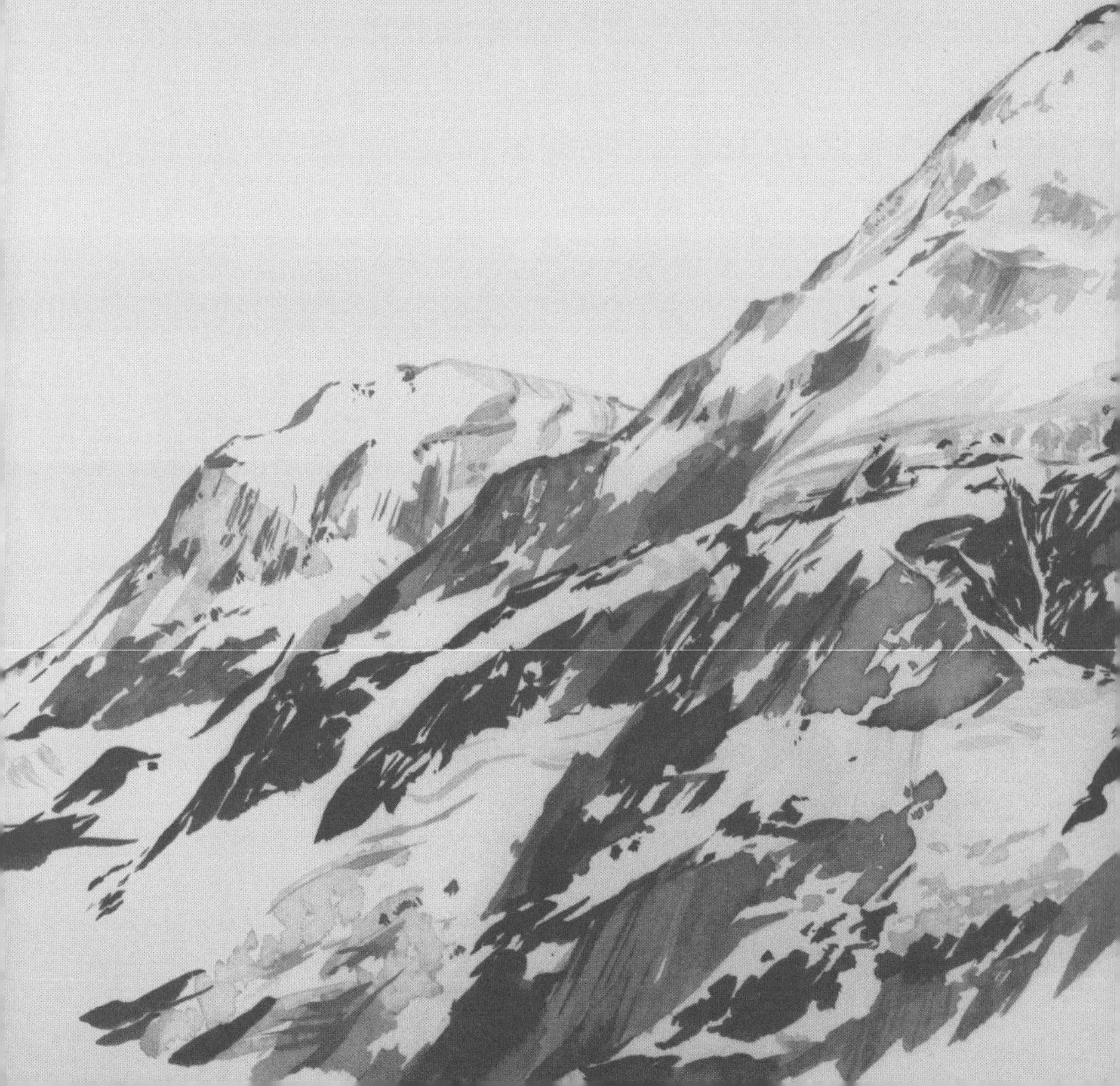

Lydia Bradey and Her Solo Ascent of Everest

The year is 1988. Imagine that you are about to embark
on the biggest climb of your life, tackling Mount Everest.
Imagine you have trained for this moment for a decade.
If you succeed, you will be the first woman to ascend
Mount Everest solo, without the use of supplemental oxygen.
Imagine you reach the summit. Exhausted but elated,
you make your way to basecamp. Now imagine that
when you arrive there, you learn that some of your
expedition team have died on their climb. The rest of
the team has abandoned you, spreading vicious rumours
denying your achievement. You are called to prove your
claim and the moment of glory is overshadowed by
doubt and jealousy; the controversy will carry on
for years. This is the story of Lydia Bradey.

LYDIA BRADEY

Nationality:
New Zealand

Born:
9 October 1961

Active:
1975-present

Opposite: Lydia Bradey on the summit of Everest, 19 May 2016.
Below: Photographer Xavier Raoux and Lydia Bradey at Everest basecamp, 1988.

Lydia Bradey was raised by a single mother in Christchurch, New Zealand. As a child, she hated sports, once vomiting out of fear before a school sports day. She much preferred writing poetry or reading books and thought that she would one day make a fine barrister. It seemed unlikely that she would end up climbing on the big walls of Yosemite or in the Himalayas, and even guide others on these massive peaks.

After a trip to the mountains of New Zealand with a youth tramping group at the age of fourteen, Bradey discovered, much to her surprise, that she quite liked walking in the fresh air among the peaks. When her instructor suggested that someday some of the youth might not just walk but climb the mountains, she became obsessed with the idea. By the time Bradey turned eighteen, she had climbed both Mount Aspiring (3,033 metres/9,951 feet) and Aoraki (3,724 metres/12,218 feet), serious mountaineering endeavours involving rope skills and glacier travel. The New Zealand Alps proved to be a perfect training ground and once she'd completed many of the classic routes in her country, she turned her attentions abroad.

Bradey flew to Alaska with bold ambitions to do the American Direct route on Denali with two climbing partners. After relentless storms, they realized that ascending Denali was no easy feat; cold temperatures, poor weather and altitude sickness plagued them and eventually the expedition fell apart, with each team member learning a valuable lesson: never underestimate the severity of your climb.

Bradey arrived in Yosemite from Alaska via Squamish, British Columbia, where she had managed her first big-wall climbs using aid technique, something she hoped to refine on the grand walls of El Capitan. At times her zeal outmatched her skills, but she eventually climbed one of the most famous aid routes on El Capitan, Zodiac, over the course of five days with a friend, John Middendorf, making her the first woman to do so. In the three summers she spent there, she would complete the first female ascent and second overall ascent of Sunkist, a difficult aid route that she and her partner knew very little about before they stepped on to the rock. Sunkist was a formative climb, a cerebral endeavour and the test piece she needed to confirm that both her body and mind could perform under challenging conditions. With ten big-wall ascents and seven first female ascents to her name, Bradey decided she was ready to try her luck above 8,000 metres (26,247 feet) in the Himalayas.

In 1984, the world's sixth highest mountain, Cho Oyu, had yet to be climbed by a woman, so Bradey jumped at the chance to join a joint British–New Zealand team. The team had an ambitious goal – to attempt a new route from the Nepali side. For its climbing permit to be approved, the

MOUNT EVEREST
SOUTH COL ROUTE

Lydia Bradey has climbed Mount Everest six times. Five of those summits were reached via the South Col route, including her first ascent without supplemental oxygen.

1. Lhotse Face – the steep ice wall leads to Camp 4 on the South Col.
2. Camp 3.
3. The Balcony.
4. South Summit.

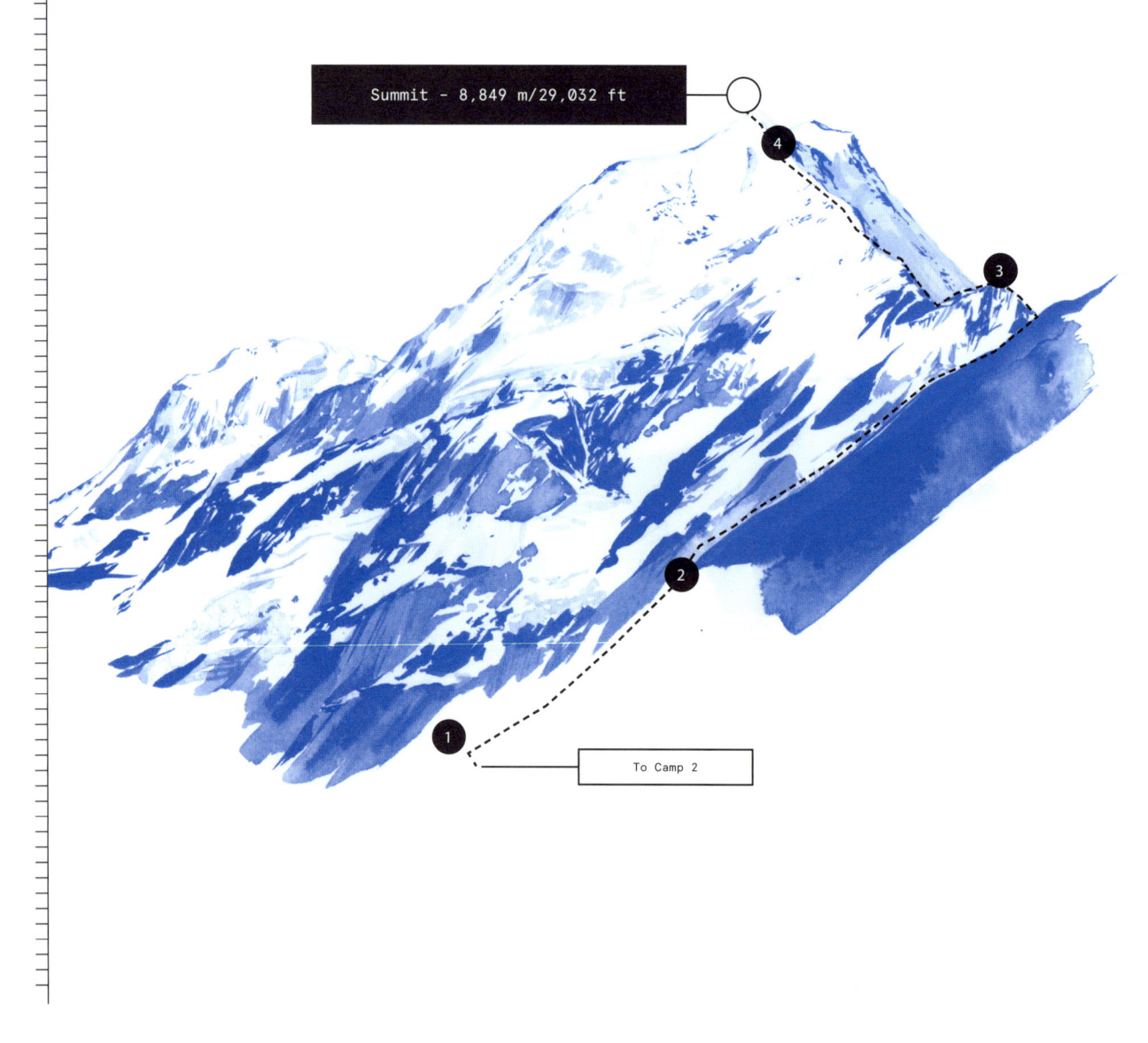

Summit – 8,849 m/29,032 ft

To Camp 2

team would have to include Nepalis as climbing members; despite the fact that Cho Oyu was in Nepal, no Nepali had been to its summit. Although Bradey did not reach the top of the mountain, she gained valuable experience on the expedition, particularly discovering how her body would react at altitude and navigating team dynamics. She wrote, 'This is what I learned from Cho Oyu; I was strong; I had done my best and not let the team down. I was determined to return, even stronger than before'.[1]

In the years that followed, Bradey was invited to join a number of expeditions to the Himalaya, including one to Gangkhar Puensum in Bhutan, as well as one to Kedarnath Dome in India and the Gasherbrums in Pakistan in 1987. The conditions on Kedarnath Dome were extremely challenging as their descent was hit by a powerful storm. After being caught in several significant avalanches, one of which buried Bradey as she slept in a snow cave, she and her climbing partner finally made it down after eight days on the mountain. Shaken but seemingly undaunted, Bradey was on her way to the Gasherbrums a week later.

In the mid-eighties, climbs in the mighty Baltoro Glacier region meant fourteen days of hiking simply to reach basecamp, a journey that takes less than half that time today. It was a remote place with little chance of immediate rescue and no modern weather forecasting. The Gasherbrum expedition was organized by New Zealand mountaineer and guide Rob Hall, who would factor heavily in Bradey's life later on. The team planned to climb Gasherbrum I via the northwest ridge, though Hall was unable to join because of an injury.

Bradey and her team made steady upwards progress in preparation for their summit bid. When four Pakistani climbers from another expedition were swept to their deaths by an avalanche, Bradey and other climbers at basecamp went up to retrieve the bodies, an episode that weighed heavily on her at such a young age. She and her companions continued their summit bid with heavy hearts but abandoned their efforts after weeks of gruelling effort.

When other climbers at basecamp started packing up to head back to Islamabad, Bradey convinced a few that they should have a go at Gasherbrum II, which seemed to have better snow conditions. They had acclimatized so well in their preparation for Gasherbrum I that they approached this climb alpine style, in a single push up the mountain from basecamp. With her summit, Bradey became the first Australasian woman to summit an 8,000-metre (26,247-foot) peak. When she spied K2 from the climb, she knew she had to add it to her list.

Along with fellow Kiwi climbers Rob Hall and Gary Ball, Bradey set to work preparing for their next Himalayan adventure. This expedition would have a double objective: climbing the world's two highest summits – K2 and Everest – in the same year without oxygen. Bradey and Ball secured sponsorship while Hall dealt with the difficult task of obtaining permits. Bradey didn't own a car, so she biked to and from prospective funder meetings all over Christchurch, which was a welcome contribution to her training regime. The team spent three months in Pakistan between May and August 1988, before transferring to Mount Everest in mid-August for a summit attempt.

The expedition was wrought with tension from the start. Not only was there political unrest in the area, but Bradey felt isolated as the only female, a sentiment exacerbated by travel through the strict Muslim country, where virtually no women were seen in public. However, her worries lifted as soon as K2 came into sight. They set up basecamp, found their daily rhythm and were soon neighbours to a US climbing team, whose members Bradey befriended immediately.

The teams worked together preparing for their summit bids. Hall chastized Bradey for spending too much time with the Americans, as well as Slovenian and Spanish teams, which created a rift between them. To make matters worse, Ball sided with him. In the end, all the disagreements were for nothing as the weather window they hoped for never materialized, dashing their hopes for a successful summit. The tensions lingered, however, and would eventually come to a head when the team moved to Nepal.

After only three days' rest in Kathmandu, the New Zealanders began the trek to Everest basecamp. Along the multi-day journey, they met up with the Slovakian team that was climbing on the same permit; while the New Zealanders had raised money for the expedition, the Slovaks provided the climbing permit and specialized equipment needed to support both groups. The Slovaks had applied to climb both Lhotse and Everest via the difficult southwest face. The New Zealanders, in theory, were meant to climb the southwest face as well but knew they lacked the technical expertise, so they planned to formally alter their route choice at basecamp once they met up with their liaison officer.

Once they reached basecamp and began rope fixing through the Khumbu Icefall, tensions rose between the Slovaks and the Kiwis, both claiming that the other team wasn't pulling its weight. Bradey was caught in the middle, but eventually sought comfort with her new Slovakian friends. They encouraged her to try and climb the mountain without oxygen. Having witnessed her physical strength during acclimatization, they felt she was fit enough. If successful, she would be the first woman to do so.

When news came from the liaison officer that the Nepali government had denied the New Zealanders' application to change their route, the team faced some tough decisions. No one was willing not to climb – they had already put in so much hard work to get there – but the southwest face route was too difficult. Hall and Ball decided they would climb without the correct permit, ascending via the South Pillar, and try to sort it out with the Nepali government when they were back in Kathmandu. Bradey remained undecided, but she leaned towards climbing Everest on her own. When a storm hit as they were positioned at Camp 2, the other New Zealanders decided to wait it out, while Bradey chose to descend. After all, the storm might last for days, and she would rest better lower down. With no high-tech forecasting reports in place, the weather was an unknown. Her decision was affirmed when the Slovaks said they would go down too. With that decision, she knew she had just sealed her fate to climb alone.

After the five-day storm had subsided, Bradey made her way back to Camp 2, where she met an exhausted Hall after his attempt on the South Pillar. He recommended that she take the easiest way to the summit, via the 'normal route', as the going was difficult anywhere else because of deep snow. That would give her the best chance of reaching the top without oxygen. Bradey agreed. She said goodbye to her fellow Kiwis, unaware that she wouldn't see them again until she reached New Zealand weeks later.

Bradey departed Camp 2 at 2 a.m. on 13 October and started to make her way up towards the top of the world… alone. It was cold and dark, and the wind was wide awake. She knew that if she could make it to the South Col by midday, she would be able to rest at Camp 4 and then make the final push for the summit the next day. Choosing to climb without supplemental oxygen meant that Bradey would ascend slowly, resting between hours of physical exertion. She would have to drink lots of fluids and be mindful of her fingers and toes. The risk of frostbite increases exponentially without oxygen at high altitude, where appendages can freeze solid and there is no hope of reviving circulation after a certain point.

Bradey followed the fixed ropes to Camp 3, where she rested, melted snow to drink and then set out again with the goal of reaching Camp 4 by noon. She made her way up the steep, icy slope known as the Lhotse Face, over the Geneva Spur and on to the plateau of the South Col itself. She felt strong, and all the weeks of acclimatization that

INFO

NOTABLE CLIMBS BY LYDIA BRADEY

1987:
Gasherbrum II, Pakistan – first Australasian woman to summit an 8,000-m (26,247-ft) peak and first New Zealander to climb an 8,000-m (26,247-ft) peak without supplemental oxygen.

1988:
Mount Everest (8,849 m/29,032 ft) – first woman to summit without supplemental oxygen. Additional summits in 2008, 2013, 2016 and 2018.

2004:
Cho Oyu (8,188 m/26,863 ft)

2010:
Ama Dablam (6,828 m/22,401 ft)
Aconcagua (6,962m/22,841 ft)

2011:
Kilimanjaro, Tanzania (5,895 m/19,340 ft)

2012:
Mount Vinson, Antarctica (4,892 m/16,050 ft)

2014:
South Pole Last Degree

2016:
Peak Lenin (7,010 m/22,999 ft)

2017:
Dhaulagiri (8,167 m/26,795 ft)

2019:
Mount Everest (from the north, Tibetan side), Broad Peak (8,051 m/26,414 ft)

2023:
Kun Peak (7,064 m/23,176 ft)

led up to that moment gave her confidence. She knew she could do it and the Slovaks believed in her too.

When Bradey left the South Col at 2 a.m. on 14 October, she was entering new territory. She had never been above the Col and there were no fixed lines to guide her. In the light of her headtorch, she placed each cramponed foot ahead of the other. She noted small landmarks as she went in case she should become disorientated on the way down. When she found her rhythm, she calculated that it would likely take her more than ten hours to reach the summit.

When she reached a feature called the Balcony, Bradey pulled out her water bottle, only to discover it was frozen solid, as was her camera. Undeterred, she continued slowly but surely to the South Summit, where she met a team of Spanish climbers and their Sherpa guides. One of the Catalonians had been overcome with cerebral oedema and they were descending after reaching the summit. It was 2.30 p.m. and Bradey realized she had about two hours to go until she reached the top. At one of her rest points, she realized she'd lost her watch, and now faced another challenge: to rely on the sun's position to give her an approximate time of day.

Bradey reached the summit alone while the sun was still shining brightly. She took in the views but struggled to breathe and stay warm as the wind whirled around her. After ten unceremonious minutes on the summit, she began to descend. She went about reversing the difficult moves on the Hillary Step in the howling wind, which threatened to blow her off the mountain. The sun was setting as she descended below the South Summit, a glorious moment where she saw Makalu, the world's fifth highest mountain, in the distance bathed in yellow and orange. Only after she had made her way down below the Balcony at 8,400 metres (27,559 feet) did Bradey realize the magnitude of her achievement. She shouted with joy into the wind. She had become the first woman to solo Mount Everest without supplemental oxygen and only the second Kiwi, after Sir Edmund Hillary, to reach the top of the world.

Bradey encountered the Catalonians again on her way to the South Col and told them that she had reached the summit. When she finally reached the South Col, exhausted from her efforts, she met Ang Rita Sherpa and told him she'd made it. He congratulated her and helped her find her tent in which to rest before continuing her descent the next day.

Down in the valley however, another story was unfolding. Her Kiwi teammates had already packed up camp (including many of Bradey's possessions and most of the expedition money) and left, making assistance impossible had she needed a rescue. The Slovakian team would also have been unable to help – it was high on the mountain dealing with its own trauma. Tragically, several of the team members died in their summit attempt.

By the time Bradey reached basecamp, news of her achievement had been tainted by disbelief from her teammates and the death of some of her Slovak friends. When they reached Kathmandu, her fellow New Zealanders publicly disputed her claim in the press, perhaps out of jealousy, perhaps because they were concerned about the repercussions for the New Zealand team members climbing without the correct permits. Whatever the reason, what should have been a celebration of a national hero turned into a controversy. There was no ceremony for Bradey once she reached basecamp, nor once she flew home. Once again, she was entirely alone.

It wasn't until six years later that Bradey was vindicated through articles that included confirmation from the Catalonians and her climb was finally recognized as the amazing feat it was. However, it was much too little, much too late. No one had called out the other team members for climbing without permits, nor had they been held accountable for abandoning her. Bradey lived with this tarnished reputation for years and it wasn't until 2008 that she returned to Mount Everest. She has done so five more times, guiding others to the top of the world. Her love of climbing big mountains continues to this day and she has made a total of ten ascents over 8,000 metres (26,247 feet) and been on more than thirty-five expeditions over 6,000 metres (19,685 feet).

Lydia Bradey at Everest basecamp with members of the US expedition, 1988.

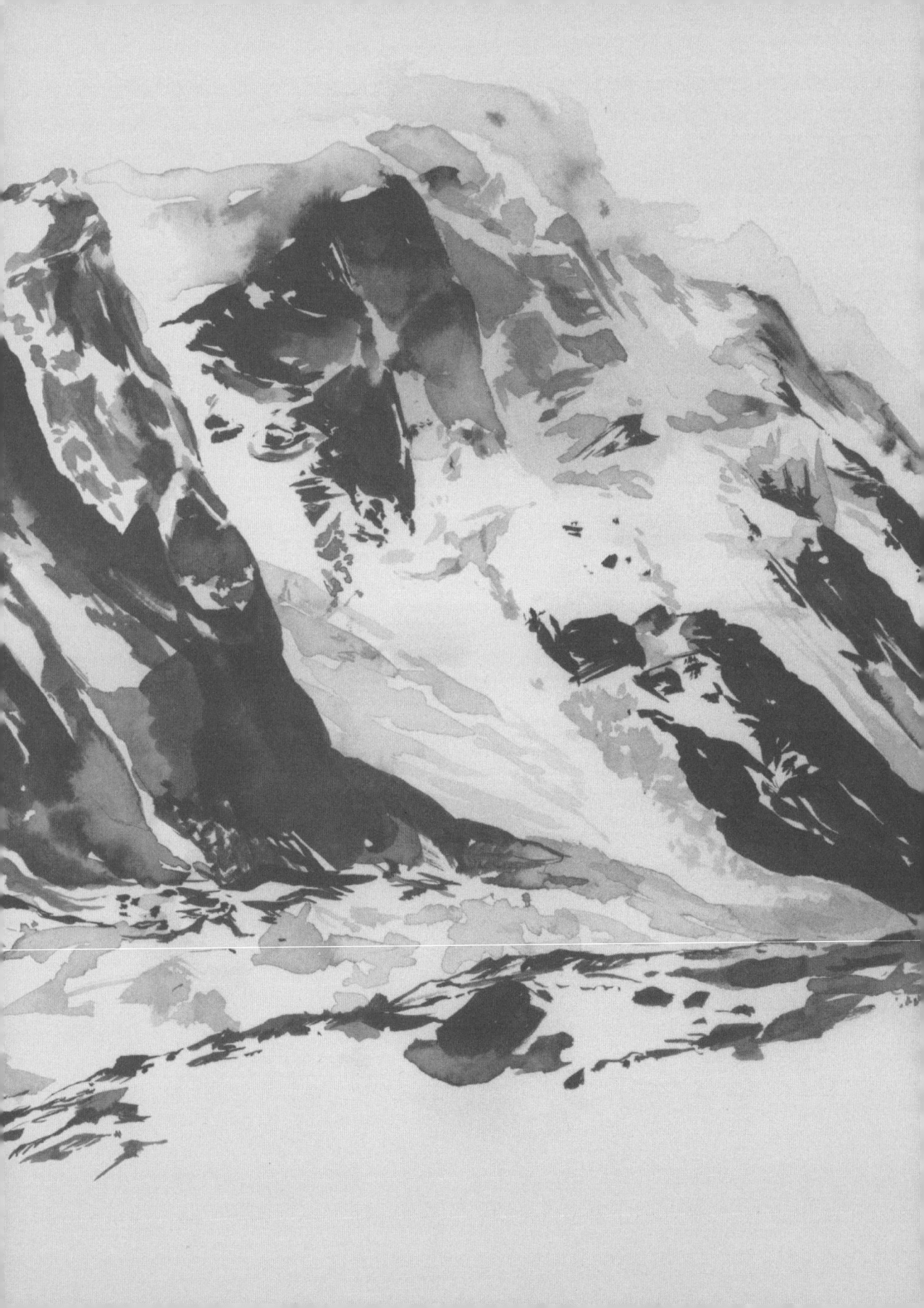

Tamara Lunger's Love and Loss on K2

Italian mountaineer Tamara Lunger had just descended to K2 Advanced Base Camp when something caught her eye. It seemed to be an object tumbling down a snow slope from Camp 1 towards her. Could it be a large rock? As the object gained momentum, she realized, to her horror, that it was a falling climber. Instinctively, she ran towards the body. Whoever it was, she hoped they were still alive.

TAMARA LUNGER

Nationality:
Italian

Born:
6 June 1986

Active:
2002–present

Opposite: Tamara Lunger at K2 basecamp, winter 2020.
Below: Tamara Lunger.

Lunger had been to K2 before, and it had captured her heart. She had ascended the peak with the help of high-altitude porters, but without supplemental oxygen, in the summer of 2014. It was everything she had hoped for in her early climbing career. She vowed to return, something she didn't often do, as she felt that each mountain had its own unique energy and she disliked diluting those feelings by repeating an expedition.

When Lunger returned to K2 in December 2020, it was the last 8,000-metre (26,427-foot) peak still unclimbed in winter – a dangerous proposition. She knew what she was getting into though. She had been to Pakistan in winter before and experienced the extreme cold first hand. In 2016, she was part of an expedition to Nanga Parbat with famous Italian Himalayan specialist Simone Moro, along with Pakistani hero Ali Sadpara and Basque mountaineer Alex Txikon. Just 70 metres (230 feet) from the summit, suffering from stomach issues and debilitating fatigue, Lunger had made the difficult decision to turn around and descend as her teammates carried on to the top of the mountain, making history as the first climbers to reach its summit in winter.

When Moro turned down her invitation to climb K2 in winter, Lunger joined forces with Romanian climber Alex Găvan. When they arrived at basecamp for weeks of acclimatization and preparation, Lunger was surprised by the number of climbers there. She noted many commercial operators with clients who had never climbed in the Himalaya or Karakoram in winter before. She knew that the smallest mistakes – losing a glove to the wind, or a faulty stove that failed to light – could be life-threatening in these severe temperatures, where simple movements like walking or pitching a tent took enormous effort and burned valuable calories. Tackling an 8,000er in winter is not for the average climber.

The pair soon found their preparation rituals differed and Lunger worried about her partner's safety more often than she had hoped. To ease tensions, they befriended two other climbers at basecamp, Juan Pablo 'JP' Mohr Prieto from Chile and Sergi Mingote from Spain.

It was returning to advanced basecamp on one of their acclimatization climbs that they saw the climber fall. They were even more horrified to discover it was Mingote, badly battered, but still breathing. They sat with him, offering comfort in his final moments. Mingote's was the first death on the mountain that season, but sadly it wouldn't be the last. By the time the winter climbing season closed in March 2021, K2 would have taken the lives of five climbers. The 'Savage Mountain' was living up to its nickname.

In the aftermath of Mingote's death, Lunger and Mohr leaned on each other for comfort, their friendship blossoming into romance. Găvan left for Islamabad, abandoning the expedition, but the two remaining climbers debated whether to continue. There were many teams vying for the winter record that year and, on the same day as Mingote's death, several Nepali teams under the leadership of Mingma G Sherpa and Nims Purja had joined forces to make the summit, a historic event for the global climbing community and the country of Nepal. When news of their success reached Lunger and Mohr, it was bittersweet. They were happy for the Nepalis but still devastated by the loss of Mingote, and they questioned if their own summit bid was now necessary.

Since the Nepalis had reached the summit with oxygen and Lunger and Mohr were planning an oxygen-less ascent, they decided that Mingote would have encouraged them to continue, and they became climbing partners. They pooled resources with Ali Sadpara, his son Sajid Sadpara and Icelandic climber John Snorri Sigurjònsson, sharing important information about the condition of the route.

As they continued to acclimatize and wait for longer weather windows, Lunger began to have doubts. There had been many bad omens since their arrival. There had been politics and drama at basecamp, and Mingote's death marked a dark turn in the season despite the success of the Nepali climbers. On her website she remarked, 'The mountain did not want us there. I went there with a positive spirit, thinking I could do anything. Instead, K2, after the Nepalese's victory, told me and everyone else that we didn't belong there.'[1]

Throughout her climbing career, Lunger had been accustomed to following her intuition; it had led to her difficult decision on Nanga Parbat, when turning around so close to the summit had possibly saved her life. The safety and comfort of a team are invaluable to lift spirits and encourage mutual success, but when it comes to summit day, climbers must trust their gut feelings to survive.

When Lunger and Mohr started up the Abruzzi Spur for their final high camp rotation and summit attempt, they knew it was risky. All the climbers made it to Camp 3 on 4 February 2021, and it was there that Lunger's instincts really kicked in. She had been suffering from stomach issues in the days before they went to the higher camps, the -50°C (-58°F) temperatures taking their toll. She was also surprised to learn that their expedition company, who managed their logistics, wanted to leave earlier than they had originally arranged. There was no time to spare. It was now or never, and Lunger wasn't feeling one hundred per cent, so she said goodbye to the others as they left their tent and ventured higher. She would remain at Camp 3 to rest in the hope of making her summit bid in the coming days.

INFO

TAMARA LUNGER'S CLIMBS

2007-09
Consistent top 10 finishes in many European ski mountaineering races.

2010
Becomes the youngest woman (23 years, 11 months) to reach the summit of Lhotse (8,516 m/27,940 ft), Nepal.

2010
Cho Oyu (8,188 m/26,863 ft) attempt, Nepal.

2011
Summit Khan Tengri (7,010 m/22,999 ft), Tien Shan Mountains, Kyrgyzstan/China and attempt of Peak Pobeda (7,439 m/24,406 ft).

2012
Summit Muztagh Ata (7,546 m/24,757 ft) and attempt of Broad Peak (8,051 m/26,414 ft), Pakistan.

2013
Summit Peak Lenin (7,134 m/23,405 ft), Kyrgyzstan, and the Great Crossing - ski-touring traverse with her father Hansjörg Lunger from Shimshal to Askole, Pakistan.

2014
K2 summit (8,611 m/28,251 ft), Pakistan, without supplemental oxygen, only the second woman to do so.

2015
Winter attempt on Manaslu (8,163 m/26,781 ft), Nepal, with Simone Moro; heavy snowfall forced them to abandon their climb.

2015-16
Attempt to be the first to summit Nanga Parbat (8,126 m/26,660 ft), Pakistan, in winter, with Simone Moro, Ali Sadpara and Alex Txikon. Lunger turns around just 70 m (230 ft) from the summit.

2017
Attempt to cross the four 8,000-m (26,247-ft) subpeaks of Kangchenjunga.

2018
First winter ascent of Peak Pobeda (3,003 m/9,852 ft) in the Chersky Mountains of Siberia, with Simone Moro, reportedly the coldest place on earth.

2019
Winter attempt on Gasherbrum I (8,080 m/26,509 ft) and Gasherbrum II (8,035 m/26,361 ft), Pakistan, with Simone Moro.

2020-21
Winter attempt on K2 (8,611 m/28,251 ft), Pakistan.

INFO

ITALIANS ON K2

Italians have long held K2 in their hearts and minds, ever since Prince Luigi Amedeo, Duke of the Abruzzi, visited the mountain in 1909 and climbed to an altitude of 6,250 m/20,505 ft) on the Southeast Spur, now known as the Abruzzi Spur. In 1954, climbers Lino Lacedelli and Achille Compagnoni reached the summit via the Abruzzi Spur. This celebrated feat was not without controversy. Up-and-coming Italian climber Walter Bonatti and Pakistani climber Amir Mehdi worked diligently to bring oxygen tanks to 8,100 m (26,575 ft) for Lacedelli and Compagnoni, an altitude much higher than they had previously agreed. Bonatti and Mehdi were caught out overnight above 8,000 m (26,247 ft) and Mehdi suffered severe frostbite to his toes, which were eventually amputated. The details were withheld from the Italian press so as not to tarnish the reputations of Lacedelli and Compagnoni. Years later, it became apparent that Compagnoni might have intentionally forced Bonatti and Mehdi to a higher altitude to tire them out as he was afraid Bonatti might summit first and steal his thunder.

K2 Summit - 8,611 m/28,251 ft

K2 SOUTH FACE

The Abruzzi Ridge is the most commonly ascended route on K2 and was first attempted in 1909 by Luigi Amedeo, Duke of the Abruzzi.

1. K2 basecamp, 5,100 m/16,732 ft.
2. K2 Advanced Base Camp and the beginning of the Abruzzi Ridge, 5,303 m/17,398 ft.
3. Abruzzi Ridge.
4. Camp 3.
5. The Shoulder.

TAMARA LUNGER

There were other climbers on K2 that day, and many abandoned their summit bids as clouds encompassed the peak and much of Camp 4. Knowing a storm must be moving in, Lunger descended quickly, longing to be with others. Normally she felt at peace alone on the mountain, but on this day, she craved company.

Earlier that day, before the bad weather rolled in, Lunger's friends had encountered tough decisions near the Bottleneck. Sajid was in trouble. He had chosen to use oxygen for the climb but the regulator for his bottle was malfunctioning; he was forced down to Camp 3 as the other three continued. By the time he reached basecamp on 6 February, there was still no news from the trio who had been on their way to the summit the day before. Sajid was not optimistic and told Lunger they had little chance of survival if they had been forced to bivouac in winter conditions above Camp 3. Had they been waiting out the storm there, they might have been able to communicate their position, although Sajid believed the batteries in their radio might also be dead.

Not only was the trio missing, but a Bulgarian climber, Atanas Skatov, had also made an error while rappelling that sent him to his death; his body was later found below Advanced Base Camp. Lunger wondered what the mountain was telling her.

Earlier on the expedition, she had had a vision. She was feeling ill, likely due to poor air quality in the dining tent because of the kerosene heater, and lack of fresh air, as the doors had been sealed against the frigid wind outside. She had escaped to her own tent, where, as she lay down and closed her eyes, K2 appeared to her as a beautiful woman with long flowing hair. The goddess of K2 expressed love and harmony, and she was wearing a full skirt in the shape of the mountain, which protected Lunger as she climbed to Camp 2. Lunger had felt reassured at the time, but as she waited for news from her friends, the K2 before them was not the one of her vision, but a nightmare.

By 8 February, the three climbers were presumed dead. As she packed up Mohr's personal belongings for the long trek out, Lunger cried continuously. The Pakistani cooks at her camp did their best to comfort her as she broke the news to her family and friends.

It took more than a year for Lunger to recover from the loss. She fell into a deep depression, lost her love for the mountains and feared going outside. She was afraid of skiing because of avalanches and rock climbing because she might fall. Even biking caused her anxiety. The icy cold from K2 had driven into her bones and she never felt warm; even during summer in the Dolomites she couldn't bring herself to wear shorts for the entire season.

Before the trip, Lunger had been a popular, highly respected climber, not only in Italy, but in climbing circles worldwide. She chose to participate in difficult expeditions and others always wanted to know what her next big goal would be. Caught in post-traumatic depression after K2, she had no idea who she was any more, and the external pressure to set a new goal weighed heavily on her.

Lunger slowly emerged from the darkness through trauma therapy and regular visits to the mountains she loved. Step by step, she began to rebuild herself, focusing on personal goals designed to enhance her connection with nature rather than conquer it. Throughout her climbing career, she had set goals based on the accomplishments of the men she admired, and she had had the physical strength to keep up with them all. Her body had suffered during the K2 climb, and the physical pain lingered in the months that followed. Her stress manifested itself in her body as pain. Now, as she climbed out of her traumatic experiences, she sought a gentler, 'more feminine' approach to climbing and mountain sports.

For a long time after Mohr's death, Lunger had held their relationship close to her heart, not revealing their secret romance. Once on her healing journey, she realized that she needed to be honest with others as well as herself. She returned to the mountains with a different mindset, one where she wouldn't try to be the fastest or the strongest, but to enjoy every precious moment. She took up paragliding again and found joy in soaring above the peaks rather than scaling them.

During her difficult Himalayan climbs, Lunger had perhaps allowed her ambition to define who she was. She describes her new outlook on life as a return to her early childhood, when she first experienced the joy of nature near her home in Bolzano. On weekend trips in the Dolomites, the family would camp and watch her father compete in mountain bike races. Now, more than ever, she is convinced that her connection with mountains is what gives her life.

Tamara Lunger is one of the best mountaineers in the world, having undertaken many successful skiing and climbing expeditions. She now works to inspire young women to find their inner strength and believe in themselves, just as she has had to do on so many expeditions.

Opposite: Tamara Lunger paragliding in the Alps.

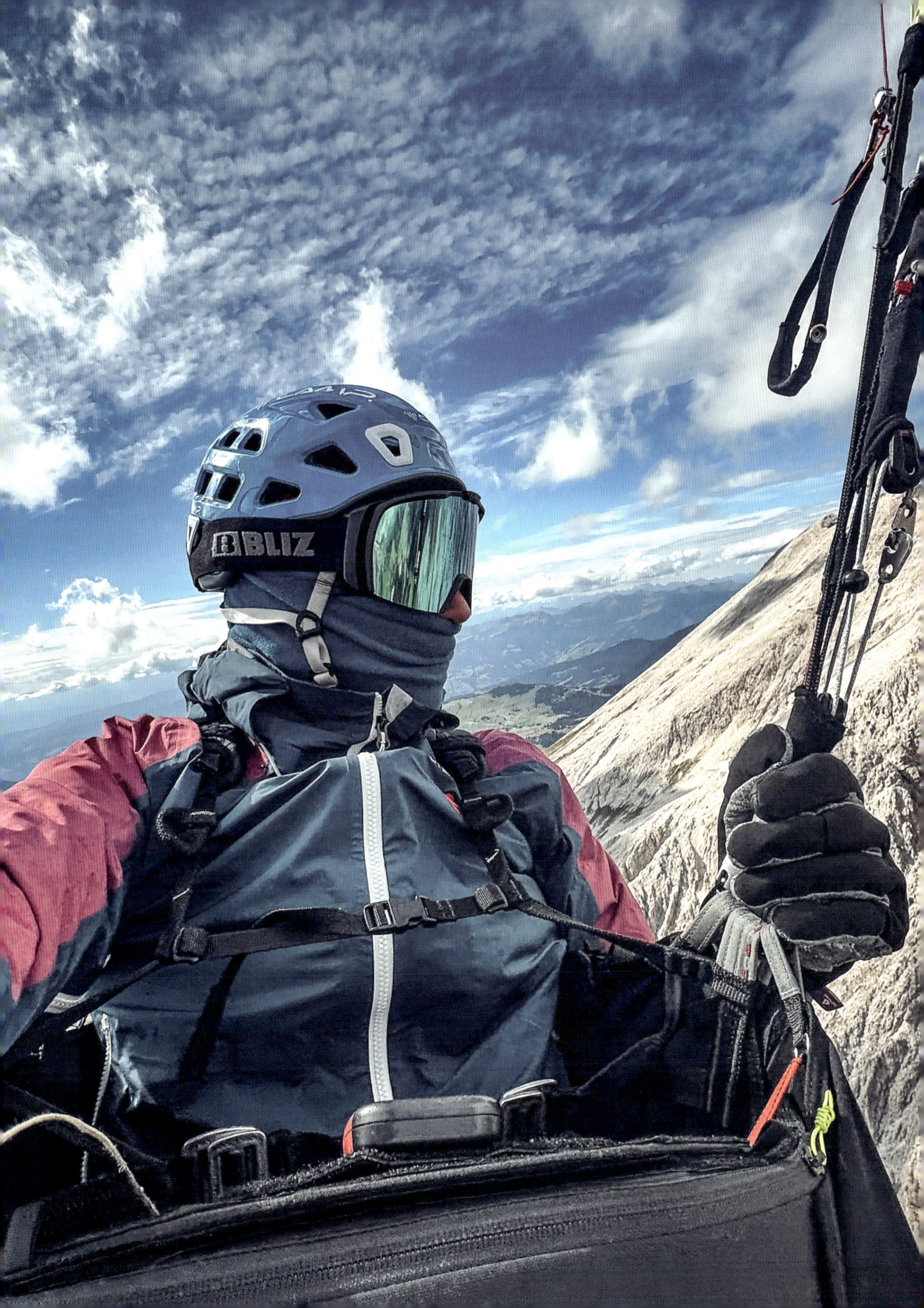
BLIZ

Above: Lydia Bradey at Everest basecamp, 1988.
Opposite: Antisana Volcano, Ecuador, March 2017. Juliana García's group can be seen packing up.

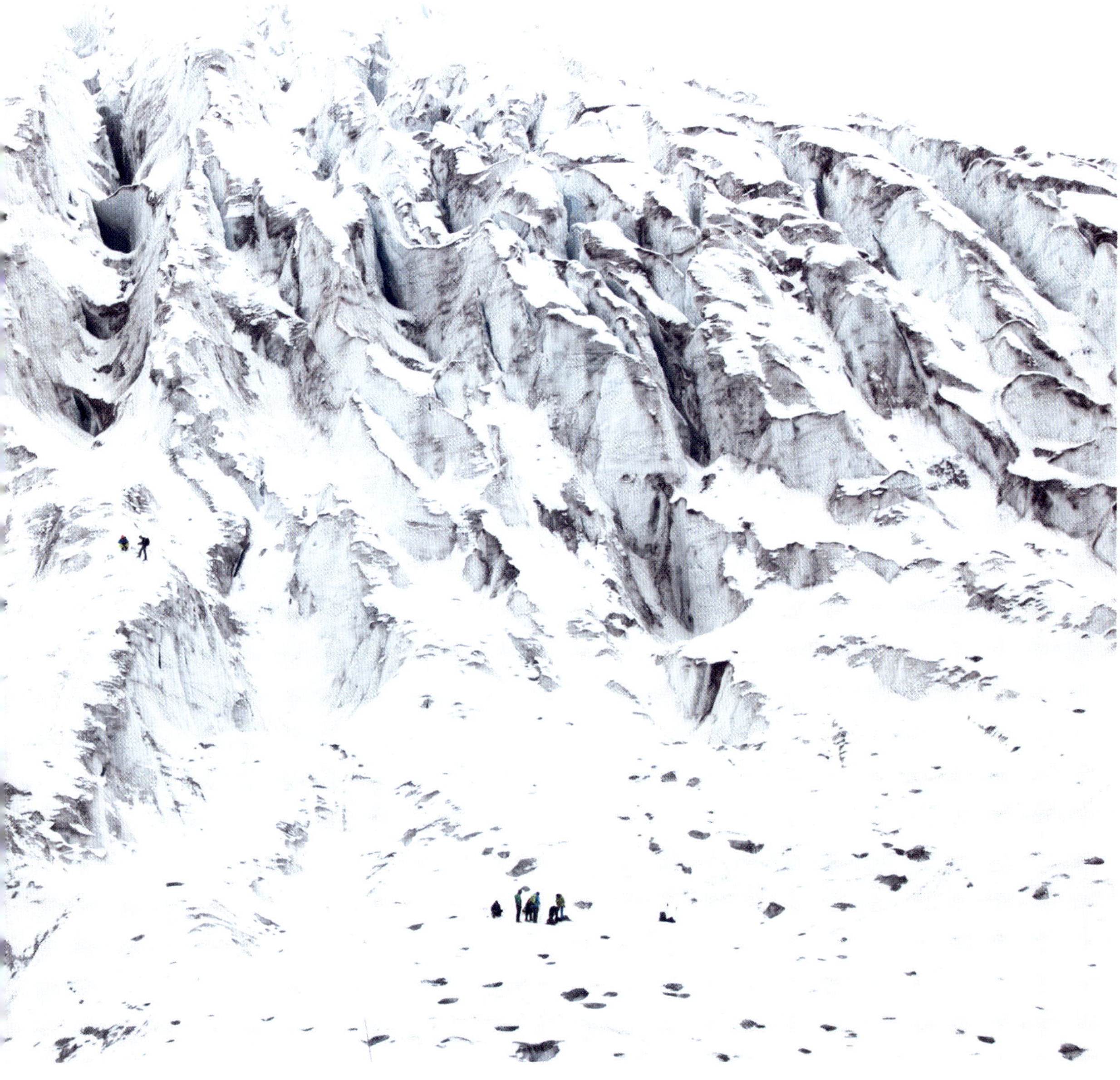

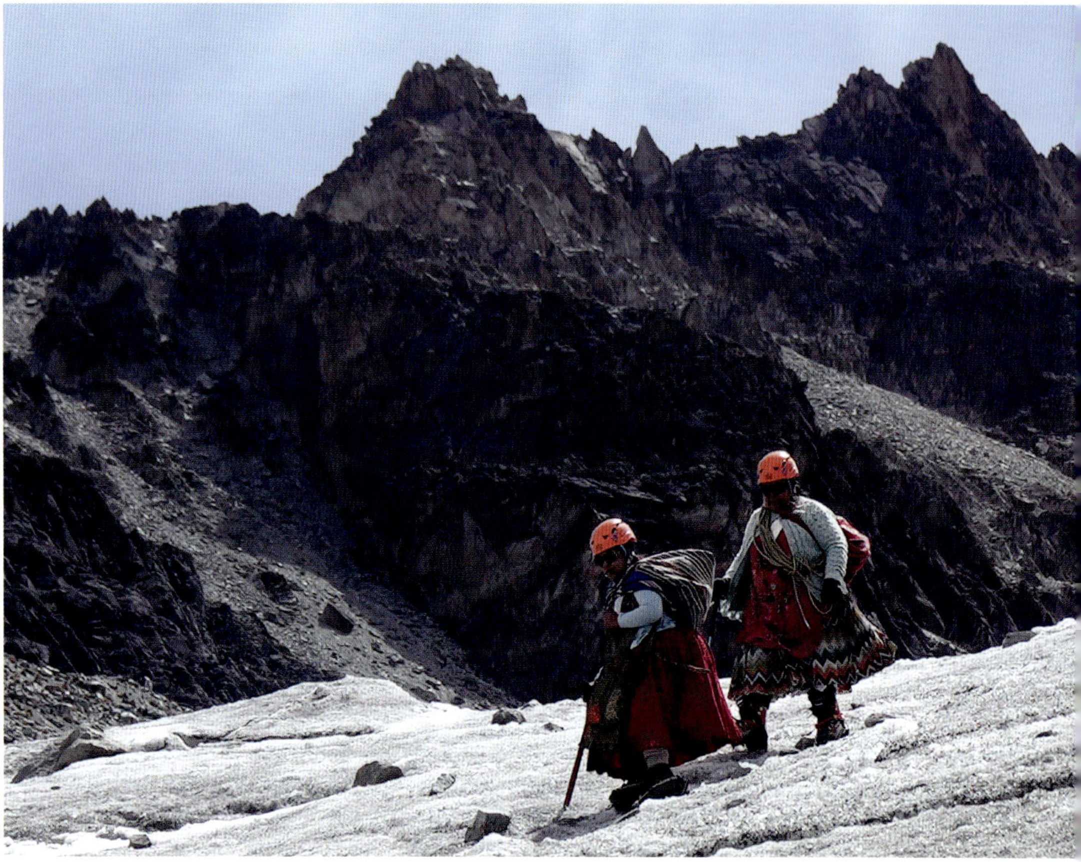

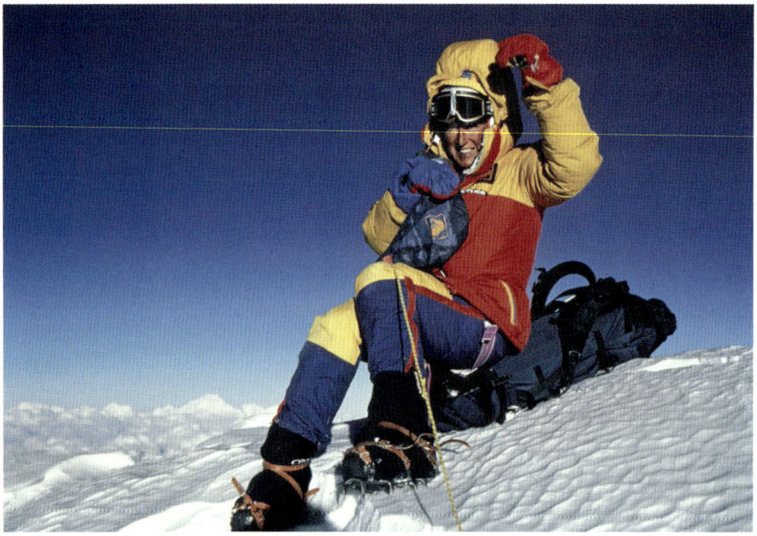

Opposite above: Aymara Indigenous guides known as 'Las Cholitas Escaladoras': Suibel Gonzales, left, and her mother Lidia Hauyllas, on Huayna Potosi, Bolivia, 2023.
Opposite below: Sharon Wood on the summit of Mount Everest, 1986.

Below: Huandoy, Peru.
Pages 230–31: Juliana García during her UIAGM exams on the Antisana Glacier.

230

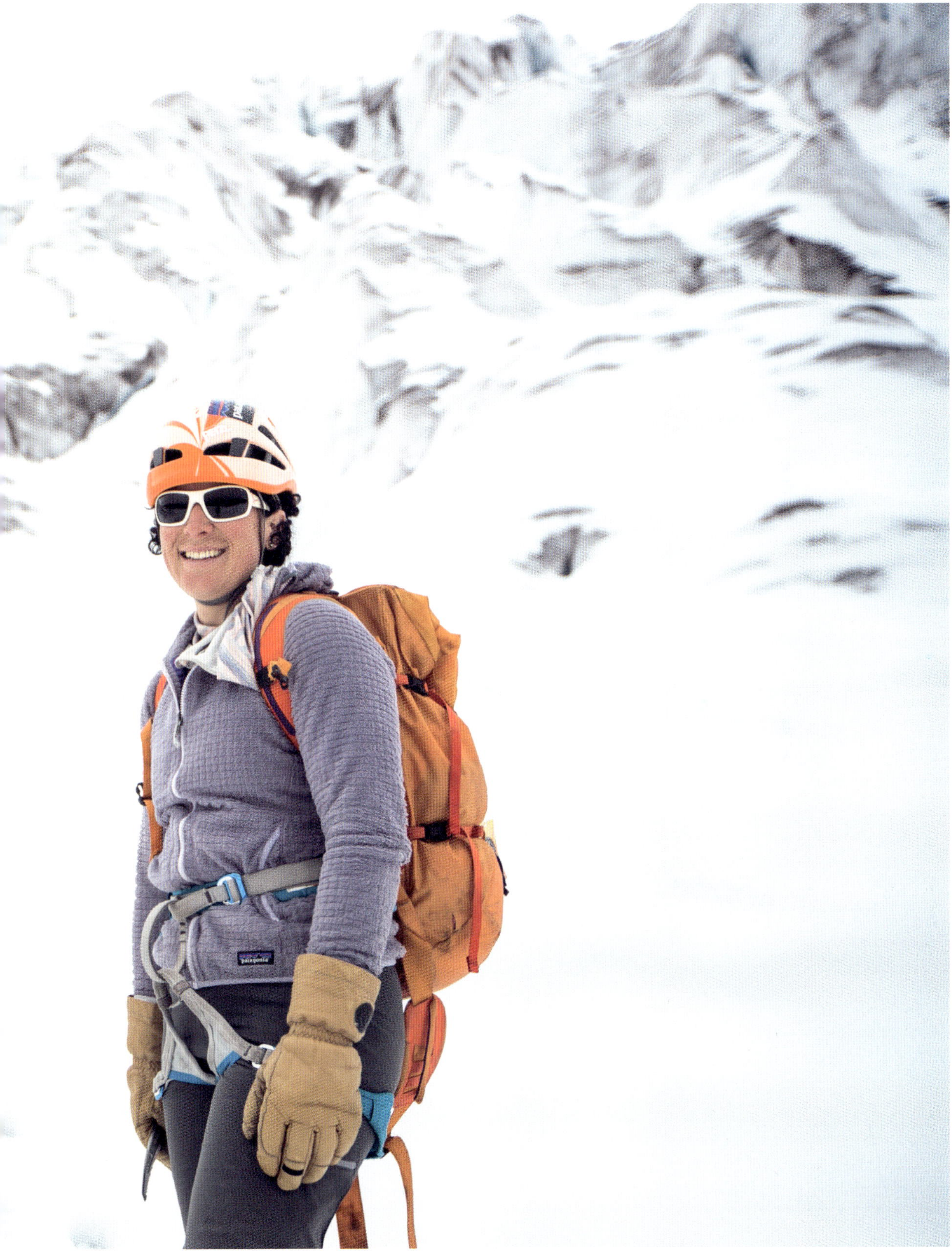
patagonia

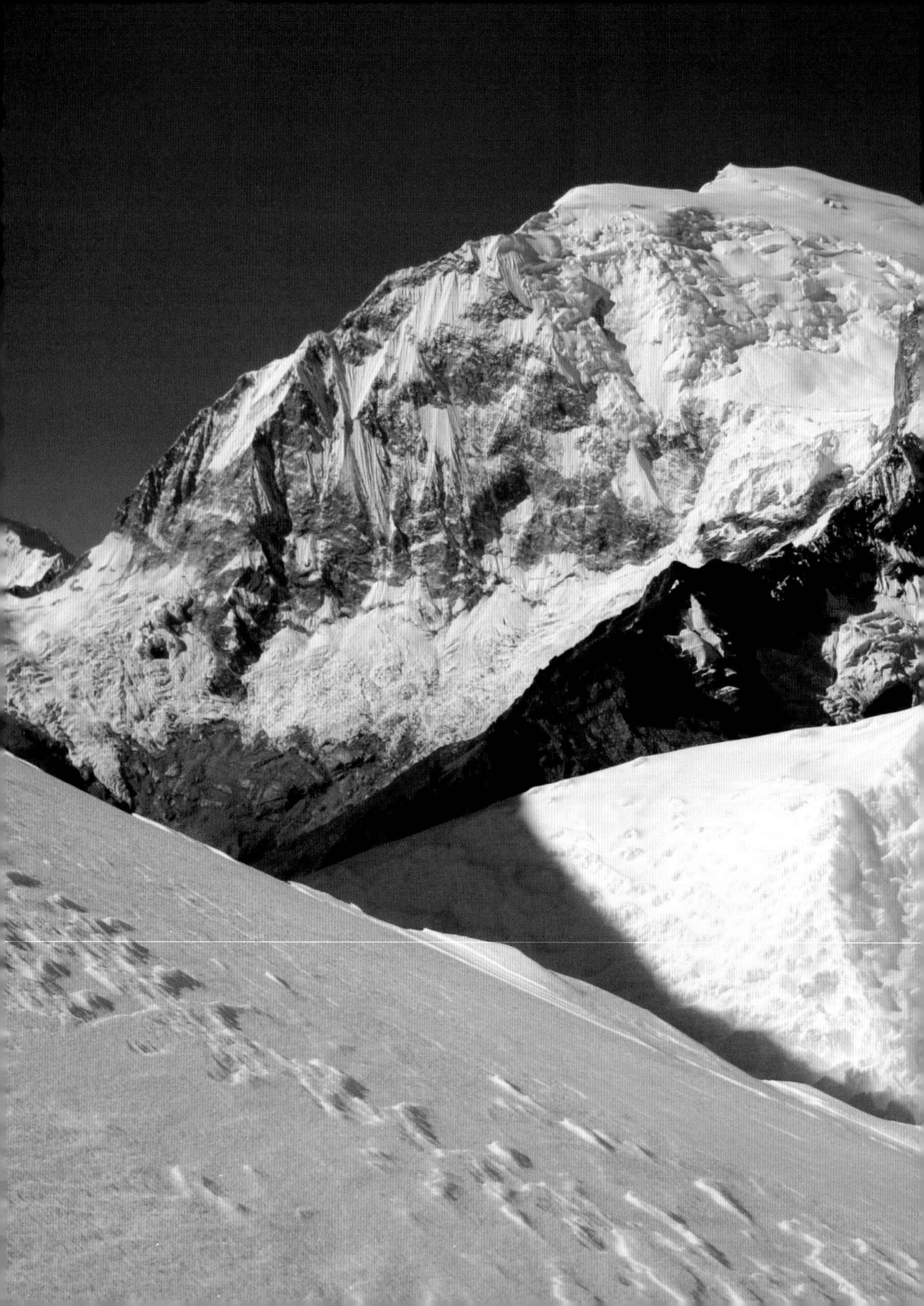

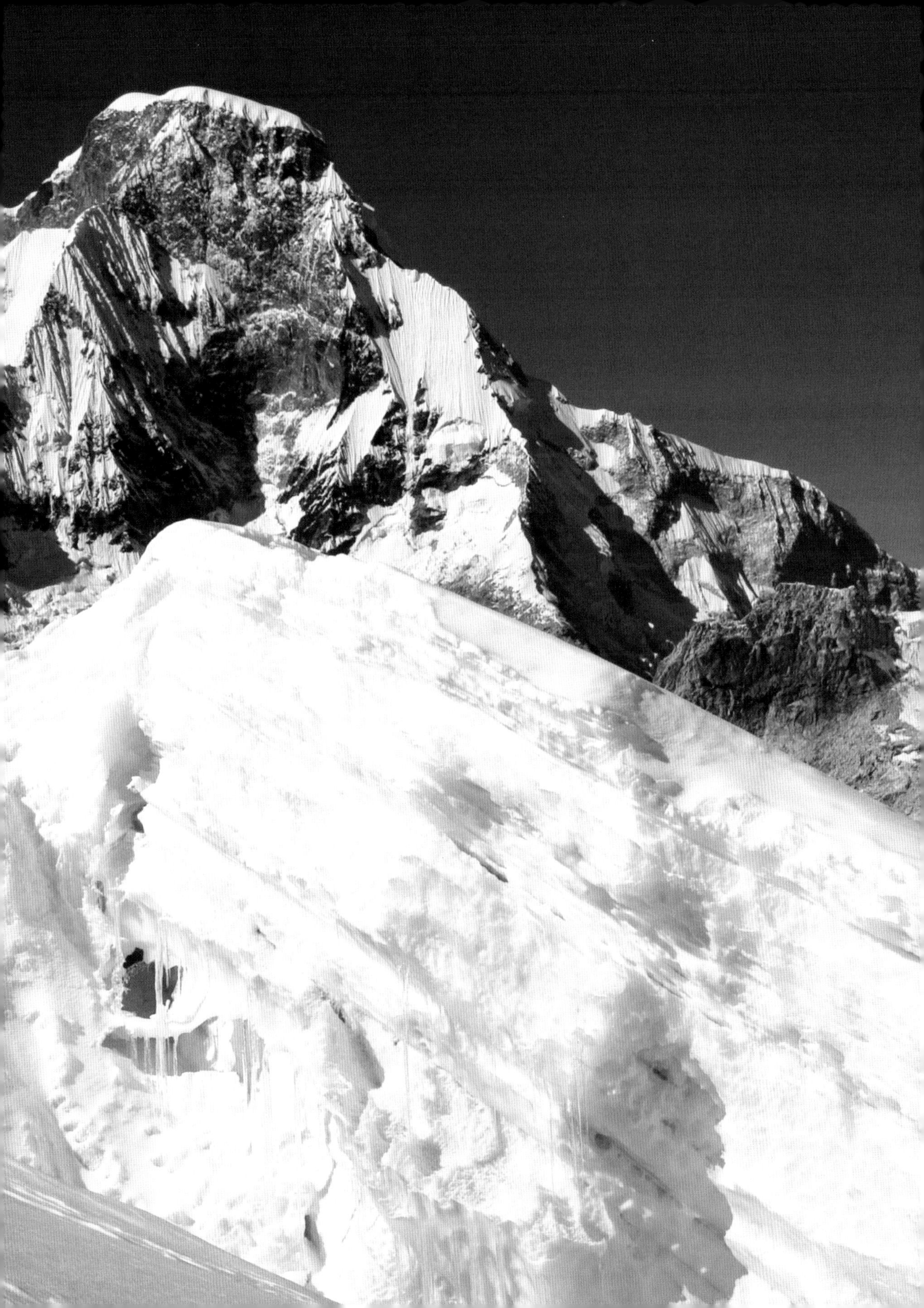

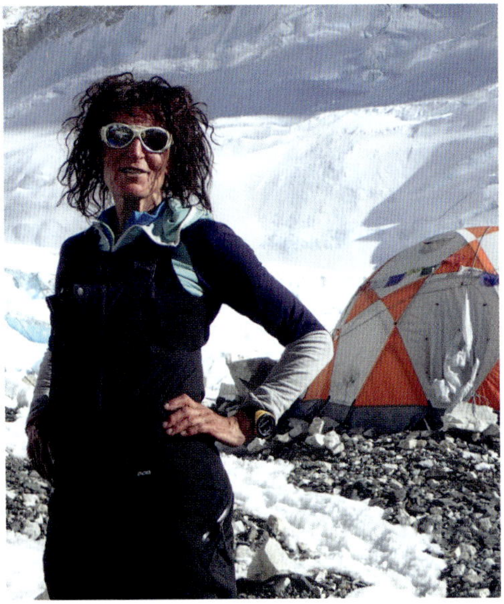

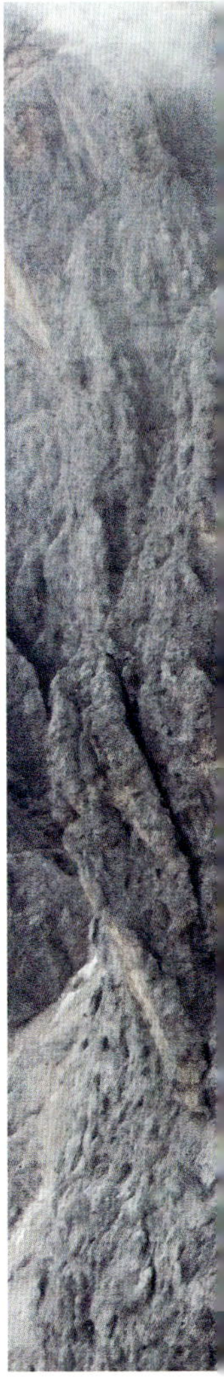

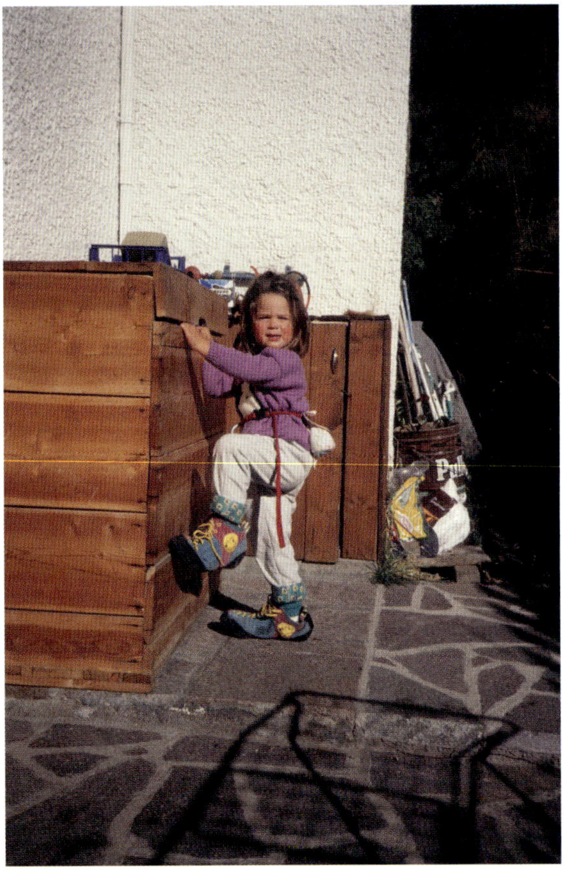

Pages 232–33: Huascarán, Peru.
Opposite above: Lydia Bradey, Camp 2, Everest, 2018.
Opposite below: Tamara Lunger as a child.

Above: Tamara Lunger climbs at the Vajolet Towers in the Dolomites.

Above: Everest basecamp dining room with Lydia Bradey and team members and visitors. Rob Hall is second from the left.
Below: Pasang Lhamu Sherpa and her husband Sonam.
Opposite: Lydia Bradey on the first female ascent of Zenith, Half Dome, Yosemite National Park.
Pages 238–39: Tamara Lunger and Simone Moro on Kanchenjunga, 2017.

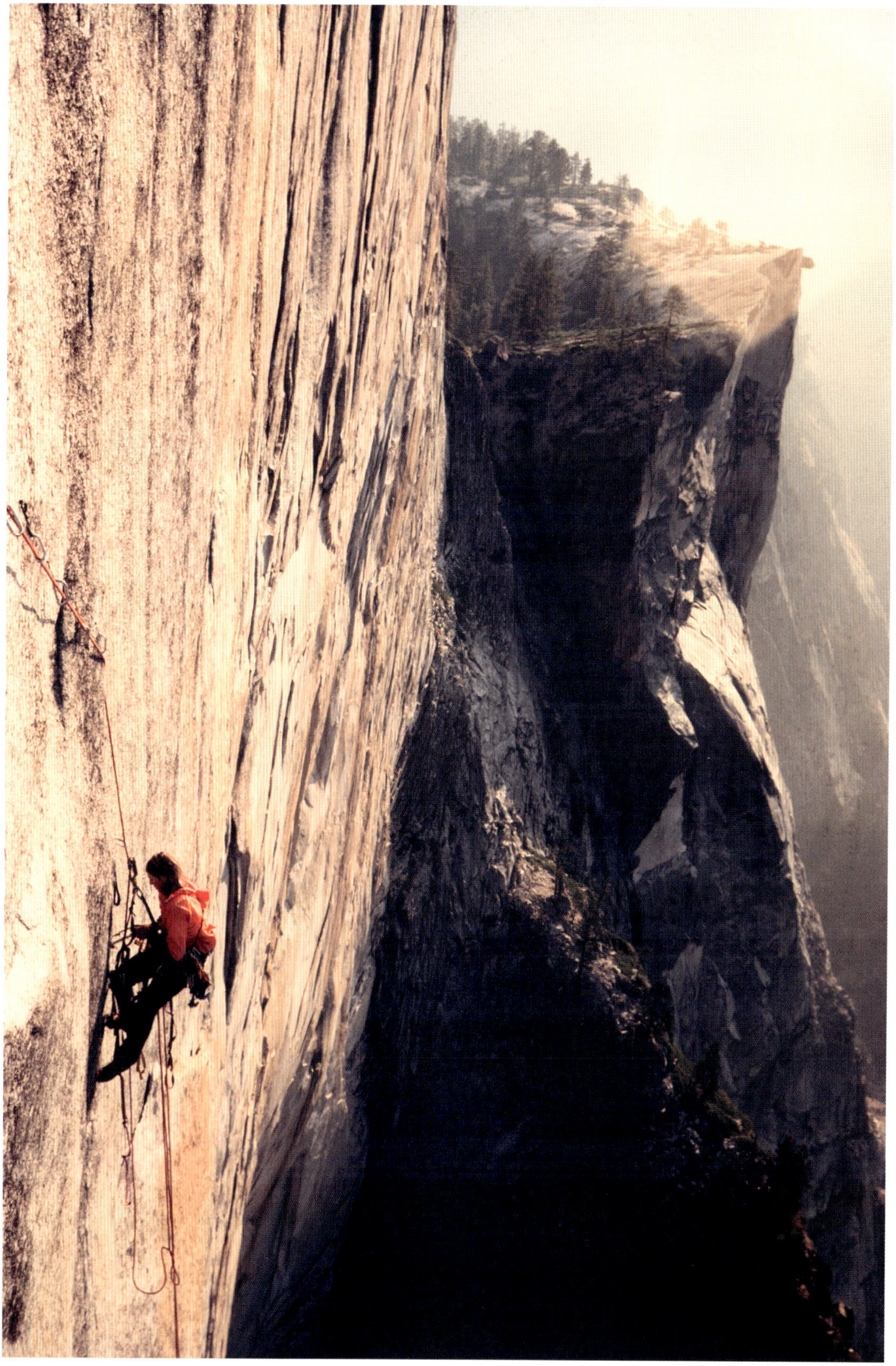

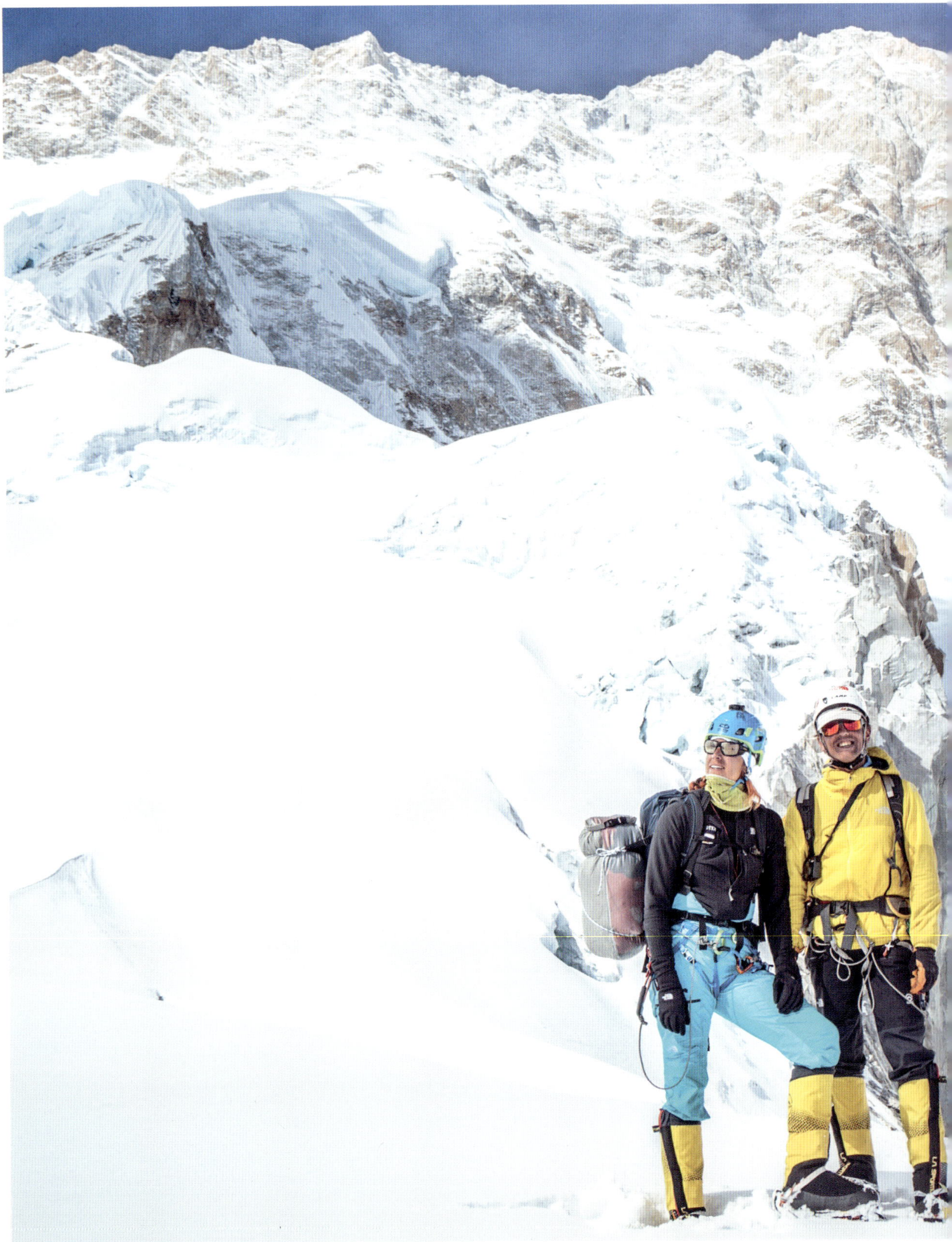

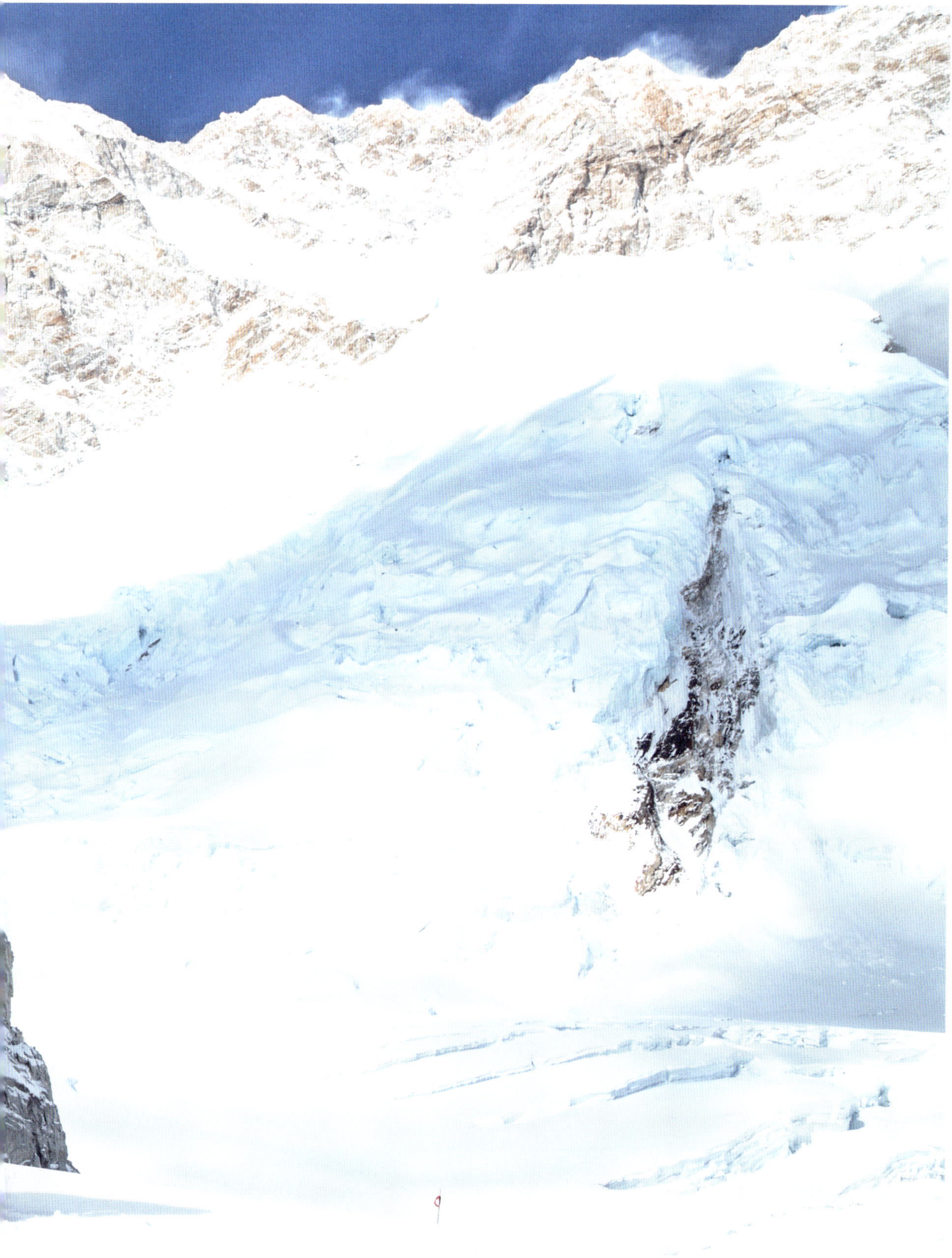

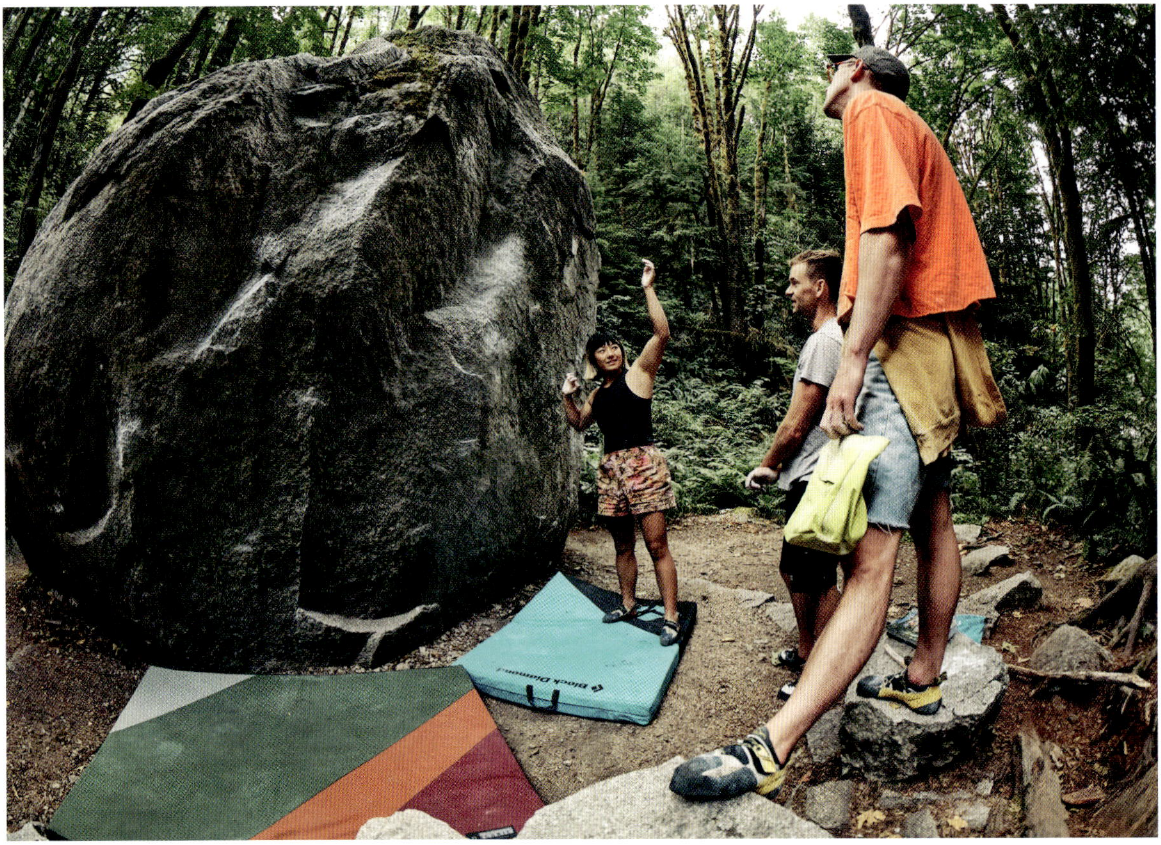
Black Diamond

THE FUTURE OF CLIMBING

Ashima Shiraishi

The first time I touched a rock, it was a boulder named for the rats that crawl around it. 'Rat Rock' is an outcrop of ancient bedrock smack in the middle of Frederick Law Olmsted and Calvert Vaux's meticulously landscaped Central Park in New York. The year was 2007, and I found myself drawn to a fringe group of climbers that happened to be climbing in the middle of Manhattan. I didn't want to go home that evening; I just wanted to keep climbing. For the 4.4 billion people around the world who live in urban areas – a figure that's expected to grow to 6 billion by 2045 – accessing the mountains isn't always an option. And at the time, there were just a few walls, like the one at Manhattan Plaza Health Club, but no dedicated climbing gyms in my native New York City. There weren't many strong or famous climbers that looked like me, either.

So much has changed in the nearly two decades that have passed since. Now, in 2024, there are brand-new gyms and chains opening up seemingly every month. A boulder in Lappnor, Finland, was given the inconceivable grade of V17 in 2016. Free-solo climbing made it into the mainstream consciousness through an Oscar-winning documentary, along with a slew of other climbing and mountaineering films that inspired audiences with their tales of human endeavour. New records and limits are being broken at every turn, and increasingly diverse faces are popping up in the climbing world from every corner of the globe. The sport made it to the Olympics by way of Tokyo in 2020, even in the face of a pandemic.

Years ago, it would have been hard to imagine just how vastly different the climbing world would look. From the early mountaineering expeditions in the high Alps to the colourful routes of today's city gyms, climbing has become increasingly accessible to a greater number of people. It'd be hard to deny the claim that rock climbing has become in part a trendy activity to post about, but to dismiss it as a fitness craze would be to overlook the real potential of what climbing can be.

Some dismiss gym climbing, which is focused on pulling on plastic. But I've seen firsthand how climbing can be a therapeutic movement that gives city kids a shift in perspective. Whether you're out in the mountains or on a man-made wall, climbing can take a person out of their normal context. It can give someone a reason to connect with nature; for others, it's a reason to move, to feel better in their own bodies. The future of climbing promises more diversity and access to those who have historically been excluded, thanks to the work of groups like Brothers of Climbing, Brown Girls Climb and Latino Outdoors. I hope to carry on this tradition through my work with AllRise, an experimental programme promoting access and inclusivity in the outdoors.

Most of all, I imagine a world where climbing is more fully represented in the public consciousness. As it is now, only a slim dimension of climbing in a modern context shows up in the media, such as competition climbing or fatalities on Mount Everest. My main hope for the future of climbing is that we see its roots and soul, that climbing will exist in pluralities, as an accessible movement that can take someone from point A (where they are) to point B (where they want to go) in the literal and metaphorical sense. That more people will realize that there are so many creative ways to interact with climbing, and through it bond with each other to create a thriving community.

Ashima Shiraishi bouldering.

I know that some might worry over the exponential growth in the number of climbers. The impact on nature must be considered, but I see the growth as a net positive. The joy of climbing, the connection found to one's own body and to a close-knit community cannot be understated. What can't be overlooked, however, is the context of climbing: that at its core, it happens in nature. That climbing can be a ritual.

Outside of the West, climbing isn't a fad or a trendy sport. Like the Inca and Sherpa women who roamed their mountains long before the European 'mountaineers' came along, for the ethnic minority Miao group in the Guizhou province of China, climbing is rooted in ritual and tradition. It was once part of a burial ritual to carry coffins of elders up the staggering cliff-sides. Centuries later, climbing remains a skill that is passed down through generations. It's a connective thread that binds the elders to the young, and also serves as an act of care for the community, since Miao climbers today ascend high cliffs to pick herbs that are used in traditional medicine. They engage in 'free soloing', but they don't do it to claim a send, name a route or pose for the cameras – but because they're carrying on an ancient tradition.

This persistence of tradition, even today, makes me hopeful. It makes me wonder, dream and imagine: how can climbing circle back to being an activity rooted in ritual and meaning? In what ways can climbing and its cousin, mountaineering, connect us to the natural environment, the geology, the flora and fauna? What other traditions and cultures that have gone unwritten and unnoticed may emerge into the climbing culture, and what subcultures and alternative ways of living and connecting can form next?

For me, the future of climbing is also philosophical, if not spiritual. Since I was young, my dad taught me the importance of quieting my mind before climbing. This meditative act was essential for my sport, but now it's taken on a much bigger meaning. Climbing now is a way to erase attachment to my self, my mind and my ego; a way to connect with the natural world; and a vehicle to cultivating appreciation of the local rock and surrounding ecology. Just as it was for many of the mountaineering women, represented in this book, who went before.

GLOSSARY

Abseil – also known as rappelling, abseiling is the controlled descent of a rock or ice wall by moving down a rope that is fixed to an anchor from above.

Aid climbing – see 'Climbing Styles: A Glossary' (page 105).

Aiguille – French for needle, a sharp pointy rock feature or peak.

Alpine climbing – a type of mountaineering involving a broad range of advanced climbing skills, including rock climbing, ice climbing and/or mixed climbing in an alpine environment.

Alpine style – an approach to climbing where small, lightly equipped teams carry all their own equipment and climb without the support of porters. It involves establishing small temporary camps that are packed up and re-established as the team moves upwards.

Anchor – an arrangement of one or more pieces of fixed protection set up to support the weight of a belay, a top rope or an abseil.

Arête – French for edge or ridge, a sharp, outward-pointing corner of rock on a climbing route.

Ascender – a mechanical device used for climbing a fixed rope, very common in aid climbing and big-wall climbing. Also known as a jumar.

Belay – the act of controlling and managing the rope as a roped climber ascends. The belayer catches a falling climber by slowing the fall using a friction device.

Bergschrund – a crevasse that forms on the upper portion of a glacier where the ice pulls away from a headwall.

Bivouac or Bivy – a crude, usually unplanned, overnight camp or shelter on a climbing route.

Bothy – a small stone hut used by climbers (usually in Scotland).

Bouldering – see 'Climbing Styles: A Glossary' (page 105).

Buttress – a projecting ridge of rock.

Carabiner – a specialized type of metal shackle with a spring-loaded gate used to connect components of protection while climbing.

Choss – loose or 'rotten' rock that makes for unpleasant, difficult, or dangerous climbing.

Cirque – French for an amphitheatre-like valley formed by glacial erosion.

Competition climbing – see 'Climbing Styles: A Glossary' (page 105).

Cornice – an overhanging edge of snow on a ridge, usually formed by high winds.

Couloir – a steep snowy chute on a mountain.

Crampons – metal spikes attached to footwear for grip on snow and ice while ice climbing and mountaineering.

Crimp – a tiny rock edge, usually just large enough for the first pad of a finger to grasp.

Crux – the most difficult portion of a climb; often the grade is defined by the difficulty of the crux.

Dihedral – an open book-shaped corner formed at the intersection of two flat rock faces.

Drytooling – a technique where ice climbing tools are used on rock rather than ice.

Etrier – a ladder made of webbing used in aid climbing.

Flash – ascending a route on the first attempt after receiving information about the route prior to climbing.

Free climbing – see 'Climbing Styles: A Glossary' (page 105).

Free soloing – see 'Climbing Styles: A Glossary' (page 105).

Ground up – when a new route is established, the first ascensionist does not inspect the features from above nor install safety devices in advance of climbing but starts upwards from the ground. If the climber falls, they return to the beginning and start again.

Hang dogging – hanging on the rope, or a piece of protection, after falling, then starting to reclimb without returning to the ground.

Hang fire – falling rock, hanging ice or a snow cornice that presents an imminent threat from above while climbing.

Haul bags – large equipment duffel bags used in big-wall climbing.

Layback – climbing an edge or crack by side-pulling with both hands and using opposing friction for the feet.

Moraine – soil and rock left behind by a moving glacier.

Névé – permanent snow that remains year round.

Onsight – ascending a route on the first attempt without having received prior information.

Pitch – one rope length, usually 50–60 metres (164–197 feet).

Piton – a peg or spike driven into a rock or crack to support a climber or a rope.

Redpoint – free-climbing a route by leading it after having already failed it or practised it beforehand.

Runnel – a narrow, waterworn channel on a rock face or on a glacier.

Sending – completing a climbing route.

Serac – an overhanging piece of glacier.

Siege style – completing a mountaineering route by any means, using all resources available. This usually means a large expedition with teams of climbers ascending pre-placed fixed ropes, staying at high camps established by porters. This is the opposite of alpine style.

Sirdar – the head porter or expedition logistics leader.

Snow mushrooms – snow formations shaped like mushrooms, caused by wet snow conditions and heavy winds.

Spindrift – small clouds or avalanches of powdery snow.

Sport climbing – see 'Climbing Styles: A Glossary' (page 105).

Topping out – reaching the top of a route.

Top roping – climbing a route with a rope already in place from above.

Traditional climbing – see 'Climbing Styles: A Glossary' (page 105).

TIMELINE

1822
MRS & MISS CAMPBELL
United Kingdom

A mother-and-daughter team are led across the Col du Géant in Chamonix by French guides who get lost on the way, forcing an unplanned bivouac high above the valley.

1871
LUCY WALKER
United Kingdom

First ascent of the Matterhorn by a woman, accompanied by her guides.

1800

1838
HENRIETTE D'ANGEVILLE
France

The second woman to ascend Mont Blanc, d'Angeville is congratulated once back in Chamonix by Marie Paradis, who declares them 'two sisters in Mont Blanc'.

1882
ELIZABETH LE BLOND
United Kingdom

Elizabeth Le Blond makes two successful summits of Mont Blanc and the Grandes Jorasses. She would go on to achieve more than one hundred other ascents.

1808
MARIE PARADIS
France

Accompanied by French guides, maid Marie Paradis climbs Mont Blanc as a publicity stunt to escape a life of poverty. Her plan works and she never climbs again after summiting.

1897
ANNIE PECK SMITH
USA

Summits Mount Orizaba (5,687 m/ 18,658 ft) and Mount Popcatepetl (5,450 m/17,881 ft) in Mexico, high altitude records at the time.

1907
ELIZABETH LE BLOND ET AL
United Kingdom

Founding of the Ladies' Alpine Club in London, the world's first mountaineering organization for women.

1947
BARBARA WASHBURN
USA

First female ascent of Denali, Alaska, North America's highest peak.

1955
FIRST ALL-WOMEN'S EXPEDITION TO THE HIMALAYAS
United Kingdom

First ascent of Gyalzen Peak.

1900

1899
FANNY BULLOCK WORKMAN
USA

First Western woman to lead an expedition/exploration of the Karakoram and the Baltoro Glacier. First ascent of a peak in the Shigar Valley, christened Mount Bullock Workman.

1934
HETTIE DYHRENFURTH
Germany

Dyhrenfurth breaks the 7,315-m (24,000-ft) ceiling for climbing women with her ascent of 7,422 m (24,350 ft) Sia Kangri, Pakistan.

1954
CLAUDE KOGAN
France

Kogan reaches a new high point in the Himalaya, 7,620 m (25,000 ft), while attempting Cho Oyu in Nepal.

1964
DAISY VOOG
Germany

German climber Daisy Voog completes the first female ascent of the Eiger's north face, along with Werner Bittner.

1969
YVETTE VAUCHER AND LOULOU BOULAZ
France

First all-women's ascent of the Cassin route on the north face of the Piz Badile.

1974
MASAKO UCHIDA, MIEKO MORI AND NAOKO NAKASEKO
Japan

First women to ascend an 8,000-m (26,247-ft) peak, Manaslu in Nepal, the world's eighth highest peak.

1986
WANDA RUTKIEWICZ
Poland

First Pole and first woman to summit K2.

—

SHARON WOOD
Canada

First North American woman to summit Mount Everest (Chomolungma), via new route from the Tibetan side.

1978
ARLENE BLUM
USA

International all-women's team expedition Annapurna I, Nepal.

1988
LYDIA BRADEY
New Zealand

Makes the first women's ascent of Everest without supplemental oxygen.

1975
JUNKO TABEI
Japan

The first woman to summit Mount Everest (Chomolungma).

1988
ALISON HARGREAVES
United Kingdom

Suffers morning sickness and vomiting while climbing the notorious north face of the Eiger while five months pregnant.

1973
WANDA RUTKIEWICZ
Poland

Polish climbers Wanda Rutkiewicz, Danuta Wach and Stefania Egierszdorff make the first all-female team ascent of the north face of the Eiger.

1985
SHARON WOOD
Canada

Huascarán Sur, Anqosh Face first ascent.

TIMELINE

1990
CATHERINE DESTIVELLE
France

First female ascent (solo) of the Bonatti Pillar on the Petit Dru, Chamonix, France.

1991
WANDA RUTKIEWICZ
Poland

Solo ascent of the south face of Annapurna, first ascent by a woman.
—
1991–1993
CATHERINE DESTIVELLE
France

Completes the Alps North Face trilogy in winter: Eiger, Grandes Jorasses and the Matterhorn.

1993
PASANG LHAMU SHERPA
Nepal

The first Nepali woman to summit Mount Everest (Chomolungma). She tragically dies on the descent but is celebrated as a national hero in Nepal for decades to come.
—
ALISON HARGREAVES
United Kingdom

First female solo ascents of six north faces in the Alps: the Eiger, the Matterhorn, Grandes Jorasses, Piz Badile, Le Petit Dru and Cima Grande.
—
LYNN HILL
USA

First person to free-climb the Nose on El Capitan, Yosemite, California.

1994
LYNN HILL
USA

Free-climbs the Nose on El Capitan, Yosemite, California, in less than 24 hours.

1995
ALISON HARGREAVES
United Kingdom

Achieves the summits of Mount Everest and K2 in a single season, both without supplemental oxygen, making her the first woman to do so.

2001, 2003, 2004 & 2006
INES PAPERT
Germany

Wins the overall World Cup (male or female) for Ice Climbing.

2000

2010
EDURNE PASABAN
Spain

First woman to ascend all fourteen 8,000-m (26,247-ft) peaks.

2015
WASFIA NAZREEN
Bangladesh

First Bangladeshi to achieve the Seven Summits.

2016
ASHIMA SHIRAISHI
USA

First woman to achieve the bouldering grade of V15.

2020
CATHERINE DESTIVELLE
France

Receives the Piolet d'Or Award for lifetime achievement.

2024
Dawa Yangzum Sherpa
Nepal

Becomes the first Nepali woman to complete the fourteen 8,000-m (26,247-ft) peaks.

2009
KEI TANIGUCHI
Japan

First woman to receive a coveted Piolet d'Or, for her ascent of the southeast face of Kamet.

2011
GERLINDE KALTENBRUNNER
Austria

First woman to ascend all fourteen 8,000-m (26,246-ft) peaks without the use of supplemental oxygen.

2017–2018
ÉLISABETH REVOL
France

Summits Nanga Parbat in winter with Tomek Mackiewicz, new route in alpine style on the west/northwest face.

2022
WASFIA NAZREEN
Bangladesh

First Bangladeshi and Bengali to summit K2.
—
LHAKPA SHERPA
Nepal

Summits Mount Everest for the tenth time, setting a record for most Everest summits to date for a woman.

MOUNTAIN PROFILES

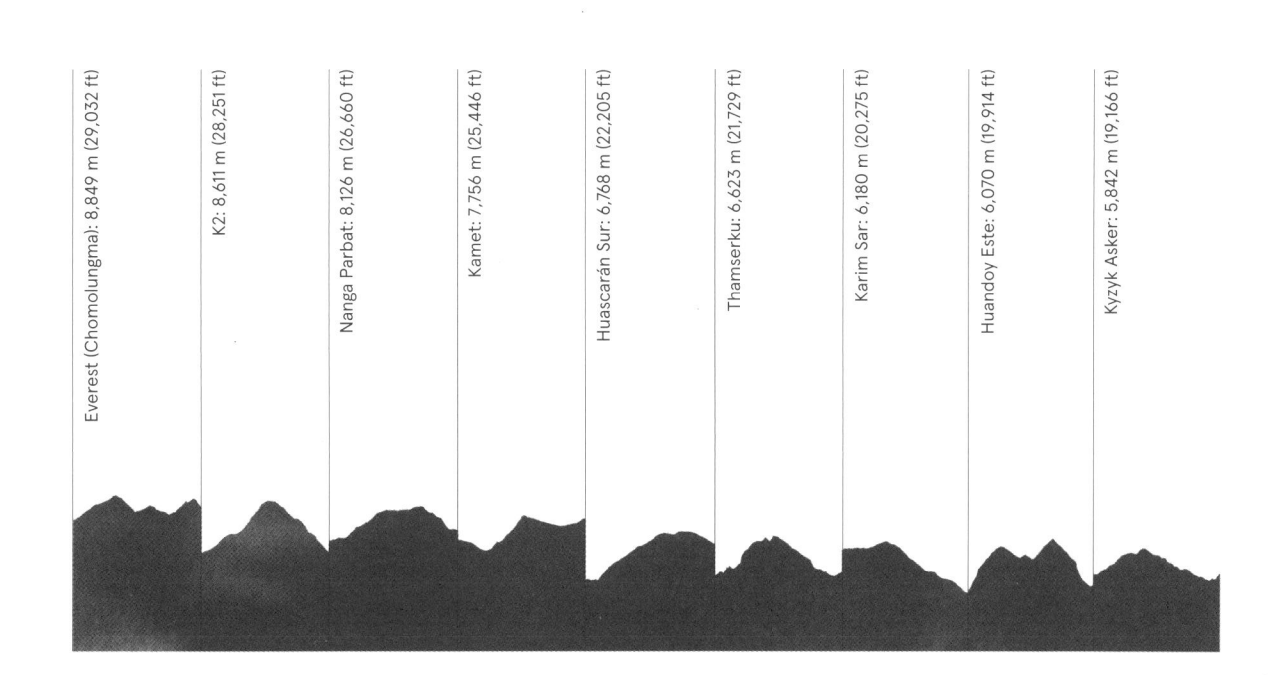

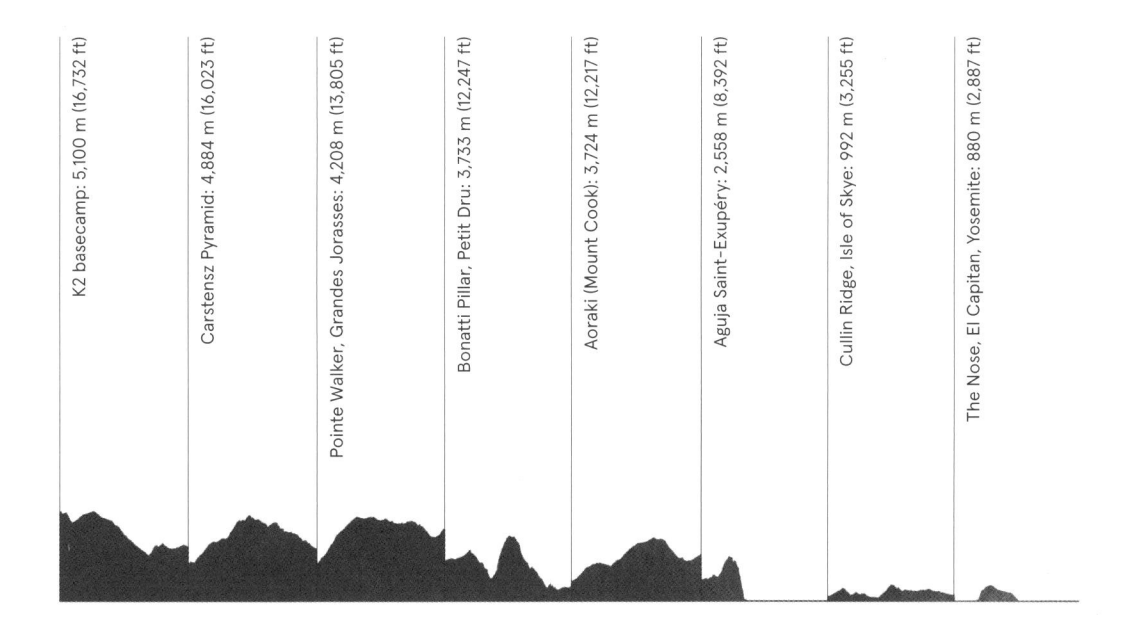

- Everest (Chomolungma): 8,849 m (29,032 ft)
- K2: 8,611 m (28,251 ft)
- Nanga Parbat: 8,126 m (26,660 ft)
- Kamet: 7,756 m (25,446 ft)
- Huascarán Sur: 6,768 m (22,205 ft)
- Thamserku: 6,623 m (21,729 ft)
- Karim Sar: 6,180 m (20,275 ft)
- Huandoy Este: 6,070 m (19,914 ft)
- Kyzyk Asker: 5,842 m (19,166 ft)

- K2 basecamp: 5,100 m (16,732 ft)
- Carstensz Pyramid: 4,884 m (16,023 ft)
- Pointe Walker, Grandes Jorasses: 4,208 m (13,805 ft)
- Bonatti Pillar, Petit Dru: 3,733 m (12,247 ft)
- Aoraki (Mount Cook): 3,724 m (12,217 ft)
- Aguja Saint-Exupéry: 2,558 m (8,392 ft)
- Cullin Ridge, Isle of Skye: 992 m (3,255 ft)
- The Nose, El Capitan, Yosemite: 880 m (2,887 ft)

MORE MOUNTAINEERING WOMEN

Chantel Astorga
Astorga received a Piolet d'Or special mention with Anne Gilbert Chase in 2017 for their new route on Nilkantha, India. In 2018, Astorga and Gilbert Chase also completed the first female ascent of the Slovak Direct, which many people consider Denali's most difficult route. In 2021, she was the first female to solo the Cassin Ridge on Denali, which she completed in 14 hours 39 minutes before skiing down from the summit.

Simone Badier
A leading French climber and alpinist during the 1960s, Badier climbed many great routes of the Mont Blanc range, including the Walker Spur and Croz Spur on the north face of Grandes Jorasses, the Central Pillar of Frêney and the Hemming-Robbins on the west face of Petit Dru. In 1973 she led the first female ascent of the south face of Aiguille du Fou via the Harlin-Hemming-Frost-Fulton route, the most difficult climb of that era.

Stéphanie Bodet
French climber known for completing difficult routes around the world. Some of her most famous ascents are Eternal Flame, Nameless Tower, Pakistan, and Rainbow Jambaia, Angel Falls, Venezuela. She has also made first ascents in Madagascar, Morocco and China.

Las Cholitas Escaladoras
Indigenous women of Aymara heritage who have formed an active climbing group in Bolivia and use modern protective equipment like helmets, crampons and ropes, but climb in the traditional dresses worn by their ancestors. Based in La Paz and El Alto, they successfully summited Huayna Potosi (6,000 m/19,685 ft) in 2015, their first Bolivian peak. Afterwards, they summitted Aconcagua. At 6,961 m (22,838 ft), it is the highest peak in South America. Las Cholitas are currently seeking certification as mountain guides and are determined to uplift the status of Indigenous women in their country.

Sasha DiGiulian
American climber with more than thirty first female ascents and over a dozen other significant first ascents, including Rolihlahla in South Africa and The Misty Wall in Yosemite National Park. In 2015, she became the first woman to free-climb Magic Mushroom (7c+), one of the most difficult routes on the north face of the Eiger.

Freda Du Faur
Australian-born Freda Du Faur was an early pioneer of women's mountaineering in New Zealand. In 1920 she became the first woman to summit Aoraki, in New Zealand. Between 1901 and 1913, she made thirty successful ascents in the New Zealand Alps, making her one of the most prolific climbers – male or female – of the age. In her final climbing summer, she achieved what was deemed impossible at the time: a complete traverse of the three main peaks of Aoraki, thereafter known as The Grand Traverse.

Janja Garnbret
Born in Slovenia, Garnbret specializes in sport climbing and competition climbing. She has won multiple competition lead climbing and bouldering events, as well as two Olympic gold medals, and is widely regarded as the greatest competition climber of all time.

Mélissa Le Nevé
After years of training and rehearsing the route, French climbing prodigy Le Nevé completed an ascent of Action Directe in 2020. Rated 9a or 5.14d, it is one of the hardest rock-climbing routes in the world. In 2024, Meroi received a special mention for lifetime achievement at the Piolets d'Or.

Nives Meroi
In 2017, Italian mountaineer Nives Meroi became the second woman (after Gerlinde Kaltenbrunner) to complete all fourteen 8,000-m (26,247-ft) peaks without the use of supplementary oxygen and climbing porters. She is the successful author of several mountaineering books.

Phyllis Munday
In 1924, Phyllis Munday, one of Canada's pioneering climbers, made the first female ascent of Mount Robson in the Canadian Rockies. Her guide, Conrad Kain, was surprised by her strength on the peak, noting that she carried as much weight as her male companions. Over the next decade, Phyllis and Don Munday mounted several expeditions to climb Mount Waddington, the highest peak in British Columbia.

Beth Rodden
American climber Rodden was the youngest woman to climb 5.14a (8b+) and is one of the only women in the world to have redpointed

a 5.14c (8c+) traditional climbing graded climb. Rodden and Tommy Caldwell completed the second free ascent of the Nose in 2005. In 2008, Rodden made the first ascent of Meltdown in Yosemite and became the first female matching the highest climbing grades of the time.

Dawa Yangzum Sherpa

In 2024, Dawa Yangzum became the first Nepali woman, and one of only a handful of women worldwide, to have ascended all fourteen 8,000-m (26,247-ft) peaks. In 2017, she received a certification from the International Federation of Mountain Guides Association and became the first female Nepali international mountain guide. She splits her guiding time between North America and the Himalaya.

Lhakpa Sherpa

In 2022, Lhakpa summited Chomolungma for the tenth time and claimed the world record for most ascents by a woman. Born one of eleven siblings in the Makalu region of Nepal, she never attended school and now lives as a single mother with her children in Connecticut, where she works odd jobs to fund her expeditions to the Himalaya.

Cecilie Skog

Norwegian adventurer Skog has made ascents of Everest, Denali, Carstenz Pyramid, Lhotse, Mount Vinson, Manaslu, Aconcagua and Cho Oyu. In August 2008, she attempted K2 with her husband, Rolf Bae, who perished during the descent along with ten other climbers, in one of K2's worst climbing seasons.

Mayan Smith-Gobat

A professional big-wall climber from New Zealand, in 2019 Smith-Gobat held the record for the fastest all-female team ascent of El Capitan's the Nose in Yosemite, with her partner Libby Sauter. Other notable ascents include her 2012 first female ascent of Punks in the Gym (5.14a) in the Arapiles, Australia, and the first all-female Half Dome/El Cap link-up in Yosemite in 2013. Smith-Gobat has made multiple attempts to free-climb Riders on the Storm, a difficult big wall on Torre Central, Torres del Paine, Patagonia.

NOTES

Introduction
1. Brown, Rebecca A., *Women on High: Pioneers of Mountaineering*, Appalachian Mountain Club, 2002, page 11.
2. Ibid. page 18.
3. Birkett, Bill & Bill Peascod, *Women Climbing: 200 Years of Achievement*, A&C Black Publishers, 1989, page 22.
4. Price, Cathryn J., *Queen of Mountaineers – The Trailblazing Life of Fanny Bullock Workman*, Chicago Review Press, 2019.
5. Bullock Workman, Fanny, *Two Summers in the Ice-Wilds of Eastern Karakoram: The Nineteen Hundred Square Miles of Mountain and Glacier*, Forgotten Books, 2019, page 282.
6. Ed. and trans. McClure, M.L. and Feltoe, C.L., *The Pilgrimage of Etheria*, Society for Promoting Christian Knowledge, 1919, page 1.
7. Purandare, Nandini & Deepa Balsavar, *Headstrap: Legends and Lore from the Climbing Sherpas of Darjeeling*, Mountaineers Books, 2024, page 172.
8. Ibid. page 172.
9. Ibid. page 173.

Junko Tabei
1. Rolfe, Helen Y. and Junko Tabei, *Honouring High Places: The Mountain Life of Junko Tabei*, Rocky Mountain Books, 2018, page 21.
2. Ibid. page 193.

Gwen Moffat
1. Moffat, Gwen, *Space Below My Feet*, Weidenfeld & Nicolson, 2013, page 27.
2. Broomhead, Rachel, 'For the Love of Rock', interview with Gwen Moffat, *Trail*, June 2023, page 42.
3. Moffat, Gwen, *Space Below My Feet*, op. cit, page 95.
4. Ibid. page 231.
5. Ibid. page 73.

Catherine Destivelle
1. McDonald, Bernadette, and John Amatt (ed.), *Voices from the Summit*, National Geographic, 2000, p. 128.

Wanda Rutkiewicz
1. Reinisch, Gertrude, *Wanda Rutkiewicz: A Caravan of Dreams*, Carreg Ltd, 2001, page 30.
2. Jordan, Jennifer, *Savage Summit: The True Stories of the First Five Women Who Climbed K2*, HarperCollins, 2005, page 51.
3. Reinisch, Gertrude, *Wanda Rutkiewicz*, op. cit, page 88.

Pat Deavoll
1. Deavoll, Pat, *Wind From a Distant Summit*, Craig Potton Publishing, 2011, page 190.
2. Deavoll, Pat, 'Karim Sar (6180m), First Ascent', *American Alpine Journal*, 2010.

Brette Harrington
1. Harrington, Brette, 'What the Heart, Only, Sees', *Alpinist Magazine*, 17 August 2015.
2. Interview with the author, 11 February 2024.

Lynn Hill
1. Hill, Lynn, with Greg Child, *Climbing Free*, Norton & Company, 2002, page 114.
2. Ibid. page 237.

Gerlinde Kaltenbrunner
1. Kaltenbrunner, Gerlinde, *Mountains in My Heart: A Passion for Climbing*, Mountaineers Books, 2014, page 71.

Ines Papert
1. Interview with the author, 15 April 2024.

Kei Taniguchi
1. Kei Taniguchi, 'Being with the Mountain', *Alpinist*, no. 52, 30 November 2015.
2. Ibid.
3. Akihiro Oishi, 'Pandora's Box: The Brief, Brilliant Life of Kei Taniguchi', *Alpinist*, no. 68, Winter 2020.
4. Kei Taniguchi, 'Being with the Mountain', *Alpinist*, no. 52, 30 November 2015.

Sarah Hueniken
1. Quoted in Mosher, Heather, *Not Alone* (film), Canada, 2021.
2. Interview with the author, 17 August 2023.

Alison Hargreaves
1. Hargreaves, Alison, *A Hard Day's Summer*, Hodder & Stoughton, 1994.
2. Rébuffat, Gaston, *Etoiles de Tempetes (Starlight and Storm)*, Modern Library, 1999.
3. Hargreaves, Alison, *A Hard Day's Summer*, op. cit.
4. Jordan, Jennifer, *Savage Summit: The True Stories of the First Five Women Who Climbed K2*, HarperCollins, 2005.

Hazel Findlay
1. Interview with the author, 12 December 2023.

Sharon Wood
1. Wood, Sharon, from a deleted/draft chapter not included in the published version of her book *Rising*, Mountaineers Books, 2019.

Lydia Bradey
1. Bradey, Lydia, *Going Up is Easy*, Penguin Random House New Zealand, 2016.

Tamara Lunger
1. tamaralunger.com

INDEX

A
Abruzzi
  Ridge 53, 223
  Spur 53, 57–60, 63, 222, 223
Aconcagua 51, 60, 201, 206, 216, 250, 251
Action Directe 251
Aguja
  de l'S 80
  Guillaumet 80
  Poincenot 80
  Rafael Juárez 77
  Saint-Exupéry 76, 77, 80
  Standhardt 80
Ahwahneechee tribe 101
Aiguille de Saussure 190
  du Dru (*see also* The Dru) 41
  Verte 130
Allain, Pierre 41, 155
Alpine Club 11
  Austrian 113
  Keiyo 137
  Ladies' 11, 37, 245
  Pakistani 52
Alps 9, 10, 13, 36, 37, 41, 45, 57, 58, 119, 150–159, 182, 224, 241, 247
  Japanese 137
  New Zealand 68, 213, 250
  Urner 122
Altai 9
Ama Dablam 113, 216
Amedeo, Prince Luigi (Duke of the Abruzzi) 63, 223
Andes 9, 10, 197–199, 202–209
Annapurna I 113–115, 246, 247
Annapurna III 21, 22
Annapurna East 130
Antisana Volcano 226
Aoraki 68, 213, 249, 250
Arapiles 251
Arwa Tower 122
Astorga, Chantel 250
Atlas Mountains 9
Auer, Hansjorg 192
Aymara guides (*see also* Cholitas Escaladoras, Las) 229, 250

B
Badier, Simone 250
Ball, Gary 215–216
Ballard, Tom 159
Baltoro Glacier 52, 215, 245
Barrard, Maurice and Liliane 60–61, 63
Bass, Malcolm 70
Batard, Marc 182
Beka Brakai Chhok 70
Ben Nevis 32
Bielecki, Adam 129, 131, 133
Birkett, Dave 189
Bodet, Stéphanie 250
Bonatti, Walter 42–43, 45, 223, 247, 249
Bonington, Chris 153
Botor, Jaroslaw 133
Bottleneck, the 53, 57, 59, 61, 63, 224
Boulaz, Loulou 246
Bradey, Lydia 68, 102, 210–217, 226, 234–237, 246
Breitwangfluh 122
Bridge, Marjory 102
Broad Peak 53, 60, 111, 114, 115, 216, 222
Buhler, Carlos 205–209
Bullock Workman, Fanny 9, 10, 12–13, 245
Byrch, Christine 71

C
Caldwell, Tommy 106, 251
Carstensz Pyramid 50–51, 251

Cassin Ridge 71, 156
Cerro
    Bonete 201
        Domo Blanco 80
        Torre 77, 78, 80
Cesen Route 110
Chacraraju 205
Charlet-Straton, Isabella 11
Chase, Anne Gilbert 250
Chersky Mountains 222
Chiaro di Luna 76, 77, 80
Chimborazo 201
Chogori (see also K2) 51, 53
Cholitas Escaladoras, Las (see also Aymara guides) 229, 250
Chomolungma (see also Mount Everest and Sagarmatha) 16, 23, 51, 83, 115, 138-139, 182, 184-185, 246, 247, 251
Cho Oyu 113, 115, 162, 213, 215, 216, 222, 245, 251
Cima Grande 122, 156, 159, 246
Cirque of the Unclimbables 122
Clark, Whitney 80
Clocher de Planpraz 44
Club Alpin Français (CAF) 41
Cobra Norte 122
Compagnoni, Achille 223
Congdon, Dwayne 209
Cordillera Blanca 196, 198-200, 205, 207
Corkscrew, the 77, 78
Cotopaxi 197, 198
Cryophobia 147, 148, 169-171
Cuatro Dedos 80
Cuillin of Skye 32-36
Culm Coast 188-189
Czerwinska, Anna 58

D
Dalai Lama 49
Danenberg, Sophia 22
d'Angeville, Henriette 10, 244
Davis, Steph 80
Davis-Robbins, Crystal 80
Death Zone 23, 53, 130
Deavoll, Pat 64-71, 80, 81
Denali Range 51, 71, 122, 139, 155, 213, 245, 250, 251
Desmaison, René 41
Destivelle, Catherine 9, 38-45, 82-83, 94-95, 105, 247, 248
Dhaulagiri 114, 115, 169, 216
DiGiulian, Sasha 250
Diran 139
Dolomites 36, 122, 159, 224, 235
Drei Blumen 12
Dru, the (see also Aiguille du Dru) 38-45, 130, 247
Du Faur, Freda 250
Dujmovits, Ralf 113-114
Dyhrenfurth, Hettie 245

E
Eastman, Barb 102
Edlinger, Patrick 42
Egierszdorff, Stefania 58, 246
Eiger 45, 58, 60, 82, 83, 122, 130, 155-159, 246, 247, 250
El Capitan 6, 7, 100-107, 190, 192, 213, 247, 249, 251
Engels Peak 71
Esclatamasters 190
Everest (see Mount Everest)

F
Fidelman, Dean 102, 104
Findlater, Sonja Johnson 146, 149
Findlay, Hazel 186-193
Fitzpatrick, Silvia 80
Fitz Roy 76, 80

G
Gangkhar Puensum 215
García, Juliana 194-201, 226, 227, 229-231
Garnbret, Janja 250
Gasherbrum I 114, 115, 130, 215, 222
Gasherbrum II 12, 60, 114, 115, 130, 215, 216, 222
Gasherbrum III 58, 60
Găvan, Alex 221-222
Gilkey, Art 63
Gilkey Memorial 58, 63
Gingery, Mari 102, 104
Godwin-Austen Glacier 58, 59
Gonzales, Suibel 228, 229
Grandes Jorasses 45, 130, 152-156, 159, 244, 247, 249, 250
Grand Traverse, the 250
Gran Gendarme del Pollone 80
Great Trango Tower 42
Grmovšek, Tanja 80
Grossglockner 9
Gyachunkang 162, 163
Gyalzen Peak 245

H
Haley, Colin 77
Half Dome 100, 102, 251, 236, 237
Hall, Rob 215, 216, 236
Harding, Warren 102, 105
Hargreaves, Alison 9, 10, 150-159, 162, 163, 168, 169, 173, 176, 246, 247
Harrer, Heinrich 153, 155
Harrington, Brette 72-79, 86-87, 122
Harrington, Sue 80
Haston, Dougal 153
Hauyllas, Lidia 228, 229
Hawkins, Ellie 102
Hechtel, Sibylle 102
Heinrich, Tommy 114
Hersey, Paul 67, 70-71, 80-81
Higgins, Molly 102
Hill, Lynn 4, 7, 42, 98-107, 247
Hillary, Edmund 15, 22, 26, 185, 217
Hillary Step 23, 26, 217
Himalaya 9, 10, 12, 13, 15, 16, 21, 26, 45, 49, 51, 58, 67, 68, 71, 113, 114, 128, 133, 136, 137, 140, 159, 181, 185, 205, 208, 213, 215, 221, 224, 245, 251
Hindu Kush 13, 67
Hiraide, Kazuya 136, 139, 140
Hornbein, Tom 205
Huandoy Este 196-200, 229, 249
Huascarán 7, 201, 204-209, 232-233, 246, 249
Huayna Potosi 229, 250
Huber, Alex 77
Huber, Christina 80
Hueniken, Sarah 2, 7, 142-149, 160, 162, 164-166, 169-173
Hydrophobia 147-149, 160, 162, 164-166

I
Inca Empire 9, 14
Indian Creek 192-193
Indigenous peoples 101, 205, 229, 250
Ingmikortilaq 190

J
Johnson, Beverly 102
Jungfrau 9, 13
Jurassic Coast 188

K
K2 (see also Chogori) 9, 12, 48, 51-53, 54-63, 68, 92-94, 110-115, 133, 156, 159, 161, 162, 169, 173, 177, 215, 218-225, 246, 247, 248, 249, 251

Kaltenbrunner, Gerlinde 9, 108-115, 161, 162, 169, 248, 251
Kambič, Monika 80
Kamet 134-141, 248, 249
Kampire Dior 67
Kanchenjunga 63, 114, 115, 236, 238-239
Kangtega 153, 156, 157, 162, 163, 173, 176, 183
Karakoram 10, 12, 13, 16, 51, 53, 67, 68, 69, 94, 97, 114, 137, 221, 245
Karim Sar 64-71, 80-81, 88, 94, 97, 249
Karl Marx Peak 71
Kearney, Alan 80
Keen, Dora 10
Kedarnath Dome 215
Khan Tengri 222
Khumbu Icefall 23, 25, 184, 215
Kilimanjaro 51, 216
Koch-e-Rank 71
Kogan, Claude 245
Koh-e-Baba Tangi 71
Koh-e-Shakawr 71
Kokshaal Too 118, 119, 122
Krüger-Syrokomska, Halina 57-58
Kukuczka, Jerzy 58
Kun Peak 216
Kusum Kanguru 173, 176
Kwangde Shar 122
Kyzyl Asker 118-123, 162, 163, 166, 173-175

L
Lacedelli, Lino 223
La Garganta 206, 207, 209
Laila Peak 138, 139
Langua-tai-Barfi 71
Lawton, Nicole 80
Le Blond, Elizabeth 8, 9, 11, 12, 14, 37, 244, 245
Le Nevé, Mélissa 251
Leclerc, Marc-André 75, 77-78
Les Courtes 130
Les Droites 130
Lewis Lloyd, Emmeline 11
Lhotse 23, 114-115, 130, 133, 214, 215, 216, 222, 251
Likhu Chuli I 122
Lindič, Luka 120, 122, 123, 162, 163
Llullaillaco 201
Lobuche 168, 169, 173
Long, John 102, 105
Lowe, Jeff 42, 44, 156
Lunger, Tamara 218-225, 234, 235, 236, 238-239
Lustenberger, Christina 78

M
Mackiewicz, Tomasz 'Tomek' 129-133, 248
Magic Mushroom 250
Makalu 113, 115, 206, 217, 251
Manaslu 90, 91, 113, 115, 130, 137, 138, 139, 141, 222, 246, 251
Manfrini, Rosanna 80
Mansail 139
Matterhorn 9, 10, 13, 22, 41, 45, 58, 60, 83, 130, 155, 156, 244, 247
Mehdi, Amir 223
Mer de Glace (Sea of Ice) glacier 41
Meroi, Nives 114, 251
Messner, Reinhold 58
Metzelin, Silvia 80
Mingote, Sergi 221-222
Moffat, Gwen 11, 28-37
Mohr Prieto, Juan Pablo 'JP' 221, 222, 224
Monnoyeur, Laurence 80
Mont Blanc 9, 10, 13, 36, 37, 41, 45, 154, 181, 182, 190, 244, 250
Monte Pissis 201
Morehouse Meek, Hope 102

Mori, Mieko 246
Moro, Simone 221, 222, 236, 238–239
Morrow, Pat 49
Mount
    Asgard 122
    Aspiring 213
    Blane 78
    Bullock Workman 13, 245
    Elbrus 51, 58
    Everest (see also Chomolungma and Sagarmatha) 7, 9, 12, 15, 16, 18–27, 51, 56, 58, 63, 83–85, 94, 96, 114, 115, 130, 133, 139, 156, 159, 162, 172, 173, 180–182, 185, 204–205, 208–209, 210–217, 226, 228–229, 234–236, 241, 246–249, 251
    Fay 78, 122
    Fuji 14
    Hunter 68
    Huntington 68, 122, 123
    Kailash 140
    Koser Gunge 13
    Kurodake 140
    Logan 206
    Orizaba 245
    Popcatepetl 245
    Robson 206, 251
    Rundle 68
    Sinai 14
    Vinson 51, 216, 251
    Waddington 122
Munday, Phyllis 250
Muztagh Ata 113, 139, 222

N
Nadin, Simon 105
Naimona'nyi 139
Nakaseko, Naoko 246
Nanga Parbat 60, 68, 113, 114, 115, 126–133, 159, 221, 222, 248, 249
Nangpa La 15
National Geographic 53, 114
Nazreen, Wasfia 12, 46–53, 248
Nevada Sajama 201
Nevada Tres Cruces 201
Nilkantha 250
Nophobia 144, 145, 147, 148
Norgay, Tenzing 15
North, Caroline 80
North Pillar 58, 60, 110, 115, 169
North Ridge 112
Nose, the 6, 7, 98–107, 247, 249, 251
Nun Kun 13
Nuptse 21, 110, 111

O
Ojos del Sabado 201
Oldenhorn 10
Once Upon a Time in the South West 189–192
Ortler 9

P
Palmowska, Krystyna 58
Papert, Ines 116–125, 162, 163, 166, 167, 247
Paradis, Maria 10, 244
Parmentier, Michel 57, 60, 61, 63
Parsons, Ian 156
Pasaban, Edurne 114, 248
Patissier, Isabelle 105
Peak Lenin 216, 222
Peak Pobeda 222
Peck, Annie Smith 8–11, 206, 245
Petit Dru 43, 155, 156, 157, 247, 249, 250
Pharilapcha 130
Pietron, Dörte 80
Pinnacle Club 11, 36

Piolets d'Or 9, 45, 140, 200, 248, 250
Pivtsov, Vassiliy 114
Piz
    Badile 155, 157, 246
    Corvatsch 11
    Palü 11
Pomme d'Or 2, 7
Profit, Christophe 42
Pumori 152, 153
Purja, Nims 222

R
Rai, Nanda 184
Rat Rock 241
Rébuffat, Gaston 41, 155
Revol, Élisabeth 126–133, 248
Rizzi, Anne-Marie 102
Robbins, Liz 102
Roberts, Quentin 78
Rockies 37, 78, 122, 145, 147, 148, 149, 160, 162, 164–165, 166, 169, 170–171, 206, 209, 251
Rodden, Beth 106, 251
Rolihlahla 250
Rutherford, Kate 80
Ruth Gorge 139
Rutkiewicz, Wanda 12, 54–63, 88, 89, 90, 92–93, 94, 96, 246, 247

S
Sabir, Nazir 52
Sadpara, Ali 221
Sadpara, Sajid 222
Sagarmāthā (see also Mount Everest and Chomolungma) 115, 182
Sandahl, Brooke 106
Sauter, Libby 251
Scott, Doug 153
Sea of Vapors 68, 149
Sentinel Rock 102
Seven Summits 12, 26, 46–53, 248
Shawangunks 105
Sherpa, Ang Rita 217
Sherpa, Ang Tsering 26, 27
Sherpa, Ani Daku 15, 16
Sherpa, Dawa Futi 22
Sherpa, Dawa Yangzum 248, 251
Sherpa, Kami Rita 22
Sherpa, Lhakpa 22, 248, 251
Sherpa, Lhakpa Phuti 184
Sherpa, Lhakpa Sonam 181
Sherpa, Mingma 53
Sherpa, Mingma G 222
Sherpa, Nima Jangmu 22
Sherpa, Pasang Lhamu 9, 15, 16, 178–185, 236, 247
Sherpa, Pemba Norbu 184
Sherpa, Sonar Tsering 184
Sherpa, Tshering Namgya 22
Shilinbar Glacier 66, 67, 69
Shiraishi, Ashima 240–242, 248
Shishapangma 45, 90, 113, 114, 115
Shivling 138, 139
Shoulder, the 53, 59, 61, 223
Siachen Glacier 13
Sigurjónsson, John Snorri 222
Silver Throne plateau 13
Sinha, Arunima 22
Skatov, Atanas 224
Skog, Cecilie 251
Smith-Gobat, Mayan 122, 251
Smythe, Frank 136, 139, 140
Snowdonia 32, 37
Spantik 138, 139

T
Tabei, Junko 7, 18–27, 90, 91, 141, 246
Tainted Love 190
Taniguchi, Kei 90, 91, 134–141, 248
Tantalus Range 75
Tatra Mountains 57
Tawiz Peak 13
Thamserku 181–183, 185, 249
Tien Shan 9, 222
Tomala, Piotr 133
Torre Central 251
Torre Egger 78, 79, 88
Torres del Paine 122, 251
Triglav 120
Trollryggen 57, 58, 60
Twight, Mark 156
Txikon, Alex 221, 222

U
Uchida, Masako 246
Unsoeld, Willi 205
Urubko, Denis 129, 131, 133

V
Vajolet Towers 235
Vasuki Parbat 71
Vaucher, Yvette 246
Verdon Gorge 41
Vision, the 78
Voog, Daisy 245

W
Wach, Danuta 58, 246
Waddington Range 75
Waiparous Valley 147, 148
Wakhan Corridor 71
Walker, Lucy 10, 11, 244
Washburn, Barbara 245
Whitehouse, Annie 209
Whymper, Edward 9, 10
Wolf, Herbert 113
Wood, Sharon 7, 22, 153, 159, 202–209, 228, 229, 246

Y
Yerupajá 201
Yosemite National Park 6, 7, 98–107, 190, 192, 212, 236, 237, 247, 249, 250, 251

Z
Zaluski, Darek 114
Zhumayev, Maxut 114
Zurita, Fabian 197

PICTURE CREDITS

Images are identified by page number

a = above, b = below

2 Photo © John Price; 4 Photo © Heinz Zak; 6 Photo © Ian Corless – all rights reserved; 8 Illustrated London News Ltd/Mary Evans; 10a Bridgeman Images; 10c Bibliothèque de Genève (inv. Rig 0501); 10b Bridgeman Images; 11a Library of Congress Prints and Photographs Division, Washington, D. C.; 11b, 12a, 12b The Lizzie Le Blond Collection. Courtesy The Martin and Osa Johnson Safari Museum, Chanute, Kansas; 13a From F. B. Workman and W. H. Workman, 'Two Summers in the Ice Wilds of the Eastern Karakoram' (New York; E. P. Dutton & Company, 1916); 13b Library of Congress Prints and Photographs Division, Washington, D. C.; 14 The Lizzie Le Blond Collection. Courtesy The Martin and Osa Johnson Safari Museum, Chanute, Kansas; 15 Photo Charles Wylie/Royal Geographical Society (with IBG); 16 Photo Alfred Gregory/Royal Geographical Society (with IBG); 20 Photo © Jim Herrington; 21, 24 Photos courtesy Tabei family archive; 27 Photo Junko Tabei. Courtesy Tabei family archive; 30 Photo © Jim Herrington; 34–35 Photo VWB photos/Getty Images; 40 Photo Craig Richards © Banff Centre for Arts and Creativity/Whyte Museum of the Canadian Rockies; 41, 44 Photos Catherine Destivelle/Sygma via Getty Images; 48, 49 Photos Pat Morrow; 52 Photo Munir Uz Zaman/AFP/GettyImages; 56, 57, 61, 62 Photos from the Wanda Rutkiewicz archive; 66 Photo © Lydia Bradey; 70 Photo © Pat Deavoll; 74, 79 Photo © Quentin L. Roberts; 81 Photo © Pat Deavoll; 82a, 82b, 83 Photos Catherine Destivelle/Sygma via Getty Images; 84–85 Photo R.M. Nunes/Adobe Stock; 86–87 Photo © Quentin L. Roberts; 88 Photo © Pat Deavoll; 88–89, 90–91 Photos from the Wanda Rutkiewicz archive; 91 Photo © Yumiko Hiraki; 92–93, 94 Photos from the Wanda Rutkiewicz archive; 94–95 Photo Catherine Destivelle/Sygma via Getty Images; 96 Photo from the Wanda Rutkiewicz archive; 97 Photo © Pat Deavoll; 100 Photo Craig Richards © Banff Centre for Arts and Creativity/Whyte Museum of the Canadian Rockies; 107 Photo © Heinz Zak; 110 Photo © Archiv Kaltenbrunner; 111 Photo © Schöffel, courtesy Archiv Kaltenbrunner; 115 Photo © Ralf Dujmovits, courtesy Archiv Kaltenbrunner; 118 Photo © Rainer Eder; 119, 124–125 Photo courtesy Ines Papert; 128 Photo © Adam Bielecki; 133 Photo Philippe Desmazes/AFP via Getty Images; 136, 141 Photo © Yumiko Hiraki; 144 Still from 'Not Alone'. Produced and directed by Heather Mosher, © Heather Mosher Media, 2021. Photo © John Price; 152, 153, 157 Photos © Mark Twight 1986; 158 Photo © Manfred Thuerig/Dreamstime.com; 160 Still from 'Not Alone', drone footage by Alex Taylor/Raven West. Produced and directed by Heather Mosher, © Heather Mosher Media, 2021; 161 Photo © Maxut Zhumayev, courtesy Archiv Kaltenbrunner; 162 Photo © Ralf Dujmovits, courtesy Archiv Kaltenbrunner; 163a Photo © Mark Twight 1986; 163b Photo courtesy Ines Papert; 164–165 Still from 'Not Alone'. Produced and directed by Heather Mosher, © Heather Mosher Media, 2021; 166, 167a, 167b Photos courtesy Ines Papert; 168–169 Photo © Mark Twight 1986; 169a Photo © Archiv Kaltenbrunner; 169b Photo © Ralf Dujmovits, courtesy Archiv Kaltenbrunner; 170–171 Still from 'Not Alone', drone footage by Alex Taylor/Raven West. Produced and directed by Heather Mosher, © Heather Mosher Media, 2021; 172a Still from 'Not Alone'. Produced and directed by Heather Mosher, © Heather Mosher Media, 2021; 172b Photo Tashi Lakpa Sherpa/AFP via Getty Images; 173 Photo © Mark Twight 1986; 174–175 Photo courtesy Ines Papert; 176 Photo © Mark Twight 1986; 177 Photo © Steve Swenson; 180, 181, 185 Photos courtesy of the Pasang Lhamu Sherpa Foundation; 188 Photo © Jonny Baker; 189 Photo © Colette McInerney; 193 Photo © Cameron Maier; 196 Photo Joshua Jarrin; 197 Photo © Roberto Espinosa Fernández (@roberef); 198 Photo © Samuel Saidel-Goley; 204 Photo Andrew Haliburton/Alamy Stock Photo; 205 Photo © Carlos Buhler; 212 Photo Mike Roberts. Courtesy Lydia Bradey; 213, 217 Photos Xavier Raoux. Courtesy Lydia Bradey; 220, 221, 225 Photos © Tamara Lunger Archive; 226a Photo courtesy Lydia Bradey; 226–227 Photo © Roberto Espinosa Fernández (@roberef); 228a Photo Juan Karita/AP Photo/Alamy Stock Photo; 228b Photo courtesy Sharon Wood; 229 Photo © Joshua Jarrin; 230–231 Photo © Roberto Espinosa Fernández (@roberef); 232–233 Photo © Jakub Cejpek/Dreamstime.com; 234a Photo Penny Webster. Courtesy Lydia Bradey; 234b Photo © Tamara Lunger Archive; 234–235 Photo © Alice Russolo. Courtesy Tamara Lunger Archive; 236a Photo Xavier Raoux. Courtesy Lydia Bradey; 236b Photo courtesy of the Pasang Lhamu Sherpa Foundation; 237 Photo © Steve Monks; 238–239 Photo © Alessandro D'Emilia. Courtesy Tamara Lunger Archive; 240 Photo © Kyle Gibson (www.kylegibsonphoto.com)

ABOUT THE CONTRIBUTORS

Joanna Croston moved to the Canadian Rockies in 1998, where she is currently the Director for the Banff Centre Mountain Film and Book Festival and World Tour. She has climbed many of the classic 3,350-metre (11,000-foot) peaks in the area, as well as travelling and skiing throughout North America, the Alps, Kashmir, Japan and the Indian Himalaya. Her writing has appeared in *Highline Magazine*, *Gripped*, *The Canadian Alpine Journal*, *Mountain Life*, *Alpinist* and *Waymaking*, an award-winning women's adventure anthology.

Jasmin Paris is a British ultrarunner. In 2014 she became the first woman to complete the Barkley Marathons, arguably the toughest footrace on Earth.

Nandini Purandare is editor of the internationally renowned *The Himalayan Journal* (THJ) and President of the Himalayan Club. She has travelled extensively in the Himalaya.

Ashima Shiraishi is a professional rock climber from New York City. She is also the co-founder of All Rise, an experimental programme in the world of DEI.

Tessa Lyons is an award-winning artist, illustrator and climber based in North Wales.

AUTHOR ACKNOWLEDGMENTS

I'm indebted to Helen Fanthorpe and Lucas Dietrich from Thames and Hudson who went out on a limb and entered the adventure game with this book. Thanks to Johanne Lian Olsen, the talented designer who made the book look so beautiful.

This book was inspired by Junko Tabei, Helen Y. Rolfe and Yumiko Hiraki's book *Honouring High Places*. They reminded me that many women's mountain stories have yet to be told. Yumiko was also instrumental in the creation of this book, acting as my liaison to the Japanese climbing community.

The stories contained within this book are not my own but born from the achievements of twenty remarkable mountain women. I'm honoured to be able to tell their stories and no words can convey my thanks to these climbers, many of whom agreed to interviews and provided feedback on my work.

My sister Anik See, a talented writer herself, read every word in advance of others – her wisdom and guidance pulled me through my first drafts. Anthony Whittome, Shannon O'Donoghue, Greg Child, Claire Carter and Bernadette McDonald offered encouragement and valuable advice. John Porter, Nancy Svendsen and Dawa Futi Sherpa all read early drafts and provided valuable input.

Nandini Purandare, Ashima Shiraishi and Jasmin Paris wrote brilliant complements to the main body of the book, providing insight into the past and future of women's climbing. I'm so delighted to be in such good company.

Tessa Lyons is responsible for creating the amazing, gorgeous illustrations that accompany these stories – she is one of a kind. Pauline Hubner worked tirelessly as researcher of photographs, for which I am so thankful. I gratefully acknowledge the remarkable photographs included in the book provided by: Jim Herrington, Carlos Buhler, Steve Swenson, Pat Morrow, Yumiko Hiraki, Shinya Tabei, Dawa Futi Sherpa, Eliza Kubarska and the Rutkiewicz family, Heather Mosher, John Price, Alex Taylor, Cameron Maier, Rolando Garibotti, Heinz Zak, Mark Twight, Quentin Roberts, Setsuko Kitamura, Tabei Kikaku, Yomiuri Shimbun, Ang Tsering, the Taniguchi family, Adam Bielecki, Craig Richards, Whyte Museum of the Canadian Rockies, Tamara Lunger, Gerlinde Kaltenbrunner, Joshua Jarrin, Pat Deavoll, Lydia Bradey, Ines Papert, Luka Lindič, Ralf Dumovits, Dwayne Congdon, Jon Griffith, Jonny Baker, Steve Monks, Lauren Baker and to anyone I may have inadvertently missed, the list of photo contributors is robust.

And finally, to my family, especially René Geber and Iyla Brewster Geber who kept me laughing and well-cared for during the entire process, love to you all.

On the front cover:
Above: Pasang Lhamu Sherpa on the summit of Mont Blanc, France.
Photo courtesy of the Pasang Lhamu Sherpa Foundation
Below left: Lynn Hill free-climbing the Nose, El Capitan, California.
Photo © Heinz Zak
Below right: Annie Smith Peck, 1911. Library of Congress Prints and Photographs Division, Washington, D. C.

On the back cover:
Hazel Findlay climbs at Indian Creek, Utah. Photo © Cameron Maier

First published in the United Kingdom in 2025 by
Thames & Hudson Ltd, 6–24 Britannia Street, London WC1X 7JD

First published in the United States of America in 2025 by
Thames & Hudson Inc., 500 Fifth Avenue, New York, New York 10110

Mountaineering Women © 2025 Thames & Hudson Ltd, London

Text © 2025 Joanna Croston
Foreword © 2025 Jasmin Paris
Introduction © 2025 Nandini Purandare
The Future of Climbing © 2025 Ashima Shiraishi
Mountain illustrations by Tessa Lyons

For full picture credits, see page 255

All Rights Reserved. No part of this publication may be reproduced or transmitted in any form or by any means, electronic or mechanical, including photocopy, recording or any other information storage and retrieval system, without prior permission in writing from the publisher.

EU Authorized Representative: Interart S.A.R.L.
19 rue Charles Auray, 93500 Pantin, Paris, France
productsafety@thameshudson.co.uk
www.interart.fr

A CIP catalogue record for this book is available from the British Library

Library of Congress Control Number 2024951838

ISBN 978-0-500-02717-2
01

Printed in Malaysia by Papercraft

Be the first to know about our new releases, exclusive content and author events by visiting
thamesandhudson.com
thamesandhudsonusa.com
thamesandhudson.com.au

Dedication
For all the strong women in my family.

Author's Note
The most difficult part of writing this book was deciding which women to include. There are so many brilliant stories yet untold, and my initial list was more than seventy climbers strong. Noticeably missing in the realm of mountain literature are celebrations of mountaineering accomplishments by women, and in particular, celebrations of Indigenous women and those of African and Asian ancestry. I've included some remarkable climbers from these under-represented groups among these pages, but even in the twenty-first century, these stories are difficult to track down. My hope is that these stories will come to the forefront in the decades to come. As the world recognizes the effects of colonialism and begins to reconcile the historical suppression of Indigenous narratives, I encourage women from mountain cultures around the globe to come forwards and share their achievements, so that together we can support and uplift each other.

In this book, we have used both the Tibetan name (Chomolungma) and the British-derived name (Everest) to describe the highest mountain on Earth, depending on what felt most appropriate to each climber and narrative. The same logic has been followed for K2 and Chogori, the name in Balti.

Sherpas often name their children after the day of the week they were born, but all share the surname Sherpa. Unlike other climbers in the book, we have used first names in the text to avoid confusion.